CBT: Science Into Practice

Series Editor

Nikolaos Kazantzis, Cognitive Behavior Therapy Research Unit
Melbourne, Australia

This series addresses topics that reflect current thinking in the field of cognitive behavior therapy, the most widely accepted form of therapy across mental health disciplines. Despite the consensus that CBT is an effective treatment modality, much of the existing clinical literature focuses on single facets, such as specific disorders or populations. Mostly it does not take into account the latest evidence for transdiagnostic change mechanisms and processes. This series provides guidance on how the latest evidence can be translated into practice. Volumes focus on enhancing flexibility in both the selection and delivery of techniques tailored to individual clients. Each provides clinical insights enhanced by case studies and vignettes to ensure relevance for the practicing professional.

Lillian Reuman • Johanna Thompson-Hollands
Editors

Enhancing CBT Through Family and Peer Engagement

Springer

Editors
Lillian Reuman
Department of Psychology
Stonehill College
North Easton, MA, USA

Johanna Thompson-Hollands
Department of Psychiatry
Boston University Chobanian & Avedisian
School of Medicine
Boston, MA, USA

ISSN 2946-5419 ISSN 2946-5427 (electronic)
CBT: Science Into Practice
ISBN 978-3-031-74837-0 ISBN 978-3-031-74838-7 (eBook)
https://doi.org/10.1007/978-3-031-74838-7

This Springer imprint is published by the registered company Springer Nature Switzerland AG
The registered company address is: Gewerbestrasse 11, 6330 Cham, Switzerland

Dedicated with love to the family I was raised by, the children I'm raising, and the partner I'm raising them with.

—LR

With gratitude to the clients and families I have worked with over the years, who inspire me daily with their resilience and care for one another.

—JTH

Foreword

I am delighted that the book *Enhancing CBT Through Family and Peer Engagement* is being published in the CBT: Science Into Practice book series. As clinicians, we constantly witness the profound influence of interpersonal environments on our clients' experiences of psychopathology and medical conditions. Family members and peers often play crucial roles, either supporting the individual within or outside sessions, and at other times may inadvertently reinforce symptoms, thus maintaining the disorder. Including these significant others in clinical assessment and treatment offers unique benefits and can augment or exceed the benefits of individual interventions. Clearly, enhancing the opportunity for family members and peers to acquire skills that support treatment elements such as behavior change, engagement with homework assignments, and session attendance represents just a selection of likely benefits.

Cognitive Behavior Therapy (CBT) was originally formulated as a therapy for individuals but has since been expanded to address a wide range of presenting concerns in individual, dyadic, or group formats. This volume highlights the diverse ways in which CBT can incorporate trusted family members and peers across community mental health centers, inpatient/hospital settings, and schools. It explores a variety of formats, such as "massed" sessions and parent/partner-only interventions.

As with other volumes in the series, this book assembles authors with distinct clinical and research expertise, and in the case of this volume, elucidates the rationale and research support for CBT in an interpersonal context. Each chapter offers a comprehensive guide to practicing CBT in such contexts, synthesizing recent research evidence and addressing clinical considerations. Every chapter concludes with a case vignette, providing practical insights into real-world applications. I applaud all the contributors to this volume for their excellent work.

The editors bring a wealth of professional experience to this volume. Dr. Lillian Reuman is a licensed clinical psychologist and an Assistant Professor at Stonehill College in Easton, MA. Dr. Reuman's clinical work and research are dedicated to understanding and treating transdiagnostic fear-based disorders. Her mixed-methods clinical research aims to directly improve the lives of individuals living with anxiety and those who interact with them. Dr. Reuman has extensive clinical training in evidence-based treatments and has provided clinical care across a range of settings. She has conducted, presented, and published research in national and international venues and has co-authored over 50 peer-reviewed articles and chapters on cognitive behavioral processes and treatments.

Dr. Johanna Thompson-Hollands is a licensed clinical psychologist, a staff investigator in the National Center for PTSD at the VA Boston Healthcare System, and Associate Professor of Psychiatry at the Boston University Chobanian and Avedisian School of Medicine. Dr. Thompson-Hollands is an expert in the field of PTSD intervention; her research focuses on the role of social factors in treatment and how best to incorporate significant others into care to improve patient outcomes. She is the developer of a brief family intervention protocol meant to support patients as they undergo exposure-based treatment for posttraumatic stress disorder. She has published over 40 peer-reviewed articles and chapters and has received multiple grants for her work from the National Institute of Mental Health and the Department of Veterans Affairs. With such backgrounds to draw on, Dr. Reuman and Dr. Thompson-Hollands are eminently qualified to offer this book, which provides a rich synthesis of evidence to guide practice.

The practice of CBT ideally considers the individual in context, within family, peer, and partner relationships. As we move toward a science for CBT that clearly identifies those processes of etiology that become processes of treatment, strengthening interpersonal relationships, including directly drawing on the support of others in the client's life, can bolster the effects of CBT. The purpose of Dr. Reuman and Dr. Thompson-Hollands' book is to inspire clinicians and researchers to continue expanding family and peer involvement across settings and conditions. By embracing the synergistic power of CBT and interpersonal support, we can create a more holistic and effective therapeutic experience for those we serve. Dr. Reuman and Dr. Thompson-Hollands have performed exceptionally well in this regard.

Conflicts of Interest

Kazantzis disclosed his royalties from the Guilford Press (*Therapeutic Relationship in Cognitive Behavior Therapy*; *Cognitive and Behavior Theories in Clinical Practice*), Routledge (*Using Homework Assignments in Cognitive Behavior Therapy*); Springer Nature publishers (CBT: Science Into Practice Book Series; *Handbook of Homework Assignments in Psychotherapy: Research, Practice, & Prevention*). He also disclosed editor stipend from the Association for Behavioral and Cognitive Therapies for his role as Editor-in-Chief for *Cognitive and Behavioral Practice* (Elsevier).

Nikolaos Kazantzis
Book Series Editor, CBT: Science Into Practice
Cognitive Behavior Therapy Research Unit
Melbourne, VIC, Australia
Beck Institute for Cognitive Behavior Therapy
Philadelphia, PA, USA

Preface

A client's experience of psychopathology or a medical condition influences—and is affected by—the interpersonal environment. Family members may also impact said conditions by engaging in behaviors that support the individual or inadvertently reinforce symptoms, thereby maintaining the disorder. Including family members and peers in clinical assessment and treatment can offer benefits above and beyond individual interventions, including symptom amelioration, enhanced individual and relationship functioning (e.g., improved communication and satisfaction), and opportunities for family members/peers to learn skills to support elements of treatment (e.g., behavior change, practice assignment completion, and attendance).

Cognitive behavioral therapy (CBT) is a gold-standard, evidence-based treatment approach that can effectively address many presenting concerns in an individual, dyadic, or group format. This edited volume highlights and synthesizes the myriad ways in which cognitive behavioral approaches can incorporate trusted family members (e.g., parents/guardians, partners) and others (e.g., peers) across a variety of settings and formats.

Cognitive behavioral approaches involve both science and art. Accordingly, this edited volume brings together authors with unique clinical and research expertise to demonstrate the rationale and research support for CBT in an interpersonal context. Each chapter includes a thorough guide to practicing CBT in an interpersonal context, a synthesis of recent research evidence, as well as clinical considerations that address diverse identities. All chapters conclude with a case vignette. This edited volume adopts a transdiagnostic approach that decenters individual diagnoses and instead focuses on the ways in which CBT can be implemented in an array of settings (e.g., community mental health centers, inpatient/hospital settings, schools) and in a variety of formats (e.g., "massed," parent/partner-only). Collectively, each chapter can serve as a comprehensive evidence-based clinical guide for how and why to use CBT in a family- or peer-inclusive format.

This edited volume first addresses evidence-based strategies for including parents/guardians and partners in cognitive behavioral assessment (both functional and diagnostic) (Part I). The intervention subsection of the edited volume discusses approaches for adults (i.e., couple/conjoint arrangements) (Part II), children and adolescents (i.e., parent/family involvement) (Part III), and peers (Part IV). The first two intervention subsections (adult and child/adolescent, respectively) begin with chapters introducing a "standard" use case of other-involvement in weekly outpatient CBT; subsequent chapters within the intervention sections address the many permutations of interpersonal involvement in CBT. It is our hope that this volume inspires clinicians and researchers to continue expanding family and peer involvement across settings and conditions, for the benefit of clients everywhere.

North Easton, MA, USA — Lillian Reuman
Boston, MA, USA — Johanna Thompson-Hollands

Contents

Abbreviations

ADHD	Attention-Deficit/Hyperactivity Disorder
ARD	Anxiety-Related Disorder
BA	Behavioral Activation
BFI	Brief Family Intervention
BPD	Borderline Personality Disorder
BPT	Behavioral Parent Training
CBCT	Cognitive Behavioral Conjoint Therapy
CBT	Cognitive Behavior Therapy
DBT	Dialectical Behavior Therapy
DSM	Diagnostic and Statistical Manual of Mental Disorders
EMA	Ecological Momentary Assessment
ERP	Exposure and Response Prevention
FM	Family Member
GAD	Generalized Anxiety Disorder
NIMH	National Institute of Mental Health
OCD	Obsessive Compulsive Disorder
PE	Prolonged Exposure
PHP	Partial Hospitalization Program
PTSD	Posttraumatic Stress Disorder
RCT	Randomized Controlled Trial
SMI	Serious Mental Illness
SPACE	Supportive Parenting for Anxious Childhood Emotions
SSRI	Selective Serotonin Reuptake Inhibitor
TFT	Trauma Focused Treatment
VA	Veterans Affairs

Part I
Assessment

Chapter 1
Multi-informant Adult and Couple Assessment

Iris Antonopoulos and Anne Wagner

1.1 Introduction

Assessment is a vital part of not only cognitive-behavioral therapy (CBT) but also psychotherapy generally. Evidence-based assessment utilizes research and theory to determine appropriate assessment targets, select suitable measures and methods, and inform the overall assessment process (Hunsley & Mash, 2007). The purposes of assessment may include determining a diagnosis, making clinical predictions, informing case conceptualization, planning treatment, and monitoring therapy processes and outcomes (Hunsley & Mash, 2008). Assessment is considered an ongoing, fluid, and dynamic process that is continuous over the course of working with a client and can be used for collaborative planning with the client and with other healthcare professionals (Drummond & Jones, 2010).

One part of evidence-based assessment is the use of multiple informants. Informants (also referred to as "collaterals" in this chapter) are defined as untrained raters who provide data about the client (De Los Reyes & Epkins, 2023). It is considered standard practice to obtain assessment data from informants such as teachers and parents in research and clinical practice with children and youth (Hunsley & Mash, 2007). However, multi-informant assessment is far less common when assessing adults; it is used more frequently for adults with certain conditions such as psychosis, cognitive limitations, substance use, or in forensic cases (Achenbach et al., 2005). Instead, assessment of adult psychopathology is frequently obtained directly from the client being assessed (Achenbach et al., 2005).

I. Antonopoulos (✉) · A. Wagner
Remedy Institute, Toronto, ON, Canada
e-mail: dr.antonopoulos@remedycentre.ca

L. Reuman, J. Thompson-Hollands (eds.), *Enhancing CBT Through Family and Peer Engagement*, CBT: Science Into Practice, https://doi.org/10.1007/978-3-031-74838-7_1

The lack of multi-informant assessment can often be attributed to clinicians holding the perspective that adult clients know best about the problems they are experiencing and that assessors can rely on their reporting (Rescorla et al., 2016). Multi-informant assessment can be used to contextualize and extend the reporting of the client. It may be used for assessing not only psychopathology, but also other aspects of functioning, personality, and satisfaction in various domains. Informants may be partners, family members, or others who have a relationship with the client. Multi-informant assessment allows for a more holistic and fuller understanding of the client being assessed and can be used with individual adult clients and couples seeking treatment. Research demonstrates that informant data provide valuable information above and beyond an individual's own report (De Los Reyes & Makol, 2022), and information gathered may enhance treatment planning and monitoring. Yet clinicians may shy away from multi-informant assessment due to various questions that arise including who should be selected as an informant, what types of assessment measures are suitable for administration, what to do when informant reports reveal inconsistencies, and how to integrate information from various informants. This chapter will address these questions and provide an overview of multi-informant assessment.

1.2 Assessment Overview and Research Evidence

1.2.1 Value of Multi-informant Assessment

A measure with strong utility assesses a construct above and beyond what the measure was developed to assess (Youngstrom, 2008). In the case of multi-informant assessment, informant reports should lead to improved clinical decision-making relative to making decisions without informant data (De Los Reyes & Makol, 2022). For instance, informant ratings may provide corroborative data related to assigning a client a particular mental health diagnosis or increase the accuracy of differential diagnoses, help clinicians make decisions about which interventions to suggest, and aid in monitoring treatment processes and response to treatment (De Los Reyes & Makol, 2022).

In a study examining the convergence of clinician, self, and collateral ratings of posttraumatic stress disorder (PTSD) symptoms, the authors found moderate to strong correlations between measures for total PTSD and symptom cluster scores (Ennis et al., 2021). According to the clinician-administered measure, 51.3% of trauma-exposed participants met the criteria for PTSD, whereas 34.2% and 29.1% met the criteria based on the self-report and collateral measures, respectively. The clinician and self-report ratings had a greater percentage of agreement (78%) for PTSD diagnosis than the clinician and collateral rating (62.4%). Examining differences in reports between informants in detail can generate additional questions clinicians may want to ask before assigning a diagnosis and proceeding with treatment, given that informants may be providing information that can provide an alternative view of what the client reports.

Multi-informant reports can be valuable for predicting long-term outcomes. Klein (2003) examined self-reports and collateral reports of clients experiencing depression. Clients and informants were interviewed separately at the initial evaluation and once again seven and a half years later. Interviews consisted of scales to assess depression, global functioning, and a clinician-administered measure of personality psychopathology. Klein (2003) found that baseline personality disorders and dimensional scores from self and collateral reports independently predicted symptoms of depression and functioning. Interestingly, only informants' reports added unique contributions to the prediction of social adjustment, suggesting that informant ratings may be especially relevant for understanding outcomes related to social functioning and are valuable beyond what is reported by clients themselves. In another study by Galione and Oltmanns (2013), self-report, informant report, and clinician-assessed personality pathology each independently predicted lifetime episodes of major depressive disorder, suggesting that multiple sources of assessment provided unique information related to clinical outcomes.

1.2.2 Selecting Informants

Clinicians may struggle to identify who should serve as an informant as it can be difficult to know who would best serve this role. In response to the question of which informants should be selected to provide reports, De Los Reyes and Makol (2022) suggest that this question is best answered with another question: "Which informants have evidence supporting their expertise as a clinically relevant information source?" (p. 2). Research on adult multi-informant assessment suggests obtaining reports from significant others in a client's life, which may include partners, family members, co-workers, or nonfamilial caregivers such as nurses in the context of older adults. De Los Reyes and Makol (2022) view the decision-making process for identifying informants to be quite similar to other aspects of clinical care, such as selecting suitable treatment interventions. Selecting informants can be based on a combination of reliance on clinical experience and guidelines from evidence-based assessment.

There are no guidelines on how many informants should be selected in clinical practice settings. The number of informants will vary across settings, and it is important to be mindful of the incremental value of involving additional informants. Clinicians should be aware of what kind of data the informant will bring to the assessment and if the information gathered will overlap or complement the information provided by other informants (De Los Reyes & Makol, 2022). In other words, the data obtained across informants should not be completely redundant. If the agreement between informants is very high, the data are less likely to be clinically valuable. Further, there is less potential for adding incremental validity than if the agreement is lower (Achenbach et al., 2005; Kraemer et al., 2003). Differing views from collaterals can imply that ratings are not interchangeable but rather that each informant has the potential to provide valuable assessment data (Hunsley & Mash, 2007). Assessors should select informants who vary in the context and perspective from which they observe the client, which will naturally lead to discrepancies in reporting (Kraemer et al., 2003). In other words, differences in data obtained across informants present an opportunity to enhance decision-making, rather than be viewed as problematic (Makol et al., 2020).

There is also a worry that adult clients may not want to identify close others to serve as informants. Additionally, clinicians may be concerned that even if informants agree, it may be challenging to obtain data from them. This concern was examined in the National Survey of Children, Youths, and Adults (Achenbach & Rescorla, 2003). Interviewers randomly selected homes to obtain self-report data that measured adaptive functioning, substance use, and other mental health issues. Participants were asked to nominate collaterals to complete a parallel measure describing the participant. The Adult Self-Report was completed by 2020 (94%) of the 2146 eligible adult individuals. Informants completed the parallel questionnaire for 81% of the clients in this sample. The researchers suggest that this indicates it is fairly easy to obtain collateral reports. Even though individuals and informants in this study were compensated $10 for participation, this monetary value was likely no more persuasive than a simple request to a loved one to complete the questionnaire. In another study where participants were recruited using listed phone numbers as part of census data and asked to provide details to contact an informant who knew them, only 9% of participants did not have an informant able to participate (Galione & Oltmanns, 2013).

1.2.3 Methods of Assessment

A recommended approach to evidence-based assessment is the use of multiple assessment methods from different assessment sources, such as self-report and collateral-report measures, clinician-administered interviews, behavioral assessments, and psychophysiological methods. Psychophysiological methods that assess bodily responses such as heart rate, blood pressure, brain activity, temperature, and perspiration are valuable measures but since these are inconvenient to administer in most clinical practice settings, we have omitted them from this section. The balance between the comprehensiveness of the assessment and client's burden needs to be weighed. Assessment methods will vary due to the goals of the assessment (e.g., screening, case conceptualization, treatment monitoring) and the selection of measures should be empirically guided (Snyder et al., 2016).

Antony (2001) discusses guiding principles for clinicians that can aid in decision-making related to assessment selection. These principles include (1) considering the assessment goals, (2) choosing several measures that target different domains of the same problem, (3) selecting measures that help with treatment planning if that is consistent with the assessment goal, (4) picking measures that can test hypotheses clinicians may have (e.g., based on earlier information from other assessment methods), and (5) using broad measures at first and then more focused measures as needed. Recommendations in couple and family assessment are that the assessment should include multiple levels (e.g., individual, dyadic, nuclear, extended family, sociocultural) and multiple perspectives (e.g., interview, observational, self-report, collateral report; Snyder et al., 2016). Relying on a single method of assessment can result in an incomplete or biased understanding of the client that has implications for diagnoses and interventions offered (Meyer et al., 2001). Multimethod assessment provides a multidimensional understanding of the client's difficulties.

1.2.3.1 Self and Collateral Report

Self-report measures involve the client themselves providing information on areas such as their cognitions, feelings, behaviors, and experiences through questionnaires. These are helpful as information is gathered directly from the client who has first-hand knowledge of their experience but can be difficult to fully rely on if clients lack insight into their problems or are not forthright in their responses (Galione & Oltmanns, 2013). Collateral-report measures are similar to self-report measures in that they ask for the informant's perspective on the client's symptoms or area being assessed. For instance, the PTSD Checklist collateral version (PCL-CO; Monson, 2012) asks the same 20 questions that a collateral completes based on their perception of the client's symptoms. Collaterals can provide valuable information from their direct experience in observing the client's very concerns that may bring them to seek assessment and treatment (De Los Reyes & Makol, 2022). Unlike clinicians, informants often have multiple opportunities to observe experiences and behaviors in one or multiple environments. Informants may provide information that the client is unable or unwilling to disclose (Gallagher et al., 1998). Self-report data, or collateral report data, can allow clients to report experiences that they may otherwise be reluctant to discuss directly with the clinician or in the context of a couple assessment, in the presence of their partner (Snyder et al., 2016). Self-administered questionnaires are convenient and relatively easy to administer (Snyder et al., 2016) can be completed by a variety of informants, and require very little time for clinicians to administer (Achenbach et al., 2005). Both self and collateral measures are subject to self-report biases that can be due to selective attention or social desirability (Möricke et al., 2016; Pu et al., 2019). There are many self-report measures available for assessing psychopathology and it should be noted that these measures do not replace a diagnostic assessment conducted by a trained clinician as clinical judgement is required for making a diagnosis. Additionally, collaterals are lay individuals who are not trained in areas such as the classification of symptoms and their report should be considered without being used as a sole diagnostic tool (De Los Reyes & Makol, 2022).

1.2.3.2 Clinician-Administered Measures

Clinicians may obtain information through unstructured clinical interviews, structured or semi-structured assessments, and/or behavioral observations of the client. The advantage of clinician-administered assessment is that it involves a trained clinician who knows what to look for and what kinds of questions to ask to obtain an understanding of the client's difficulties. In unstructured interviews, clinicians ask any questions they believe are appropriate for assessing diagnostic features or relevant clinical characteristics (Rowa et al., 2008), which may aid in establishing rapport with the client and more naturally obtaining a client's narrative. A drawback of unstructured interviews is that clinicians may seek confirmatory evidence for their initial impressions and neglect assessing other important areas (Galione & Oltmanns, 2013). Research also suggests that rates of diagnostic agreement using unstructured interviews are no better than chance (Rowa et al., 2008). Interviews that are more standardized increase reliability by using clear language and specific steps for sequencing and rating items (Galione & Oltmanns, 2013). Structured diagnostic assessments involve specific standardized questions that the clinician asks, which then determines the presence of diagnoses based on an algorithm (De Los Reyes & Makol, 2022). Structured interview questions are read verbatim and are limited in their flexibility of ratings (Galione & Oltmanns, 2013). Semi-structured interviews include specific prompts that assessors use to determine the presence of a symptom, and assessors then may follow up with unstructured questions which can help determine how much the client understood the original question as well as the severity and context of the occurrence of the symptom (De Los Reyes & Makol, 2022). Semi-structured interviews allow clinicians to rely more on clinical judgment rather than solely relying on the client's responses (Galione & Oltmanns, 2013).

In working with couples, the initial clinical interview is often conducted with both partners present (Snyder et al., 2016). There is debate about whether the couple's intake interview should be conducted with both partners interviewed together, separately, or a combination of both (Snyder et al., 2016). Some research indicates that the convergent validity of disclosure on delicate topics such as sex, infidelity, and violence is higher from separate interviews than from conjoint interviews (Haynes et al., 1981; Whisman & Snyder, 2007). Clients may be unwilling to disclose issues such as violence in the initial assessment session due to feeling embarrassed, minimizing the issue, or a fear of retaliation (Rathus & Feindler, 2004; Snyder et al., 2016). Treatments such as integrative behavioral couple therapy recommend an initial joint session with both partners, followed by individual sessions with each partner for a comprehensive assessment (Christensen et al., 2014).

An example of an informant interview could also be used with a friend, parent, or sibling sharing about their experience of their loved one's substance use, which could include descriptions of the impact on their relationship and of the client's ability to meet role expectations. Similarly, this type of assessment could be used for cognitive impairment. An adult child might be involved in the intake process for a client's neuropsychological assessment for dementia. This involvement could include both unstructured clinical interviews, as well as self-report measures completed by the child to document their perception of their parent's functioning, including instrumental activities of daily living (e.g., Hackett et al., 2020). Factors that may impact informants' reporting of functional impairment include caregiver burnout and cohabitation. Additionally, adult children may be less accurate in assessing everyday functioning compared to spouses (Loewenstein et al., 2001). Although there may be discrepancies in reporting between clients and their informants in these presentations, it is useful to enable triangulation to understand what a comprehensive picture may look like.

1.2.3.3 Behavioral and Observational Methods

Behavioral assessments involve observing the individual's behavior in real-life situations. Ecological momentary assessment (EMA) methods collect data in real-time from the client repeatedly within the client's natural environments and rely less on insight or retrospection in the way that self-report measures do (Shiffman et al., 2008). EMA may involve self-monitoring of a variety of behaviors (e.g., eating behaviors, sleep habits, or self-harm) and include thoughts or emotions the client is experiencing at the same time. This form of assessment is particularly useful as it can provide information on the behavior as it occurs in real-time and allows the client and clinician to better understand the behavior outside of the context of the clinical office (Shiffman et al., 2008). Collaterals can monitor the client's behavior which may provide additional information beyond what the client reports themselves. For instance, an adult child can monitor the frequency of memory issues that they observe in their parent with dementia. Electronic diary methods are also used in couples and can be helpful for assessing interpersonal processes (Snyder et al., 2016).

In working with couples, observational methods may include a communication task proposed to elicit verbal and nonverbal behaviors of interest related to areas including effect, behavioral engagement, communication skills, problem-solving, power, and intimacy (Snyder et al., 2016). There are specific tasks that can be assigned to the couple and then measured with coding instructions which can be difficult to administer in routine clinical practice settings (Snyder et al., 2016). Alternatively, the clinician may propose a communication sample, in which the couples are asked to discuss a moderately distressing topic while the clinician observes their interaction and notes strengths and weaknesses in their communication (Monson & Fredman, 2012).

1.2.4 Assessment Domains

Recommendations in couples therapy include a sequential strategy in which initial clinical inquiry is used to understand relationship problems, which is then followed by brief structured interviews or self-report measures and can be followed up with more detailed assessment methods for higher levels of relationship distress (Snyder et al., 2016). A similar approach may be applied to working with individuals where a clinician-administered assessment is first conducted, followed up with self-report measures, and then asking for the involvement of collaterals to obtain further data. Self-report and collateral-report data can be more easily compared if collaterals complete parallel forms that assess the same domains of functioning in similar formats and are scored the same way (Achenbach et al., 2019). Computer software can be used to examine side-by-side comparisons from self and other reports on each item within a scale, making it easy to examine which items are agreed upon and which items have disagreements that warrant further inquiry (Achenbach et al., 2005).

Various measures of psychopathology and individual functioning exist and some of these have parallel measures that assess a close other's perception of the client's symptoms or functioning. For instance, the Behavior Rating Inventory of Executive Function—Adult Version (BRIEF-A) assesses executive functions and self-regulation has self-report and informant-report formats (Roth et al., 2005). The Posttraumatic Stress Disorder Checklist (PCL-5; Weathers et al., 2013) that assesses self-reported PTSD symptoms also has a parallel collateral version, the PCL-CO (Monson, 2012). The Adult Self-Report (ASR) and Adult Behavior Checklist (ABCL) developed by Achenbach and Rescorla (2003) are parallel measures that assess problems, personal strengths, and adaptive functioning.

Snyder et al. (2016) discuss the importance of assessing relationship behaviors, cognitions, and affect for case conceptualization and treatment planning in couple therapy. For instance, clinicians may want to understand how frequent and intense the couple's conflicts are, what standards the partners hold for the relationship, and how much various feelings are expressed with one another (Snyder et al., 2016). These areas can be assessed from a variety of methods described below. Individual mental health functioning (e.g., depression, anxiety, substance use, violent behavior) is also important to assess as this can impact the relationship (Snyder et al., 2016).

Dimensions of relationship functioning including areas such as dyadic distress, communication patterns, and accommodation can be assessed in multiple ways for both individuals and couples. The Dyadic Adjustment Scale (Spanier, 1976), the Kansas Marital Satisfaction Scale (Schumm et al., 1986), and the Couples Satisfaction Index (Funk & Rogge, 2007) are examples of measures that assess aspects of relationship satisfaction; identical measures can be given to partners or collaterals to better understand their own perspective of the relationship. The adapted version of the Frequency and Acceptability of Partner Behavior Inventory (Doss & Christensen, 2006) assesses behaviors between partners in domains related to affection, closeness, demands, and relationship violations. The Communication Patterns Questionnaire (Christensen, 1987) measures communication patterns before, during, and after conflict. There are also various measures of family functioning that can be administered (e.g., the Family Assessment Device; Epstein et al., 1983). Physical and psychological aggression can be assessed using the revised Conflict Tactics Scale (Straus & Douglas, 2007) and the Multidimensional Measure of Emotional Abuse (Murphy & Hoover, 1999). These measures of conflict may be particularly helpful to administer if clinicians are completing intake interviews in a joint format to increase a sense of privacy for each individual. Partner accommodation may be important to assess in couple therapies being delivered to one or both clients who have a mental health disorder as well as in individual treatments when there may be interpersonal factors influencing the client. For instance, in clients with PTSD, close loved ones may accommodate by avoiding feared places with the client, participating in safety behaviors, or suppressing thoughts and feelings related to the relationship which can contribute to or maintain symptoms and relationship distress (Fredman et al., 2022). Accommodation can occur in clients with a variety of mental health disorders and can be assessed by the clinician asking the client or informant about accommodation behaviors or using a measure developed to assess accommodation such as the Significant Others' Responses to Trauma Scale (SORTS; Fredman et al., 2014). These measures can be used for initial assessment and for screening purposes (Snyder et al., 2016), as well as administered throughout the course of treatment to help clinicians decide if accommodation should be further targeted clinically.

1.2.5 Correlations Between Multi-informant Ratings

In the adult literature on multi-informant reporting, Meyer et al. (2001) found small to moderate associations between self-reported personality and clinical diagnoses and other sources of data including reports from loved ones, peers, clinicians, performance tasks, and observed behaviors. In a meta-analysis examining agreement between informant ratings for adults with psychopathology, the authors found a correlation of $r = .68$ for substance use, $r = .43$ for internalizing issues (e.g.., anxiety, depression), and $r = .44$ for externalizing problems (aggression, lying; Achenbach et al., 2005). Out of the 50,000 studies that the authors screened for eligibility, only 108 (0.2%) included information on multi-informant assessment, indicating that very little research obtains data from close others of adults. Different instruments had a slightly smaller overall correlation ($r = .30$) than parallel instruments completed by self and others. The authors found no studies that used observational measures. Additionally, there were no significant effects of clinical interviews compared to questionnaires versus multi-informant reporting.

In a study by Rescorla et al. (2016), the authors analyzed multi-informant correlations between problem scale scores on the Adult Self-Report and Adult Behavior Checklist (collateral measure). These measures are parallel to one another assessing DSM-oriented scales, internalizing and externalizing problems, and other specific issues (e.g., aggressive behavior). They recruited a large sample ($N = 8203$) from 14 societies differing in economic, political, ethnic, religious, and cultural characteristics to better understand similarities and differences across societies in collateral reports of adult issues. They reported a mean correlation of $r = .47$ across all problem scales in the 14 societies, which is similar to the correlations reported in Achenbach et al. (2005)'s meta-analysis. Overall, these small to moderate correlations between various informants suggest there are differences in reporting. If informants reported the same type of information, a high correlation would be expected (greater than $r = .70$), and this information would be less valuable as it would be redundant (Alexander et al., 2017; Kraemer et al., 2003). This body of research suggests that single assessment methods provide an incomplete picture of what the client is experiencing (Meyer et al., 2001).

1.2.6 Reasons for Discrepancies Across Informants

Inconsistent findings between informants were initially thought to be due to measurement issues stemming from problems such as rater biases or random error (De Los Reyes & Epkins, 2023). Because of this, it was suggested that low levels of agreement between informants were problematic and indicated issues related to poor validity and reliability. Current research suggests that large discrepancies can still occur between informant reports on measures that are psychometrically sound, suggesting that measurement error does not solely explain disagreement (De Los Reyes, 2011). Conflicting information obtained through different assessments allows clinicians an opportunity to consider the nature of the information gathered from each test, idiosyncrasies in the way different measures assess a construct, psychometrics of a test, and the motivational and environmental factors that may influence test responses (Meyer et al., 2001).

There are several reasons why there may be differences in reports from unique informants. Collaterals may fail to report symptoms that are not observable as informant reports often rely on observations or inferences about the individual's behavior. Some research indicates that there is greater agreement between the client and close others who serve as informants on visible symptoms (e.g., behavioral avoidance) than less visible (e.g., physiological) symptoms (Ennis et al., 2021). Discrepancies may be due to variations in the client's behavior that are seen in different contexts (De Los Reyes & Makol, 2022). Collaterals cannot observe another person's behavior in situations in which they are not present and certain behaviors may be more prominent in certain contexts (Rescorla et al., 2016). For instance, an individual may be anxious when giving a presentation at work which may be best observed by co-workers, but the individual may not experience performance-related anxiety when they are at home with their loved ones.

The interpersonal nature of the relationship between the individual and the informant may also differ with the degree of closeness and intimacy (Achenbach et al., 2019). For instance, the way an individual behaves around another, topics that are discussed, or activities that they engage in together will likely vary depending upon if the informant is a romantic partner versus a sibling. Relationship factors such as satisfaction can impact reports about an individual due to leniency bias or halo effects, where ratings about specific attributes are based on the general perception of the individual (Pu et al., 2019). In romantic couples, a sentient override can occur in which high levels of affection or disaffection for one's partner creates a cognitive filter (Pu et al., 2019). Discrepancies in ratings from different collaterals may also be due to the way the informant interacts with the client (Achenbach et al., 2019). These discrepancies due to individual differences may arise even between informants who play a similar role in the client's life (e.g., pairs of siblings or colleagues). For instance, a colleague who is hostile will likely elicit a different behavior from the client than a colleague who is warm.

Self and collateral ratings can also be influenced by intrapersonal personality traits (e.g., narcissistic, antisocial) and cognitive characteristics that impact an individual's perception of the world around them (Achenbach et al., 2019). These characteristics can impact how they perceive or remember another individual's behavior, leading to reporting discrepancies. Perceived stress and psychopathology such as depression can influence the information the individual pays attention to and may distort what is perceived (Pu et al., 2019). For example, a person who feels anxious may subjectively perceive the way another person speaks to be critical of them.

In relation to treatment, agreement across various informants of a behavior (e.g., aggression) would imply that interventions should target this behavior generally (i.e., across contexts), whereas if this behavior is only reported by one informant, clinicians can focus on the informant's perception of the client or on addressing behavior as it arises in the relationship with that particular client and collateral (Achenbach et al., 2005). Differences in self and collateral ratings may help identify issues that are not recognized by the individual client (Achenbach et al., 2005). Discrepancies have implications for clinical practice including exploring symptoms and domains of functioning the client is having issues with that warrant further support, as well as whether the treatment being delivered leads to improvement in the issues (Marsh et al., 2020).

1.2.7 Integrating Multi-informant Assessments

Discrepancies increase uncertainty in decision-making in clinical practice. Clinicians are prone to making clinical decisions that favors one informant's report over another when there is a discrepancy in reporting (De Los Reyes & Makol, 2022; Marsh et al., 2020). This may be due to clinicians making judgments regarding which informant has the most insight into the problem, causing the clinician to focus on one informant's reporting. However, there is no evidence that one informant provides more precise information in comparison to the other informants and this approach is problematic as it neglects the data provided by other sources (De Los Reyes & Makol, 2022; Marsh et al., 2020). Achenbach et al. (2019) suggest that rather than asking "who should I believe" when information is inconsistent, a better approach is to examine the discrepancies to understand possible reasons for them. It is recommended that clinicians conceptualize the client in a manner that synthesizes all the assessment data in the context of the client's history, referral information, and observation (Meyer et al., 2001).

In research, there are various approaches to integrating informant reports, and in considering each approach, De Los Reyes and Makol (2022) recommend asking "what is gained, and perhaps more importantly, what is lost when using one of these approaches" (p. 12). Researchers sometimes create an "and" rule, meaning that at least two or more informants must endorse the presence of a target behavior for that behavior to be considered present. Alternatively, the "or" rule requires that a behavior be reported by at least one informant for it to be considered present. Evidence is lacking to suggest that these combined strategies improve clinical decision-making (De Los Reyes et al., 2015) and both methods neglect the contextual information related to the data (De Los Reyes & Makol, 2022). Researchers may also take a composite-score approach to integrating data, whereby scores across informant reports are averaged. However, this approach treats reporting discrepancies as measurement errors and does not account for the distance between scores or the differences in informants (De Los Reyes & Makol, 2022).

Recommendations for clinical practice are that clinicians create hypotheses about patterns they expect to see across informant reports and test these hypotheses through additional assessment as needed (De Los Reyes & Makol, 2022). The Satellite Model (Kraemer et al., 2003) also referred to as the trait-score approach (Makol et al., 2020) may be used as a tool to integrate informant reports. In this model, informants who systematically vary in terms of context (e.g., home, work) and perspective (e.g., self, other) in their observations of the client should be selected. This method produces a trait score, which captures the behaviors that manifest across contexts and perspectives and accounts for the positioning and relative distance of informants (Makol et al., 2020). In a study examining the trait-score method in assessments of social anxiety for adolescents, the trait-score method outperformed reports from individual informants and composite scores of informant reports in predicting observed anxiety during social interaction tasks and referral status (Makol et al., 2020). Furthermore, Alexander et al. (2017) present a simplified version of the Operations Triad Model (De Los Reyes et al., 2013) that focuses on context (i.e., physical environment, social environment, timing of when behaviors occur) and insight (i.e., cognitive abilities of the individual). They suggest that multiple informants may provide unique information when either context or insight is a relevant factor (Alexander et al., 2017). For instance, if the individual's behavior varies across settings (making context relevant), or if the individual has limited self-awareness of their symptoms or behaviors (making insight relevant). Both approaches described emphasize the appreciation for variability in informant reporting.

1.2.8 Ethical Considerations

One of the first questions clinicians may ask themselves when deciding to involve collaterals in the assessment or treatment process is "who is the client?". The American Psychological Association's "Ethical Principles of Psychologists and

Code of Conduct" (American Psychological Association [APA], 2017) discusses ethical principles when psychologists work with multiple individuals. Standard 10.02a of the APA Ethics Code states "(a) When psychologists agree to provide services to several persons who have a relationship (such as spouses, significant others, or parents and children), they take reasonable steps to clarify at the outset (1) which of the individuals are clients/patients and (2) the relationship the psychologist will have with each person. This clarification includes the psychologist's role and the probable uses of the services provided or the information obtained" (p. 14). This means clinicians should clarify the differences in the nature of the relationship with a client versus an informant. In individual work, the client seeking services is the client, whereas in couples therapy both members of the couple are considered to be the client (Ellis, 2012). Since the purpose of a collateral is to further the clinical interests of a client, collaterals are not considered clients (Jasper, 2016).

The Canadian Code of Ethics for Psychologists under standard I.26 states "Clarify the nature of multiple relationships to all concerned parties, including collateral contacts, before obtaining consent, if providing services or conducting research at the request of or for the use of a retaining or other third party. This would include, but not be limited to clarifying: the purpose of the service or research; the role and responsibilities of the psychologist; the reasonably anticipated use that will be made of the information collected; access to records or the information contained therein; the limits of privacy and confidentiality; and any special legal requirements or limitations" (Canadian Psychological Association [CPA], 2017, p. 15). Depending on the level of involvement of the collateral, therapists may wish to use written consent forms. For instance, if the therapist plans to meet with the collateral and conduct an interview, having a written consent form may be helpful to ensure that areas mentioned in the CPA code have been thoroughly addressed. If the individual client is going to be simply giving their loved one a collateral measure to complete and the client is bringing this measure back, going through an informed consent process with the collateral may be unnecessary. The Trust Practice and Risk Management Association (TrustPARMA) has developed a consent form that can be used in practice with collaterals that is available online (https://parma.trustinsurance.com/Resources/Articles/sample-outpatient-services-agreement-for-collaterals).

The role of the collateral during assessment and therapy should be discussed, as collateral roles may vary. For instance, the clinician may consider whether the collateral will be providing information about the client's symptoms and functioning that may be helpful in clarifying a diagnosis or if the collateral is providing information about the interpersonal environment and the relationship between the client and the informant. The rationale for involving collaterals should be explained to clients and potential risks and benefits should also be discussed. The client may have concerns about whether their personal information will be shared by the clinician with the collateral. Clinicians can remind clients of their right to confidentiality and answer any questions they may have. The clinician should explain the level of involvement they believe the collateral will have in the client's care. For example, will they be only completing questionnaires as part of the assessment process, or will they attend one or multiple sessions either separately or with the client? Documenting in the client's chart the purpose of the collateral and the client's response to collateral involvement is also recommended (Jasper, 2016).

Bennett et al. (2006) provide an example of a psychologist who is treating a wife individually and during treatment, the husband attends conjoint sessions as an informant. Their relationship ends, and they both wish to have individual sessions with the psychologist. In this example, it would have been ideal for the psychologist to have explained at the first conjoint session that the wife is the client and that the husband is the collateral contact whose purpose is to further the wife's treatment. This would then increase the likelihood of the husband being able to understand that the primary treatment obligation is to the wife, and the psychologist could refer him to a therapist of his own (Bennett et al., 2006). The consent form template by TrustPARMA includes information on who a collateral is and the roles of collaterals in therapy. It also describes the reasons why collaterals are referred out for their own therapy (avoiding dual relationships and helping the clinician stay focused on the care of the original client).

Collaterals should be provided information regarding the clinician's practice, policies, and procedures that will further help the informant understand their role and provide them with an opportunity to ask any questions before participating in the assessment (Jasper, 2016). Collaterals should also be aware that the client's therapy records will not be shared with them and that the collateral does not have a right of access. The collaterals should also not have an expectation of confidentiality with the information disclosed, though they do have a right to privacy. Jasper (2016) states that collaterals have a general right to privacy on topics such as finances, sexual history, physical, or mental health. If a third party requests the client's records, it is recommended that any personal information about the collateral be redacted to ensure that the collateral's privacy is upheld (Jasper, 2016). Clinicians should also have a plan for how to respond if a collateral discloses information that relates to the well-being of the collateral. For instance, if the collateral reports experiencing suicidality themselves, since the collateral is not a client, clinicians do not have a legal obligation to intervene or breach confidentiality for safety purposes. However, ethically, the clinician may choose to help find ways to support the collateral such as referring them to a therapist or providing crisis resources.

If conducting interviews with collaterals, clinicians need to make the decision as to whether interviews with the collateral will be done separately or while the client is present. In a couple therapy context, clinicians would have to decide if the collateral would be interviewed separately, with one partner present at a time, or with both partners present. Generally, joint interviews can have benefits such as being more efficient, allowing for the client and informant to participate in an active way that can create opportunities for a shared understanding of the issues, and allowing the clinician to observe relational dynamics and communication styles between the client and a close other. Discrepancies that were noted from other measures (e.g., self-report and collateral report) can also be discussed with both individuals present. Simultaneous interviews can also have drawbacks such as the informant being uncomfortable discussing sensitive information with the client present. Separate interviews can potentially increase the sense of privacy and allow a collateral to share information more freely as well as allow for more focused questions to understand the collateral's relationship and experience with the client. In qualitative studies conducted with couples, separate interviews with each partner can be perceived to be a test of whether responses between partners will match (Blake et al., 2021; Mellor et al., 2013; Taylor & de Vocht, 2011). However, separate interviews conducted with couples in one of the studies allowed for greater self-reflection which may have been otherwise unexpressed in a joint format (Blake et al., 2021).

If sensitive information is disclosed by a collateral privately to the clinician (e.g., during an individual interview or through measures that were completed), the clinician should be mindful of whether sharing this with the client would be beneficial. For instance, if the collateral discloses to the clinician a mental health issue that was previously unreported by the client due to lack of insight (e.g., delusional thinking), clinicians should consider how sharing this information with the client can impact the client, the therapeutic alliance, and the relationship between the client and collateral. Similarly, if the collateral discloses something clinically important about the client's history (e.g., childhood sexual abuse) that was denied or unreported by the client, clinicians should be thoughtful about whether they will bring up this information to the client and how to do so in a way that does not damage rapport or trust. In another example, if the collateral indicates that the client is physically abusive toward them, clinicians may not want to directly report this to the client that this is what was reported by the collateral due to concerns that this could escalate aggression. Instead, clinicians may provide resources to the collateral for them to obtain support and further assess the client for aggressive behaviors. In all of these instances where delicate and unexpected information is disclosed by the collateral, clinicians should consider how disclosing versus not disclosing the information to the client will impact the client's care. Discussing the risks and benefits of involving collaterals with the client before doing so can help prepare both clients and clinicians for handling unexpected disclosures.

1.3 Clinical Considerations for Diverse Identities

In conducting assessments with clients who have unique cultural identities (defined as an individual's affiliation or identification with a particular group or groups; Substance Abuse and Mental Health Services Administration [SAMHSA], 2014), clinicians should strive to practice cultural competence and cultural humility to offer culturally responsive care. The APA guidelines for Psychological Assessment and Evaluation (2020) state that "Psychologists who conduct psychological testing, assessment, and evaluation strive to practice with cultural competence" (p. 18). Cultural competence emphasizes that healthcare systems must recognize a client's cultural perspectives and background and that individuals from various cultural groups can have different beliefs and practices (Betancourt et al., 2002; SAMHSA, 2014). Increasing a clinician's general knowledge about cultures (e.g., how culture influences communication patterns, clinical presentations, behavioral norms within and outside of sessions) can increase one's cultural competence (SAMHSA, 2014; Stubbe, 2020). A lack of cultural competence can lead to breakdowns in communication between the client and clinician, delay appropriate treatments, cause misdiagnosis, lower treatment compliance, and result in poorer treatment outcomes (Barr, 2008; Carpenter-Song et al., 2009; Dixon et al., 2011).

Cultural humility focuses less on the knowledge of cultures one holds and instead emphasizes self-evaluation and critique as well as an open, curious approach that focuses on interpersonal relationships with a willingness to learn from others (Stubbe, 2020). Cultural humility implies that one does not know and is willing to learn from clients about their experiences, while being aware of one's own culture (Lekas et al., 2020). It involves being aware of one's own biases, increasing self-understanding, being interpersonally sensitive, and developing an appreciation for the multifaceted domains of each person (Stubbe, 2020).

Hays (2016) outlines the ADDRESSING framework which can be applied to both clinicians undergoing self-assessment to understand cultural influences on their own attitudes and beliefs, as well as cultural factors to consider when working with clients and collaterals. The ADDRESSING acronym stands for Age and generational influences, Developmental or other Disability, Religion and spirituality, Ethnic and racial identity, Socioeconomic status, Sexual orientation, Indigenous heritage, National origin, and Gender. These factors are all important for clinicians to consider during the assessment process and clinicians should recognize that clients may have multiple intersecting identities that influence their lived experience. Similarly, collaterals cannot be defined in terms of a generic cultural identity as even loved ones from the same racial background or ethnic heritage can be quite different from one another (SAMHSA, 2014). A multidimensional approach is necessary for understanding the role of culture for clients and collaterals (SAMHSA, 2014). Bhugra and De Silva (2000) recommend that therapists take a systems approach when working with couples, which can also be applied to clients and collaterals as well. This entails understanding cultural factors within the individual, dyad, and in relation to extended family, society, or subcultures. Therapists can also examine their own relationship with each member of the dyad as this may be relevant. For instance, in situations where the therapist is from a similar cultural background to one of the partners, therapists can be mindful of how the therapeutic alliance with each person may be impacted (Bhugra & De Silva, 2000).

The APA guidelines for Psychological Assessment and Evaluation (2020) recommend that psychologists understand how test administration, results, and interpretation can be impacted by factors such as age, disability, race, ethnicity, gender, religion/spirituality, sexual orientation, social class, language, acculturation, and immigration/refugee status. Individuals from nondominant cultures can demonstrate their symptoms in a unique way, as well as have different levels of awareness and explanations for their concerns (Sue & Sue, 2013). The assessment methods and language used should be appropriate for the age group the clinician is working with. Financial barriers may impact participation in aspects of the assessment for both clients and collaterals and clinicians can try to be flexible in terms of where (e.g., in-person office versus virtual) and when services are offered to increase accessibility. Clinicians should strive to understand the client's views on gender roles, expectations, and societal messages and how these interact with presenting concerns. It is recommended that clinicians be mindful of how their own identities may limit understanding of the client as well as interact with the identities of the client (Hays, 2016).

A course of action can be recommended to the client in a collaborative manner. Although not all clients have a desire to be involved in treatment planning, the clinician can openly offer that the client participates in treatment planning especially if a client's beliefs and practices can serve as a healing framework for treatment. Collaboration should also include understanding the client's preferences for involving family and community members in the assessment and treatment process. Different cultures can have different norms related to privacy and involvement of loved ones and individual preferences which may or may not fit with the individual's culture may also influence a person's views on the inclusion of loved ones.

The Association for Assessment in Counseling and Education (2012) has developed tips for culturally responsive screening and assessment. They recommend knowing the client's primary language and language proficiency prior to the assessment as clinicians may need to arrange for having an interpreter present or to be mindful of this as they decide which test instruments to use. Clinicians can also ask the client questions about the collateral's culture to be prepared for these arrangements. They also caution clinicians to not assume that translations of test materials exactly match the language of the client as it is possible that the translations do not fit with the client's own way of thinking or speaking. Clinicians should consider how acculturation may influence responses during the assessment with both clients and collaterals. Finally, understanding how the test was developed and if normative data are available for the population being worked with is important. Individuals who are not appropriately represented in the normative sample increase the likelihood of misinterpretation of test results due to individual and cultural characteristics (APA, 2020).

Hays (2016) recommends that extra time is included during the initial assessment for obtaining informed consent in case the client has limited language or comprehension abilities, fears about signing written documents, distrust of authority figures, or financial concerns. Extra time should also be made for the end of the session to ask if the client felt understood, if they have any questions about the process, or if they would like to tell the clinician any other information to be further understood at this time (Stubbe, 2020). A flexible, dynamic, hypothesis-testing approach to culturally informed assessment is also recommended (Hays, 2016). This includes choosing tests that match the referral question and client's characteristics, culture, and preferences and understanding the reasons for a client's test performance (Hays, 2016). This is similar to the hypothesis-driven approach (De Los Reyes & Makol, 2022) for understanding discrepancies collaterals may have as well.

1.4 Case Vignette

1.4.1 Case Overview and Individual Assessment Measures

Mr. Andrews is a 35-year-old White male. His family doctor referred him to Dr. Clark for psychological assessment and treatment in a private practice setting. The referral information stated that the client was in a car accident 6 months ago. Since then, Mr. Andrews has experienced low mood, increased anxiety, as well as difficulties in interpersonal relationships including at work and with his partner.

During the initial meeting with Mr. Andrews, Dr. Clark began the assessment with an informal interview and asked Mr. Andrews about his current struggles and questions related to demographics, background history, and culture. Mr. Andrews indicated that since his car accident, he has had increased trouble sleeping, feels more on edge throughout the day, has had less interest in his usual activities, and has had issues with concentration at work and at home. Mr. Andrews shared that he was born and raised in Canada and currently lives by himself. He reported that his parents live a few hours away from him, and he has little contact with them. He stated that he had a good childhood, though his mother experienced depression at different points in his life growing up. He indicated currently having "okay" social support, with a few friends he sees from time to time. Mr. Andrews reported that he was in a relationship with a woman, with whom he had been dating for over a year. He reported working full-time at a bank and stated that he found it difficult to connect with his colleagues. He indicated noticing he has had a shorter fuse over the last while, finding himself to be more irritable around others including his partner. Dr. Clark observed that the client's thought processes appeared logical and that his speech and motor movements appeared normal. Dr. Clark noticed that Mr. Andrews made little eye contact with her as he spoke and although he was cooperative, appeared somewhat guarded.

To assess for psychopathology related to mood disorders, anxiety disorders, and trauma-related disorders, Dr. Clark decided to use a semi-structured psychodiagnostic interview. Dr. Clark chose to use the Diagnostic Assessment Research Tool (DART; McCabe et al., 2017) as it offers a variety of modules to assess mental health conditions and the modules that are not relevant for the client can be skipped, making it efficient to administer in a private practice setting. Additionally, Dr. Clark thought it would be helpful to have Mr. Andrews complete several self-report measures to provide his perception of his own symptoms and functioning. Given his presenting concerns of issues related to mood, anxiety, difficulties in interpersonal relationships as well as observed poor eye contact, Dr. Clark decided to use measures that would assess these domains. She chose to use the Patient Health Questionnaire (PHQ-9; Kroenke et al., 2001), the Generalized Anxiety Disorder measure (GAD-7; Spitzer et al., 2006), the Social Phobia Inventory (SPIN; Connor et al., 2000), the PTSD Checklist for DSM-5 (PCL-5; Weathers et al., 2013), and the Couples Satisfaction Index (CSI; Funk & Rogge, 2007). As these measures are all brief, it took very little time to administer the measures and for Mr. Andrews to complete them.

Self-report measure scores were mild on the PHQ-9 (total score of 9) and severe on the GAD-7 (total score of 15). The total score on the SPIN was 12, indicating few symptoms of social anxiety and the total score on the PCL-5 was 40, indicating a probable PTSD diagnosis. The client's CSI score was 98, suggestive of relationship dissatisfaction. With regard to the information gathered from the administration of the DART, the client's symptoms met the criteria for PTSD and though he endorsed some symptoms related to generalized anxiety and a major depressive episode, these symptoms appeared to be best accounted for by the PTSD diagnosis. While assessing his trauma history, Mr. Andrews reluctantly shared with Dr. Clark that he had had an uncomfortable sexual experience as a child. Dr. Clark thanked Mr. Andrews for letting her know this and validated that these experiences can be difficult to talk about and that they are important discussions for understanding him holistically. Mr. Andrews further disclosed that he was sexually abused by a male babysitter at the age of 9 years old. He indicated he had not thought about this trauma for years. However, since the accident, he described having several instances of flashbacks and intrusive thoughts related to the sexual abuse.

1.4.2 Collateral Assessment

Dr. Clark thought that it may be helpful to have data from informants to assist with the assessment results gathered so far given the client's presenting concerns were impacting him in various domains of his life and affecting his relationships. During the second session, the following dialogue occurred:

Dr. Clark: I think it would be useful to have someone who knows you or perhaps multiple people who know you involved in the assessment process as a collateral. I would do an assessment with your close other to help me form a more comprehensive understanding of your current struggles by understanding the viewpoints from other people in your life.

Mr. Andrews: Who is typically included as a collateral?

Dr. Clark: Well, there are lots of options. We can jointly discuss who might be a good fit and why. Sometimes, people might ask partners to participate. In other circumstances, it can be useful to have a work colleague, or a close friend contribute. If you feel that each person has a unique perspective on the issues you are struggling with, we can invite more than one person to participate as a collateral.

Mr. Andrews: I don't feel very close to my family or friends, and I wouldn't feel comfortable asking my work colleagues to participate. I'm open to the idea of my partner being a collateral if you think that would be useful. One concern I have is will this end up turning into a couples therapy if we involve her?

Mr. Clark: I think your partner would make sense to involve as a collateral. No, this would not turn into couple therapy. The purpose of involving your partner would be to serve as a collateral in the service of your assessment and treatment. You would still continue to be my client. I will also make that clear to her when I speak with her.

They further discussed how involved the collateral would be and the risks and benefits of involving an informant. Dr. Clark proposed that Mr. Andrews' partner complete collateral measures about her perception of his symptoms and their relationship, as well as complete a brief interview with Dr. Clark. Mr. Andrews indicated he would feel more comfortable with the interview being conducted while he was present, and Dr. Clark explained the benefits and drawbacks of conducting an interview in a private versus joint format. Mr. Andrews continued to state his preference that the interview be conducted jointly and requested that the clinician not share his information related to his sexual abuse trauma, as he had not told his partner about this yet and did not want to "scare her off." Dr. Clark indicated respecting his decision for a joint interview and further discussed with Mr. Andrews the types of questions she would like to ask his partner and if there was any other information that Mr. Andrews did not want Dr. Clark discussing in the presence of his partner. Dr. Clark requested that Mr. Andrews ask his partner if she would be willing to serve as a collateral and Dr. Clark offered that she could further explain what this means by phone to his partner if his partner had any questions. He agreed to this request. The initial session ended after Dr. Clark asked Mr. Andrews if he had any questions or concerns with anything discussed or the assessment process, as well as checking in to see how he was now feeling. He reported feeling comfortable with the plan they discussed, feeling more hopeful that treatment would help him, and feeling understood by Dr. Clark.

Dr. Clark received an email several days after their appointment that the partner, Ms. Choy, would be happy to provide collateral information. Dr. Clark began the next session with both Mr. Andrews and Ms. Choy together, and first went over a collateral consent form (e.g., TrustPARMA; https://parma.trustinsurance.com/Resources/Articles/sample-outpatient-services-agreement-for-collaterals), to ensure Ms. Choy understood the purpose of this assessment, what her role would be, risks and benefits of collateral assessment, and answered any questions that Ms. Choy had before signing. Following the signing of the consent form, Ms. Choy was asked what she noticed about Mr. Andrews' struggles and how this has been impacting her and the relationship. She shared that since the car accident, Mr. Andrews seems to have less patience for her and is more closed off. She shared that they have been seeing each other less often than when they first started dating and no longer do activities that they used to enjoy together such as driving to local parks and lakes for day trips or going to new restaurants. This has in turn made her withdraw from initiating plans with Mr. Andrews.

Ms. Choy was then given several collateral measures to complete including the PCL-CO (Monson, 2012) to assess her perceptions of Mr. Andrews' trauma symptoms, the SORTS (Fredman et al., 2014) to assess for accommodation behaviors related to trauma, and the CSI to assess for relationship satisfaction. Ms. Choy's PCL-CO score (31) was substantially lower than Mr. Andrews' reported PCL-5 score (40). Her score on the SORTS indicated a high level of partner accommodation and her CSI total score of 96 was similar to Mr. Andrews' CSI score (98). Comparing the PCL-5 and PCL-CO side by side allowed Dr. Clark to examine items that were discrepant between the partners. Dr. Clark noticed that items related to avoidance of trauma reminders and symptoms of hyperarousal (e.g., being hypervigilant, being jumpy) were rated slightly more highly by Ms. Choy than Mr. Andrews. Items that related to reexperiencing trauma symptoms (e.g., disturbing dreams, flashbacks) and some internal experiences (e.g., strong negative feelings, strong negative beliefs about oneself) were rated to be lower than Mr. Andrews' scores on these items. Dr. Clark hypothesized that these discrepancies may be due to factors such as the partners not living together which may create more limited opportunities for Ms. Choy to observe various symptoms (e.g., sleep disturbance), internal symptoms being more difficult for collaterals to detect, as well as Mr. Andrews' symptoms such as avoidance and feelings of estrangement may be impacting communication between the partners. Examining the items of the SORTS that were scored highly gave Dr. Clark further information as to how the client's trauma symptoms were impacting the relationship. For example, Ms. Choy reported that several times per week she avoids Mr. Andrews because of his irritable or angry mood, frequently avoids bringing up the car accident to not upset him, and often cancels or rearranges plans because he does not want to engage in them. This provided Dr. Clark with further information on why their overall relationship satisfaction was low and how Mr. Andrews' trauma symptoms were impacting the relationship.

1.4.3 Treatment Plan

Dr. Clark shared the results of the collateral assessment measures with Mr. Andrews in the following individual session.

Dr. Clark: If we look at these measures side by side, what you'll notice is that some of the items such as the ones related to avoiding the trauma or feeling quite aroused in your body when the trauma is activated for you are rated differently by and your partner. I think this is an important discrepancy to try to understand. Do you have a sense of why there might be a difference in these ratings?

Mr. Andrews: Well, my partner has been mentioning to me more recently that she's upset we've stopped doing so many activities we used to do together like driving to a hiking trail outside of the city, driving to new restaurants, or renting a cottage up north. When I think about why I don't want to do this, it's because I'm avoiding driving, so I think she is definitely picking up on that.

Dr. Clark: Ahh yes, that makes sense that those are activities that you two used to do together and she has noticed a shift in your behavior since the accident.

Mr. Andrews: I also don't really like to tell her when I'm experiencing things like nightmares or flashbacks because I worry that she will think I'm unable to get over what happened. It's hard to open up about these kinds of things so I tend to keep it all to myself.

Dr. Clark: I appreciate you sharing that. It's common that trauma makes it difficult to share what is going on internally for a person and that sometimes people worry about being judged if they share. I think it's helpful that we now know how much your trauma is also impacting your relationship. We have a few different options for how we might target what you are struggling with that I want to let you know more about and we can decide together what makes most sense for you.

Dr. Clark explained to Mr. Andrews that his symptoms could be targeted through a trauma-focused cognitive-behavioral treatment for PTSD. Dr. Clark stated that his relationship dissatisfaction could also be targeted with these treatments, such as through incorporating exposures where his partner could join him or through targeting thoughts related to trusting loved ones. Mr. Andrews was appreciative that the individual therapy could benefit not only his trauma-related symptoms but also his relationship distress, and he agreed with this treatment plan. Overall, multi-informant assessment in this case helped Dr. Clarke better understand Mr. Andrews' presenting concerns and led to a more specific and tailored treatment plan for the client.

References

Achenbach, T. M., & Rescorla, L. A. (2003). *Manual for the ASEBA adult forms & profiles*. University of Vermont, Research Center for Children, Youth, and Families.

Achenbach, T. M., Krukowski, R. A., Dumenci, L., & Ivanova, M. Y. (2005). Assessment of adult psychopathology: Meta-analyses and implications of cross-informant correlations. *Psychological Bulletin, 131*(3), 361–382. https://doi.org/10.1037/0033-2909.131.3.361

Achenbach, T., Ivanova, M., & Rescorla, L. (2019). Multi-informant assessment of psychopathology from preschool through old age. In M. Sellbom & J. Suhr (Eds.), *The Cambridge handbook of clinical assessment and diagnosis* (pp. 123–134). Cambridge University Press. https://doi.org/10.1017/9781108235433.011

Alexander, L. A., McKnight, P. E., Disabato, D. J., & Kashdan, T. B. (2017). When and how to use multiple informants to improve clinical assessments. *Journal of Psychopathology and Behavioral Assessment, 39*(4), 669–679. https://doi.org/10.1007/s10862-017-9607-9

American Psychological Association. (2017). *Ethical principles of psychologists and code of conduct.* American Psychological Association. https://www.apa.org/ethics/code/

American Psychological Association, APA Task Force on Psychological Assessment and Evaluation Guidelines. (2020). *APA guidelines for psychological assessment and evaluation.* https://www.apa.org/about/policy/guidelines-psychological-assessment-evaluation.pdf

Antony, M. M. (2001). Assessment of anxiety and the anxiety disorders: An overview. In M. M. Antony, S. M. Orsillo, & L. Roemer (Eds.), *Practitioner's guide to empirically based measures of anxiety* (pp. 9–17). Kluwer Academic/Plenum.

Association for Assessment in Counseling and Education. (2012). *Standards for multicultural assessment* (4th ed.). Association for Assessment in Counseling and Education.

Barr, D. A. (2008). *Health disparities in the United States: Social class, race, ethnicity, and health.* Johns Hopkins University Press.

Bennett, B. E., Bricklin, P. M., Harris, E., Knapp, S., VandeCreek, L., & Younggren, J. N. (2006). *Assessing and managing risk in psychological practice: An individualized approach.* The Trust.

Betancourt, J. R., Green, A. R., & Carrillo, J. E. (2002). *Cultural competence in health care: Emerging frameworks and practical approaches [field report].* https://www.commonwealthfund.org/sites/default/files/documents/___media_files_publications_fund_report_2002_oct_cultural_competence_in_health_care__emerging_frameworks_and_practical_approaches_betancourt_culturalcompetence_576_pdf.pdf

Bhugra, D., & De Silva, P. (2000). Couple therapy across cultures. *Sexual and Relationship Therapy, 15*(2), 183–192. https://doi.org/10.1080/14681990050010763

Blake, S., Janssens, A., Ewing, J., & Barlow, A. (2021). Reflections on joint and individual interviews with couples: A multi-level interview mode. *International Journal of Qualitative Methods, 20*, 160940692110167. https://doi.org/10.1177/16094069211016733

Canadian Psychological Association. (2017). *Canadian code of ethics for psychologists* (4th ed.). Canadian Psychological Association. https://cpa.ca/docs/File/Ethics/CPA_Code_2017_4thEd.pdf

Carpenter-Song, E., Whitley, R., Lawson, W., Quimby, E., & Drake, R. E. (2009). Reducing disparities in mental health care: Suggestions from the Dartmouth–Howard collaboration. *Community Mental Health Journal, 47*(1), 1–13. https://doi.org/10.1007/s10597-009-9233-4

Christensen, A. (1987). Detection of conflict patterns in couples. In K. Hahlweg & M. J. Goldstein (Eds.), *Understanding major mental disorder: The contribution of family interaction research* (pp. 250–265). Family Process Press.

Christensen, A., Doss, B. D., & Jacobson, N. S. (2014). *Reconcilable differences* (2nd ed.). Guilford Press.

Connor, K. M., Davidson, J. R. T., Churchill, L. E., Sherwood, A., Foa, E. B., & Weisler, R. H. (2000). Psychometric properties of the Social Phobia Inventory (SPIN): New self-rating scale. *British Journal of Psychiatry, 176*(4), 379–386. https://doi.org/10.1192/bjp.176.4.379

De Los Reyes, A. (2011). Introduction to the special section: More than measurement error: Discovering meaning behind informant discrepancies in clinical assessments of children and adolescents. *Journal of Clinical Child & Adolescent Psychology, 40*(1), 1–9. https://doi.org/10.1080/15374416.2011.533405

De Los Reyes, A., Thomas, S. A., Goodman, K. L., & Kundey, S. M. (2013). Principles underlying the use of multiple informants' reports. *Annual Review of Clinical Psychology, 9*, 123–149.https://doi.org/10.1146/annurev-clinpsy-050212-185617

De Los Reyes, A., & Epkins, C. C. (2023). Introduction to the special issue. A dozen years of demonstrating that informant discrepancies are more than measurement error: Toward guidelines for integrating data from multi-informant assessments of youth mental health. *Journal of Clinical Child and Adolescent Psychology, 52*(1), 1–18. https://doi.org/10.1080/15374416.2022.2158843

De Los Reyes, A., & Makol, B. A. (2022). Informant reports in clinical assessment. *Comprehensive Clinical Psychology*, 105–122. https://doi.org/10.1016/b978-0-12-818697-8.00113-8

De Los Reyes, A., Augenstein, T. M., Wang, M., Thomas, S. A., Drabick, D. A. G., Burgers, D., & Rabinowitz, J. (2015). The validity of the multi-informant approach to assessing child and adolescent mental health. *Psychological Bulletin, 141*(4), 858–900. https://doi.org/10.1037/a0038498

Dixon, L., Lewis-Fernandez, R., Goldman, H., Interian, A., Michaels, A., & Kiley, M. C. (2011). Adherence disparities in mental health. *Journal of Nervous & Mental Disease, 199*(10), 815–820. https://doi.org/10.1097/nmd.0b013e31822fed17

Doss, B. D., & Christensen, A. (2006). Acceptance in romantic relationships: The frequency and acceptability of partner behavior inventory. *Psychological Assessment, 18*(3), 289–302. https://doi.org/10.1037/1040-3590.18.3.289

Drummond, R. J., & Jones, K. D. (2010). *Assessment procedures for counselors and helping professionals* (7th ed.). Pearson.

Ellis, E. M. (2012). What are the confidentiality rights of collaterals in family therapy? *The American Journal of Family Therapy, 40*(5), 369–384. https://doi.org/10.1080/01926187.2012.677705

Ennis, N., Sijercic, I., Wanklyn, S. G., & Monson, C. M. (2021). Assessing posttraumatic stress disorder with close others' collateral reports: Convergence with self- and clinician reports. *Journal of Family Psychology, 35*(2), 258–263. https://doi.org/10.1037/fam0000803

Epstein, N. B., Baldwin, L. M., & Bishop, D. S. (1983). The McMaster family assessment device. *Journal of Marital and Family Therapy, 9*(2), 171–180.

Fredman, S. J., Vorstenbosch, V., Wagner, A. C., Macdonald, A., & Monson, C. M. (2014). Partner accommodation in posttraumatic stress disorder: Initial testing of the Significant Others' Responses to Trauma Scale (SORTS). *Journal of Anxiety Disorders, 28*(4), 372–381. https://doi.org/10.1016/j.janxdis.2014.04.001

Fredman, S. J., Le, Y., Renshaw, K. D., & Allen, E. S. (2022). Longitudinal associations among service members' PTSD symptoms, partner accommodation, and partner distress. *Behavior Therapy, 53*(6), 1161–1174. https://doi.org/10.1016/j.beth.2022.05.005

Funk, J. L., & Rogge, R. D. (2007). Testing the ruler with item response theory: Increasing precision of measurement for relationship satisfaction with the Couples Satisfaction Index. *Journal of Family Psychology, 21*(4), 572–583. https://doi.org/10.1037/0893-3200.21.4.572

Galione, J. N., & Oltmanns, T. F. (2013). Identifying personality pathology associated with major depressive episodes: Incremental validity of informant reports. *Journal of Personality Assessment, 95*(6), 625–632. https://doi.org/10.1080/00223891.2013.825624

Gallagher, J. G., Riggs, D. S., Byrne, C. A., & Weathers, F. W. (1998). Female partners' estimations of male veterans' combat-related PTSD severity. *Journal of Traumatic Stress, 11*, 367–374. https://doi.org/10.1023/A:1024411422586

Hackett, K., Mis, R., Drabick, D. A. G., & Giovannetti, T. (2020). Informant reporting in mild cognitive impairment: Sources of discrepancy on the functional activities questionnaire. *Journal of the International Neuropsychological Society, 26*(5), 503–514. https://doi.org/10.1017/S1355617719001449

Haynes, S. N., Jensen, B. J., Wise, E., & Sherman, D. (1981). The marital intake interview: A multimethod criterion validity assessment. *Journal of Consulting and Clinical Psychology, 49*(3), 379–387. https://doi.org/10.1037/0022-006X.49.3.379

Hays, P. A. (2016). *Addressing cultural complexities in practice: Assessment, diagnosis, and therapy* (3rd ed.). American Psychological Association.

Hunsley, J., & Mash, E. J. (2007). Evidence-based assessment. *Annual Review of Clinical Psychology, 3*(1), 29–51. https://doi.org/10.1146/annurev.clinpsy.3.022806.091419

Hunsley, J., & Mash, E. J. (2008). *A guide to assessments that work*. Oxford University Press.

Jasper, S. (2016, March 16). *Understanding the role of collaterals in psychotherapy*. California Association of Marriage and Family Therapists. https://www.camft.org/Resources/Legal-Articles/Chronological-Article-List/understanding-the-role-of-collaterals-in-psychotherapy

Klein, D. N. (2003). Patients' versus informants' reports of personality disorders in predicting 7 1/2-year outcome in outpatients with depressive disorders. *Psychological Assessment, 15*(2), 216–222. https://doi.org/10.1037/1040-3590.15.2.216

Kraemer, H. C., Measelle, J. R., Ablow, J. C., Essex, M. J., Boyce, W. T., & Kupfer, D. J. (2003). A new approach to integrating data from multiple informants in psychiatric assessment and research: Mixing and matching contexts and perspectives. *American Journal of Psychiatry, 160*(9), 1566–1577. https://doi.org/10.1176/appi.ajp.160.9.1566

Kroenke, K., Spitzer, R. L., & Williams, J. B. W. (2001). The PHQ-9: Validity of a brief depression severity measure. *Journal of General Internal Medicine, 16*(9), 606–613. https://doi.org/10.1046/j.1525-1497.2001.016009606.x

Lekas, H. M., Pahl, K., & Fuller Lewis, C. (2020). Rethinking cultural competence: Shifting to cultural humility. *Health Services Insights, 13*, 117863292097058. https://doi.org/10.1177/1178632920970580

Loewenstein, D. A., Arguelles, S., Bravo, M., Freeman, R. Q., Arguelles, T., Acevedo, A., & Eisdorfer, C. (2001). Caregivers' judgments of the functional abilities of the alzheimer's disease patient: A comparison of proxy reports and objective measures. *The Journals of Gerontology, Series B, 56*(2), P78. https://doi.org/10.1093/geronb/56.2.P78

Makol, B. A., Youngstrom, E. A., Racz, S. J., Qasmieh, N., Glenn, L. E., & De Los Reyes, A. (2020). Integrating multiple informants' reports: How conceptual and measurement models may address long-standing problems in clinical decision-making. *Clinical Psychological Science, 8*(6), 953–970. https://doi.org/10.1177/2167702620924439

Marsh, J. K., Zeveney, A. S., & De Los Reyes, A. (2020). Informant discrepancies in judgments about change during mental health treatments. *Clinical Psychological Science, 8*(2), 318–332. https://doi.org/10.1177/2167702619894905

McCabe, R. E., Milosevic, I., Rowa, K., Shnaider, P., Pawluk, E. J., Antony, M. M., & the DART Working Group. (2017). *Diagnostic Assessment Research Tool (DART)*. St. Joseph's Healthcare/McMaster University.

Mellor, R. M., Slaymaker, E., & Cleland, J. (2013). Recognising and overcoming challenges of couple interview research. *Qualitative Health Research, 23*(10), 1399–1407. https://doi.org/10.1177/1049732313506963

Meyer, G. J., Finn, S. E., Eyde, L. D., Kay, G. G., Moreland, K. L., Dies, R. R., Eisman, E. J., Kubiszyn, T. W., & Reed, G. M. (2001). Psychological testing and psychological assessment: A review of evidence and issues. *American Psychologist, 56*(2), 128–165. https://doi.org/10.1037/0003-066x.56.2.128

Monson, C. M. (2012). *The posttraumatic stress disorder checklist-close other version*. Unpublished Instrument, Ryerson University.

Monson, C. M., & Fredman, S. J. (2012). *Cognitive-behavioral conjoint therapy for PTSD: Harnessing the healing power of relationships* (1st ed.). The Guilford Press.

Möricke, E., Buitelaar, J. K., & Rommelse, N. N. J. (2016). Do we need multiple informants when assessing autistic traits? The degree of report bias on offspring, self, and spouse ratings. *Journal of Autism and Developmental Disorders, 46*(1), 164–175. https://doi.org/10.1007/s10803-015-2562-y

Murphy, C. M., & Hoover, S. A. (1999). Measuring emotional abuse in dating relationships as a multifactorial construct. *Violence and Victims, 14*(1), 39–53. https://doi.org/10.1891/0886-6708.14.1.39

Pu, D. F., Rodriguez, C. M., & Baker, L. R. (2019). When couples disagree: Predicting informant differences in adults' emotion regulation. *Journal of Child and Family Studies, 28*(6), 1548–1557. https://doi.org/10.1007/s10826-019-01401-z

Rathus, J. H., & Feindler, E. L. (2004). *Assessment of partner violence: A handbook for researchers and practitioners*. https://doi.org/10.1037/10685-000

Rescorla, L. A., Achenbach, T. M., Ivanova, M. Y., Turner, L. V., Árnadóttir, H., Au, A., Caldas, J. C., Chen, Y. C., Decoster, J., Fontaine, J., Funabiki, Y., Guðmundsson, H. S., Leung, P., Liu, J., Maraš, J. S., Marković, J., Oh, K. J., da Rocha, M. M., Samaniego, V. C., et al. (2016). Collateral reports and cross-informant agreement about adult psychopathology in 14 societies. *Journal of Psychopathology and Behavioral Assessment, 38*(3), 381–397. https://doi.org/10.1007/s10862-016-9541-2

Roth, R. M., Isquith, P. K., & Gioia, G. A. (2005). *BRIEF-A: Behavior rating inventory of executive function-adult version: Professional manual*. Psychological Assessment Resources.

Rowa, K., McCabe, R. E., & Antony, M. M. (2008). Specific phobia and social phobia. In J. Hunsley & E. J. Mash (Eds.), *A guide to assessments that work* (pp. 207–228). Oxford University Press.
Schumm, W. R., Paff-Bergen, L. A., Hatch, R. C., Obiorah, F. C., Copeland, J. M., Meens, L. D., & Bugaighis, M. A. (1986). Concurrent and discriminant validity of the Kansas Marital Satisfaction Scale. *Journal of Marriage and the Family, 48*, 381–387.
Shiffman, S., Stone, A. A., & Hufford, M. R. (2008). Ecological momentary assessment. *Annual Review of Clinical Psychology, 4*(1), 1–32. https://doi.org/10.1146/annurev.clinpsy.3.022806.091415
Snyder, D. K., Heyman, R. E., Haynes, S. N., Carlson, C. I., & Balderrama-Durbin, C. (2016). Couple and family assessment. In J. C. Norcross, R. Krishnamurthy, D. K. Freedheim, & G. R. VandenBos (Eds.), *APA handbook of clinical psychology: Vol. 3. Applications and methods* (pp. 201–217). American Psychological Association.
Spanier, G. B. (1976). Measuring dyadic adjustment: New scales for assessing the quality of marriage and similar dyads. *Journal of Marriage and the Family, 38*(1), 15. https://doi.org/10.2307/350547
Spitzer, R. L., Kroenke, K., Williams, J. B. W., & Löwe, B. (2006). A brief measure for assessing generalized anxiety disorder. *Archives of Internal Medicine, 166*(10), 1092. https://doi.org/10.1001/archinte.166.10.1092
Straus, M. A., & Douglas, E. M. (2007). A short form of the revised Conflict Tactics Scales, and typologies for severity and mutuality. *Violence and Victims, 19*(5), 507–520. https://doi.org/10.1891/088667004780927800
Stubbe, D. E. (2020). Practicing cultural competence and cultural humility in the care of diverse patients. *Focus, 18*(1), 49–51. https://doi.org/10.1176/appi.focus.20190041
Substance Abuse and Mental Health Services Administration. (2014). *Improving cultural competence*. Treatment Improvement Protocol (TIP) Substance Abuse and Mental Health Services Administration. https://store.samhsa.gov/sites/default/files/d7/priv/sma14-4849.pdf
Sue, D. W., & Sue, D. (2013). *Counseling the culturally diverse: Theory & practice* (6th ed.). Wiley.
Taylor, B., & de Vocht, H. (2011). Interviewing separately or as couples? Considerations of authenticity of method. *Qualitative Health Research, 21*(11), 1576–1587. https://doi.org/10.1177/1049732311415288
Weathers, F. W., Litz, B. T., Keane, T. M., Palmieri, P. A., Marx, B. P., & Schnurr, P. P. (2013). *The PTSD checklist for DSM-5 (PCL-5)*. Scale available from the National Center for PTSD at www.ptsd.va.gov
Whisman, M. A., & Snyder, D. K. (2007). Sexual infidelity in a national survey of American women: Differences in prevalence and correlates as a function of method of assessment. *Journal of Family Psychology, 21*(2), 147–154. https://doi.org/10.1037/0893-3200.21.2.147
Youngstrom, E. A. (2008). Evidence-based strategies for the assessment of developmental psychopathology: Measuring prediction, prescription, and process. In D. J. Miklowitz, W. E. Craighead, & L. Craighead (Eds.), *Developmental psychopathology* (pp. 34–77). Wiley.

Chapter 2
Child Assessment with Corroborative Parent Report

Kristine Lee, Anamika Dutta, Justine Lee, and Donna B. Pincus

2.1 Introduction

As rates of psychopathology rise globally in children and adolescents, it is crucial that effective, evidence-based care is tailored to their needs (Kyu et al., 2016; Deighton et al., 2016; Ribeiro et al., 2023). A critical first step in providing this care is conducting a diagnostic and functional assessment of children's presenting concerns, using a multimethod, multi-informant, cognitive behavioral assessment approach. The last several decades have resulted in tremendous growth in research on child and family assessment. Clinical assessment tools have been designed to effectively capture the nuances of child and family functioning. Current "gold standard" assessment methods are typically multimodal, incorporating a combination of interviews, self-reports, and observational measures, and are completed by multiple informants. Given the range of developmental considerations when working with children, assessment methods are also carefully tailored to the child's age and presenting problems. Parents and guardians are crucial to the assessment process, as they are almost always included in reporting on observations of their children's symptoms and daily functioning across multiple settings. As a result of a thorough clinical assessment that combines both the child report and the parent/guardian report, clinicians can make informed recommendations about whether treatment is

K. Lee (✉)
ATTN: Center for Anxiety and Related Disorders, Boston, MA, USA

Boston University, Boston, MA, USA
e-mail: klee01@bu.edu

A. Dutta · J. Lee · D. B. Pincus
Boston University, Boston, MA, USA
e-mail: anamikad@bu.edu; justine@bu.edu; dpincus@bu.edu

L. Reuman, J. Thompson-Hollands (eds.), *Enhancing CBT Through Family and Peer Engagement*, CBT: Science Into Practice, https://doi.org/10.1007/978-3-031-74838-7_2

warranted, and about the type and format of treatment that will likely be most helpful.

Although a comprehensive assessment typically precedes treatment, assessment is also an ongoing process throughout treatment. For example, clinicians must continually assess for suicidal risk and must assess whether the treatment being implemented is having an impact in decreasing distressing symptoms and simultaneously improving quality of life. Furthermore, circumstances in the child's life can change during treatment (e.g., through experiencing a trauma), which can necessitate reassessment of clinical symptoms. There are numerous, well-researched assessment tools that have been designed to effectively capture ongoing or sudden changes in child functioning.

This chapter will highlight best practices in the multimethod cognitive behavioral assessment of child and adolescent anxiety disorders, focusing specifically on incorporating parents and guardians throughout the process. The chapter begins with a guide to conducting child and adolescent multimethod assessments with parent corroborative reporting. We discuss the "gold standard" measures used in the field of child anxiety assessment and how they are most effectively used to integrate both child and parent reports. We then proceed to discuss existing research studies that illustrate the value of gaining both child and parent perspectives on a child's presenting problems. Cultural considerations are presented to provide clinicians with guidance on methods for assessing children and families with diverse identities. Lastly, the chapter concludes with a case vignette that demonstrates how a parent can be meaningfully incorporated into the assessment process. We present a case overview of a client named "Rosalie," describing the rationale for the battery of measures that were considered and those that were administered, and the treatment plan that resulted from the functional multimodal assessment.

2.2 Assessment Overview

2.2.1 Diagnostic Interviews

In clinical settings, structured evidence-based assessment (EBA) or semi-structured clinical interviews are recommended as the "gold standard" for the diagnostic evaluation of anxiety disorders (Ford-Paz et al., 2020; Silverman & Ollendick, 2005; Spence, 2018). Data collected through structured EBA or semi-structured clinical interviews inform the evaluation of diagnostic criteria symptoms; symptom frequency, severity, onset, and duration; degree of associated distress and functional impairment; developmental and medical considerations; and physical symptoms (Walters et al., 2020). Numerous EBA have been well-researched for their psychometric validity and reliability, such as the Anxiety Disorders Interview Schedule for Children/Parents (ADIS-C/P; Silverman & Albano, 1996), the Schedule for Affective Disorders and Schizophrenia for School-Age Children (K-SADS;

Kaufman et al., 1997), and the NIMH Diagnostic Interview Schedule for Children-IV (NIMH DISC-IV; Shaffer et al., 2000). The K-SADS, ADIS-C/P, and NIMH DISC-IV all include parent and child versions to capture multi-informant responses. Multi-informant responses to EBA are often standardized, where parent and child informants are asked to report on the same domains of anxiety assessment measures and their own perceived severity and interference of each domain. The most commonly used anxiety assessments capture how the child feels in different situations, what they think or worry about, how they behave in response to those thoughts and feelings, and what body sensations they experience in trigger situations from the perspective of parents and the child. The length of the assessment may be adjusted based on developmental and clinical indications as well. For example, if a briefer assessment battery is preferable while still adhering to the standardized structure, the ADIS-C/P or K-SADS would be appropriate to consider as both instruments were designed with screening questions that allow for shorter administration time.

Utilizing EBA allows for precise evaluation of psychological symptoms across diagnostic classifications. Comorbidity among mental health disorders is high, and these comorbidities may heighten distress and functional impairment and impact treatment outcomes (Leyfer et al., 2013; Melton et al., 2016). Each comorbid disorder may influence the treatment planning process, as well as the selection of the treatment approach. Therefore, thorough assessment and identification of relevant disorders (i.e., neurodevelopmental disorders, posttraumatic stress, medical conditions, and physical disabilities) are crucial in the diagnostic assessment process.

Research suggests that using EBA, in addition to modes of direct observation at home or school, can improve clinical decision-making by reducing clinician bias (Mash & Hunsley, 2005; Smith & Dumont, 2002). Despite the strong research base supporting the use of EBA, unstructured clinical interviews remain the most common method of assessing psychological concerns for children and adolescents. Major limitations to unstructured clinical interviews include poor interrater reliability, high likelihood of error, and high variance in the use of diagnostic criteria (Rettew et al., 2009). It is notable that less than 10% of clinicians use EBA for the evaluation of child and adolescent anxiety (Whiteside et al., 2016). Many report significant barriers to implementing EBA, including time constraints, lack of access to materials, lack of training, and high costs (Van Meter et al., 2014; Whiteside et al., 2016). At a structural level, obstacles to implementing evidence-based anxiety assessment for children and adolescents in clinical practice remain prevalent and continue to warrant addressing.

2.2.2 Informants

Parent/guardian corroborative reporting is beneficial to multimethod assessment. Using a multi-informant EBA approach allows both parents and their children the opportunity to elaborate on their perception of symptoms, symptom timeframes, and perceived severity and/or impairment. Children and adolescents may overlook impairment or interference at home, school, or in peer relationships, and young children may specifically lack the understanding or vocabulary necessary for communicating symptoms and distress. For the assessment of anxiety-related concerns, incorporating parents' perspectives allows clinicians to gain insight into the consistency or inconsistency of anxiety concerns across contexts (Dirks et al., 2012). Wei et al. (2014) found that using multiple informants (i.e., children and parents) improved the accuracy of predicting the severity and diagnosis of anxiety disorders. It is well supported that involving parents or guardians and the child/adolescent in the assessment process is considered the best practice for child psychological assessment (Hunsley & Mash, 2007).

2.2.2.1 Discrepancy in Parent–Child Report

Evidence suggests that a multi-informant approach is appropriate for gaining a complete diagnostic profile of a given child's symptom presentation (Grills & Ollendick, 2003; Ollendick & Hersen, 1993) even when there is discordance among respondents (Charamut et al., 2022). One complication of multi-informant reporting is that disagreement is common and expected. Numerous studies and meta-analyses have found low to moderate concordance between child-report and parent-report (De Los Reyes et al., 2015, 2019; Rescorla et al., 2013). Data from 25 countries demonstrated that adolescents self-report greater internalizing symptoms compared to their parents' report (Rescorla et al., 2013). Moreover, a recent meta-analysis examined parent–child report comparisons and found, when specifically analyzing agreement on externalizing and internalizing concerns, that reporting of the latter is substantially more prone to disagreement (De Los Reyes et al., 2015). Differences in reports of anxiety concerns may occur given that respondents are observing the child or adolescent in a context-dependent manner. For example, in cases of social anxiety, parents may be able to report on perceived avoidance of social situations but less able to assess their child's inner thoughts and feelings during social interactions with peers, as parents are not typically present in these situations or may underestimate their child's internalized experience. Despite the existing challenges of weak agreement between informants, it remains crucial to include data from multiple sources to gather corroborating evidence of anxiety problems across different settings. Factors such as a child's age, developmental stage, cognitive capacity to understand assessment questions, and cognitive insight into their emotional experience should be considered by clinicians when weighing a child's self-report. It is also important to understand a parent's daily level of contact with their child, their own expectations of normative child behavior, and family stressors, which are factors that may influence a parent's report. For example, if one parent has primary custody of the child but both parents have legal decision-making for the child, it is important to capture both parents' perspectives; however, if the child spends the majority of their time in one primary household with the parent, then that parent's report may be weighed more due to their daily proximity to the child. Clinicians must use their clinical judgment to integrate all of the information to produce a better understanding of the child's emotional experience, cognitions, behaviors, and physiological symptoms.

2.2.2.2 Additional Informants

If a child has various parents, guardians, or primary adult caretakers (i.e., stepparents, grandparents, foster parents, adoptive parents, and other relatives) involved in their daily life, clinicians must consider who should be included in the assessment process and their level of involvement. Clinicians must obtain consent and authorization from the child's legal guardians to involve other adults in the assessment as additional informants. Depending on the relationship, proximity to the child, and level of engagement in their daily activities, clinicians should involve those who will be able to provide the most reliable and accurate assessment of the child's daily functioning. This may be particularly relevant if a child spends a significant amount of time being cared for by a relative or in situations where the child splits their time living in different households. Clinicians may experience limitations, such as time constraints or insurance limitations, in being able to include all informants in the EBA; therefore, utilizing standardized questionnaires to capture additional informant's perspectives of the child's functioning may be appropriate and should be considered (refer to Sect. 2.2.5).[1]

2.2.3 *Evaluation Structure*

A diagnostic interview for anxiety includes the parent and client, either separately, together, or both, as developmentally and clinically indicated. One challenge in the assessment of child anxiety disorders is that children at younger ages may have difficulties in communicating cognitive functioning, emotions, and avoidance, as well as the associated distress and impairment (Beesdo et al., 2009). This highlights the importance of a developmentally sensitive approach that may use multiple age-appropriate assessment techniques (e.g., direct and indirect questioning, interactive techniques, pictures/images, storytelling, and symptom rating scales) (Spence, 2018). Clinicians may determine that a young child is not able to provide a reliable report of their own symptoms, and therefore weigh parent reports more heavily in their clinical conceptualization. In some cases, adolescents may be less willing to report on symptoms that they perceive as less "socially acceptable," such as

[1] The term "parent" has been referred to throughout this chapter, but it is important to acknowledge that other informants may be relevant in any given case.

separation anxiety, thus leading to underreporting. Conversely, parents may not have a clear understanding of generalized worries that adolescents may feel at school and in the community, therefore underscoring the importance of collecting self-report data from the adolescent (Wei et al., 2014). Moreover, when assessing adolescents, levels of parent involvement in the assessment process may vary depending on the adolescent's desire for increased autonomy, self-awareness, and insight, and the pattern of parent–child interactions in the context of anxiety-related concerns (Cardy et al., 2020). Interviewing parents and adolescents separately should be considered to ensure accuracy in reporting and protected space for disclosure, specifically for the adolescent. Overall, weighing the differential reports of parents/guardians and their children when deciding on diagnoses and treatment plans must account for a child's cognitive capacity to understand the assessment questions and the developmental appropriateness of the questions (Spence, 2018). For example, the child version of the K-SADS and ADIS-C is designed and validated for children between 6 and 18 years old, while the NIMH DISC-IV youth version is validated for 9–17-year-old children/adolescents. Therefore, it is generally preferable for children under the minimum age required to complete the child report of the selected EBA to be concurrently interviewed with a parent. For older children and adolescents, separate interviews are often more appropriate. Behavioral observation in the clinic, home, or school is also useful in the assessment. Behavioral observations with parents/guardians and the child may reveal environmental reinforcement factors, levels of parental accommodation, parental reactivity, and observations of parenting styles and behaviors (Stiede et al., 2023; Walters et al., 2020). For example, for children who present with symptoms of selective mutism, behavioral observations during the assessment process may provide a baseline observation about parent–child interactions and mimic what happens when children with selective mutism need to speak with someone other than their parents. This allows for opportunities to observe parents' own verbal response styles and rescuing behaviors and may give insight into parents' threshold for distress. Using direct behavioral observation also allows clinicians to distinguish patterns of parent–child interaction that may contribute to the reinforcement and maintenance of anxiety.

2.2.4 Risk Assessment

Assessment of suicidal thoughts and risk should be standard practice during any intake evaluation. Screening children and adolescents for suicide risk is important to identify youth who need psychiatric services and to prevent suicide attempts and deaths (Cwik et al., 2020). Suicide screening tools with the most robust validation data and wide use across a variety of settings among children and adolescents are the Patient Health Questionnaire—9 Item (PHQ-9; Kroenke et al., 2001), Columbia Suicide Severity Rating Scale—Screen Version (C-SSRS; Posner et al., 2011), and the Ask Suicide-Screening Questions (ASQ; Horowitz et al., 2012). A common concern of both clinicians and clients is limits to confidentiality. It is standard practice for a clinician to inform parents and clients about the limitations to confidentiality during the consent/assent process prior to the start of any assessment. The most common situations that are considered limitations to confidentiality include disclosure of immediate danger to self, duty to warn, and suspected abuse/neglect of a child or elderly person. Whether or not the child/adolescent expresses concern about limits to confidentiality, clinicians have an ethical, legal, and therapeutic responsibility to discuss it before inquiring about suicidal thoughts and behaviors (Pettit et al., 2018). Youth should never feel surprised or "blind-sided" in the event that clinicians break confidentiality. Clinicians may approach broaching confidentiality and its limits with an example statement such as: "Before we go any further, I want to remind you that what we talk about today will be private and I will not talk about it with other people, unless it is necessary to keep you safe once you leave this session. If I have concerns for your safety, I may need to speak with other people about that, including your parents. However, I will only share information that is necessary to keep you safe—I will not share other things we discuss."

When discussing suicidal thoughts or behaviors, skilled assessment often involves genuine concern for the child's well-being, being supportive of their autonomy, and willingness to engage in open and empathic dialogue about sensitive topics. Clinicians should begin with an explanation of the importance of the topic and ask for permission to proceed. When introducing the topic of suspected suicidal risk, normalizing the experience of suicidal thoughts and behavior, and approaching it in a matter-of-fact manner tend to lower defenses and may lead to more open disclosure. Asking for permission to discuss these topics conveys respect for the client's autonomy and often further lowers defenses. If a client does not grant permission, the clinician should take the time to explore their concerns about discussing the topic (e.g., concerns it will lead to hospitalization, concerns about parent's reaction) and then reiterate the importance of the topic. An open and empathic dialogue about the client's concerns opens the door to building rapport and for the clinician to demonstrate that their priority is the client's well-being and safety, above all else. Nevertheless, suicide risk assessment is not optional. The best practice for navigating a skilled risk assessment is for clinicians to be transparent about their ethical and professional responsibility to ensure the safety of their clients and to communicate that they may need to take further steps, which may include hospitalization if suspected risk cannot be assessed (Pettit et al., 2018).

Clinicians can use the same approach of explaining the importance of the topic, asking permission, addressing concerns, and then returning to risk assessment when meeting with parents and guardians. However, considering the level of parent involvement in the assessment of suicidal risk requires deliberate decision-making from clinicians. Although parents can provide necessary information about family and external risk factors, it is important to be aware of the impact their involvement will have on treatment engagement and therapeutic alliance with the child or adolescent (Barrio, 2007). In families where the adolescent perceives low family support, has a history of suicide attempts, and parents have less mental health literacy, parents may be unaware of the nature and extent of their child's suicidality. In these cases, it is crucial to involve parents in the adolescent's short- and long-term safety planning and treatment to increase parental awareness and help them provide a safe environment for the adolescent (Klaus et al., 2009). Prior to creating a safety plan, it is also important to consider the optimal level of involvement of parents in collaboratively developing and implementing the safety plan. With young children, it is often advantageous to create a safety plan with children and caregivers together, as children may need more support in developing and utilizing the plan. With adolescents, parent involvement may vary. For some adolescents, it can be useful for maintaining rapport and fostering independent mastery of skills to develop the initial safety plan before bringing in parents to review the rationale for the safety plan, and then discussing how parents can create safer environments at home (e.g., removing access to objects used for self-harm, locking up medication) and support the adolescent in implementing the safety plan. For other adolescents, specifically, those who may have limited insight into their thoughts, emotions, and behaviors, it may be more helpful to involve parents in the development of the entire plan.

2.2.5 *Measurement-Based Care*

Measurement-based care is the process of tracking clients' symptoms at regular intervals to monitor progress and modify treatment if needed (Scott & Lewis, 2015). Assessment of anxiety symptoms should be an ongoing, routine process throughout treatment with children and adolescents. As treatment progresses, clinicians should readminister questionnaires completed during intake by all reporters to gauge whether symptoms are increasing, decreasing, or maintaining at the same frequency and/or severity. Although the literature has primarily focused on the utility of measurement-based care in adult populations, emerging literature suggests that children in measurement-based care have greater symptom reduction for a range of mental health concerns relative to children not in measurement-based care (Tam & Ronan, 2017). A recent study found significant improvement in anxiety severity among children and adolescents who participated in a digital measurement-based care intervention (Huffman et al., 2023). Based on responses, clinicians can gauge whether symptoms are improving across different contexts, such as social, familial, and academic domains. Additionally, continually assessing symptoms using parent-report measures can help provide insight into whether treatment is addressing key concerns at home (e.g., behavioral concerns, level of accommodation being requested by the child, impairment in family life).

2.2.6 Measures of Anxiety

A variety of measures have been developed and validated for the purpose of assessing child anxiety. Some of these measures are explicitly designed to be completed by the child (i.e., self-report), but also have parent-report counterparts. Although they differ in length and content, three child- and parent-report anxiety measures are consistently used in routine clinical and research settings: the Screen for Child Anxiety Related Emotional Disorders (SCARED; Birmaher et al., 1997), the Spence Children's Anxiety Scale (SCAS; Spence, 1997), and the Multidimensional Anxiety Scale for Children (MASC; March et al., 1999). A recent meta-analysis by Kook et al. (2022) compared the content overlap between these psychometrically validated measures as well as other youth-report anxiety measures and found weak mean overlap. Across all possible content categories, only items relating to worry and social fear were consistent across the seven measures.

The parent-report versions of these measures provide a valuable comparison to the child-report of presenting symptoms. For example, the SCAS-Parent Report (SCAS-P) is recommended as a diagnostic tool in clinical settings (Nauta et al., 2004). The SCARED-Parent Report has demonstrated good psychometric properties, moderate parent–child agreement, and sensitivity to treatment response (Birmaher et al., 1999). The MASC-Parent (MASC-P) has excellent internal reliability and validity, such that this measure can reliably discriminate between children with and without an anxiety disorder (Villabø et al., 2012). As discussed earlier, using multiple informants during the assessment process is valuable in attaining the most comprehensive, accurate, and relevant information for treatment. Similar to the administration of child self-report measures, the decision to use a given parent-report measure should be intentional and dependent upon the types of concerns one is hoping to assess.

It is evident that not all measures will capture the same constructs of anxiety, and some may be more suited for certain presenting concerns than others. For example, school-related anxiety is measured differently in each measure, with some assessing physical manifestations of school anxiety, others assessing school refusal, and others assessing academic worry (Kook et al., 2022). In essence, with many psychometrically sound child-report measures available, it is critical that clinicians choose measures that capture the features of anxiety most relevant to the child or adolescent. If a young child presents with concerns of selective mutism, clinicians may consider administering the Selective Mutism Questionnaire (SMQ; Bergman et al., 2008). The SMQ is a parent-report questionnaire that assesses the frequency of selective mutism symptoms over the preceding two weeks, in three domains: at school, speech in home/family environments, and in community or social settings.

2.3 Cultural Considerations in Psychological Assessments

EBA is an integral part of the therapy process, as the clinical information obtained influences diagnostic impressions, case conceptualization, and treatment planning in a way that represents a client's needs (Sanchez et al., 2022). Cultural considerations are also crucial to the assessment process and should be deliberately and intentionally factored into a client's diagnostic assessment. With this in mind, it is important to note that research continues to demonstrate the presence of bias and lack of cultural equivalence (i.e., in assessment measures) given to determine child and adolescent psychopathology (Liang et al., 2016). Racially and ethnically marginalized populations may face poorer quality of care due to a lack of diagnostic accuracy and disregard for relevant social and environmental contributing factors to their psychopathology (Liang et al., 2016). To prevent misdiagnosis in marginalized groups, many cultural considerations should be carefully noted throughout the assessment process. The following section will highlight some important cultural considerations, such as clinician–client language differences, clients' views about therapy, cultural context, and race/ethnicity.

2.3.1 *Clinician–Client Language Differences*

A client's native language or primary spoken language is a major consideration that clinicians must plan for in advance of the assessment, specifically if it differs from the clinician's native language. When considering which EBA to conduct, the client's native language will most likely influence which assessment is most appropriate for them. This is not without limitations, as the ADIS-C/P is only validated for English speakers. Moreover, the NIMH DISC-IV offers both English and Spanish versions and the K-SADS has been validated in English, Spanish, Japanese, and Farsi, to date. In order to prevent linguistic barriers to treatment, it is vital that clinicians improve linguistic access by including translators in sessions if need be (Cooley & Boyce, 2004). If the EBA does not have a translated version and/or the primary clinician does not speak the client's native language, then utilizing a translator is appropriate. If a client speaks English as a second language, it is not sufficient to focus on a client's proficiency in the language. Rather, clinicians must also consider how certain ideas, messages, and colloquialisms are explained and interpreted across cultures. For example, in some East Asian cultures, it is appropriate for children to be attuned to others' emotional states in order to promote well-being within a group, but this could be misconstrued in Western-created measures that categorize "worrying when someone is angry" as an indicator of a mental illness (Gee, 2004). This is particularly important to the assessment process since many psychological assessments were designed with Western cultural ideals in mind, and what is considered a symptom of anxiety in Western culture can be part of everyday life in other cultures (Gee, 2004).

Translated written materials (i.e., consent forms, measures, handouts) must be provided as well. Child- and parent-report anxiety measures should be selected based on clinical appropriateness, as well as accessibility of a validated, translated version. From the measures aforementioned, the SCARED has been translated and validated across the greatest number of languages other than English, including Dutch, Chinese, Arabic, Portuguese, Italian, and Spanish. Translated versions of the SCAS (i.e., English, Portuguese, and Urdu) and the MASC (i.e., English, Portuguese, and Taiwanese) are limited. Regardless of the limitations, providing translated written materials must be considered carefully in a client's native language to ensure that the client can easily read and understand the written materials provided to them.

2.3.2 *Cultural Views About Mental Health*

Cultural differences regarding views on therapy and mental health are another key consideration during the assessment process. Gaining a thorough understanding of the client's cultural identity lends insight into how cultural beliefs and values influence the client's behavior and responses to questions during the assessment (Gee, 2004). Asking the client about their connectedness to their cultural identity and/or values after therapeutic alliance and trust provides another lens through which clinicians can interpret behaviors. Clinicians can begin learning about a client's culture by exploring if and how they have encountered stigma and/or racism, as well as their beliefs about mental illness and treatment (Naeem et al., 2019). It is important to consider the ways in which multiethnic families may have varying cultural values that have led to certain biases surrounding mental health, which can influence both reporting of symptom presentation and perceived interference/distress during an assessment. Cultural formulation is an essential component of any comprehensive psychiatric assessment and clinicians should utilize cultural assessment tools within EBA to obtain cultural information in a client-centered way (Lewis-Fernández et al., 2010).

Using EBA is critical with children and adolescents from minority groups, as unstructured clinical interviewing can be susceptible to clinician bias and potential misdiagnosis (Gee, 2004; Turner & Mills, 2016). For example, Asian youth could underreport somatic symptoms of anxiety such as lack of sleep, trouble concentrating, and/or low appetite during unstructured assessments if these are not directly asked about (Gee, 2004), which subsequently omits crucial information to inform accurate diagnoses. Established measures, such as the Multigroup Ethnic Identity Measure (Phinney, 1992), can be used during the assessment process to ensure information about cultural identity is best captured. The Multigroup Ethnic Identity Measure assesses ethnic identity through interviews with just the child or adolescent and can aid clinicians in understanding the strength of the client's cultural ties (Williams et al., 2020). The Diagnostic and Statistical Manual of Mental Disorders, Fifth Edition Cultural Formulation Interview (DSM-5 CFI; Lewis-Fernández et al., 2010) is another well-researched evidence-based tool that can be used during assessments to gain a better perspective of the aforementioned factors to determine how a client views their cultural identity and how their cultural community views mental health (Sanchez et al., 2022). The CFI can help clinicians use the client's cultural strengths to employ therapeutic skills and coping, furthering the therapeutic alliance between the clinician and client (Sanchez et al., 2022). For example, familial relationships are a top in some cultures, and spending time with family as a coping skill is a way to draw on this cultural strength.

2.3.3 *Cultural Context*

Recent literature has highlighted the importance of understanding a client's sociocultural context while conducting clinical assessments (Gee, 2004; Naeem et al., 2019). As mentioned previously, a multi-informant interview approach with the primary parent/guardian is one way to capture background information about the family. Clinicians can not only obtain information regarding symptomatology of the presenting concerns, but must also seek to understand other important contextual factors such as the family's generational status, reasons for immigration, and degrees of acculturation. In addition, clinicians can inquire about the perceived root of their client's mental health concerns as a way to explore any spiritual and religious factors attributed to the causes of mental illness. Spiritual and religious beliefs can also be used to determine client strengths that can be maximized over the course of treatment (Williams et al., 2020). Conversations about the client's broader family structure and/or dynamics can also act as a gateway to understanding the client's values and ways of thinking.

2.3.4 *Racial and Ethnic Identity*

In order to address the cultural considerations discussed, it is crucial that a clinician carefully consider and acknowledge the race- or ethnicity-based differences between them and their client. This acknowledgment can open space for the client to discuss their racial/ethnic identity and serve as an open invitation to continue to have conversations about their identity in treatment (Beck, 2019). Due to the effect of racism on mental health, recent literature has recommended that mental health providers utilize tools to assess race-based stress (e.g., PTSD symptoms that may develop due to chronic fear and paranoia of experiencing microaggressions) in relation to mental illness (Williams et al., 2014). These tools can be used to ensure clinicians are able to identify the effects of racism on psychopathology instead of attributing responses to racism to other factors (Williams et al., 2014). There likely may not be enough time to administer such a tool during the assessment process, but research has shown that it can even be helpful to ask clients if they are comfortable discussing their background (Beck, 2019). This also allows room for the client to reject conversations about race and ethnicity, signaling that greater rapport must be established through future sessions.

2.4 Case Vignette

2.4.1 Case Overview

"Rosalie," a 16-year-old who identifies as a biracial, cisgender female, indicated on her online initial prescreening questionnaire that she is a first-generation, US born, Chinese/Mexican American and that she was seeking help because of "uncontrollable anxiety." She indicated on her clinic intake form that she found the clinic herself by doing an online search and had never received help for her mental health but was "desperate" for someone to help her.

When the clinic phone screener called to gather some standard demographic and background information about her presenting problems, Rosalie and her mother were asked to provide information separately due to Rosalie's age and developmental appropriateness. First, Rosalie's mother described that Rosalie was having "nervous attacks" at school in anticipation of tests, eating in the lunchroom, and during classes in which she did not have any friends. Rosalie's mother stated that she worried what kind of effects these attacks were having on Rosalie's body, and whether they could cause a heart attack. After speaking to Rosalie's mother, the phone screener asked Rosalie the same questions related to her presenting problems. Rosalie described distressing symptoms of dizziness, heart racing, fears of dying and going crazy, and terror. Rosalie described that she has always felt strong feelings of anxiety since she was a child, and that the only person who typically could make her feel less anxious was her mother. She indicated that her mother was very supportive of her getting help but that others in her family did not truly understand her condition and how upsetting it was.

Rosalie reported that her anxiety has caused a lot of interference in her daily activities. She recently got a job as a server at a local restaurant to help make money for her family but reported that she got fired from her job because she frequently had to leave the restaurant to "get air" to "calm herself down" when her rushes of anxiety started coming on. Rosalie reported that she was desperate for help in order to get her job back and not have anxiety at school. Rosalie described that she became extremely terrified when she experienced an anxiety attack at home, which made her feel like her problem was out of her control. Rosalie reported that she typically has about six to eight anxiety attacks per week, but that most recently she has had as many as two or three per day. As a result of her anxiety, Rosalie reported that sometimes she will leave school. In response to Rosalie's anxiety, Rosalie's mother typically picks her up from school and comforts her until the symptoms subside. Rosalie reported that she worries not only about the anxiety attacks but also about many other things, such as her siblings' well-being, her mother's well-being, her family finances, unsettling world events, weather events like hurricanes, school, and her future. Rosalie also reported that she had trouble being far from her mother, for fear that she would have an anxiety attack and not have access to her. As a result,

Rosalie often turned down requests to spend time with friends outside of their immediate local area. She denied any suicidal ideation but stated that her avoidance of many social activities and school has started making her feel down and depressed.

2.4.2 Selection of the Assessment Battery

Prior to Rosalie and her mother arriving at the clinic, the clinician created a core battery of questionnaires based on Rosalie's presenting problems. The clinician decided to administer the Anxiety Disorders Interview Schedule Child and Parent Versions (ADIS-C/P) to assess all the major domains of anxiety and other co-occurring symptoms. The English version of the ADIS-C/P was selected because English is the family's primary language spoken at home. Given that Rosalie is 16 years old, the clinician met briefly with both Rosalie and her mother at the start of the assessment to outline the assessment plan. Limits to confidentiality, specifically related to immediate danger to self, duty to warn, and suspected abuse or neglect of a child or elderly person were explained to both Rosalie and her mother. Both were given the opportunity to ask questions or express any concerns regarding limits to confidentiality. The assessor conducted the ADIS interview first with Rosalie and then with her mother, separately. The Diagnostic and Statistical Manual of Mental Disorders, Fifth Edition Cultural Formulation Interview (DSM-5 CFI), administered to Rosalie only, includes questions on cultural identity after general questions on how the client defines their problem and perceives its causes, context, and sources of support. While Rosalie was being interviewed, her mother filled out a battery of questionnaires, and when Rosalie's interview was complete, she completed a short battery of questionnaires.

To reduce the burden on Rosalie and her mother during the assessment session, the clinician carefully selected only a few self-report questionnaires that would add incremental knowledge about Rosalie's presenting problems. The clinician selected the Panic Disorder Severity Scale for Adolescents (PDSS-A; Elkins et al., 2014) The PDSS-A was chosen to be administered to Rosalie and her mother because Rosalie described symptoms that were consistent with panic disorder. In addition to the PDSS-A, the clinician asked Rosalie to complete the Columbia Suicide Severity Rating Scale (C-SSRS)—Screen Version for initial screening purposes attempting to assess suicidal ideation severity and suicidal behaviors. The Multidimensional Anxiety Scale for Children, 2nd Edition (MASC-2) was also included as a self-report measure because it is a very thorough multi-rater assessment of anxiety dimensions in children and adolescents, and there are both parent and child report forms. Both Rosalie and her mother completed the MASC separately. This self-report measure was chosen to complement the ADIS interview method of gathering data about Rosalie's range and severity of anxiety symptomatology. Lastly, in the parent assessment questionnaire packet, Rosalie's mother completed a Background

Questionnaire to gain further information about Rosalie's history, such as her developmental milestones, school and learning history, medical background, past and current medication use, history of receiving psychological treatment, and family mental health history.

Finally, the clinician recorded behavioral observations about Rosalie's mood and behavior during the assessment, as well as observations about Rosalie and her mother's interactions. By selecting measures to be completed by different informants (i.e., client, parent), and by using various formats of measures (i.e., semi-structured clinical interview, self-report questionnaires, parent questionnaires), the assessor was aiming to gain an in-depth clinical picture of Rosalie's current problems. The assessor was also hoping to compile the data gleaned by these different sources to arrive at a functional assessment of the major problems Rosalie was experiencing and the factors that might be maintaining her self-reported panic, anxiety, sadness, and distress.

2.4.3 Review of Relevant Diagnostic and Functional Assessments

During the ADIS interview, Rosalie reported symptoms that were consistent with panic disorder, including worry about panic attacks occurring, and avoidance of places where she thought panic might arise. She endorsed almost every physical symptom of panic, including dizziness, hands tingling, heart racing, shortness of breath, and fears of going crazy. However, significant discrepancies existed in the information reported by Rosalie and her mother. Rosalie's mother reported that Rosalie only worried about her panic and that the attacks were mostly caused by difficulties in school. Rosalie, however, reported that her panic occurred all the time, and did not have one particular trigger, but rather came on "out of the blue." Rosalie reported that there were many places and situations in which her panicky feelings increased, such as when riding in the back seat of the car, riding in the subway or buses, being in class, and exercising at the gym. Rosalie's report of the frequency of her panic was much greater than her mother's report. Rosalie reported during the ADIS interview that she "does not tell her mother half of what she worries about" and "does not ever tell her mother how sad she gets" to try to protect her mother from worrying about her.

Rosalie also reported that she had many other worries in addition to panic. During the ADIS interview, Rosalie met the criteria for Generalized Anxiety Disorder in addition to the criteria for Panic Disorder. She endorsed that her worry gets in the way of her sleep (i.e., falling asleep, staying asleep). Rosalie also endorsed many more symptoms of depression than her mother reported her having. There were also discrepancies between Rosalie's and her mother's report on the MASC questionnaire, with Rosalie endorsing more severity of anxiety than her mother reported. On the C-SSRS, Rosalie endorsed many symptoms of sadness and anhedonia but did not endorse any suicidal ideation.

During the ADIS interview, Rosalie's mother reported that she has "tried everything" to make Rosalie feel better when she panics, including making her warm drinks, wrapping her in blankets, and soothing her. She stated that she no longer asks Rosalie to do chores around the house for fear of "stressing her out." She also stated that she appreciated the feeling of being "needed" by Rosalie, as she was "the only one in the world who could make her feel better."

During the CFI, Rosalie was asked about the important aspects of her background and identity, such as the communities she belongs to, the languages spoken, where her family are from, racial/ethnic background, gender or sexual orientation, and faith/religion. She was asked to describe aspects of her background/identity that make a difference to her anxiety and mood, and if there were aspects of identity that make things challenging or difficult for her. The assessor also inquired about the role of social barriers (i.e., money, work or family commitments, stigma or discrimination, or lack of services that understand the native language or background) to help seeking, access to care, and problems engaging in previous treatment.

2.4.4 Treatment Plan as Informed by the Assessments

Although Rosalie's mother and Rosalie had somewhat discrepant reports about the severity of anxiety, the clinician decided to rely more heavily on Rosalie's report given her age. Rosalie met DSM-5 criteria for Panic Disorder as well as for Generalized Anxiety Disorder. Rosalie was also displaying some symptoms of depressed mood, though she did not meet full criteria for a depressive disorder. Taking all the information provided by the parent report and Rosalie's report, it was clear that Rosalie could benefit from a course of cognitive behavioral therapy (CBT) for anxiety and worry. It was also determined that Rosalie's mother should receive parent training to gain skills for understanding panic and the most effective ways to help her daughter. As part of the results of the functional assessment, it was determined that increasing Rosalie's knowledge of anxiety and its effective management strategies could help increase her feelings of control over her panic attacks and decrease her fear about them. It was also determined that Rosalie's mother's responses to Rosalie's panic could be inadvertently reinforcing the panic. The assessor planned to continually assess Rosalie's mood state throughout treatment, to monitor whether her depressed feelings subside after learning skills for managing anxiety, and after reentering developmentally appropriate activities and situations. Plans were also made to inform Rosalie's teacher about the best strategies to use when Rosalie reported feeling anxious at school.

Once Rosalie received a full course of CBT for anxiety, it would then be determined whether she needed any additional sessions to help teach her other specific strategies for improving her mood and sleep. The clinician's overall goals were to help decrease Rosalie's frequency and severity of her panic, decrease Rosalie's avoidance of developmentally appropriate situations, and increase Rosalie's social interactions. Additional goals of therapy were to decrease Rosalie's worry, and to improve her sleep and her mood. This was routinely monitored using measurement-based assessment, as the clinician readministered questionnaires completed during intake to gauge whether symptoms were increasing, decreasing, or maintaining at the same frequency and/or severity. These results were shared with Rosalie and her mother to track treatment progress and to inform the level of parental support needed in assisting with out-of-session practice or at home reinforcement of skill use. Overall, the goal of treatment was to help Rosalie return to healthier and happier daily functioning.

References

Barrio, C. A. (2007). Assessing suicide risk in children: Guidelines for developmentally appropriate interviewing. *Journal of Mental Health Counseling, 29*(1), 50–66. https://doi.org/10.17744/mehc.29.1.1x8qu2axd1v6rv3q

Beck, A. (2019). Understanding Black and minority ethnic service user's experience of racism as part of the assessment, formulation and treatment of mental health problems in cognitive behaviour therapy. *The Cognitive Behaviour Therapist, 12*, e8. https://doi.org/10.1017/S1754470X18000223

Beesdo, K., Knappe, S., & Pine, D. S. (2009). Anxiety and anxiety disorders in children and adolescents: Developmental issues and implications for DSM_V. *The Psychiatric Clinics of North America, 32*(3), 483–524. https://doi.org/10.1016/j.psc.2009.06.002

Bergman, R. L., Keller, M. L., Piacentini, J., & Bergman, A. J. (2008). The development and psychometric properties of the selective mutism questionnaire. *Journal of Clinical Child and Adolescent Psychology, 37*(2), 456–464. https://doi.org/10.1080/15374410801955805

Birmaher, B., Khetarpal, S., Brent, D., Cully, M., Balach, L., Kaufman, J., & Neer, S. M. (1997). The Screen for Child Anxiety Related Emotional Disorders (SCARED): Scale construction and psychometric characteristics. *Journal of the American Academy of Child and Adolescent Psychiatry, 36*(4), 545–553. https://doi.org/10.1097/00004583-199704000-00018

Birmaher, B., Brent, D. A., Chiappetta, L., Bridge, J., Monga, S., & Baugher, M. (1999). Psychometric properties of the Screen for Child Anxiety Related Emotional Disorders (SCARED): A replication study. *Journal of the American Academy of Child and Adolescent Psychiatry, 38*(10), 1230–1236. https://doi.org/10.1097/00004583-199910000-00011

Cardy, J. L., Waite, P., Cocks, F., & Creswell, C. (2020). A systematic review of parental involvement in cognitive behavioural therapy for adolescent anxiety disorders. *Clinical Child and Family Psychology Review, 23*(4), 483–509. https://doi.org/10.1007/s10567-020-00324-2

Charamut, N. R., Racz, S. J., Wang, M., & De Los Reyes, A. (2022). Integrating multi-informant reports of youth mental health: A construct validation test of Kraemer and colleagues' (2003) Satellite Model. *Frontiers in Psychology, 13*, 911629. https://doi.org/10.3389/fpsyg.2022.911629

Cooley, M. R., & Boyce, C. A. (2004). An introduction to assessing anxiety in child and adolescent multiethnic populations: Challenges and opportunities for enhancing knowledge and practice. *Journal of Clinical Child & Adolescent Psychology, 33*(2), 210–215. https://doi.org/10.1207/s15374424jccp3302_1

Cwik, M. F., O'Keefe, V. M., & Haroz, E. E. (2020). Suicide in the pediatric population: Screening, risk assessment and treatment. *International Review of Psychiatry, 32*(3), 254–264. https://doi.org/10.1080/09540261.2019.1693351

De Los Reyes, A., Augenstein, T. M., Wang, M., Thomas, S. A., Drabick, D. A. G., Burgers, D. E., & Rabinowitz, J. (2015). The validity of the multi-informant approach to assessing child and adolescent mental health. *Psychological Bulletin, 141*(4), 858–900. https://doi.org/10.1037/a0038498

De Los Reyes, A., Ohannessian, C. M., & Racz, S. J. (2019). Discrepancies between adolescent and parent reports about family relationships. *Child Development Perspectives, 13*(1), 53–58. https://doi.org/10.1111/cdep.12306

Deighton, J., Argent, R., De Francesco, D., Edbrooke-Childs, J., Jacob, J., Fleming, I., et al. (2016). Associations between evidence-based practice and mental health outcomes in child and adolescent mental health services. *Clinical Child Psychology and Psychiatry, 21*(2), 287–296. https://doi.org/10.1177/1359104515589637

Dirks, M. A., Reyes, A. D. L., Briggs-Gowan, M., Cella, D., & Wakschlag, L. S. (2012). Embracing not erasing contextual variability in children's behavior: Theory and utility in the selection and use of methods and informants in developmental psychopathology. *Journal of Child Psychology and Psychiatry, and Allied Disciplines, 53*(5), 558–574. https://doi.org/10.1111/j.1469-7610.2012.02537.x

Elkins, R. M., Pincus, D. B., & Comer, J. S. (2014). A psychometric evaluation of the panic disorder severity scale for children and adolescents. *Psychological Assessment, 26*(2), 609–618. https://doi.org/10.1037/a0035283

Ford-Paz, R. E., Gouze, K. R., Kerns, C. E., Ballard, R., Parkhurst, J. T., Jha, P., & Lavigne, J. (2020). Evidence-based assessment in clinical settings: Reducing assessment burden for a structured measure of child and adolescent anxiety. *Psychological Services, 17*(3), 343–354. https://doi.org/10.1037/ser0000367

Gee, C. B. (2004). Assessment of anxiety and depression in Asian American youth. *Journal of Clinical Child & Adolescent Psychology, 33*(2), 269–271. https://doi.org/10.1207/s15374424jccp3302_7

Grills, A. E., & Ollendick, T. H. (2003). Multiple informant agreement and the anxiety disorders interview schedule for parents and children. *Journal of the American Academy of Child and Adolescent Psychiatry, 42*(1), 30–40. https://doi.org/10.1097/00004583-200301000-00008

Horowitz, L. M., Bridge, J. A., Teach, S. J., Ballard, E., Klima, J., Rosenstein, D. L., Wharff, E. A., Ginnis, K., Cannon, E., Joshi, P., & Pao, M. (2012). Ask Suicide-Screening Questions (ASQ): A brief instrument for the pediatric emergency department. *Archives of Pediatrics & Adolescent Medicine, 166*(12), 1170–1176. https://doi.org/10.1001/archpediatrics.2012.1276

Huffman, L. G., Lawrence-Sidebottom, D., Huberty, J., Roots, M., Roots, K., Parikh, A., Guerra, R., & Weiser, J. (2023). Using digital measurement-based care for the treatment of anxiety and depression in children and adolescents: Observational retrospective analysis of bend health data. *JMIR Pediatrics and Parenting, 6*, e46154. https://doi.org/10.2196/46154

Hunsley, J., & Mash, E. J. (2007). Evidence-based assessment. *Annual Review of Clinical Psychology, 3*, 29–51. https://doi.org/10.1146/annurev.clinpsy.3.022806.091419

Kaufman, J., Birmaher, B., Brent, D., Rao, U., Flynn, C., Moreci, P., Williamson, D., & Ryan, N. (1997). Schedule for affective disorders and schizophrenia for school-age children-present and lifetime version (K-SADS-PL): Initial reliability and validity data. *Journal of the American Academy of Child and Adolescent Psychiatry, 36*(7), 980–988. https://doi.org/10.1097/00004583-199707000-00021

Klaus, N. M., Mobilio, A., & King, C. A. (2009). Parent–adolescent agreement concerning adolescents' suicidal thoughts and behaviors. *Journal of Clinical Child & Adolescent Psychology, 38*(2), 245–255. https://doi.org/10.1080/15374410802698412

Kook, M., Clinger, J. W., Lee, E., Schneider, S. C., Storch, E. A., & Guzick, A. G. (2022). A content analysis of self-report child anxiety measures. *Child Psychiatry & Human Development*. https://doi.org/10.1007/s10578-022-01455-z

Kroenke, K., Spitzer, R. L., & Williams, J. B. W. (2001). The PHQ-9: Validity of a brief depression severity measure. *Journal of General Internal Medicine, 16*(9), 606–613. https://doi.org/10.1046/j.1525-1497.2001.016009606.x

Kyu, H. H., Pinho, C., Wagner, J. A., Brown, J. C., Bertozzi-Villa, A., Charlson, F. J., Coffeng, L. E., Dandona, L., Erskine, H. E., Ferrari, A. J., Fitzmaurice, C., Fleming, T. D., Forouzanfar, M. H., Graetz, N., Guinovart, C., Haagsma, J., Higashi, H., Kassebaum, N. J., Larson, H. J., et al. (2016). Global and national burden of diseases and injuries among children and adolescents between 1990 and 2013: Findings from the Global Burden of Disease 2013 study. *JAMA Pediatrics, 170*(3), 267–287. https://doi.org/10.1001/jamapediatrics.2015.4276

Lewis-Fernández, R., Hinton, D. E., Laria, A. J., Patterson, E. H., Hofmann, S. G., Craske, M. G., Stein, D. J., Asnaani, A., & Liao, B. (2010). Culture and the anxiety disorders: Recommendations for DSM-V. *Depression and Anxiety, 27*(2), 212–229. https://doi.org/10.1002/da.20647

Leyfer, O., Gallo, K. P., Cooper-Vince, C., & Pincus, D. B. (2013). Patterns and predictors of comorbidity of DSM-IV anxiety disorders in a clinical sample of children and adolescents. *Journal of Anxiety Disorders, 27*(3), 306–311. https://doi.org/10.1016/j.janxdis.2013.01.010

Liang, J., Matheson, B. E., & Douglas, J. M. (2016). Mental health diagnostic considerations in racial/ethnic minority youth. *Journal of Child and Family Studies, 25*(6), 1926–1940. https://doi.org/10.1007/s10826-015-0351-z

March, J. S., Sullivan, K., & Parker, J. (1999). Test-retest reliability of the Multidimensional Anxiety Scale for Children. *Journal of Anxiety Disorders, 13*(4), 349–358. https://doi.org/10.1016/S0887-6185(99)00009-2

Mash, E. J., & Hunsley, J. (2005). Evidence-based assessment of child and adolescent disorders: Issues and challenges. *Journal of Clinical Child and Adolescent Psychology, 34*(3), 362–379. https://doi.org/10.1207/s15374424jccp3403_1

Melton, T. H., Croarkin, P. E., Strawn, J. R., & McClintock, S. M. (2016). Comorbid anxiety and depressive symptoms in children and adolescents: A systematic review and analysis. *Journal of Psychiatric Practice, 22*(2), 84–98. https://doi.org/10.1097/PRA.0000000000000132

Naeem, F., Phiri, P., Rathod, S., & Ayub, M. (2019). Cultural adaptation of cognitive–behavioural therapy. *BJPsych Advances, 25*(6), 387–395. https://doi.org/10.1192/bja.2019.15

Nauta, M. H., Scholing, A., Rapee, R. M., Abbott, M., Spence, S. H., & Waters, A. (2004). A parent-report measure of children's anxiety: Psychometric properties and comparison with child-report in a clinic and normal sample. *Behaviour Research and Therapy, 42*(7), 813–839. https://doi.org/10.1016/S0005-7967(03)00200-6

Ollendick, T. H., & Hersen, M. (1993). Child and adolescent behavioral assessment. In T. H. Ollendick & M. Hersen (Eds.), *Handbook of child and adolescent assessment* (pp. 3–14). Allyn & Bacon.

Pettit, J. W., Buitron, V., & Green, K. L. (2018). Assessment and management of suicide risk in children and adolescents. *Cognitive and Behavioral Practice, 25*(4), 460–472. https://doi.org/10.1016/j.cbpra.2018.04.001

Phinney, J. S. (1992). The multigroup ethnic identity measure: A new scale for use with diverse groups. *Journal of Adolescent Research, 7*(2), 156–176. https://doi.org/10.1177/074355489272003

Posner, K., Brown, G. K., Stanley, B., Brent, D. A., Yershova, K. V., Oquendo, M. A., Currier, G. W., Melvin, G. A., Greenhill, L., Shen, S., & Mann, J. J. (2011). The Columbia-Suicide Severity Rating Scale: Initial validity and internal consistency findings from three multisite studies with adolescents and adults. *The American Journal of Psychiatry, 168*(12), 1266–1277. https://doi.org/10.1176/appi.ajp.2011.10111704

Rescorla, L. A., Ginzburg, S., Achenbach, T. M., Ivanova, M. Y., Almqvist, F., Begovac, I., Bilenberg, N., Bird, H., Chahed, M., Dobrean, A., Döpfner, M., Erol, N., Hannesdottir, H., Kanbayashi, Y., Lambert, M. C., Leung, P. W. L., Minaei, A., Novik, T. S., Oh, K.-J., et al. (2013). Cross-informant agreement between parent-reported and adolescent self-reported problems in 25 societies. *Journal of Clinical Child and Adolescent Psychology, 42*(2), 262–273. https://doi.org/10.1080/15374416.2012.717870

Rettew, D. C., Lynch, A. D., Achenbach, T. M., Dumenci, L., & Ivanova, M. Y. (2009). Meta-analyses of agreement between diagnoses made from clinical evaluations and standardized diagnostic interviews. *International Journal of Methods in Psychiatric Research, 18*(3), 169–184. https://doi.org/10.1002/mpr.289

Ribeiro, W. S., Grande, A. J., Hoffmann, M. S., Ziebold, C., McDaid, D., Fry, A., et al. (2023). A systematic review of evidence-based interventions for child and adolescent mental health problems in low-and middle-income countries. *Comprehensive Psychiatry, 121*, 152358.

Sanchez, A. L., Comer, J. S., & LaRoche, M. (2022). Enhancing the responsiveness of family-based CBT through culturally informed case conceptualization and treatment planning. *Cognitive and Behavioral Practice, 29*(4), 750–770. https://doi.org/10.1016/j.cbpra.2021.04.003

Scott, K., & Lewis, C. C. (2015). Using measurement-based care to enhance any treatment. *Cognitive and Behavioral Practice, 22*(1), 49–59. https://doi.org/10.1016/j.cbpra.2014.01.010

Shaffer, D., Fisher, P., Lucas, C. P., Dulcan, M. K., & Schwab-Stone, M. E. (2000). NIMH Diagnostic Interview Schedule for Children Version IV (NIMH DISC-IV): Description, differences from previous versions, and reliability of some common diagnoses. *Journal of the American Academy of Child and Adolescent Psychiatry, 39*(1), 28–38. https://doi.org/10.1097/00004583-200001000-00014

Silverman, W. K., & Albano, A. M. (1996). *Anxiety Disorders Interview Schedule for DSM-IV: Parent interview schedule*. Oxford University Press.

Silverman, W., & Ollendick, T. (2005). Evidence-based assessment of anxiety and its disorders in children and adolescents. *Journal of Clinical Child and Adolescent Psychology, 34*, 380–411. https://doi.org/10.1207/s15374424jccp3403_2

Smith, J. D., & Dumont, F. (2002). Confidence in psychodiagnosis: What makes us so sure? *Clinical Psychology & Psychotherapy, 9*(4), 292–298. https://doi.org/10.1002/cpp.336

Spence, S. H. (1997). Structure of anxiety symptoms among children: A confirmatory factor-analytic study. *Journal of Abnormal Psychology, 106*(2), 280–297. https://doi.org/10.1037/0021-843X.106.2.280

Spence, S. H. (2018). Assessing anxiety disorders in children and adolescents. *Child and Adolescent Mental Health, 23*(3), 266–282. https://doi.org/10.1111/camh.12251

Stiede, J. T., Trent, E. S., Viana, A. G., Guzick, A. G., Storch, E. A., & Hershfield, J. (2023). Cognitive behavioral therapy for children and adolescents with anxiety disorders. *Child and Adolescent Psychiatric Clinics of North America, 32*(3), 543–558. https://doi.org/10.1016/j.chc.2022.12.001

Tam, H. E., & Ronan, K. (2017). The application of a feedback-informed approach in psychological service with youth: Systematic review and meta-analysis. *Clinical Psychology Review, 55*, 41–55. https://doi.org/10.1016/j.cpr.2017.04.005

Turner, E. A., & Mills, C. J. (2016). Culturally relevant diagnosis and assessment of mental illness. In A. M. Breland-Noble, C. S. Al-Mateen, & N. N. Singh (Eds.), *Handbook of mental health in African American youth* (pp. 21–35). Springer International Publishing. https://doi.org/10.1007/978-3-319-25501-9_2

Van Meter, A., Youngstrom, E., Youngstrom, J. K., Ollendick, T., Demeter, C., & Findling, R. L. (2014). Clinical decision making about child and adolescent anxiety disorders using the Achenbach system of empirically based assessment. *Journal of Clinical Child and Adolescent Psychology, 43*(4), 552–565. https://doi.org/10.1080/15374416.2014.883930

Villabø, M., Gere, M., Torgersen, S., March, J. S., & Kendall, P. C. (2012). Diagnostic efficiency of the child and parent versions of the Multidimensional Anxiety Scale for Children. *Journal of Clinical Child and Adolescent Psychology, 41*(1), 75–85. https://doi.org/10.1080/15374416.2012.632350

Walters, R., Leslie, S. J., Polson, R., Cusack, T., & Gorely, T. (2020). Establishing the efficacy of interventions to improve health literacy and health behaviours: A systematic review. *BMC Public Health, 20*(1), 1040. https://doi.org/10.1186/s12889-020-08991-0

Wei, C., Hoff, A., Villabø, M. A., Peterman, J., Kendall, P. C., Piacentini, J., McCracken, J., Walkup, J. T., Albano, A. M., Rynn, M., Sherrill, J., Sakolsky, D., Birmaher, B., Ginsburg,

G., Keeton, C., Gosch, E., Compton, S. N., & March, J. (2014). Assessing anxiety in youth with the Multidimensional Anxiety Scale for children. *Journal of Clinical Child & Adolescent Psychology, 43*(4), 566–578. https://doi.org/10.1080/15374416.2013.814541

Whiteside, S. P. H., Deacon, B. J., Benito, K., & Stewart, E. (2016). Factors associated with practitioners' use of exposure therapy for childhood anxiety disorders. *Journal of Anxiety Disorders, 40*, 29–36. https://doi.org/10.1016/j.janxdis.2016.04.001

Williams, M. T., Malcoun, E., Sawyer, B. A., Davis, D. M., Nouri, L. B., & Bruce, S. L. (2014). Cultural adaptations of prolonged exposure therapy for treatment and prevention of posttraumatic stress disorder in African Americans. *Behavioral Sciences, 4*(2), 102–124. https://doi.org/10.3390/bs4020102

Williams, M. T., Rouleau, T. M., Torre, J. T. L., & Sharif, N. (2020). Cultural competency in the treatment of obsessive-compulsive disorder: Practitioner guidelines. *The Cognitive Behaviour Therapist, 13*, e48. https://doi.org/10.1017/S1754470X20000501

Part II
Interventions with Adults

Chapter 3
Weekly Outpatient Conjoint Treatment for Adult Psychopathology

Donald H. Baucom, Alexandra K. Wojda-Burlij, and Melanie S. Fischer

3.1 Introduction

Typically, when adult individuals experience some form of psychopathology, they are treated individually. Similarly, when couples experience relationship distress, they are typically seen for couple therapy to address their relationship concerns. Whereas this logic regarding the form of intervention sounds intuitive, in the current chapter, we describe a broadened paradigm in which a couple might be seen as the basis for improving one person's psychopathology within outpatient treatment settings (e.g., private practice and academic medical centers), along with a consideration of depression and obsessive-compulsive disorder (OCD) as clinical examples within this framework. For a fuller explanation of the clinical aspects of our couple-based interventions for these and other disorders, we refer the reader to our recent book on the treatment of relationship distress and psychopathology (Baucom et al., 2020). A more detailed discussion of the empirical evidence for the couple-based interventions discussed here is provided in Baucom and Fischer (2023). Thus, the current chapter is intended as an overview to delineate important principles that can be adapted to a number of disorders treated within a couple context.

D. H. Baucom (✉)
University of North Carolina, Chapel Hill, NC, USA
e-mail: don_baucom@unc.edu

A. K. Wojda-Burlij
Philadelphia VAMC, Philadelphia, PA, USA

M. S. Fischer
Philipps-Universität Marburg, Marburg, Germany

L. Reuman, J. Thompson-Hollands (eds.), *Enhancing CBT Through Family and Peer Engagement*, CBT: Science Into Practice, https://doi.org/10.1007/978-3-031-74838-7_3

3.2 Why and How to Employ Couples in the Treatment of Psychopathology

Many investigations using various methodologies conclude that relationship functioning and individual well-being are inextricably linked, with each influencing the other in a reciprocal manner over time. For example, the Harvard Study of Adult Development has followed participants for more than 80 years, and the investigators conclude that the single best long-term predictor of individual functioning—and even longevity—is the quality of close relationships (Waldinger, 2015). Reviewing studies including different methodologies such as genetically informed samples in twin studies as well as treatment outcome investigations, Whisman et al. (2021) concluded that relationship discord is an important causal risk factor for one partner developing depression and that intervening in the couple's relationship can modify that risk. Thus, whether looking at broad patterns of well-being across the lifespan or more fine-grained views of specific disorders, the conclusion is the same: Individuals experience various forms of individual psychopathology, yet these disorders do not exist in a vacuum. Instead, they exist in a social context, and that context (particularly individuals' close relationships) can impact the magnitude and course of those disorders in various ways.

3.2.1 Impact of Relationship Functioning on Psychopathology

Couples' relationships influence the degree and trajectory of one partner's psychopathology at two distinct levels. First, on a broad level, the overall quality of the relationship creates a social environment within which each partner lives day-to-day. A positive, supportive relationship environment can contribute to an optimal context for individual well-being, particularly for partners vulnerable to various psychological disorders. On the other hand, relationship distress often includes high levels of hostility and criticism from a partner. Such interaction patterns can serve as a chronic, diffuse stressor on an individual and exacerbate or maintain various forms of psychopathology. Both the couple communication literature (Heyman, 2001) and the family psychopathology literature with a particular emphasis on expressed emotion (EE; Hooley & Miklowitz, 2018) demonstrate the toll that such negative interactions have on individuals experiencing psychopathology. Thus, if couples are experiencing relationship distress, helping them alleviate this distress can alter the overall social environment and lower or eliminate a chronic, diffuse stressor in the individual.

Second, relationships impact individual psychopathology at a much more specific level, including the ways in which two partners interact around the disorder itself. Often, due to a lack of understanding, even well-meaning partners in happy relationships behave in ways that are maladaptive, and in turn, the couple develops interaction patterns that maintain or exacerbate the disorder. These partner responses have been widely noted, particularly in anxiety and fear-based disorders, and are referred to as symptom accommodation (e.g., Reuman & Abramowitz, 2018). For example, if a person with social anxiety disorder is reluctant to attend a social gathering, a caring partner might agree for the couple to decline the invitation. Such responses might alleviate distress temporarily but maintain the disorder long-term through continued avoidance.

There can be various reasons why a partner accommodates symptoms (see Fredman et al., 2014, Renshaw et al., 2020 for a discussion regarding PTSD). Whereas understanding the reasons for accommodation can help to shape treatment, on a broad level, the impact is the same regardless of the reasons: It functions to maintain the disorder over time. What is important to note, however, is that such interaction patterns around various symptoms of the disorder do not presume the presence of relationship distress. In fact, such patterns often exist among happy couples in which a partner is attempting to be helpful but does not understand how best to accomplish that goal. Thus, even in satisfied couples, helping the two partners work together without accommodation can be quite effective. Of course, at times, relationship distress co-exists with maladaptive interaction patterns around the disorder. In this case, effective intervention must target both broad relationship issues as well as how the couple interacts specifically around the disorder.

3.2.2 Broad Principles and Common Interventions for Working with Couples with Psychopathology

3.2.2.1 Roles for the Partner

Given the potential value of working with the couple to target one partner's individual disorder, the question arises regarding how to include a partner in treatment in an outpatient setting. This question is important given that different clinicians and researchers have approached this issue in numerous ways. For example, Thompson-Hollands (see current volume) has developed an intervention for PTSD in which family members are seen briefly without the identified patient present, whereas Fredman et al. (see current volume) employ a conjoint form of PTSD treatment with both partners seen together. Still, other clinicians might conduct mostly individual therapy, bringing the partner in at selected points in treatment for conjoint sessions around key issues. Our own work has largely involved working with the couple conjointly across outpatient sessions, what we refer to as *couple-based interventions for psychopathology*. This label is meant to clarify that the treatment works with the couple *together*, but the goal is to alleviate or lessen one or both people's *psychopathology*.[1] This contrasts with couple therapy where the primary goal is to improve relationship functioning for its own sake.

---

[1] One exception is when treating adult anorexia nervosa. Due to the complexity of the disorder, the treatment is multi-faceted, including our couple-based intervention, individual therapy, medical management, and dietary interventions (see Baucom et al., 2020 for description).

As we discuss below, there are specific aspects for each type of psychopathology that are important to consider in couple-based interventions. In addition, there are several overarching ways to include a partner in treatment that we have described in more detail elsewhere (Baucom & Fischer, 2023; Baucom et al., 2020). First, a person with an individual disorder often needs to make specific individual changes, and the current approach draws from individual cognitive-behavioral interventions (CBT) to delineate those changes. In such instances, a partner can assist the individual with a disorder and serve as a support and coach to help the person make those changes; these we have referred to as *partner-assisted interventions*. Such an approach does not focus on changing the couple's relationship; the partner is serving as a support for individual change. In addition, the couple might need to alter the specific ways they interact around the disorder. For example, a couple with agoraphobia might need to shift roles and responsibilities such that the person with the disorder begins to do the shopping and transporting the children to events. We have labeled this type of intervention as a *disorder-specific intervention* because it involves altering the couple's relationship specifically around the disorder. Neither of these two types of interventions assumes relationship distress on a broad level. However, when broad relationship distress is present and serves as a stressor on the person, then elements of *general couple therapy* are needed to improve the overall relationship.

3.2.2.2 Common Elements

The above approaches to couple-based treatment often involve the following broad interventions, frequently in the order outlined below. These interventions typically can be completed within a course of 10–20 weekly conjoint sessions, with an additional 1–2 "booster" sessions as needed. Importantly, these broad approaches are individualized to the needs of the particular couple, along with specific interventions for the disorder under consideration. First, often within the context of treatment planning, the therapist provides psychoeducation about the specific disorder, what we know about effective interventions for the disorder (typically based on principles from individual therapy), how the couple can work together to address the disorder, and what they might attempt to change from their current way of interacting around the disorder. The goal is to make certain that everyone is "on the same page" about what they will be attempting in treatment. This is particularly important since some interventions might seem counterintuitive to the partner, such as being involved in exposure when a person has great fear in certain situations (see Baucom et al., 2020 for an in-depth discussion of couple-based psychoeducation). Second, adapting communication guidelines from cognitive-behavioral couple therapy (CBCT; Baucom et al., 2020), the therapist teaches the couple to communicate effectively, (a) sharing their thoughts and feelings and (b) making effective decisions specifically around the disorder. Third, and the bulk of the treatment, the couple employs partner-assisted and disorder-specific interventions to address specific symptoms focal to the given disorder, for example, behavioral activation for depression, exposure for anxiety disorders, or balanced eating for various eating disorders. During this phase, interventions from individual therapy are adapted for a couple context, along with aspects of the relationship that typically are considered less extensively in individual treatment (e.g., the couple's sexual relationship or rewarding joint activities). Finally, if the couple experiences overall relationship distress, broader relationship issues beyond the disorder are considered. Whereas these broader relationship issues might be addressed later in therapy, if the couple is so acrimonious that they cannot work together effectively to address one partner's disorder, then relationship distress is considered early in treatment.

Below, we provide examples of how this third element of treatment—that is, how the couple can work together around specific elements of a given disorder—can be utilized in treating two disorders often seen in outpatient settings—depression and anxiety. In our discussion of anxiety, we will focus on OCD, but it is important to note that the principles of exposure hold across anxiety disorders currently included in the DSM-5-TR.

3.3 A Cognitive-Behavioral, Couple-Based Intervention for Depression

As noted earlier, psychopathology and relationship functioning often have a reciprocal effect on each other, and these recursive influences appear to be particularly strong within the context of depression. That is, if one partner is depressed, the depression significantly increases the likelihood that the couple will experience relationship distress within the next year (Whisman et al., 2021). Similarly, if the couple is experiencing relationship dissatisfaction, this distress significantly increases the likelihood of one partner becoming depressed within the next year (Whisman et al., 2021). Furthermore, as discussed above, even within satisfied relationships, the couple often develops interaction patterns that can inadvertently maintain or exacerbate depression. Therefore, addressing different aspects of depression by working with the couple within a conjoint therapeutic framework holds promise.

Following an initial assessment that includes a discussion of both the depression and the couple's relationship, treatment typically begins with psychoeducation about depression in an interpersonal context along with a discussion of what the couple has experienced relative to the depression. The therapist and couple discuss treatment goals, strategies that will be employed to achieve these goals, and how the couple can work together to address specific aspects of depression. The most common elements of depression, along with maladaptive and constructive couple interaction patterns that are noted and targeted for treatment, are discussed below.

3.3.1 Communication Training to Optimize Healthy Emotional Expression and Decision-Making

Effective communication is central to optimal couple functioning in general, and within the context of treating depression, it takes on particular salience for two reasons. First, communication is an important behavior in and of itself and can either have a positive or negative impact on the depressed person (and the partner). Second, the couple needs to be able to discuss various aspects of the depression, either (a) sharing their thoughts and feelings about the depression and/or (b) making good decisions about how to address various elements of the depression consistent with treatment guidelines (e.g., how to enact behavioral activation).

One communication pattern that is particularly detrimental to depressed individuals (as well as other forms of psychopathology) involves a partner's high rate of hostility (general negative sentiments expressed about the individual) and criticism (negative comments targeted to specific aspects of behavior; Hooley & Miklowitz, 2018). Whereas these responses are perhaps not surprising when interacting with a depressed person who has withdrawn, they can contribute to the downward spiral of depression. Thus, it is important to teach both partners how to express concerns and negative feelings in a constructive manner.

In addition, the couple needs to be skilled in making decisions to counteract multiple aspects of depression (e.g., low energy, lack of motivation, and frequent withdrawal). Consistent with the application of CBCT across many contexts, the therapist can provide psychoeducation and broad principles of intervention that are salient for a specific aspect of the couple's functioning. Following a discussion between the couple and therapist about the applicability of this principle to their relationship, the couple typically has a decision-making conversation about how they might bring this principle to fruition in their everyday lives. For example, the couple may decide to increase pleasurable activities through date nights, consistent with a discussion of behavioral activation (as described below).

3.3.2 Behavioral Activation to Address Withdrawal or Overreliance on a Partner

Depressed individuals often doubt themselves and their abilities and experience overall low motivation. This often manifests in one of two couple interaction patterns. First, depressed individuals withdraw from the world around them, including their partners. This may involve (a) difficulty accomplishing chores, (b) avoiding challenging tasks or even tasks that previously seemed simple, and (c) declining or avoiding opportunities to spend time with their partner in previously rewarding activities. Second, low self-efficacy can result in overreliance on the partner, asking for advice or wanting the partner to assist in activities the depressed person previously handled on their own. Both patterns can be addressed using principles of behavioral activation (BA), which has been shown to be efficacious in individual therapy for depression.

BA is geared toward helping a depressed person participate in activities that have the potential to bring them pleasure or joy, a sense of mastery, or that are values focused (Martell et al., 2021). Given that individuals seem to benefit from both a sense of connectedness and autonomy in a couple context, BA can be adapted to promote these important needs depending on the behavioral patterns noted above. Thus, we differentiate between (a) couple-level BA, in which the couple engages in activities together and (b) individual-level BA, in which the couple discusses what the depressed person might do individually with the partner's support.

If the depressed person has generally withdrawn from a wide range of activities (including those that involve the partner), both couple-level and individual-level BA might be helpful. In such instances, intervention might begin with couple-level BA because the direct involvement of the partner in the activities often can assist in successful follow-through. This might include activities such as a date night to increase pleasurable activities, working on a household task together geared toward mastery or engagement in community service consistent with the couple's values. Likewise, individual-level BA might be helpful to ensure that the depressed person does not re-engage only when the partner is present. Conversely, if the depressed person presents with overreliance on the partner, individual-level BA might be emphasized, for example, getting together with friends without the partner present, yet using the partner's support to discuss how they might arrange their schedules to facilitate this activity.

Inherent in BA is a discussion of how it can serve to disrupt overdependence or withdrawal from the partner. Thus, both partners need to understand accommodation and how a partner's well-intended efforts to help (e.g., taking over chores for the depressed person) might alleviate distress for the depressed person momentarily but long term serve to maintain the disorder. This understanding is crucial so that if a partner (a) is not compliant with the depressed person's requests or (b) engages in a notable behavioral change to support the depressed individual's increasing autonomy, the intent is not interpreted as a lack of care or ill will.

3.3.3 Cognitive Restructuring and Guided Discovery to Address Distorted Cognitions

A cardinal symptom of depression involves distorted, negative cognitions that can include a person's negative view of themselves, their relationships, and their world. Within individual CBT, the therapist often employs cognitive restructuring via Socratic questioning (Beck, 2020). For an individual to be open to such exploration, the person must be willing to acknowledge that there are more adaptive ways to think about what is occurring. This approach can become difficult within distressed couples because acknowledging one's distorted thinking in front of an accusatory partner can feel unsafe and expose the person to unhelpful criticism. As a result, guided discovery can be used to create experiences that might lead the depressed person to think about things differently without directly focusing on their "distorted thinking" (Baucom et al., 2020; Epstein & Baucom, 2002). This might include assisting the couple to have a conversation where each person speaks for themselves and the partner listens carefully to gain new perspectives. This contrasts with partners mind-reading each other's motivations, which sets the stage for negative thinking to flourish. Similarly, the therapist and couple might decide on couple-level activities outside of the session that can counteract the depressed person's distorted beliefs, such as believing their partner does not want to spend time with them. Having concrete behavioral experiences with a partner can be quite facilitative toward changing beliefs about the relationship (e.g., "Our relationship has no chance of succeeding; we've lost our ability to enjoy each other and have fun as a couple").

Additionally, helping the partner assume appropriate roles when the depressed person makes distorted statements is valuable. Many partners (either out of concern or wanting to defend themselves) often feel the need to "straighten out" the depressed person's thinking and tell them why their thinking is wrong. Oftentimes, such efforts can feel invalidating to the depressed person; thus, we recommend that partners generally not attempt to change the depressed person's thinking. Instead, it can be helpful to follow good listening guidelines that include acceptance of what the other person is feeling and thinking without necessarily agreeing with them. At the same time, the partner needs the opportunity to express their own perspectives: "It must feel horrible to experience that you are a major burden to me and the kids. I know that you feel really bad about yourself, and we'll keep working through this together. Also, I want you to know I see you very differently. You're the most important person in the world to me."

3.3.4 Addressing Additional Aspects of Depression

Numerous other aspects of the disorder also can be addressed depending on how depression is expressed within a given relationship. For example, depression and some antidepressants often lead to a lessening of interest in sexual activities or physical interactions more broadly. When both partners agree that they are ready to approach their physical relationship, a gradual, hierarchical approach to increasing intimate interactions can be employed, along with psychoeducation about depression and sexual functioning. Furthermore, given that many couples have rarely discussed their physical relationship, providing a safe context with good communication about their physical relationship can be valuable.

Perhaps one of the most frightening aspects of depression involves suicidal ideation and possible self-harm. It is important to realize that such thoughts exist in the depressed person's everyday life and in an interpersonal context, whether the couple has discussed the issue or not. Therefore, we help couples talk about such concerns. This can be viewed as an exposure experience in which the couple learns to talk together about this very frightening topic that they previously avoided. Rather than having a depressed person deal with suicidal thoughts on their own, we note the value of having an intimate partner provide an outside perspective, without making the partner responsible for the depressed person's safety. We discuss how they can make good decisions about whether they need to act or consult with their therapist when safety concerns do arise (see Baucom et al., 2020 for a fuller discussion of this important topic).

In summary, in addition to addressing common aspects of depression in an interpersonal context, there are a host of additional domains that can be addressed with couple-based behavioral, cognitive, and emotional interventions via a contextual framework. As noted below, the empirical evidence to date indicates that working with the couple to treat depression can be a highly efficacious approach.

3.3.5 Empirical Status of Couple-Based Interventions for Depression

Several randomized controlled trials (RCTs) and open trials focused on couple-based intervention for depression have been conducted, one of the largest sets of couple-based treatment studies for any outpatient disorder. The results of many of these investigations are included in a meta-analysis of 14 studies conducted by Barbato and D'Avanzo (2020). Their review compared what they referred to as couple therapy for depression (some studies included partner-assisted and disorder-specific interventions) versus either individual psychotherapy, drug treatment, or minimal intervention. Their findings indicated that couple therapy and individual therapy are equally efficacious in alleviating depression at the end of treatment and at follow-up. They also found that couple therapy results in greater increases in relationship adjustment than individual therapy. Some of the investigations included couples who were not relationally distressed, and the advantage of couple therapy in improving relationship adjustment was even stronger when the couple was relationally distressed when treatment began. This later finding is important, given that relationship distress is a risk factor for subsequent depression. Therefore, when both depression and relationship distress are present, couple-based interventions that lead to improvement in both domains should be considered.

In Barbato and D'Avanzo's (2020) meta-analysis, couple therapies from different theoretical orientations were included, speaking to the robustness of including partners in treatment. To provide some initial indications of the effectiveness of the specific CBT-oriented, couple-based intervention described in this chapter, an open trial employing this intervention for depression was conducted in London, England, within the National Health Service (NHS) in routine community treatment settings (Baucom et al., 2018). Within the NHS, clients decide which among several empirically supported interventions to receive. In the Baucom et al. (2018) investigation, most clients selected either individual therapy (largely CBT or interpersonal psychotherapy for depression) or our couple-based intervention. That is, couples were not randomized to treatment conditions. The findings showed a depression recovery rate of 57% for the couple-based intervention, compared to 41% recovery for other depression treatments in the same London clinics. Nonclient partners who also were depressed or anxious (yet not the focus of treatment) demonstrated a 48% recovery rate with the couple-based intervention, suggesting that a single couple-based intervention can be helpful when both partners are struggling.

3.4 A Cognitive-Behavioral, Couple-Based Intervention for OCD and Anxiety Disorders

Across anxiety and other fear-based disorders (e.g., OCD and PTSD), individuals experience frequent, intense fear that is (a) out of proportion to the actual threat in a given situation and (b) maintained through avoidance, escape, and other safety behaviors. Although OCD and PTSD are categorized separately from anxiety disorders in the DSM-5-TR (American Psychiatric Association, 2022), there is significant overlap across these disorders in terms of their clinical features. For example, an individual with panic disorder fears their own physiological sensations (e.g., increased heart rate) and avoids situations in which these sensations may occur (e.g., going to the gym). Similarly, someone with OCD experiences intrusive, distressing thoughts and engages in compulsions to either "neutralize" these thoughts and/or prevent a feared consequence (e.g., excessive hand washing to prevent contracting AIDS). Likewise, after experiencing a traumatic event, an individual with PTSD may have distorted beliefs about the safety of the world around them and avoid anxiety-provoking situations. Thus, anxiety disorders, OCD, and PTSD can be conceptualized in similar ways, with the primary differences across disorders being the source of perceived threat or anxiety.

Similar to depression, these disorders also occur in social contexts wherein the disorder and the couple's relationship functioning reciprocally impact one another. Often, the person with the disorder relies on their partner in a variety of ways to decrease their sense of danger. As such, partners may engage in symptom accommodation, which can range from the partner participating in the rituals established by the person with the disorder (e.g., checking windows and doors) to providing excessive reassurance (e.g., reiterating that the individual is safe many times a day) or altering their roles and responsibilities to helping the individual avoid emotional distress (e.g., shopping at stores that are "off-limits" for the person with the disorder). As this behavioral avoidance continues, the couple's lives may begin to "shrink" over time. To avoid anxiety-provoking situations, places that were once a source of joy or meaning might be eliminated from the couple's lives. Furthermore, partners may find it difficult to sustain accommodation over time, with the very act of accommodation experienced as frustrating and burdensome. In fact, Boeding et al. (2013) found that higher rates of OCD symptom accommodation were correlated with greater relationship distress for partners.

In addition to the overlapping conceptualization across disorders, the principles used in their treatment also share similar features. Using a combination of behavioral exposures and cognitive restructuring, cognitive-behavioral treatments often help the individual re-evaluate that their feared situation or stimuli are not as dangerous as they once thought. Given these treatment similarities, we focus here on presenting our couple-based intervention for OCD as an example of how to address anxiety and fear-based disorders within a couple context (Abramowitz et al., 2013). (For a discussion of intensive couple-based interventions for PTSD, see Fredman in the current volume.) Notably, the general principles employed in treating OCD are conceptually consistent with those applied in the treatment of anxiety disorders and PTSD, with the couple and individual approaching situations that the individual experiences as dangerous.

Couple-based interventions for OCD center around several core treatment targets. These include: (a) counteracting avoidance via partner-assisted exposures around feared stimuli, (b) reducing partner accommodation to increase alternative strategies for couple engagement, and (c) generalizing these newfound skills to other aspects of the relationship (Abramowitz et al., 2013; Baucom et al., 2020). These goals are explained to the couple following (a) assessment of the individual's symptoms and the couple's relationship, (b) psychoeducation on the nature and maintenance of the disorder, and (c) review of the treatment rationale for couple-based exposure and response prevention (ERP). Psychoeducation can serve as an early intervention to address maladaptive cognitions common in OCD (e.g., thought-action fusion in which the person believes that thinking something will make it happen) as well as the partner's misattributions for the OCD person's behavior (e.g., "He won't spend time with me because he finds me repulsive" versus "It is hard for him to touch me because of his symptoms"). Furthermore, communication skills training is integrated early in therapy to help the couple not only talk about the disorder with increased empathy but also decide how to execute various aspects of treatment (e.g., increase approach behaviors and decrease avoidance). As with depression, psychoeducation and communication skills training are the foundations upon which subsequent interventions are built, giving couples the information and skills needed to address the OCD as a team. We elaborate on these OCD-specific interventions below, beginning first with partner-assisted exposures.

3.4.1 Partner-Assisted Exposures

Using the same principles as individual ERP, partner-assisted exposures involve partners serving as a "coach" during exposure exercises. In this role, the partner helps the individual to implement the exposures adaptively. Their task is to ensure that the person confronts what they perceive as dangerous (whether it be a taboo thought or some external situation), stays in that situation, and does not engage in their typical actions used to neutralize or escape from the threat (i.e., their compulsions such as ritualized hand washing). In tandem, this process allows the individual with OCD to learn that obsessional fears are exaggerated or unrealistic and that anxiety eventually declines even when avoidance and other compulsive behaviors are not employed.

To accomplish this process, the couple is introduced to four phases of completing an exposure (Abramowitz et al., 2013). First, prior to the exposure, the couple uses communication skills to decide on their exposure scenario and to share how they feel about the upcoming practice. Second, the individual completes the exposure with the partner present, telling their partner how they feel throughout. This enables the individual to confront distressing feelings and provides the partner with useful information about the individual's experience (including avoidance urges). In response, the partner acknowledges their own feelings, provides support, and offers reinforcement without accommodation (e.g., "I know how hard this is, and I'm really proud of you. You're doing a great job!"). Importantly, within healthy relationships, the partner may find it upsetting to see the individual with OCD experience high levels of distress. As such, ERP may likewise be a form of exposure for the partners themselves, as they resist the temptation to distract the individual, provide reassurance, or use other strategies to reduce distress.

Third, there may be times when the individual with OCD experiences overwhelming anxiety during an exposure and wants to end the exposure. When this happens, the individual is instructed to inform their partner, who may once again acknowledge their distress, provide empathy, and remind the individual that their distress will decrease over time. However, these statements of support may not be enough at the moment, and the individual may want to exit the exposure. In such instances, a brief time-out might take place, with the partner providing individual support using strategies that do not include accommodation behaviors. For example, the partner can discuss with the individual what might have gone awry during the exposure and together think through ways of resuming. If the couple decides to continue with exposure, they might decide to choose a less distressing scenario for the time being, primarily to ensure that the individual does not end their practice with an escape and avoidance response.

Finally, after the exposure, the couple is encouraged to evaluate how it went, including what the individual with OCD learned, what they found helpful, and how they felt about the experience overall. The partner has an opportunity to provide praise as appropriate for what went well, along with a discussion of how they might adapt in the future if needed. This step helps the individual consolidate any corrective information they may have gathered about their obsessional fears and provides the couple with an opportunity to feel more united as a team.

As with many behavioral interventions in which the client demonstrates increasing autonomy as treatment progresses, it is important for the partner to eventually "fade out" of their role as "coach" during exposures. That is, to optimize the individual's sense of self-efficacy, they will be encouraged to complete exposures gradually on their own. Thus, while the partner might still discuss these independent experiences and troubleshoot future exposure practices, they typically are no longer present during the exposure, unless the partner is an inherent part of the situation that creates distress (e.g., concerns about bodily fluids during sex). This step can be particularly valuable for couples in which the person with OCD sees their partner as a safety signal and has trouble confronting distressing situations without their partner. In addition to avoiding accommodation during exposure outings, it is important to decrease partner accommodation in other domains of life as well.

3.4.2 Joint Decision-Making to Reduce Partner Accommodation

Although partner-assisted exposures can be effective in reducing OCD symptoms, often they only partially address the role of the couple's relationship in the maintenance of OCD, including partner accommodation. Some accommodations may decrease notably as progress continues with other interventions (including psychoeducation and exposure practices). Yet, some accommodation may remain, either because the behavior has become a significant part of the way in which the partner shows love and concern for the person with OCD or because the avoidance may have become gradually integrated into the roles and responsibilities shared between partners. For example, one partner may cook all of the couple's meals due to the other person's contamination-related fears regarding handling raw meat. Although the individual could likely benefit from counteracting their avoidance of touching raw meat, the couple may not question this distribution of cooking responsibilities or recognize the partner's accommodation because they have divided their roles in this way for many years.

Therefore, the therapist helps the couple use decision-making skills to find ways of promoting exposure in everyday situations where accommodation might be present. For couples where accommodation may be an expression of care and concern, the therapist can help the partners express these feelings in ways that are unrelated to the individual's disorder. In fact, some partners report that in the absence of accommodation, they no longer feel connected or close to one another. Therefore, the therapist should work to help the couple engage in other shared activities, provide emotional support more broadly, or increase affection without focusing on caring in terms of OCD.

3.4.3 Couple Therapy Interventions to Optimize the Relationship

The goal of partner-assisted exposures and reducing symptom accommodation is to help the couple progress toward a life in which they can increasingly confront feared situations without giving in to compulsive or avoidance urges. As the couple makes progress toward this goal and OCD symptoms decrease, the couple may begin to consider how to use these principles to enhance their overall relationship or address topics unrelated to the OCD. For example, to continue building a sense of closeness and connection into their lives, some couples may engage in informal exposure outings, such as spending time with friends in places that were previously "off-limits" due to the OCD or participating in new, unfamiliar activities. Here, the couple aims to "expand" their world that was once restricted by OCD-related avoidance. This has the potential to improve relationship functioning overall but also can indirectly target OCD symptoms by asking the individual to tolerate uncertainty across situations and engage with the world in new ways. Similarly, other couples may elect to improve their relationship by focusing on issues beyond the disorder. In these circumstances, the therapist may rely on general couple therapy techniques, such as using communication skills, to help the couple interact effectively around challenging topics. For example, for a couple who frequently argue over finances, the therapist might lead the partners through a decision-making conversation in which they discuss how to approach difficult topics in their daily lives. Thus, while this phase of the work may be less focused on OCD, it can play a crucial role in the maintenance of OCD treatment gains, as the couple works to address and reduce relationship distress or enhance their lives by living in an unrestricted manner that had become part of the interpersonal context of OCD.

3.4.4 Empirical Status of Couple-Based Interventions for OCD and Anxiety Disorders

The field remains in the early stages of its empirical investigation of couple-based treatments for OCD and anxiety disorders. However, findings thus far are promising. An open trial of the OCD treatment outlined above (Abramowitz et al., 2013) demonstrated significant reductions in the magnitude of OCD, both post-treatment and at a one-year follow-up. Moreover, benchmark comparisons with meta-analytic findings from individual ERP for OCD indicated that the treatment gains from couple-based treatment for OCD were larger than what is typical for individual OCD treatment (Abramowitz et al., 2013). Relationship adjustment also improved for participants. Similarly, a meta-analysis on family- and couple-based CBT for OCD in adults (with family member involvement varying widely across a broader range of formats) showed greater reductions in OCD symptoms and accommodation when compared to other treatments (Stewart et al., 2020). Thus, while controlled trials directly comparing individual and couple-based treatments have yet to be conducted, these initial results are encouraging.

3.5 Clinical Considerations for Diverse Identities

Working with couples from diverse populations requires extra attention to the social context in which partners are rooted. Although there are common factors that affect relationship functioning across all couples (e.g., communication difficulties), individuals with marginalized identities are often exposed to unique contextual stressors that can undermine psychological and relationship well-being. For example, in the face of stressors such as discrimination and financial insecurity, individuals may experience feelings of powerlessness and lack of control over their lives, heightening threat vigilance, negative expectations about the future, and perceived lack of self-efficacy (Kraus et al., 2011; Williams, 2018). Also, some individuals may experience internalized forms of oppression in which they devalue themselves based on their identity (e.g., internalized racism or homonegativity; Lavner, 2017). Such self-directed negativity has been associated with feelings of worthlessness and low self-esteem (Frost & Meyer, 2009; Kwate & Meyer, 2011) as well as anxiety (Gale et al., 2020) among racial and sexual minority groups. At the level of the couple's relationship, contextual stressors may likewise constrain couples' ability to interact effectively or spend time together in certain settings, increasing the likelihood of relationship distress (Neff & Karney, 2017).

Overall, research on couples-based interventions for psychopathology is limited among culturally diverse samples. However, in recent years, more attention has been given to culturally specific adaptations of (a) couple therapies for relationship distress and (b) CBT interventions for individual treatment among diverse populations. The initial results of this work are promising. Findings suggest that CBCT, CBCT-based relationship education programs, and other behaviorally based couple interventions might be effective with diverse couples, including same-sex female relationships (Pentel et al., 2021), African American couples (Barton et al., 2018), and low-income couples (Doss et al., 2020). Similarly, although further research is needed, culturally tailored interventions have been found to enhance the effect of CBT for Black, Asian, and Latino Americans with a variety of mental health challenges (Huey et al., 2023). Given that couple-based treatments involve the adaptation of interventions that are effective in individual therapy and expand upon these by integrating couple therapy strategies to address relationship dynamics (e.g., communication skill training), there is reason to believe these interventions might be used cross-culturally if clinicians remain sensitive to the issues relevant to a given cultural group. Therefore, in many instances, treatment can proceed by using the overarching framework and principles outlined in this chapter, while making certain adaptations as appropriate. Because other resources provide more thorough recommendations for working with couples with marginalized identities via couple therapy (e.g., Pentel & Baucom, 2022) and individual treatment (e.g., Hays, 2009), we focus on several overarching, guiding principles.

First, it is important to evaluate the extent to which a couple's intersecting identities impact the psychopathology that one partner is experiencing. That is, the centrality of cultural concerns can vary widely among couples of diverse backgrounds

(Pentel & Baucom, 2022). For example, one partner within a same-gender couple may be struggling with depression due to a pile-up of stressors (e.g., transition to parenthood and long hours at work) that are largely unrelated to their sexual minority identity. At other times, experiences of identity-related stress may be present, but the individual and the couple cope with them well as a team. Yet, in other instances, stressors such as discrimination against a marginalized individual and a lack of family support might be major factors in understanding one partner's depression. Thus, affirming care adjusts the degree to which such concerns are addressed based on their relevance, a process referred to as *dynamic sizing* (Kelly et al., 2014).

Also, therapists should consider the extent to which negative experiences for one partner or the couple are (a) being approached in a constructive, realistic manner or (b) whether they are being addressed in an unhelpful way by the couple that contributes to one partner's psychopathology. For example, if an African American couple reports anxiety after being the victim of race-based violence, their anxiety would be viewed as an understandable emotional response to a situation in which their lives were in danger. The clinician would then work with the couple to understand whether their response to the danger has resulted in widespread avoidance that now is interfering with adaptive functioning, and if so, help the couple address how to navigate the danger without unduly compromising their own well-being.

Importantly, when identity-related stressors (e.g., racism, sexual minority discrimination, and economic marginalization) become a focal part of couple-based treatment, therapists should help the couple assess the *controllability* of the situations contributing to the partner's symptoms and adapt accordingly. Many of the interventions discussed here (e.g., behavioral activation and exposure therapy) involve couples interacting with their environment rather than avoiding it. Implied in such interventions are two assumptions: (a) it is relatively *safe* for couples to interact with the world around them and (b) couples have the *means* to change various aspects of their lives. However, it is important to recognize that neither assumption is universally true, particularly for some couples from marginalized groups—either because they do not have adequate resources or because they live in environments where psychological or physical danger may be present. That is, as described in more detail below, negative cognitions are not always distorted, and avoidance of dangerous situations can be adaptive. In such cases, the therapist's role is to help the couple decide how to navigate such circumstances and the extent to which they can (and elect to) alter the environment in which they live, both to address an individual's psychopathology and the couple's relationship.

For example, when working with a racial minority couple in which one partner has contamination-related OCD but also a recent history of public harassment, initial in vivo exposures may need to take place in certain environments deemed safe (e.g., at home). To increase the generalization of the exposure, the couple might next use imaginal exposures that ask the partner with OCD to "visualize" what it would be like to encounter contaminants in other places (on the street, etc.), and finally encourage exposure in other settings that seem realistically safe. Similarly, a lower-income couple struggling to make ends meet may not be able to afford a date night as part of their couple-level BA for depression. Instead, the therapist may work with the couple to employ their decision-making skills and help them creatively decide how else to spend their time together (e.g., making dinner together or going for a walk).

Of note, some couples might benefit from assistance in judging the controllability of various aspects of their environment. Some individuals with psychopathology may believe that they "should" be able to control situations that they objectively cannot; conversely, some might engage in widespread avoidance after a negative experience when they realistically can engage in many safe contexts. In other words, consistent with the cognitive style of depression and anxiety disorders, an individual's perception of their life circumstances may at times be distorted or extreme. In such instances, the two partners may not hold the same perspective regarding the safety of their environment and how to respond to it. This difference in perspective can be particularly complicated when the two partners have different individual identities—for example, if one person is a member of a minority group that has experienced much discrimination and the other partner is not. Given that social contexts and other individuals' more subtle reactions to the couple involve subjective interpretation, the two partners might reach different conclusions about how people are reacting to them. For example, a partner might express to the depressed individual who is an ethnic minority that they are "overreacting": "I think the people at the next table were frustrated by the poor service that we also were experiencing. It probably wasn't about us being a mixed-race couple." In such instances, it is important for the therapist not to take sides (while taking into account that one partner has much more extensive experiences of microaggressions and might more readily notice such instances), but to help the couple accept each other's experiences and to help the couple decide how to handle such situations in the future.

Thus, in many instances, culturally tailored couple-based treatment might not require new types of interventions per se. Instead, it is essential that the therapist has the comfort level needed to address identity-related concerns openly and focus treatment around these concerns as appropriate. Thus, the behavioral, cognitive, and emotional interventions employed to address psychopathology with a couple context have broad applicability, yet the content of what various couples experience and the intersection of those experiences can become an important consideration in treatment.

3.6 Case Vignette

In the following case, the couple experiences a range of complications related to their major presenting complaint of psychopathology in one partner, a somewhat common situation. Neil (age 35), a White cisgender man, and Sarah (age 33), an Asian-American cisgender woman, have been married for 3 years and have an 18-month-old daughter, Madeleine. They contacted a couple therapist following Sarah's disclosure that she had become very frustrated by Neil's struggle with contamination-related OCD. Not only did she believe that his symptoms have had a negative impact on their relationship; she also believed they have affected his role as a stay-at-home caregiver for their daughter. During the initial assessment, Neil completed the Yale-Brown Obsessive-Compulsive Scale (Y-BOCS; Goodman et al., 1989) and had a score of 31, indicating severe OCD symptoms. They both also scored as moderately relationally distressed on the Couple Satisfaction Index (CSI; Funk & Rogge, 2007) with Sarah indicating greater distress, and both demonstrated mild depression on the Patient Health Questionnaire (PHQ-9; Kroenke et al., 2001), with Sarah scoring a bit higher.

During their first two sessions, the therapist assessed Neil's symptoms and the couple's relationship, including how the partners interacted around Neil's OCD and its overall impact on the relationship. The therapist learned that Neil had long been preoccupied with intrusive fears about the cleanliness of household surfaces (e.g., kitchen counters) and other environments (e.g., grocery stores, restaurants, and parks). To control this distress, Neil avoided places that provoked such fears; for example, he would not eat at certain restaurants without first calling to inquire about their food safety procedures. He also refused to participate in certain household chores (such as cooking meals that involved raw meat) and frequently scrubbed counters and other surfaces with bleach. While these behaviors were concerning to Sarah, she often went along with them, assuming they would dissipate as life became more focused on their young child as Neil assumed stay-at-home parent responsibilities.

However, to Sarah's dismay, Neil's obsessional fears were exacerbated after Madeleine was born. His contamination fears generalized to the belief that their daughter might contract a fatal illness resulting from contamination. Thus, in addition to cleaning rituals, Neil adopted several other safety behaviors, including wearing latex gloves while interacting with their daughter and taking showers multiple times per day. The idea of leaving home with their daughter provoked extreme anxiety for fear that she would come into contact with germs; therefore, several places such as the neighborhood park were deemed "off-limits." Sarah reported that if she did not participate in his cleaning rituals, he would become angry with her. Their interactions would then quickly devolve into escalating mutual criticism with her telling him that he was mentally disturbed, followed by Sarah's indignant complying with Neil's rituals to prevent further conflict. Neil felt invalidated by Sarah's criticism of his OCD rituals, believing that he simply wanted to keep himself and their family "safe." Sarah worried that if his OCD symptoms did not improve, their relationship would further deteriorate and as Madeleine became older, she also might start to experience the world as dangerous and copy some of Neil's extreme behaviors.

Based on the initial assessment, the therapist recognized the importance of treating Neil's OCD and their relationship distress defined by mutual conflict and hostility. For this reason, the therapist was concerned the couple might be uncooperative with one another if they were to address the OCD immediately. Therefore, the therapist elected first to address their relationship distress before turning to the OCD. Two initial goals focused on (a) introducing psychoeducation about OCD and ERP and (b) teaching communication skills to help the couple share their thoughts and feelings. These joint goals aimed to help both partners build insight into the nature of Neil's OCD (including its maintenance via avoidance and ritualistic cleaning), normalize their frustrations, and reduce ongoing maladaptive expressions of resentment and criticism. Moreover, the presence of mild depression for both partners was important to consider. It was unclear whether the depression primarily resulted from relationship distress or was somewhat independent. Because both partners continued to be active and engaged on a daily basis, the therapist decided to hold off on focusing on depression and assess whether the depression lifted as other issues were addressed or would need its own focus.

Psychoeducation had its intended therapeutic impact to some degree. Neil began to understand that his current contamination fears were based largely on his tendency to overestimate the likelihood and severity that Madeleine would contract an illness. Similarly, Sarah, who often criticized Neil for going "overboard" as a parent, acknowledged that Neil was a loving father who cared deeply about the well-being of their family. To capitalize on this early progress and build a sense of mutual caring, Neil and Sarah were taught expressive and empathic listening skills and encouraged to share with one another (a) the positive qualities they still value about each other and (b) their shared hopes for their relationship and their daughter. During these discussions, the therapist helped the couple join around their mutual goals, guiding Neil and Sarah to realize that they shared a great deal of common ground. The therapist asked the couple to practice these skills between sessions, with a focus on discussing positives about their day and about the other person. This intervention also was intended to address the couple's selective attention toward negative aspects of their relationship. By recognizing and openly sharing positives, the couple's global relationship perspective began to change over time.

As the couple demonstrated increased facility with these skills and were less negative in their interactions with each other, the therapist shifted the focus of sessions to address Neil's OCD within the context of the relationship. This included a focus on partner-assisted ERP, and with the therapist's help, they constructed a fear hierarchy that initially included confrontation of "contaminated" items with both partners present (e.g., door handles and kitchen counters). Eventually, they incorporated exposures focal to their daughter, for example, playing together as a family without wearing gloves or taking a walk through the neighborhood park. Across these exposures, Neil was encouraged to resist his decontamination rituals and Sarah to support him through this process. Instead of assuring him that everything would be fine, she expressed confidence in his ability to continue despite his concerns. Afterward, Neil and Sarah were also asked to evaluate how the exposure went, with Sarah providing Neil with praise for a job well done whenever appropriate.

Over the course of their progress with ERP, the couple hit some roadblocks along the way. In particular, exposures became much more difficult when Madeleine was involved. Whereas Neil would take a chance that *he* might become ill, the idea of Madeline contracting an illness was "absolutely unbearable," and he viewed himself as a bad parent for putting Madeleine in "harm's way." Also, Sarah continued some unhelpful accommodation at home. She began to offer reassurance when Neil voiced negative beliefs about himself as a parent and the likelihood of Madeleine becoming sick. She found these beliefs "too painful to listen to" and was reluctant to have him feel anxious when there were ways of helping him feel better immediately. Although her behavior was intended to express care for Neil and alleviate his notable distress, it was in direct contrast to the goals of exposure. Such reassurance ultimately prevented Neil from learning (a) that he can tolerate his contamination fears, both regarding Madeline and himself and (b) that effective parenting involves bringing one's child into the world to learn both about its richness and how to cope with uncertainty (rather than keeping the child in an overly restricted environment).

To target this pattern between Sarah and Neil, the therapist addressed the concept of accommodation, while normalizing Sarah's urge to accommodate. They discussed that it may serve several purposes, such as wanting to help Neil feel better immediately and to lower Sarah's own experience of distress as he becomes anxious. However, these behaviors worsen OCD symptoms by encouraging avoidance and reassurance as ways of continued coping over time. In addition, the therapist helped Neil and Sarah identify other patterns of accommodation in their relationship (e.g., Sarah preemptively cleaning Madeleine's toys before Neil could voice fear-related concerns) and helped them make decisions about how to change Sarah's responses. The couple agreed that Sarah would express empathy for Neil's anxiety and offer emotional support (e.g., a hug) while encouraging him to tolerate his distress. The therapist also helped Sarah identify possible coping strategies to manage her own negative emotional arousal without providing reassurance (e.g., deep breathing, reminding herself that they may need to currently engage in distress tolerance to make progress on this OCD for the future).

Additionally, the couple was guided toward thinking of ways to resume the Madeleine-focused exposures without accommodation. Such decisions included Neil handling impromptu exposures with Madeleine, such as changing her diapers without first stopping to put on gloves or allowing other people into their home without cleaning the living room and Madeleine's toys in a ritualized way. In addition, the couple agreed to focus attention on the positive aspects of the world around them and embrace Madeleine's delight with dogs and flowers in the park as they ventured as a family into a broader world. As exposure continued, Neil at times took Madeleine on outings without Sarah, learning that he did not need to rely upon Sarah to ensure safety. Across the next several sessions, Sarah's reassurance behaviors decreased, and Neil began experiencing concomitant decreases in his OCD symptoms. The couple remarked that a major motivating factor in exposure was their joint commitment to raising Madeleine in a healthy, positive manner. This joint commitment to their daughter and positive family outings also led to increasing positive interactions between Neil and Sarah, and their depressions began to lift without explicitly focusing on depression per se. They actually had been engaging in couple and family-level behavioral activation for pleasure without labeling it as such.

During their final stage of treatment, the therapist and couple reflected on their progress, noting they had successfully completed most exposures on their initial hierarchy. Now that the couple demonstrated marked improvements in their understanding of OCD symptoms and how to handle them, the therapist helped the couple generalize their newfound skills to other areas of their relationship. For example, to increase their feelings of intimacy and enjoyment, the couple had several decision-making conversations about visiting places that were previously "off-limits" due to Neil's OCD (e.g., certain restaurants, children's play arenas, and travel by airplane). The couple now planned to spend time with friends and engage in new activities as a couple and a family which maintained their exposure practice in an informal way. Ultimately, treatment for Neil and Sarah had created a context for the couple in which they were able to apply exposure-based principles to their everyday life on an ongoing basis, fundamentally altering patterns that were the basis on their relationship distress prior to the first session.

By the end of treatment, Neil's Y-BOCS score was 7, indicating subclinical symptoms and substantial overall improvements in his OCD. Both partners were now in the normal range on the PHQ-9 as a measure of depression, reported greater relationship satisfaction, and felt better equipped to have more open and constructive conversations about Neil's anxiety. Whereas the couple and therapist all agreed that they had made notable progress, they discussed how the couple needed to make ongoing efforts to (a) interact with the world in an open and engaging way, thus providing ongoing exposure, and (b) communicate effectively, particularly when difficulties arise. By doing so, they could help maintain gains regarding Neil's OCD, their relationship satisfaction, and the depression that they both had experienced (which ultimately seemed to be a consequence of relationship distress).

References

Abramowitz, J. S., Baucom, D. H., Wheaton, M. G., Boeding, S., Fabricant, L. E., Paprocki, C., & Fischer, M. S. (2013). Enhancing exposure and response prevention for OCD: A couple-based approach. *Behavior Modification, 37*, 189–210. https://doi.org/10.1177/0145445512444596

American Psychiatric Association. (2022). *Diagnostic and statistical manual of mental disorders* (5th ed., text rev.) [DSM-5-TR]. American Psychiatric Publishing.

Barbato, A., & D'Avanzo, B. (2020). The findings of a Cochrane meta-analysis of couple therapy in adult depression: Implications for research and clinical practice. *Family Process, 59*(2), 361–375. https://doi.org/10.1111/famp.12540

Barton, A. W., Beach, S. R. H., Wells, A. C., Ingels, J. B., Corso, P. S., Sperr, M. C., Anderson, T. N., & Brody, G. H. (2018). The Protecting Strong African American Families Program: A randomized controlled trial with rural African American couples. *Prevention Science, 19*, 904–913. https://doi.org/10.1007/s11121-018-0895-4

Baucom, D. H., & Fischer, M. S. (2023). Couple-based interventions for adult psychopathology. In H. S. Friedman & C. H. Markey (Eds.), *Encyclopedia of mental health* (Vol. 1, pp. 516–525). Elsevier.

Baucom, D. H., Fischer, M. S., Worrell, M., Corrie, S., Belus, J. M., Molyva, E., & Boeding, S. E. (2018). Couple-based intervention for depression: An effectiveness study in the National Health Service in England. *Family Process, 57*(2), 275–292. https://doi.org/10.1111/famp.12332

Baucom, D. H., Fischer, M. S., Corrie, S., Worrell, M., & Boeding, S. E. (2020). *Treating relationship distress and psychopathology in couples: A cognitive-behavioural approach*. Routledge.

Beck, J. S. (2020). *Cognitive behavior therapy: Basics and beyond*. Guilford.
Boeding, S. E., Paprocki, C. M., Baucom, D. H., Abramowitz, J. S., Wheaton, M. G., Fabricant, L. E., & Fischer, M. S. (2013). Let me check that for you: Symptom accommodation in romantic partners of adults with obsessive–compulsive disorder. *Behaviour Research and Therapy, 51*(6), 316–322. https://doi.org/10.1016/j.brat.2013.03.002
Doss, B. D., Knopp, K., Roddy, M. K., Rothman, K., Hatch, S. G., & Rhoades, G. K. (2020). Online programs improve relationship functioning for distressed low-income couples: Results from a nationwide randomized controlled trial. *Journal of Consulting and Clinical Psychology, 88*(4), 283–294. https://doi.org/10.1037/ccp0000479
Epstein, N. B., & Baucom, D. H. (2002). *Enhanced cognitive-behavioral therapy for couples: A contextual approach*. American Psychological Association. https://doi.org/10.1037/10481-000
Fredman, S. J., Vorstenbosch, V., Wagner, A. C., Macdonald, A., & Monson, C. M. (2014). Partner accommodation in posttraumatic stress disorder: Initial testing of the Significant Others' Responses to Trauma Scale (SORTS). *Journal of Anxiety Disorders, 28*(4), 372–381. https://doi.org/10.1016/j.janxdis.2014.04.001
Frost, D. M., & Meyer, I. H. (2009). Internalized homophobia and relationship quality among lesbians, gay men, and bisexuals. *Journal of Counseling Psychology, 56*(1), 97–109. https://doi.org/10.1037/a0012844
Funk, J. L., & Rogge, R. D. (2007). Testing the ruler with item response theory: Increasing precision of measurement for relationship satisfaction with the Couples Satisfaction Index. *Journal of Family Psychology, 21*(4), 572. https://doi.org/10.1037/0893-3200.21.4.572
Gale, M. M., Pieterse, A. L., Lee, D. L., Huynh, K., Powell, S., & Kirkinis, K. (2020). A meta-analysis of the relationship between internalized racial oppression and health-related outcomes. *The Counseling Psychologist, 48*(4), 498–525. https://doi.org/10.1177/0011000020904454
Goodman, W. K., Price, L. H., Rasmussen, S. A., Mazure, C., Fleischmann, R. L., Hill, C. L., Heninger, G. R., & Charney, D. S. (1989). The Yale-Brown Obsessive Compulsive Scale. I. Development, use, and reliability. *Archives of General Psychiatry, 46*(11), 1006–1011. https://doi.org/10.1001/archpsyc.1989.01810110048007
Hays, P. A. (2009). Integrating evidence-based practice, cognitive–behavior therapy, and multicultural therapy: Ten steps for culturally competent practice. *Professional Psychology: Research and Practice, 40*(4), 354–360. https://doi.org/10.1037/a0016250
Heyman, R. E. (2001). Observation of couple conflicts: Clinical assessment applications, stubborn truths, and shaky foundations. *Psychological Assessment, 13*(1), 5–35. https://doi.org/10.1037/1040-3590.13.1.5
Hooley, J. M., & Miklowitz, D. J. (2018). Families and mental disorders. In J. N. Butcher & J. M. Hooley (Eds.), *APA handbook of psychopathology: Psychopathology: Understanding, assessing, and treating adult mental disorders* (pp. 687–703). American Psychological Association. https://doi.org/10.1037/0000064-028
Huey, S. J., Park, A. L., Galán, C. A., & Wang, C. X. (2023). Culturally responsive cognitive behavioral therapy for ethnically diverse populations. *Annual Review of Clinical Psychology, 19*, 51–78. https://doi.org/10.1146/annurev-clinpsy-080921-072750
Kelly, S., Bhagwat, R., Maynigo, P., & Moses, E. (2014). Couple and marital therapy: The complement and expansion provided by multicultural approaches. In F. T. L. Leong, L. Comas-Díaz, G. C. Nagayama Hall, V. C. McLoyd, & J. E. Trimble (Eds.), *APA handbook of multicultural psychology, Vol. 2. Applications and training* (pp. 479–497). American Psychological Association. https://doi.org/10.1037/14187-027
Kraus, M. W., Horberg, E. J., Goetz, J. L., & Keltner, D. (2011). Social class rank, threat vigilance, and hostile reactivity. *Personality and Social Psychology Bulletin, 37*(10), 1376–1388. https://doi.org/10.1177/0146167211410987
Kroenke, K., Spitzer, R. L., & Williams, J. B. (2001). The PHQ-9: Validity of a brief depression severity measure. *Journal of General Internal Medicine, 16*(9), 606–613. https://doi.org/10.1046/j.1525-1497.2001.016009606.x

Kwate, N. O. A., & Meyer, I. H. (2011). On sticks and stones and broken bones: Stereotypes and African American health. *Du Bois Review: Social Science Research on Race, 8*(1), 191–198. https://doi.org/10.1017/S1742058X11000014

Lavner, J. A. (2017). Relationship satisfaction in lesbian couples: Review, methodological critique, and research agenda. *Journal of Lesbian Studies, 21*(1), 7–29. https://doi.org/10.1080/10894160.2016.1142348

Martell, C. R., Dimidjian, S., & Herman-Dunn, R. (2021). *Behavioral activation for depression: A clinician's guide*. Guilford.

Neff, L. A., & Karney, B. R. (2017). Acknowledging the elephant in the room: How stressful environmental contexts shape relationship dynamics. *Current Opinion in Psychology, 13*, 107–110. https://doi.org/10.1016/j.copsyc.2016.05.013

Pentel, K. Z., & Baucom, D. H. (2022). A clinical framework for sexual minority couple therapy. *Couple and Family Psychology: Research and Practice, 11*(2), 177–191. https://doi.org/10.1037/cfp0000187

Pentel, K. Z., Baucom, D. H., Weber, D. M., Wojda, A. K., & Carrino, E. A. (2021). Cognitive-behavioral couple therapy for same-sex female couples: A pilot study. *Family Process, 60*(4), 1083–1097. https://doi.org/10.1111/famp.12696

Renshaw, K. D., Allen, E. S., Fredman, S. J., Giff, S. T., & Kern, C. (2020). Partners' motivations for accommodating posttraumatic stress disorder symptoms in service members: The Reasons for Accommodation of PTSD Scale. *Journal of Anxiety Disorders, 71*, 102199. https://doi.org/10.1016/j.janxdis.2020.102199

Reuman, L., & Abramowitz, J. S. (2018). Predictors of accommodation among families affected by fear-based disorders. *Child Psychiatry & Human Development, 49*, 53–62. https://doi.org/10.1007/s10578-017-0728-x

Stewart, K. E., Sumantry, D., & Malivoire, B. L. (2020). Family and couple integrated cognitive-behavioural therapy for adults with OCD: A meta-analysis. *Journal of Affective Disorders, 277*(1), 159–168. https://doi.org/10.1016/j.jad.2020.07.140

Waldinger, R. (2015). *What makes a good life? Lessons from the longest study on happiness*. Retrieved from https://www.ted.com/talks/robert_waldinger_what_makes_a_good_life_lessons_from_the_longest_study_on_happiness?language=en

Whisman, M. A., Sbarra, D. A., & Beach, S. R. (2021). Intimate relationships and depression: Searching for causation in the sea of association. *Annual Review of Clinical Psychology, 17*, 233–258. https://doi.org/10.1146/annurev-clinpsy-081219-103323

Williams, D. R. (2018). Stress and the mental health of populations of color: Advancing our understanding of race-related stressors. *Journal of Health and Social Behavior, 59*(4), 466–485. https://doi.org/10.1177/0022146518814251

Chapter 4
Intensive, Multi-couple Group Treatment

Steffany J. Fredman, Tabatha H. Blount, Vanessa Jacoby, Candice M. Monson, and Alan L. Peterson

4.1 Introduction

Posttraumatic stress disorder (PTSD; American Psychiatric Association, 2013) is a psychological condition marked by unwanted intrusions of the traumatic event (e.g., distress with reminders and nightmares), avoidance of trauma reminders, negative thoughts and feelings that began or worsened after the event (e.g., exaggerated self or other blame for the event and negative affect), and dysregulated arousal and reactivity that began or worsened after the event (e.g., irritability and hypervigilance). PTSD symptoms are associated with a range of intimate relationship difficulties, including relationship discord, intimate partner aggression, and partner psychological distress (Lambert et al., 2012; Taft et al., 2011). Trauma survivors' interpersonal relationships can facilitate or impede clients' ability to profit from evidence-based trauma-focused individual psychotherapies for PTSD. For example, significant other encouragement for clients to participate in treatment and approach, rather than avoid, their distress is associated with a higher likelihood of clients remaining in treatment (Meis et al., 2019). At the same time, clients whose close relationships are characterized by high levels of negativity and/or low levels of perceived support experience less improvement in PTSD symptoms (Price et al., 2013; Tarrier et al.,

S. J. Fredman (✉)
The Pennsylvania State University, University Park, PA, USA
e-mail: sjf23@psu.edu

T. H. Blount · V. Jacoby · A. L. Peterson
University of Texas Health Science Center at San Antonio, San Antonio, TX, USA
e-mail: blountt@uthscsa.edu; jacobyv@uthscsa.edu; petersona3@uthscsa.edu

C. M. Monson
Department of Psychology, Toronto Metropolitan University, Toronto, ON, Canada
e-mail: candice.monson@torontomu.ca

L. Reuman, J. Thompson-Hollands (eds.), *Enhancing CBT Through Family and Peer Engagement*, CBT: Science Into Practice, https://doi.org/10.1007/978-3-031-74838-7_4

1999) because stressful interpersonal interactions can reinforce the perception of interpersonal threat and negative appraisals of self and others. Significant others' accommodation of PTSD symptoms (e.g., participating in avoidance and safety behaviors and constraining one's own self-expression to avoid conflict regarding PTSD-related symptoms) can also interfere with clients' ability to benefit from treatment by reinforcing avoidance and homework noncompliance (Campbell et al., 2017; Howard et al., 2023). The recent increased interest in providing caregiver support for partners of PTSD clients (Shepherd-Banigan et al., 2018) may be having an unintended negative consequence in increasing partner accommodation.

4.2 Cognitive-Behavioral Conjoint Therapy for PTSD

Cognitive-behavioral conjoint therapy (CBCT) for PTSD (Monson & Fredman, 2012) was developed to address the bidirectional linkages between PTSD symptoms and intimate relationship adjustment and to capitalize on the potential for treatment to "follow the patient home" by optimizing the client's interpersonal environment to support cognitive, behavioral, and affective changes needed to promote recovery from the disorder and healthy relationship functioning. CBCT for PTSD is a 15-session disorder-specific couple therapy with the dual goals of treating PTSD symptoms and enhancing intimate relationship functioning. It includes: (1) psychoeducation about PTSD and relationships and instruction in conflict management skills; (2) behavioral skills to promote communication and affective expression and to reduce avoidance and accommodation of PTSD symptoms; and (3) a dyadic cognitive process to promote healthy meaning making about the trauma and its impact on the client, partner, and the couple's relationship. Couples are taught to conceptualize PTSD as an external entity against which the couple is united, and all skills taught and practiced throughout the treatment are conceptualized as helping the couple work together to "shrink" the salience of PTSD in their relationship.

Couples may be eligible for CBCT for PTSD if at least one member of the couple meets diagnostic criteria for PTSD (or has clinically significant PTSD symptoms) and has an intimate partner willing to participate in treatment. Common comorbidities among clients with PTSD include depression, anxiety, anger, insomnia, substance misuse, and suicidal ideation. In addition, partners often present with their own trauma histories and/or mental health difficulties. Couples in which one or both members endorse current substance misuse and/or suicidal ideation may be eligible for treatment if no immediate intervention is warranted (e.g., detox) and the substance misuse does not interfere with the PTSD focus of the treatment (e.g., by using substances as an avoidance strategy), and if there is not an imminent risk for suicide or homicide. Bipolar and psychotic disorders are not exclusionary if they are well controlled. The typical couple presenting for CBCT for PTSD includes at least one member of the dyad who is relationally distressed and ambivalent about staying in the relationship. Relationally distressed couples may be good candidates for CBCT for PTSD if both members of the couple are committed to working on the relationship and staying together as a couple through treatment. CBCT for PTSD is also appropriate for couples who are not relationally distressed per se but may be engaging in maladaptive PTSD-relevant relationship behaviors, such as couple-level accommodation of the PTSD symptoms (e.g., conjointly avoiding places, situations, people, and feelings). Couples experiencing minor physical intimate partner aggression (e.g., pushing, shoving, slapping, and throwing objects) may be appropriate for CBCT for PTSD if they agree to the elimination of aggression as a treatment goal and neither partner fears the other one. In contrast, couples engaging in severe intimate aggression (e.g., punching with a closed fist, causing injury sufficient to warrant medical attention, and using threats of harm to intimidate and control the other partner) within the prior 6 months are not considered appropriate for conjoint treatment and are typically referred for individual therapy.

The 15-session CBCT for PTSD protocol is typically delivered weekly to individual couples over 4–5 months. However, it can be difficult for couples to complete treatment due to the logistical challenges of needing to have both members of the couple participate during routine clinic hours. Indeed, approximately half of the couples who began CBCT for PTSD at a Veterans Affairs Medical Center PTSD specialty clinic did not complete treatment (Pukay-Martin et al., 2022). Evidence-based, trauma-focused individual psychotherapies for PTSD are normally delivered over the course of 8–12 sessions spanning 2–3 months but are also associated with high rates of dropout (Berke et al., 2019; Goetter et al., 2015). These individual therapies can be delivered in an intensive format over 1–3 weeks, which helps to reduce dropout (Ehlers et al., 2014; Foa et al., 2018; Peterson et al., 2023; Zalta et al., 2018). It is not feasible for most couples to participate in daily massed couple therapy for PTSD treatment delivered over 2–3 weeks. However, program evaluation data from a clinical program conducted outside of a research context (Monk et al., 2016, 2017) have shown that a retreat-style program for veterans with PTSD and their significant others delivered over 4 or 7 days was associated with improvements in veterans' self-reported PTSD symptoms, partners' well-being, and relationship adjustment. This program included trauma-relevant psychoeducation and group and conjoint therapeutic sessions, along with complementary activities (e.g., equine and art therapy) and therapeutic recreation (e.g., yoga and massage).

4.3 Treatment Overview

4.3.1 Abbreviated, Intensive, Multi-couple Group CBCT for PTSD

To enhance CBCT for PTSD's treatment efficiency and retention, we developed an abbreviated, intensive, multi-couple group version of CBCT (AIM-CBCT) for PTSD (Fredman et al., 2020) in which CBCT for PTSD content is delivered in a compressed, weekend format to multiple couples at the same time. There are also two individual meetings with couples conducted, one in the two weeks prior to the retreat and one in the two weeks after the retreat.

The weekend retreat component of AIM-CBCT for PTSD consists of approximately 12 hours of CBCT for PTSD content delivered over 2 consecutive days, with a primary focus on content from the first seven sessions of CBCT for PTSD. This includes psychoeducation about PTSD and relationship functioning, the rationale for treatment, and strategies to promote physical and emotional safety in the relationship (e.g., recognizing early warning signs of anger and negotiated time out). Couples are then introduced to behaviorally oriented skills (e.g., paraphrasing) and activities that are designed to decrease PTSD-related experiential and behavioral avoidance, safety behaviors, and partner accommodation of symptoms and to increase emotional intimacy and couple engagement. For example, couples are taught paraphrasing ("speaker listener technique") to facilitate sharing PTSD-related thoughts and feelings and to identify dyadic approach exercises. Couples are also taught a dyadic cognitive strategy (the "Big Picture" technique) designed to increase cognitive flexibility and challenge maladaptive thoughts held by either member of the couple that can maintain PTSD and/or relationship difficulties (e.g., "Crowds are always dangerous," "I must control my environment at all times," and "It's not safe to let others know what I'm feeling"). AIM-CBCT for PTSD content is delivered in seven modules or lessons lasting approximately 60–90 min each that correspond to the content of Sessions 1–7 from the 15-session parent protocol and an eighth module that corresponds to parent protocol Session 15. The eighth module is designed to help couples consolidate what they have learned over the weekend and to plan for continued skill use after they return home. Couples are also encouraged to practice their skills with other important people in their lives, such as their children, other family members, and friends. In contrast to the 15-session version of CBCT for PTSD, AIM-CBCT for PTSD does not formally instruct couples to engage in historical reappraisals of the client's trauma(s). Instead, the value of trauma-related disclosure to a supportive other is noted throughout the weekend. Couples are encouraged to use specific skills to share their thoughts and feelings about the patients' trauma(s) and offered guidance on how partners can respond supportively to the disclosure to facilitate the development of a cogent trauma narrative.

Several factors should be considered for AIM-CBCT for PTSD venues. First, the retreat space should be able to accommodate multi-couple groups. For example, the therapy room should be large enough to accommodate 4–8 couples and 2 therapists, with space and accessibility to use a projector for slide show didactic content. The space should also include semi-private areas where couples can go for "couple time" (couple breakout sessions) for skills practice. Second, it is helpful for the retreat to be in a location that is different from the couple's typical environment. This provides a "getaway" experience, and the effort taken to travel to the location promotes motivation to make the most of the experience. Ideal settings for the retreat are hotels with group conference spaces close to restaurants, shopping, and recreational activities (for ease of practicing approach assignments).

Retreats are typically co-led by two group therapists. AIM-CBCT for PTSD therapists complete an initial eight-hour training consisting of the conceptual and practical components of the treatment. They then observe at least one AIM-CBCT for PTSD retreat facilitated by an experienced provider prior to conducting the therapy themselves. The therapist then co-conducts at least one retreat with an experienced provider and receives supervision or consultation (in the case of licensed providers) from that co-therapist. Although not required, AIM-CBCT for PTSD therapists benefit from having prior experience conducting trauma-focused evidence-based individual psychotherapy for PTSD.

AIM-CBCT for PTSD content is taught to the multi-couple group using a workshop format using slides adapted from a standardized two-day training for clinicians learning CBCT for PTSD. The format for each AIM-CBCT for PTSD module is as follows: (a) psychoeducation on the effects of PTSD on some aspect of intimate relationships (e.g., the contribution of PTSD to conflict management difficulties); (b) introduction of a skill to address PTSD in a relational context (e.g., negotiated time out); (c) co-therapist role-play of that skill; (d) a break-out session in which individual couples practice the skill(s) and therapists provide coaching, (e) group debrief of the break-out session; and (f) a review of that module's main points. At the end of Day 1 and at the end of the retreat, therapists summarize key concepts to help couples consolidate learning and encourage skill use outside of the formal retreat setting. Commonalities in presenting problems across couples are highlighted throughout the weekend to help normalize participants' experiences, and interactions with other group members serve as opportunities to facilitate balanced thinking about unfamiliar others. Group-level debriefing of skill use after the break-out sessions is also used to promote normalization of challenges, vicarious learning, and social support among the couples.

Consistent with the 15-session CBCT for PTSD protocol, in vivo approach assignments are included throughout the retreat, while also capitalizing on the multi-couple group format. For example, to target clients' hypervigilance and increase their comfort sitting near windows and with others sitting behind them, couples are asked to switch seats multiple times throughout the retreat. On the Saturday evening of the retreat, couples also participate in a dyadic out-of-workshop approach exercise that doubles as a date (e.g., eating dinner at a crowded restaurant and having the client sit with their back to the door to prevent scanning for threats).

The pre-retreat and post-retreat meetings are conducted with individual couples and typically last 1–1.5 hours. At the pre-retreat meeting, therapists conduct an interview designed to facilitate rapport and orient couples to the upcoming weekend retreat. After confirming the client's diagnosis of PTSD with the couple, therapists briefly introduce CBCT for PTSD and the rationale for delivering it in the abbreviated, intensive, multi-couple group format. The therapist then discusses with the couple their relationship history and strengths, relationship domains impacted by PTSD (e.g., conflict management and communication, intimacy) and desired improvements in these domains, and their reasons for wanting to participate in AIM-CBCT for PTSD. The session concludes with therapists helping the couple to identify one or two PTSD-related relationship goals. The therapist also asks the couple to provide written responses to questions regarding the impact of PTSD on their relationship as well as what they think their relationship will be like if the salience of PTSD in their relationship decreases prior to the start of the weekend. At the post-retreat meeting, the therapist assesses each dyad member's perception of the client's current PTSD symptoms, asks about the implementation of specific skills taught at the retreat since the couple has returned home, and discusses plans for continued skill use to promote further gains with respect to PTSD symptoms and the couple's relationship.

4.4 Research Evidence

A randomized controlled trial and several small uncontrolled trials have demonstrated that the 15-session CBCT for PTSD protocol is associated with large and significant reductions in client PTSD and comorbid symptoms that are on par with those from evidence-based, trauma-focused individual psychotherapy (see Liebman et al., 2020, for a review). CBCT for PTSD is also associated with improvements in partners' mental health and couple relationship adjustment (Liebman et al., 2020). Moderation analyses indicate that clients' improvements in PTSD symptoms do not depend on either member of the couple's pretreatment relationship satisfaction (Shnaider et al., 2015). That is, clients benefit with respect to their PTSD symptoms across a range of client and partner relationship satisfaction. However, clients with higher perceived social support from their partners before starting treatment appear to exhibit greater reductions in PTSD symptoms over the course of treatment (Shnaider et al., 2017).

An uncontrolled pilot study of AIM-CBCT for PTSD delivered to 24 couples that included a post-9/11 service member or veteran with PTSD and their romantic partners (Fredman et al., 2020, 2021; Macdonald et al., 2022) provided initial support for its safety and feasibility. In that study, all couples completed treatment (0% treatment dropout). By 3 months after treatment, there were significant reductions in clients' PTSD symptoms according to clinician, client, and partner ratings, relative to baseline. There were also significant improvements in clients' comorbid symptoms and in PTSD-related psychosocial impairment, partners' mental health, and couples' relationship functioning. In general, clients' improvements in PTSD and comorbid symptoms did not depend on pretreatment relationship characteristics; in contrast, partners who were more accommodating and/or less relationally satisfied experienced greater reductions in mental health symptoms and bigger improvements in relationship satisfaction by three-month follow-up (Fredman et al., 2024).

There have since been other published studies of adaptations of CBCT for PTSD that involved either an abbreviated format or massed dosing. These include a randomized controlled trial in which veteran couples receive the first seven sessions of CBCT for PTSD integrated with mindfulness in a multi-couple group weekend retreat, followed by individual couple delivery of the remaining eight sessions of CBCT for PTSD plus mindfulness, or a modified version of CBCT that included communication skills training from Phases 1 and 2 of CBCT without PTSD-specific content followed by two additional monthly multi-couple group sessions (Davis et al., 2021). Another randomized controlled trial compared a brief, eight-session version of CBCT for PTSD consisting of the first two phases of CBCT for PTSD, delivered in-person or at home via clinical video teleconferencing, to eight-sessions of couple-based PTSD psychoeducation in veteran couples (Morland et al., 2022). In the Morland et al. (2022) study, treatment was delivered weekly to individual couples for each of the three conditions. The magnitude of change for reductions in clinician-rated PTSD symptoms for the CBCT for PTSD conditions in the Davis et al. (2021) and Morland et al. (2022) studies was similar to that observed for AIM-CBCT for PTSD. However, the treatment dropout rates were higher (26% in Davis et al., 2021, and 26–30% in Morland et al., 2022 compared to 0% in Fredman et al., 2020).

We are currently conducting a randomized controlled trial funded by the U.S. Department of Defense (W81XWH-22-1-0985) to test the efficacy of AIM-CBCT for PTSD relative to the Prevention and Relationship Education (PREP; Markman et al., 2010), a general couple-based relationship education program not focal to PTSD. PREP has been disseminated in the military for more than 20 years and has been tested in a multi-couple group retreat format using a large, nonclinical sample of active-duty military couples (see Allen et al., 2015, for a review). Future research on AIM-CBCT for PTSD includes examining outcomes for subgroups of participants (e.g., couples identifying as African American/Black) and examining the effect of AIM-CBCT for PTSD on parenting.

4.5 Clinical Considerations for Diverse Identities

To date, all couples treated with AIM-CBCT for PTSD have included at least one member of the dyad who was an active duty service member or veteran with PTSD. However, there has been considerable diversity across couples with respect to race, ethnicity, gender of the identified client, gender composition of the couple (e.g., mixed gender and same sex), sexual orientation, racial composition of the couple (e.g., same race and inter-racial), socio-economic status, age, comorbid mental and physical health diagnoses, military status (e.g., active duty versus veteran), and nature of the identified client's index trauma (e.g., combat, sexual trauma, and childhood physical or sexual abuse). Couples have also varied with respect to whether only one member of the couple was a service member or veteran or whether they were dual military, whether the partner also had PTSD, and whether they had children and, if so, whether the children were under 18 or adults. That is, although the experience of having served in the military may have been universal among couples who have participated in CBCT for PTSD, the lived experience of each individual and couple varied considerably across couples as these characteristics and identities intersected in unique ways for each member of the couple and the dyad. Thus, as part of case conceptualization for each couple, we have found it helpful to apply an intersectional frame (Crenshaw, 1989) to situate each individual and dyad within a broader socio-cultural and ecological context (Monson et al., 2010) to consider how cognitive, behavioral, and affective factors within and between members of the couple may manifest in the context of individuals' or couples' unique lived experiences and to target these processes accordingly through treatment.

For the AIM-CBCT for the PTSD protocol, culturally informed case conceptualization typically begins with information gleaned during the pre-retreat meeting, when therapists meet with individual couples to learn more about them prior to the group-based portion of the treatment delivered during the retreat. When reviewing the couple's relationship history, the therapists are attuned to ecological stressors that the couple may have experienced by virtue of any minoritized identities in the context of their military service or other lived experiences and how this has shaped their learning history and cognitions. For example, we have worked with same-sex couples who felt rejected by their families of origin and/or by fellow service members due to their sexual orientations and held cognitions about not being able to trust their partners or other people in general. For many of those couples, the experience of addressing PTSD and interpersonally relevant cognitions about safety and trust while participating in a group-based setting in which they felt safe and accepted by the larger group was very therapeutic. (See Blount et al., 2017, and Fedynich et al., 2021, for case studies of CBCT for PTSD applied to couples in which one or both members identified as lesbian, gay, bisexual, or transgender.)

Being attuned to the cultural context of couples' strengths and desired areas for improvement can also assist with case conceptualization and targeting of the treatment to couples' particular needs. For example, we have worked with couples in which intersecting gender, military, and racial/ethnic cultural norms to minimize and invalidate the experience and expression of emotions have maintained both PTSD symptoms and intimate relationship difficulties. Beliefs that emotions are an indication of weakness and/or make one vulnerable to interpersonal threat can both reinforce emotions serving as a trauma cue and interfere with couples' abilities to communicate effectively and feel close (see Fredman et al., 2023 for a fuller discussion on this point). We have found that highlighting the individual's desire to be a loving and engaged spouse and parent, which is often congruent with their cultural and spiritual values, can motivate them to try to be more flexible in how they think about and behave in response to their own and their family members' emotions. The increased closeness resulting from this cognitive and behavioral flexibility can then become interpersonally reinforcing across multiple levels of the family system (the couple subsystem, the co-parent subsystem, the parent–child subsystem, and the extended family). Relatedly, we have found it useful to assess who else features prominently in the couple's social environment, given the salience of children, extended family, and fictive kin for individuals and couples whose cultural backgrounds promote the centrality of the family, family cohesion, and collectivistic approaches to coping. Aligning treatment goals to reduce PTSD-related irritability, numbing, and withdrawal with a desire to be more harmonious as a couple and a family more broadly may be particularly resonant and culturally congruent for such individuals and couples (see case vignette as an example).

4.5.1 Other Considerations

Retreat-style interventions require extra considerations around participant cost. Couples of low er socioeconomic status may struggle to pay the expenses related to driving to the retreat location, staying in a hotel, acquiring child and/or pet care, or taking time off of work if needed. We recommend partnering with local businesses, foundations, and grant funders to assist in accommodating the needs of families who might require financial support for AIM-CBCT for PTSD services. For example, our group partnered with a local hotel to negotiate a lower room rate and acquired foundation grant funds to support participant room payment as well as travel and approach assignment expenses with a $75 gift card. If such additional resources are not available to support couples in need, it is still possible to conduct AIM-CBCT for PTSD in a compressed, multi-couple group format over two days but without delivering it in a retreat setting.

The skills learned in AIM-CBCT for PTSD have been shown to improve couple relationship satisfaction. However, these skills can be generalized and used effectively for any close relationships, including relationships with children, other close family members, and friendships. For example, when working with diverse families who may live in multi-generational homes or interact frequently with members of the extended family, other family relationships may be of similar importance to the couple's relationship. In these cases, an AIM-CBCT for PTSD therapist would emphasize and discuss with the couple how to use these skills specifically in the context of these other important relationships. The therapist would also discuss how these skills might be adapted to be appropriate for children. For example, when sharing thoughts and feelings about PTSD with one's child, it would be important not to over-share or put undue responsibility on the child. However, it may be helpful for the parent–child relationship to discuss PTSD symptoms in a developmentally appropriate way, emphasizing that the reactions (e.g., avoidance of family activities and irritability) are not the child's fault. A free resource packet to assist parents in having conversations with children about PTSD is available from the VA's Mental Illness Research Education and Clinical Center (Sherman et al., 2015). One example of children's books that explain parental PTSD in military families are *Why is Dad so mad?* and *Why is Mom so mad?* (Kastle, 2015a, b). Parents may be encouraged to review and discuss these resources with each other before sharing them with their children as a way to approach and share previously avoided thoughts and feelings.

4.6 Case Vignette

The following is a case vignette based on a couple who participated in AIM-CBCT for PTSD as part of a clinical program for veterans and families. The couple provided consent for the case vignette. To protect their privacy, pseudonyms are used, and minor details regarding their backgrounds have been altered.

Marcus, a Mexican American cisgendered male in his thirties, served 11 years in the United States Marines. He deployed three times in support of post-9/11 operations before separating from the military. He presented with an extensive trauma history; however, he reported that he was most bothered by combat experiences that occurred when he was deployed to Southwest Asia in 2009. His mental health history included PTSD, depression, anxiety, and suicidality. Approximately four months before participating in the retreat, he had an interrupted suicide attempt, which he attributed to his mental health symptoms. He had recently completed a four-week, intensive outpatient program that offered Cognitive Processing Therapy (CPT; Resick et al., 2017) for PTSD from the local US Veterans Administration Medical Center and was participating in a veteran support group. Although he described CPT as helpful in decreasing his shame and guilt related to his traumas, he was still experiencing significant distress and psychosocial impairment secondary to PTSD.

Jackie, Marcus' wife, was a Mexican American cisgendered female in her thirties with no prior military service. She endorsed a trauma history that included childhood sexual abuse. Her mental health history was otherwise unremarkable. She denied past mental health diagnoses, suicidality, or mental health treatment. Marcus and Jackie started dating in high school. At the time of the intake, they had been married for almost 13 years. They had 3 children ranging in age from 5 to 11 years and were expecting their fourth child. During their relationship, they experienced several military-related separations and a miscarriage. Two years prior to presenting for treatment, they participated in general couple therapy for six months, which helped them improve their communication skills.

4.6.1 Intake Assessment

Marcus and Jackie completed the intake assessments individually. They provided informed consent and expressed an understanding of the limits of confidentiality. Both completed the Life Events Checklist for DSM-5 (LEC-5; Weathers et al., 2013a), PTSD Checklist for DSM-5 (PCL-5; Weathers et al., 2013b), Patient Health Questionnaire-9 (PHQ-9; Kroenke et al., 2001), General Anxiety Disorder-7 (GAD-7; Spitzer et al., 2006), and Couple Satisfaction Index-32 (CSI-32; Funk & Rogge, 2007). Jackie also completed a collateral version of the PCL-5 (PCL-5-C; Ennis et al., 2021), which assessed her perceptions of Marcus' PTSD symptoms.

Marcus' score of 59 on the PCL-5 was consistent with clinically significant PTSD symptoms (scores of 31–33 or higher indicate probable PTSD; Bovin et al., 2016). He also endorsed clinically significant depressive and anxiety symptoms (PHQ-9 = 21; GAD-7 = 16). He endorsed recent passive suicidal ideation but denied imminent plans, preparation, or intent. He collaborated with one of the group therapists to develop a crisis response plan (Bryan et al., 2024), which identified warning signs, triggers, individual coping strategies, social support, professional resources, and reasons for living. Jackie did not endorse any clinically elevated symptoms on the self-report measures regarding her own mental health. Jackie's ratings of

Marcus' PTSD symptoms (53 on the PCL-C) fell in the clinical range. Notably, there was a strong concurrence between Marcus' PCL-5 and Jackie's PCL-5-C scores. Finally, Marcus' score of 137 and Jackie's score of 125 placed each of them in the relationally satisfied range on the CSI-32 (CSI scores $\geq$ 104.5; Funk & Rogge, 2007).

4.6.2 Pre-retreat Meeting

Approximately 10 days before the retreat, the couple attended a 60-min pre-retreat meeting with their assigned AIM-CBCT for PTSD therapist over a HIPAA-Compliant video call. The purpose of the pre-retreatment meeting was threefold: (1) to provide the couple with information about the retreat (i.e., the empirical basis for the treatment; targets of the treatment; and logistics of the weekend); (2) to learn more about the couple (i.e., share intake assessment results; gather information about their relationship history; and begin establishing mutually agreed upon treatment goals); and (3) to prepare for the weekend (i.e., introduce group expectations; problem solve any barriers to attending the weekend; and assign pre-retreat work). The pre-retreat work included instruction to continue identifying treatment goals, reading a "PTSD and Relationships" psycho-educational handout, and writing responses to questions regarding how PTSD and trauma have impacted their relationship as well as what they imagine their relationship will look like as the PTSD takes up less space in their relationship.

The couple was open and respectful to each other, had a shared understanding of their relationship history, and were able to easily agree upon treatment goals regarding reducing Marcus' PTSD symptoms and enhancing the couple's relationship. They stated that they had decided to participate in the retreat because Marcus had benefited from individual trauma-focused treatment but was still symptomatic and had felt he was "on his own" after graduating from the intensive outpatient program. The couple had experienced significant improvement in their relationship over the past year and were looking for "more tools in their toolbox" to promote Marcus' recovery from PTSD and maintain a healthy pattern of interacting as a couple.

As the therapist talked with the couple, she listened to how avoidance, safety behaviors, and emotional numbing were impacting the couple's functioning and relationship satisfaction. The couple reported that Marcus had difficulty sleeping in the same bed as Jackie at night. When he tried, his anxiety would spike, causing him to depart to the guest room. This avoidance behavior caused multiple problems for their relationship and family. For example, their older children seemed confused and worried by this pattern, asking questions about potential marital problems. Both Marcus and Jackie shared the desire to sleep together and established a post-retreat goal of spending at least three nights a week in the same bed.

On days when Marcus felt particularly symptomatic from PTSD, he would withdraw from the family. Although Jackie was supportive of Marcus taking individual time away from the family for his mental health needs, she was distressed by his sudden withdrawal without explanation. Therefore, the couple had the additional goal of improving communication (i.e., sharing more thoughts and feelings to address emotional numbing and avoidance, particularly during times when Marcus felt triggered). Jackie also discussed their difficulties with Marcus avoiding extended family members and family gatherings. She stated that, as a Mexican American, having a close relationship with her extended family was very important to her. Although she understood that Marcus avoided these gatherings due to his PTSD, she was saddened and frustrated that they could not spend more meaningful time with their extended family, as this felt culturally incongruent with her values regarding *familismo*. Jackie and Marcus set a goal of attending more family gatherings.

4.6.3 Retreat Format

The retreat was offered over a weekend with both days starting at 8:00 am and ending by 5:00 pm. The retreat was facilitated by one licensed psychologist, two second-year postdoctoral fellows, and one first-year postdoctoral fellow. A psychology intern attended as an observer but did not participate. Each of the lessons followed a similar format: (1) skill introduction (group didactic); (2) breakout session to practice skills (individual couples with their therapist); (3) processing of break out session (group activity); and (4) review of main ideas from the lesson (group activity). Additionally, on Saturday night, couples were asked to have a date night and apply their new skills.

4.6.4 Group Composition

Marcus and Jackie attended the retreat with seven other couples. Six of the couples (including Marcus and Jackie) consisted of a male veteran and a female civilian. The seventh was a dual-veteran, mixed-gender couple, and the eighth was a dual-military, same-sex couple. The couples varied in age, racial and ethnic identity, marital status (married versus cohabiting), relationship length, family composition (children, no children), and military experience.

4.6.5 Weekend Retreat

4.6.5.1 Lesson 1: PTSD and Relationships

Marcus and Jackie arrived on time and with their pre-retreat assignment completed. Following group introductions, a conjoint framework for PTSD was presented that highlighted the bidirectional interactions between PTSD and relationship functioning. Couples were encouraged to consider PTSD as an external entity "taking up space" in their relationship versus an individual problem. Couples learned about the cycle of PTSD symptoms and the cognitive-behavioral mechanisms that maintain this cycle within relationships (e.g., avoidance and emotional numbing). Couples, including Marcus and Jackie, shared examples of how they experienced these symptoms in their relationships. The group format allowed Marcus and Jackie to hear other couples' responses and relate to their own experiences. This normalized their trauma reactions and gave them an opportunity to respond empathically to other couples. Finally, the targets for this treatment were outlined. During the breakout session, all couples were asked to catch something nice the partner had done, share their responses to the Trauma Impact Questionnaire, and reaffirm their goals for the retreat.

Jackie expressed appreciation that Marcus had recently planned a family gathering with her extended family (something that he typically avoided), cleaned up after the dogs, and reminded her that it was okay for her to rest. Marcus expressed appreciation for her support and encouragement to focus on his mental health needs. While reviewing their answers to the Trauma Impact Questionnaire, Jackie reported that the presence of PTSD in their relationship made her feel lonely. She stated that she felt she had to accommodate Marcus' PTSD symptoms by "walking on eggshells," which left her feeling unable to communicate her feelings. She reported a previously held belief that everyone leaves at some point and stated that PTSD sometimes causes her to worry that Marcus will abandon the family or forget her. She acknowledged that she also accommodated PTSD by keeping her guard up to protect herself, their children, and sometimes even Marcus. Marcus shared that PTSD caused him to feel significant shame and guilt and made him believe that he was failing the family. In response to these thoughts and feelings, he would withdraw from the family, which subsequently increased his sense of failure and shame. During this exercise, the couple used the language introduced in Lesson 1, which externalizes and puts the blame for their difficulties onto PTSD, rather than each other (e.g., "The PTSD is making you feel shame and guilt"). They both agreed that they would be happier and less stressed when PTSD took up less space in their relationship.

4.6.5.2 Lesson 2: Shrinking PTSD by Increasing Safety

The connections between PTSD and anger were discussed, and the impact of harmful anger expression (e.g., hostility) on relationships was examined. Instructions for individual and couple-level anger management skills were provided to promote physical and emotional safety in couples' relationships. Individuals shared their earliest warning signs of anger with their partner and what they noticed about their partner's earliest warning signs. For example, Marcus shared that his body temperature increased, his face flushed, he clenched his teeth, and he started slamming doors when he was angry. In contrast, they noticed that Jackie was more likely to make sarcastic comments. During the breakout session, the couple practiced calling a time-out. They had no difficulties identifying a nonverbal time-out signal and agreed to a 30-min time-out period in which they would physically separate before reengaging.

4.6.5.3 Lesson 3: Shrinking PTSD by Active Listening and Approaching

The third lesson focused on the role of avoidance in exacerbating PTSD and relationship issues and how active listening and effective communication can address behavioral and experiential avoidance. During the group didactic, couples were taught to use paraphrasing to communicate better and learned how hypervigilance and avoidance can also take the form of safety behaviors and accommodation of their partner's avoidance behaviors. The group discussed their own safety behaviors, such as keeping one's head on a "swivel," scanning others' hands for weapons, always facing the entrance/exits, and arranging the furniture to allow for "door watching." Group discussion of accommodation included examples of "walking on eggshells" to avoid upsetting their partner, always allowing their partner to drive for their partner to feel in control, allowing their partner to choose where and when all outings occurred, and taking over childcare duties to reduce partner frustration.

During the breakout session, Marcus and Jackie practiced paraphrasing as they talked through how PTSD caused them to avoid family gatherings, Jackie's extended family, Marcus' father, watching certain movies, going to movie theaters, talking to their children about PTSD, and vulnerable feelings. Jackie noticed that she had been accommodating the PTSD by serving as an intermediary between Marcus and their children. During this conversation, she advocated for better direct communication between him and the children. In particular, she recommended that they have developmentally appropriate conversations with the children about PTSD.

Following the breakout session, the group was taught how to maximize behavioral approach activities to facilitate posttraumatic learning and promote recovery. These approach activities should be objectively safe activities that the couple avoids because they feel more dangerous than they did before the trauma (e.g., driving on the highway, sitting in a busy restaurant) or they are emotionally painful trauma reminders (e.g., watching certain movies, connecting with friends associated with the military). Engaging in approach assignments provides the couple the opportunity to disconfirm unhelpful and unrealistic beliefs that have developed since the trauma, such as "Crowds are dangerous" or "My partner can't handle these situations." Doing these activities repeatedly helps trauma survivors relearn a sense of safety, and the couple's distress will reduce over time as they learn they are objectively safe and competent at navigating these situations. Finally, activities that allow for the opportunity to experience positive emotions (e.g., watching their child win a basketball game or trying new foods together) promote couple closeness and satisfaction.

Each couple identified a date night activity for that evening. Since it was their thirteenth wedding anniversary, Marcus and Jackie decided to go to a nearby Brazilian steakhouse. They planned to minimize safety and accommodative behaviors while sharing more thoughts and feelings.

4.6.5.4 Lesson 4: Shrinking PTSD by Sharing Feelings

In the fourth lesson, psychoeducation about sharing feelings and emotional expression within the context of PTSD was provided. The group learned how sharing their feelings with their partner "pushes back" on PTSD by reducing emotional avoidance and numbing and increasing intimacy. The therapists also explained that couples could use their skills for sharing feelings to talk about the feelings that the identified clients have about their traumatic experience(s), as this facilitates recovery from PTSD by reducing avoidance of trauma memories, promoting adaptive disclosure, and helping couples to feel more emotionally connected. During the breakout session, the couples shared their PTSD-related feelings while paraphrasing each other's responses. Marcus shared that PTSD caused him to feel angry, annoyed, irritated, and depressed all the time. He further elaborated that what he experienced in combat left him feeling guilty and ashamed. Jackie shared that she felt down, numb, cautious, and anxious. They agreed that they would feel delighted, ecstatic, relieved, and peaceful after shrinking the presence of PTSD in their relationship.

Before the group broke out to practice the Sharing Feelings skill, they were asked to silently note to themselves how close and connected they felt to their partner on a scale of 1–10. When the group returned for group-wide processing after the breakout, everyone was again asked to silently note how close they felt to their partner using the same scale. As was true for most of the group, Marcus and Jackie noticed that they felt more connected with each other than before the breakout session, even though they were talking about vulnerable emotions. The lead therapist highlighted this important point for the group, emphasizing that "sharing emotions is the glue that holds relationships together," and that, except for hostility, sharing an emotion (whether negative or positively valenced) with a partner tends to promote emotional closeness.

4.6.5.5 End of Day 1

At the end of Day 1, the couples reviewed the main ideas from the first four lessons. Everyone shared the main idea that they had taken away from Day 1, and the couples reaffirmed their plans for their date night. Marcus and Jackie left the first day of the retreat optimistic about the evening and their ability to shrink PTSD.

4.6.5.6 Return on Day 2

The next morning, prior to starting Lesson 5, the couples reported on their date night and reviewed the main ideas from Day 1. Marcus and Jackie appeared distressed and were the last to share how their evening went with the group. They reported that the dinner at the Brazilian steakhouse went well. They engaged in meaningful conversation, and Marcus reduced safety behaviors by sitting with his back to the door. However, when they returned to the hotel, Marcus began watching *Knocked Up* on television. The pregnancy-themed movie triggered Jackie's memories of her miscarriage and her anxieties about their current pregnancy. She reported that she shut down emotionally, which contributed to Marcus withdrawing physically and emotionally. They were still distressed the next morning, and there was distance between them when they returned for Day 2. Jackie was tearful while they shared. The therapists praised Marcus and Jackie for their willingness to be vulnerable and share their feelings of disappointment with the group. Further, the therapists suggested that it appeared they were using some of their skills, even though the end of the evening was difficult and stressful. For example, the fact that Jackie was able to describe her thoughts and feelings in response to the movie, as well as how she was feeling that morning, were examples of using skills to identify and share her feelings. Lastly, one of the therapists reflected on the amount of pressure they felt to have a "perfect anniversary night" and encouraged them to consider a "do-over" to promote cognitive and behavioral flexibility.

4.6.5.7 Lesson 5: Shrinking PTSD by Sharing Thoughts

The fifth lesson provided psychoeducation about the association between thoughts and feelings within the context of PTSD. During the breakout session, the couple was asked to share which thoughts and related feelings they experienced because of PTSD in their relationship. They were instructed to use paraphrasing to facilitate a productive conversation. The breakout session also allowed the couple and the therapist to process the date night experience more privately. Tearfully, Jackie expressed the belief that she had not only ruined the night but had also ruined their chance for recovery from PTSD. She also shared the thoughts: "I ruined everything," "My husband is not attracted to me," "My husband is going to leave me," and "I am failing my husband." In turn, Marcus shared "My wife does not trust me," "My efforts are worthless," and "I am a failure."

4.6.5.8 Lesson 6: Shrinking PTSD by Considering Alternative Thoughts

During the sixth lesson, the group was introduced to the idea of "tunnel vision" or rigid, unhelpful thoughts that contribute to PTSD, relationship difficulties, and distress in the long term. To counter tunnel vision thinking, the group was taught how to use "Big Picture" sheets to facilitate dyadic cognitive restructuring. Together, the group practiced the process of two common PTSD-related thoughts. During the breakout session, the couples were asked to work on challenging at least two tunnel vision thoughts using the Big Picture sheets, one thought for each member of the couple (see Tables 4.1 and 4.2). Jackie and Marcus prioritized Jackie's thought "I am failing my husband in the way I support him" since it was interfering with her ability to rebound from the previous night and fully re-engage in the retreat. Together, they were able to generate alternative thoughts that they deemed more

Table 4.1 Marcus's big picture worksheet

Tunnel Vision Thought: *I am failing all aspects of my life*
Alternative Thoughts:
Nobody is perfect
I am allowed to have bad days
My job does not define me
Most people hate working in call centers
I have strong relationships with my children
I am providing emotional support for my family
Selected Thought(s) to Practice:
I am providing emotional support for my family
New Feelings and Behaviors with Alternative Thoughts:
"Changes everything"
Feels less shame, guilt, and sadness
Keep Practicing Alternative Thoughts:
Remind one another

realistic and helpful (see Table 4.2). Jackie selected the thoughts "I don't have to be 100%, 100% of the time" and "My support has helped my husband stay alive" to practice moving forward. They agreed to remind each other of their new thoughts.

Marcus decided to work with Jackie on a tunnel vision thought related to both his military experiences and his current career. He shared with Jackie that his deployment experiences caused him to view himself as a failure and feel chronically ashamed. He further explained that his current employment situation exacerbated his shame, increased his depression, caused him to withdraw from family activities, and strengthened his belief that he was failing his family. They agreed to work on his thought "I am failing in all aspects of my life." Together, they were able to generate several alternatives and selected the thought "I AM providing emotional support for my family" (see Table 4.1).

4.6.5.9 Lesson 7: Shrinking PTSD by Problem-Solving/Decision-Making

The seventh lesson introduced a dyadic problem-solving process, which the couples used to continue strategizing ways to reduce PTSD-related behavioral and experiential avoidance and to increase their emotional intimacy. Marcus and Jackie agreed to stick to the time-out procedure while discussing sensitive topics for the first week. They agreed that if that were successful, they would share more feelings while taking evening walks three times a week during the second week.

The couple also agreed to use their local family support system more so that they could have more couple time together. This was especially important for Jackie. The PTSD-related withdrawal from Jackie's extended family had felt culturally incongruent and values inconsistent for her. Additionally, it led to confusion and relational strain with the extended family. By using this problem-solving skill, along

Table 4.2 Jackie's big picture worksheet

Tunnel Vision Thought: *I am failing my husband in the ways I support him*
Alternative Thoughts:
My husband does not think I am failing in how I support him
PTSD is failing our relationship
I don't have to be 100%, 100% of the time
The PTSD in our relationship comes from trauma I did not cause
It is not my job to fix my husband
The supportive things that I have done have led to improvements
My support has helped my husband stay alive
Selected Thoughts to Practice:
I don't have to be 100%, 100% of the time
My support has helped my husband stay alive
New Feelings and Behaviors with Alternative Thoughts:
"Changes everything"
Feels less shame, guilt, and sadness
Keep Practicing Alternative Thoughts:
Remind one another

with sharing their thoughts and feelings, they were able to plan for both to engage more with the family generally and to use them as a resource. In line with using this resource, they also agreed to re-celebrate their anniversary within the next two weeks.

4.6.5.10 Lesson 8: Review of Skills and Planning for the Future

During the final lesson, information and skills acquired over the past two days were reviewed. The couples discussed ways that they planned to incorporate these skills into their lives. Finally, couples processed their experiences of participating in AIM-CBCT for PTSD and shared their main takeaways from the treatment. These included: "PTSD exists within the relationship. It's not just a 'me' or 'you' problem," "It's important to share feelings to push back against PTSD, especially the bad feelings," and "Paraphrasing is a great skill to slow conversations down and actually hear each other."

4.6.6 Group Process During the Retreat

Throughout the retreat, Marcus and Jackie engaged in meaningful and supportive interactions with the other seven couples. Overall, group cohesion was high, and the couples exchanged phone numbers with one another at the end of the retreat.

4.6.7 End of Retreat Feedback

At the end of the retreat, Marcus and Jackie completed the Client Satisfaction Questionnaire—8 Item (CSQ-8; Attkisson & Greenfield, 2004; possible score range = 8 to 32, with higher scores indicating greater satisfaction with treatment), along with a qualitative exit survey. Marcus indicated high satisfaction with the treatment (CSQ-8 Total Score = 32). In his exit interview, he wrote "I learned a lot of useful tools to help deal with my PTSD and how it has impacted my relationships. I took for granted how much my PTSD has affected my family, and I am ready to fight back. [This program] helped me to better express my emotions, how to listen better, and express myself better. I learned skills I want to use and rely on forever. My wife and I attended the retreat on our thirteenth wedding anniversary. I could not think of a better present to give to us than to allow us to grow as a couple. My only suggestion would be to hopefully allow the program to continue. We need programs like this to heal, grow, and repair our relationships. We need our battle buddies. Our lives depend on it." Jackie also endorsed high satisfaction with the treatment (CSQ-8 Total Score = 32) and provided similar post-retreat feedback as her husband on her exit interview (e.g., "I honestly think that this will shape the years to come in a big way!").

4.6.8 Two-Week Post-Retreat Check-In and Review of Outcomes

Prior to participating in their 2-week, post-retreat check-in, the couple independently completed the PCL-5, PHQ-9, GAD-7, and CSI-32. Additionally, Jackie completed the PCL-5-C. They attended their 60-minute post-retreat meeting through a HIPAA-compliant video call. They reported that they had made notable changes to their household, including Jackie changing job positions and Marcus taking on more household responsibilities while he engaged in vocational retraining. Consistent with their treatment goals, Marcus was now consistently sleeping in bed with his wife. They also reported continued use of their skills, including catching positive behaviors in each other, paraphrasing, sharing thoughts and feelings, and challenging tunnel vision thoughts related to PTSD and their relationship. The time-out procedure was not needed since the retreat; however, they reported being comfortable with using the steps if the need arose. They reported that they were able to successfully "re-do" their anniversary celebration and were looking forward to additional date nights in the future. They also planned to start having conversations with their older children about PTSD in the family. The therapist praised Jackie and Marcus for their hard work during and after the retreat and predicted further reductions in symptoms with continued practice of their skills.

Marcus reported a 22-point reduction in his PTSD symptoms from before treatment to the 2-week follow-up assessment (baseline PCL-5 = 59; follow-up PCL-5 = 37), which was consistent with a reliable improvement in PTSD symptoms (e.g., Sloan et al., 2018). Jackie's ratings of Marcus' symptoms showed an almost identical pattern (baseline PCL-5 collateral = 53; follow up PCL-5 collateral = 31). Marcus' reduction in depressive and general anxiety symptoms is also notable. His initial PHQ-9 score of 21 placed him in the *severe* range of depressive symptoms, whereas his follow-up score of 4 placed him in the *minimal* range. Similarly, his initial GAD-7 score of 16 placed him in the *severe* range for anxiety, whereas his follow-up score of 5 placed him in the *mild* range post-retreat. In addition, although both members of the couple began treatment relationally satisfied, they each reported increases in relationship satisfaction, with Marcus' scores on the CSI-32 increasing from 137 to 144 and Jackie's scores increasing from 125 to 146. Altogether, these pre- and post-retreat scores indicate robust improvements in multiple domains of trauma-related symptoms and in relationship satisfaction, with the expectation that symptoms and relationship functioning would continue to improve over the coming months with ongoing skill use.

Acknowledgements This work was supported by award number W81XWH-22-1-0985 from the U.S. Department of Defense, Congressionally Directed Medical Research Program, Traumatic Brain Injury and Psychological Health Research Program (TBIPHRP) and the Edna P. Bennett Faculty Fellowship in Prevention Research from the College of Health and Human Development at The Pennsylvania State University.

References

Allen, E., Rhoades, G., Markman, H., & Stanley, S. (2015). PREP for strong bonds: A review of outcomes from a randomized clinical trial. *Contemporary Family Therapy, 37*(3), 232–246. https://doi.org/10.1007/s10591-014-9325-

American Psychiatric Association. (2013). *Diagnostic and statistical manual of mental disorders* (5th ed.). American Psychiatric Publishing. https://doi.org/10.1176/appi.books.9780890425596

Attkisson, C. C., & Greenfield, T. K. (2004). The UCSF client satisfaction scales: I. The client satisfaction questionnaire-8. In M. E. Maruish (Ed.), *The use of psychological testing for treatment planning and outcomes assessment* (pp. 1333–1346). Lawrence Erlbaum Associates Publishers.

Berke, D. S., Kline, N. K., Wachen, J. S., McLean, C. P., Yarvis, J. S., Mintz, J., Young-McCaughan, S., Peterson, A. L., Foa, E. B., Resick, P. A., Litz, B. T., & For the STRONG STAR Consortium. (2019). Predictors of attendance and dropout in PTSD treatment for active duty service members. *Behaviour Research and Therapy, 118*, 7–17. https://doi.org/10.1016/j.brat.2019.03.003

Blount, T. H., Peterson, A. L., & Monson, C. M. (2017). A case study of cognitive-behavioral conjoint therapy for combat-related PTSD in a same-sex military couple. *Cognitive and Behavioral Practice, 24*(3), 319–328. https://doi.org/10.1016/j.cbpra.2016.05.004

Bovin, M. J., Marx, B. P., Weathers, F. W., Gallagher, M. W., Rodriguez, P., Schnurr, P. P., & Keane, T. M. (2016). Psychometric properties of the PTSD checklist for diagnostic and statistical manual of mental disorders–Fifth edition (PCL-5) in veterans. *Psychological Assessment, 28*(11), 1379–1391. https://doi.org/10.1037/pas0000254

Bryan, C. J., Bryan, A. O., Khazem, L. R., Aase, D. M., Moreno, J. L., Ammendola, E., Bauder, C. R., Hiser, J., Daruwala, S. E., & Baker, J. C. (2024). Crisis response planning rapidly reduces suicidal ideation among U.S. military veterans receiving massed cognitive processing therapy for PTSD. *Journal of Anxiety Disorders, 102*, 102824. https://doi.org/10.1016/j.janxdis.2023.102824

Campbell, S. B., Renshaw, K. D., Kashdan, T. B., Curby, T. W., & Carter, S. P. (2017). A daily diary study of posttraumatic stress disorder and romantic partner accommodation. *Behavior Therapy, 48*(2), 222–234. https://doi.org/10.1016/j.beth.2016.04.006

Crenshaw, K. W. (1989). Demarginalizing the intersection of race and sex: A Black feminist critique of antidiscrimination doctrine, feminist theory, and antiracist politics. *University of Chicago Legal Forum, 1*(8), 139–167. http://chicagounbound.uchicago.edu/uclf/vol1989/iss1/8

Davis, L. W., Luedtke, B. L., Monson, C., Siegel, A., Daggy, J. K., Yang, Z., Bair, M. J., Brustuen, B., & Ertl, M. (2021). Testing adaptations of cognitive-behavioral conjoint therapy for PTSD: A randomized controlled pilot study with veterans. *Couple and Family Psychology: Research and Practice, 10*(2), 71–86. https://doi.org/10.1037/cfp0000148

Ehlers, A., Hackmann, A., Grey, N., Wild, J., Liness, S., Albert, I., Deale, A., Stott, D., & Clark, D. M. (2014). A randomized controlled trial of 7-day intensive and standard weekly cognitive therapy for PTSD and emotion-focused supportive therapy. *American Journal of Psychiatry, 171*(3), 294–304. https://doi.org/10.1176/appi.ajp.2013.13040552

Ennis, N., Sijercic, I., Wanklyn, S. G., & Monson, C. M. (2021). Assessing posttraumatic stress disorder with close others' collateral reports: Convergence with self- and clinician reports. *Journal of Family Psychology, 35*(2), 258–263. https://doi.org/10.1037/fam0000803

Fedynich, A. L., Birkley, E. L., & Chard, K. M. (2021). Cognitive-behavioral conjoint therapy for PTSD: A case study of a transgender male co-parenting with former spouse and perpetrator of domestic violence. *Cognitive and Behavioral Practice, 28*(3), 435–443. https://doi.org/10.1016/j.cbpra.2020.06.005

Foa, E. B., McLean, C. P., Zang, Y., Rosenfield, D., Yadin, E., Yarvis, J. S., Mintz, J., Young-McCaughan, S., Borah, E. V., Dondanville, K. A., Fina, B. A., Hall-Clark, B. N., Lichner, T., Litz, B. T., Roache, J., Wright, E. C., Peterson, A. L., & For the STRONG STAR Consortium. (2018). Effect of prolonged exposure therapy delivered over 2 weeks vs 8 weeks vs present-centered therapy on PTSD symptom severity in military personnel: A randomized clinical trial. *Journal of the American Medical Association, 319*(4), 354–364. https://doi.org/10.1001/jama.2017.21242

Fredman, S. J., Macdonald, A., Monson, C. M., Dondanville, K. A., Blount, T. H., Hall-Clark, B. N., Fina, B. A., Mintz, J., Litz, B. T., Young-McCaughan, S., Hancock, A. K., Rhoades, G. K., Yarvis, J. S., Resick, P. A., Roache, J. D., Le, Y., Wachen, J. S., Niles, B. L., McGeary, C. A., Keane, T. M., Peterson, A. L., & For the Consortium to Alleviate PTSD. (2020). Intensive multi-couple group therapy for PTSD: A non-randomized pilot study with military and veteran dyads. *Behavior Therapy, 51*(5), 700–714. https://doi.org/10.1016/j.beth.2019.10.003

Fredman, S. J., Le, Y., Macdonald, A., Monson, C. M., Rhoades, G. K., Dondanville, K. A., Blount, T. H., Hall-Clark, B. N., Fina, B. A., Mintz, J., Litz, B. T., Young-McCaughan, S., Jenkins, A. I. C., Yarvis, J. S., Keane, T. M., Peterson, A. L., & For the Consortium to Alleviate PTSD. (2021). A closer look at relational outcomes from a pilot study of abbreviated, intensive, multi-couple group cognitive-behavioral conjoint therapy for PTSD with military dyads. *Family Process, 60*(3), 712–726. https://doi.org/10.1111/famp.12654

Fredman, S. J., Fischer, M. S., Baucom, D. H., Le, Y., Taverna, E. C., Chow, S.-M., Ram, N., & Marshall, A. D. (2023). PTSD symptom cluster severity predicts momentary emotion dynamics during couple conversations. *Behavior Therapy, 54*(2), 330–345. https://doi.org/10.1016/j.beth.2022.09.004

Fredman, S. J., Le, Y., Monson, C. M., Mogle, J. A., Macdonald, A., Blount, T. H., Hall-Clark, B. N., Fina, B. A., Dondanville, K. A., Mintz, J., Liz, B. T., Young-McCaughan, S., Yarvis, J. S., Keane, T. M., Peterson, A. L., & For the Consortium to Alleviate PTSD. (2024). Pretreatment relationship characteristics predict outcomes from an uncontrolled trial of intensive, multi-

couple group PTSD treatment. *Journal of Family Psychology, 38*(3), 502–509. https://doi.org/10.1037/fam0001185
Funk, J. L., & Rogge, R. D. (2007). Testing the ruler with item response theory: increasing precision of measurement for relationship satisfaction with the Couples Satisfaction Index. *Journal of Family Psychology, 21*(4), 572–583. https://doi.org/10.1037/0893-3200.21.4.572
Goetter, E. M., Bui, E., Ojserkis, R. A., Zakarian, R. J., Brendel, R. W., & Simon, N. M. (2015). A systematic review of dropout from psychotherapy for posttraumatic stress disorder among Iraq and Afghanistan combat veterans. *Journal of Traumatic Stress, 28*(5), 401–409. https://doi.org/10.1002/jts.22038
Howard, K. P., Spoont, M. R., Polusny, M. A., Eftekhari, A., Rosen, C. S., & Meis, L. A. (2023). The role of symptom accommodation in trauma-focused treatment engagement and response. *Journal of Traumatic Stress, 36*(3), 524–536. https://doi.org/10.1002/jts.22912
Kastle, S. (2015a). *Why is dad so mad?* Tall Tale Press.
Kastle, S. (2015b). *Why is mom so mad?* Tall Tale Press.
Kroenke, K., Spitzer, R. L., & Williams, J. B. W. (2001). The PHQ-9: Validity of a brief depression severity measure. *Journal of General Internal Medicine, 16*(9), 606–613. https://doi.org/10.1046/j.1525-1497.2001.016009606.x
Lambert, J. E., Engh, R., Hasbun, A., & Holzer, J. (2012). Impact of posttraumatic stress disorder on the relationship quality and psychological distress of intimate partners: A meta-analytic review. *Journal of Family Psychology, 26*(5), 729–737. https://doi.org/10.1037/a0029341
Macdonald, A., Fredman, S. J., Taylor, D. J., Pruiksma, K. E., Blount, T. H., Hall-Clark, B. N., Fina, B. A., Dondanville, K. A., Mintz, J., Litz, B. T., Young-McCaughan, S., Le, Y., Jenkins, A. I. C., Monson, C. M., Yarvis, J. S., Keane, T. M., Peterson, A. L., & For the Consortium to Alleviate PTSD. (2022). Secondary individual outcomes following multi-couple group therapy for PTSD: An uncontrolled pilot study with military dyads. *Journal of Traumatic Stress, 35*(1), 321–329. https://doi.org/10.1002/jts.22729
Markman, H. J., Stanley, S. M., & Blumberg, S. L. (2010). *Fighting for your marriage: A deluxe revised edition of the classic best-seller for enhancing marriage and preventing divorce*. Jossey-Bass Publishers.
Meis, L. A., Noorbaloochi, S., Hagel Campbell, E. M., Erbes, C. R., Polusny, M. A., Velasquez, T. L., Bangerter, A., Cutting, A., Eftekhari, A., Rosen, C. S., Tuerk, P. W., Burmeister, L. B., & Spoont, M. R. (2019). Sticking it out in trauma-focused treatment for PTSD: It takes a village. *Journal of Consulting and Clinical Psychology, 87*(3), 246–256. https://doi.org/10.1037/ccp0000386
Monk, J. K., Ogolsky, B. G., & Bruner, V. (2016). Veteran couples integrative intensive retreat model: An intervention for military veterans and their relational partners. *Journal of Couple & Relationship Therapy, 15*, 158–176. https://doi.org/10.1080/15332691.2015.1089803
Monk, J. K., Oseland, L. M., Nelson Goff, B. S., Ogolsky, B. G., & Summers, K. (2017). Integrative intensive retreats for veteran couples and families: A pilot study assessing change in relationship adjustment, posttraumatic growth, and trauma symptoms. *Journal of Marital and Family Therapy, 43*, 448–462. https://doi.org/10.1111/jmft.12230
Monson, C. M., & Fredman, S. J. (2012). *Cognitive-behavioral conjoint therapy for posttraumatic stress disorder: Harnessing the healing power of relationships*. Guilford Press.
Monson, C. M., Fredman, S. J., & Dekel, R. (2010). Posttraumatic stress disorder in an interpersonal context. In J. G. Beck (Ed.), *Interpersonal processes in the anxiety disorders: Implications for understanding psychopathology and treatment* (pp. 179–208). American Psychological Association.
Morland, L. A., Knopp, K. C., Khalifian, C. E., Macdonald, A., Grubbs, K. M., Mackintosh, M.-A., Becker-Cretu, J. J., Sautter, F. J., Buzzella, B. A., Wrape, E. R., Glassman, L. H., Webster, K., Sohn, M. J., Glynn, S. M., Acierno, R., & Monson, C. M. (2022). A randomized trial of brief couple therapy for PTSD and relationship satisfaction. *Journal of Consulting and Clinical Psychology, 90*(5), 392–404. https://doi.org/10.1037/ccp0000731

Peterson, A. L., Blount, T. H., Foa, E. B., Brown, L. A., McLean, C. P., Mintz, J., Schobitz, R. P., DeBeer, B. R., Mignogna, J., Fina, B. A., Evans, W. R., Synett, S., Hall-Clark, B. N., Rentz, T. O., Schrader, C., Yarvis, J. S., Dondanville, K. A., Hansen, H., Jacoby, V. M., Lara-Ruiz, J., et al. (2023). Massed vs intensive outpatient prolonged exposure for combat-related posttraumatic stress disorder: A randomized clinical trial. *JAMA Network Open, 6*(1), e2249422. https://doi.org/10.1001/jamanetworkopen.2022.49422

Price, M., Gros, D. F., Strachan, M., Ruggiero, K. J., & Acierno, R. (2013). The role of social support in exposure therapy for Operation Iraqi Freedom/Operation Enduring Freedom veterans: A preliminary investigation. *Psychological Trauma: Theory, Research, Practice and Policy, 5*(1), 93–100. https://doi.org/10.1037/a0026244

Pukay-Martin, N. D., Fredman, S. J., Martin, C. E., Le, Y., Haney, A., Sullivan, C., Monson, C. M., & Chard, K. M. (2022). Effectiveness of cognitive-behavioral conjoint therapy for PTSD in a VA PTSD clinic. *Journal of Traumatic Stress, 35*(2), 644–658. https://doi.org/10.1002/jts.22781

Resick, P. A., Monson, C. M., & Chard, K. M. (2017). *Cognitive processing therapy for PTSD: A comprehensive guide*. Guilford Press.

Shepherd-Banigan, M. E., McDuffie, J. R., Shapiro, A., Brancu, M., Sperber, N., Mehta, N. N., van Houtven, C. H., & Williams, J. W., Jr. (2018). *Interventions to support caregivers or families of patients with TBI, PTSD, or polytrauma: A systematic review*. Department of Veterans Affairs (US).

Sherman, M. D., Straits-Troster, K., Larsen, J., & Gress-Smith, J. (2015). *A veteran's guide to talking with kids about PTSD*. Veteran's Affairs South Central Mental Illness Research, Education & Clinical Center. http://www.mirecc.va.gov/visn16/ClinicalEducationProducts.asp

Shnaider, P., Pukay-Martin, N. D., Sharma, S., Jenzer, T., Fredman, S. J., Macdonald, A., & Monson, C. M. (2015). A preliminary examination of the effects of pre-treatment relationship satisfaction on treatment outcomes in cognitive-behavioral conjoint therapy for PTSD. *Couple and Family Psychology: Research and Practice, 4*(4), 229–238. https://doi.org/10.1037/cfp0000050

Shnaider, P., Sijercic, I., Wanklyn, S. G., Suvak, M. K., & Monson, C. M. (2017). The role of social support in cognitive-behavioral conjoint therapy for posttraumatic stress disorder. *Behavior Therapy, 48*(3), 285–294. https://doi.org/10.1016/j.beth.2016.05.003

Sloan, D. M., Marx, B. P., Lee, D. J., & Resick, P. A. (2018). A brief exposure-based treatment vs cognitive processing therapy for posttraumatic stress disorder: A randomized noninferiority clinical trial. *JAMA Psychiatry, 75*(3), 233–239. https://doi.org/10.1001/jamapsychiatry.2017.4249

Spitzer, R. L., Kroenke, K., Williams, J. B., & Lowe, B. (2006). A brief measure for assessing generalized anxiety disorder: The GAD-7. *Archives of Internal Medicine, 166*(10), 1092–1097. https://doi.org/10.1001/archinte.166.10.1092

Taft, C. T., Watkins, L. E., Stafford, J., Street, A. E., & Monson, C. M. (2011). Posttraumatic stress disorder and intimate relationship problems: A meta-analysis. *Journal of Consulting and Clinical Psychology, 79*(1), 22–33. https://doi.org/10.1037/a0022196

Tarrier, N., Sommerfield, C., & Pilgrim, H. (1999). Relatives' expressed emotion (EE) and PTSD treatment outcome. *Psychological Medicine, 29*(4), 801–811. https://doi.org/10.1017/S0033291799008569

Weathers, F. W., Blake, D. D., Schnurr, P. P., Kaloupek, D. G., Marx, B. P., & Keane, T. M. (2013a). *The life events checklist for DSM-5 (LEC-5)*. Instrument available from the National Center for PTSD. www.ptsd.va.gov

Weathers, F. W., Litz, B. T., Keane, T. M., Palmieri, P. A., Marx, B. P., & Schnurr, P. P. (2013b). *The PTSD checklist for DSM-5 (PCL-5)*. Instrument available from the National Center for PTSD. www.ptsd.va.gov

Zalta, A. K., Held, P., Smith, D. L., Klassen, B. J., Lofgreen, A. M., Normand, P. S., Brennan, M. B., Rydberg, T. S., Boley, R. A., Pollack, M. H., & Karnik, N. S. (2018). Evaluating patterns and predictors of symptom change during a three-week intensive outpatient treatment for veterans with PTSD. *BMC Psychiatry, 18*, Article 242. https://doi.org/10.1186/s12888-018-1816-6

Chapter 5
Family-Only Adjunctive Treatment

Johanna Thompson-Hollands

5.1 Introduction

The interrelationship between social/family support and posttraumatic stress disorder (PTSD) is one of the most robust and longstanding findings in the field of trauma (e.g., Brewin et al., 2000; Galovski & Lyons, 2004; Ozer et al., 2008). The relationship is bidirectional, with a dearth of social support being associated with heightened risk of meeting diagnostic criteria for the disorder and/or greater symptom severity (e.g., Ozer et al., 2008), and the diagnosis and/or higher symptomatology being associated with poorer social functioning and more relationship distress (e.g., Fredman et al., 2017; Galovski & Lyons, 2004; Sayers et al., 2009; Sippel et al., 2019). Family members (FMs) of patients with PTSD report higher levels of distress, relationship burden, and conflict compared to FMs of individuals without PTSD (e.g., Lambert et al., 2012). Without question, the social environment of PTSD patients impacts—and is impacted by—the course of their disorder.

Multiple models have been developed to describe and predict the impact of PTSD within a social system or relationship. These include the Couple Adaptation to Traumatic Stress (CATS) model (Nelson Goff & Smith, 2005), the Cognitive Behavioral Interpersonal model (Monson et al., 2010) and the Dyadic Responses to Trauma model (Marshall & Kuijer, 2017), each of which outlines a number of individual and dyad-relevant features that interact to produce behavioral responses in the face of traumatic exposure. These theoretical contributions have been invaluable in grounding empirical work to understand and address how trauma impacts relationships and how to align families and significant others to help patients recover.

J. Thompson-Hollands (✉)
Department of Psychiatry, Boston University Chobanian & Avedisian School of Medicine, Boston, MA, USA
e-mail: hollands@bu.edu

L. Reuman, J. Thompson-Hollands (eds.), *Enhancing CBT Through Family and Peer Engagement*, CBT: Science Into Practice, https://doi.org/10.1007/978-3-031-74838-7_5

The latter element is critical; although a substantial amount of research documents the potentially devastating impact of PTSD on social relationships and vice versa, there is also robust evidence that families can be an invaluable source of motivation, support, and meaning to patients. Individuals with PTSD frequently cite their family relationships as a key reason that they are seeking treatment (e.g., Sayer et al., 2009), and family behaviors/functioning have been shown to predict treatment outcomes (Evans et al., 2009; Howard et al., 2023). To leave these powerful interpersonal forces unaddressed would be a great oversight and a disservice to our patients.

In the remainder of this chapter, I outline a family-inclusive approach to PTSD treatment, the Brief Family Intervention (BFI). I describe the key elements of this short intervention and discuss the basis upon which key design decisions for the treatment (e.g., length and lack of patient participation) were made. I then describe the current empirical support for the BFI and provide a case example. It is my hope that this chapter provides a robust introduction to conducting the BFI and inspiration for experimentation with other adjunctive family-inclusive interventions for non-PTSD disorders.

5.2 Treatment Overview

The BFI is a two-session adjunctive intervention delivered to an adult family member of a patient who is pursuing trauma-focused treatment [TFT, e.g., Cognitive Processing therapy (CPT; Resick et al., 2016), Prolonged Exposure (PE; Foa et al., 2019), Written Exposure Therapy (WET; Sloan & Marx, 2019)]. BFI sessions are approximately 60 minutes long and are conducted 1 week apart. The BFI is intended to be delivered early in the patient's course of treatment (typically, before Session 4 of TFT content); alternatively, the protocol may be delivered immediately prior to the patient starting TFT.

The goals of the BFI are (1) to reduce the likelihood of dropout from individual TFT, and (2) to reduce the patient's level of avoidance in daily life (e.g., through reducing accommodation and/or increased engagement in activities with the FM). That is, despite the fact that only the FM attends the BFI sessions (for a discussion of this choice, see below), the intention of the BFI is to enhance the *patient's* treatment outcomes. The FM may also experience some direct benefits from participating in the BFI. For example, psychoeducation provided as part of the BFI may help the FM to feel less personally responsible for the PTSD symptoms or allow the FM to make sense of the patient's symptoms as a response to the traumatic event (Renshaw et al., 2014). Furthermore, the BFI can stimulate behavioral changes on the part of the FM that then provoke a positive cascade within the patient–FM relationship; improvements in relationship functioning and/or the patient's symptomatology may result in improvements in the FM's mood, relationship satisfaction, or functioning.

Prior to beginning Session 1 of the BFI, the clinician gathers some preliminary information; specifically, it is important to establish which trauma-focused treatment the patient will be pursuing (or has begun), as that treatment will be described to the FM in some detail. The clinician also assesses the current level of FM symptom accommodation. Accommodation is measured using the Significant Others' Responses to Trauma Scale (SORTS; Fredman et al., 2014; Thompson-Hollands et al., 2024) in order to provide a psychometrically valid baseline and to help anchor discussions of particular behaviors. Finally, it can be helpful for the clinician to know generally what index trauma the patient will focus on in TFT. This is not necessary, as details of the trauma are not shared with the FM during the BFI, but it can assist in conceptualizing the patient's presentation and tailoring the BFI content.

Session 1 of the BFI is scheduled for 1 hour. At the beginning of the session, the clinician reminds the FM of the structure of the program (two 1-hour sessions, scheduled roughly 1 week apart). It is beneficial to review confidentiality at the start of the BFI program, as FMs are often unsure about what they might be "allowed" to say, and likewise may not understand the clinician's obligations with regard to confidentiality. The clinician clearly states that the FM is welcome to share any details, observations, or questions they may have, and that these will not be shared with the patient. The clinician further notes that they will not be sharing any specific information from/about the patient in terms of trauma exposure symptoms and treatment progress.

The clinician begins the main portion of Session 1 by asking some introductory questions about the patient and FM's relationship, such as how long they have known one another, how they have been getting along lately, what PTSD symptoms the FM notices in daily life, and if the FM knew the patient prior to (what the FM understands to be) the index trauma. The clinician also assesses the FM's level of knowledge about the trauma itself. These questions are meant to be a nonchallenging entry point for the FM, as the FM is able to share their experience and hopefully become comfortable participating actively in the session. The questions also serve to help the clinician understand more about the dyad's relationship and begin to develop a conceptualization of aspects such as relationship satisfaction, burden, emotional disclosure, and interpersonal skills. These features in turn contribute to how the clinician will later guide the FM with respect to enhancing supportive behaviors and/or reducing accommodation later in the protocol.

Next, the clinician reviews the FM's responses on the SORTS. For each item that the FM has endorsed (e.g., "How often did you 'bite your tongue' or hold back from trying to discuss any relationship issues with [NAME]?"), the clinician asks for a more descriptive example of the behavior, how often it occurs, and any other relevant details. The clinician also attends to items that the FM did not endorse, but that based on clinical experience and knowledge of the patient's trauma/symptom presentation (if the clinician has such information) might be expected. Because the SORTS items are worded generally, and because accommodation can become almost second nature to FMs, they may not have immediately recognized all the ways that they have shifted their own behavior to "make space" for PTSD.

Following the review of the SORTS, the clinician begins the psychoeducational content of the session. First, they review the symptoms of PTSD, particularly normalizing any symptoms that the FM particularly mentioned in the earlier part of the session or that tend to be highly observable to others (e.g., nightmares, jumpiness/physical reactivity, irritability). FMs may have attributed some of these symptoms to the trauma (e.g., nightmares), yet others may not be as immediately connected to their loved one's experiences. It can be a great relief for them to hear that numbness, irritability, and other more diffuse behaviors are trauma-relevant sequelae and would be expected to improve following successful treatment.

Next, the clinician begins to provide an overview of the development and maintenance of PTSD, emphasizing both cognitive and behavioral aspects. Avoidance is highlighted as a key maintaining feature; the clinician emphasizes the negatively reinforcing nature of avoidance in order to give context to this behavior. The discussion of maintaining features of PTSD then leads into a discussion of the patient's treatment course. As noted above, the BFI clinician will be aware of which trauma-focused treatment the patient is pursuing so that the discussion of the treatment rationale and procedures is specific to the relevant approach (i.e., CPT, PE, or WET). The clinician gives examples of specific treatment activities, both in session and any that may be assigned for homework, and also describes the common timing for each of these components. Results from prior qualitative research with FMs of veterans engaged in CPT or PE revealed that FMs did not feel that they received much information about treatment from the veterans, either in the form of specific descriptions of session activities or insight into the veteran's emotional experience while in treatment (Thompson-Hollands et al., 2021a). Providing this level of detail as part of the BFI not only helps to make the treatment course clearer to the FM but also can prepare the FM for periods when the patient may be struggling more with treatment (e.g., having to write a trauma narrative in CPT following Session 3).

During the discussion of PTSD symptoms, and especially the overview of and rationale for trauma-focused treatment, the clinician must be attentive to subtle or overt signs of resistance to the treatment model. It is clear from research with clinicians that even professionals may hold negative beliefs about TFT or have concerns about the safety of these approaches (Becker et al., 2004; Frueh et al., 2006). These views may also be shared by some FMs but could be alleviated through direct conversations with the BFI provider. Regardless of whether the FM conveys particular concerns about the treatment, the clinician makes a point to emphasize that TFT is challenging and can be unpleasant at times, especially early in the treatment course.

Ideally, the conversation about challenges in treatment serves to prepare the FM for any temporary increase in symptoms and/or distress that the patient may experience. If the FM is able to tolerate their own distress in the face of such exacerbations, they will be better able to support the patient through them. Enhancing the FM's ability to demonstrate support for the patient is an important target of the BFI, as the underlying theoretical model of the BFI proposes that perceived support from the FM will result in greater engagement in treatment activities and less attrition. The clinician therefore spends a portion of Session 1 discussing ways the FM might demonstrate practical and emotional support while the patient is in treatment. Practical support can consist of things such as providing private space and quiet time for the patient to complete homework activities. Although these functional adjustments can be helpful to identify, often the bulk of the conversation around support centers on explicit verbal support for the patient's work in treatment. The BFI clinician provides a handout with simple phrases that the FM can consider using, such as "I'm so proud of you for starting treatment" or "It's great for our kids to see you working on yourself in this way." FMs respond quite positively to being provided with example language. The BFI clinician also encourages the FM to use their attendance at Session 1 as a starting point for conversations around treatment generally; for example, the FM might say "I had that family session at the clinic today. It was nice to meet the doctor and hear more about what your sessions are going to be like. It sounds like the treatment is really promising, and also that there are parts that could be tough. I'd be happy to hear about how you feel like things are going if you're open to that, but I'm really glad that I could learn a bit today."

The last portion of Session 1 focuses on a discussion of the function of accommodation in PTSD and preliminary planning for a reduction in accommodation behaviors. The clinician draws parallels between avoidance that the patient may be engaging in independently and the function that accommodation may play in the family. The clinician is careful to frame this discussion in a manner that does not convey blame for the family members' actions or imply that accommodation prevented the patient from recovering from PTSD. Rather, the focus is on taking advantage of the patient's current momentum (i.e., their having initiated an episode of TFT) to align the family member's behavior with the goals of that treatment. The clinician returns to the SORTS items that were identified earlier in the session and uses these to begin a discussion of what behaviors could be shifted in order to reduce the patient's overall avoidance. We typically recommend a gradual approach to reducing accommodation. The FM is encouraged to have a conversation with the patient about the behaviors that they are hoping to reduce or eliminate and to explicitly connect this change to support the patient's treatment goals.

The primary focus of Session 1 is to convey psychoeducational content to the FM. However, there are also a number of pieces of information that the clinician is attempting to gather, either through direct questioning or observation. For example, during the course of the session, the clinician is attempting to understand (1) how the patient's PTSD symptoms are exhibited in the family context and how this impacts the FM and others in the home, and (2) the FM's general level of comfort with emotions (especially negative emotions) and interpersonal skill in addressing emotionally laden topics. The former will inform the clinician's conceptualization of the dyad/family's functioning and may guide the clinician's selection of behaviors or symptoms to focus on in the discussion; the latter will impact the clinician's messaging to the FM and which behavioral changes they may recommend making. With FMs who appear to struggle with experiencing negative emotions themselves or witnessing such emotions from the patient, or who appear less comfortable or skilled in having emotionally open conversations, the BFI sessions will focus more on emphasizing the rationale for and safety of asking the patient to tolerate negative emotions, and the discussion of FM behavioral change will likely emphasize supportive behaviors rather than changes to accommodation (see below).

The second BFI session has a less standardized structure, as its content largely depends upon what was emphasized in Session 1. In all cases, the clinician will begin the session by checking in about how things have been since the prior session, including any major conflict in the dyad, changes in symptoms the FM may have noticed, and whether there has been any conversation within the dyad about the BFI sessions or the patient's experience in therapy. The clinician offers praise for efforts on the FM's part to initiate conversation around these topics and guidance on how to indicate openness to further conversations without undue pressure. Next, the clinician revisits any other plans established in the prior session regarding specific supportive behaviors and/or changes to accommodation. The FM may be asked to engage in a role-play to troubleshoot any challenging interactions. The session also includes time for the FM to raise any other issues or questions they might have about PTSD or treatment, or navigating daily life with the patient.

5.2.1 *BFI as an Adjunct to Individual Trauma-Focused Treatment Rather Than a Standalone Intervention*

Several fully dyadic approaches to PTSD treatment have been developed and tested to varying degrees (Johnson, 2002; Monson & Fredman, 2012; Sautter et al., 2015). These approaches are intended as stand-alone interventions to address both PTSD symptomology and relationship functioning. The BFI is not intended to replace or compete with these fully dyadic treatments. Many families, however, are unable or unwilling to devote 15 or more sessions to dyadic treatment. Furthermore, it may be that some families can be helped by briefer interventions and do not require or benefit from further sessions. In a landscape of healthcare scarcity (Harvey & Gumport, 2015), briefer interventions have an important role to play.

Additionally, the BFI was developed and tested within the Veterans Health Administration (VHA) system. The VHA has invested massively in the dissemination and implementation of CPT and PE for the treatment of PTSD. These efforts began in 2006 and have encompassed clinician training programs, increased staffing in mental health service lines, and mandated availability of CPT and PE at all VHA facilities (Bernardy et al., 2011; Karlin & Cross, 2014). Given the historic levels of investment and institutional momentum behind the use of CPT and PE in VHA, developing a family-inclusive treatment that could be delivered adjunctively to either of those treatments (and also to WET) appeared both prudent and efficient. The BFI is therefore designed to complement rather than replace or supplant individual TFT interventions.

5.2.2 *Structure of the BFI and Delivery Considerations*

The BFI is specifically intended to be delivered just prior to the patient's initiation of TFT or, if the patient has already begun the TFT protocol, before Session 4 of the protocol content. Dropout from TFT is very likely to occur early in the course of therapy (Gutner et al., 2016; Thompson-Hollands et al., 2023). Administering the BFI early in treatment maximizes the chance that FMs can provide critical early support and encouragement. Furthermore, as noted above, part of the BFI content includes educating FMs about the risk of dropout and encouraging them to be aware of any indication that the patient is considering ending therapy. The earlier FMs receive guidance, the more likely it is that they can attempt to intervene.

The BFI is intended to be delivered by a clinician who is not the patient's individual therapist. The decision to have the family component conducted by a separate provider was guided by early interviews that I (JTH) conducted with VHA clinicians. Those providers expressed hesitancy about meeting with an FM of one of their patients without that patient being present. They felt that such a meeting had the potential to damage trust and rapport. As the goal of the BFI is first and foremost to support and enhance TFT outcomes, a decrease in trust in the TFT clinician would obviously be unacceptable. Additionally, nothing about the BFI content requires specific knowledge of the patient's index trauma, the content of individual sessions, etc. Indeed, when offering the BFI program to patients, many appear to be reassured by the fact that their FM can receive some general information and support while the patient's individual sessions remain highly private.

As noted previously, existing family-inclusive treatments for PTSD are lengthy, consisting of more than 4 months of weekly sessions in most cases. There is growing attention to the fact that such extensive courses of treatment may be infeasible or unappealing in some cases. For example, among dyads who initiated CBCT in one pilot study, 66% dropped out within 2 months of treatment (Morland et al., 2019). In response to these patterns, the most recent large-scale trial of CBCT (the largest randomized-controlled trial of dyadic treatment for PTSD ever conducted) used an 8-session format rather than the original 15-session intervention (Morland et al., 2019). In developing the BFI protocol, the goal was to create a protocol that was maximally efficient while still including content and skills that were likely to be effective. Although a single-session intervention would be the least time-intensive format, I felt that having the opportunity to follow-up with the FM and offer possible corrections to any suggested interventions was valuable enough to warrant a second session. Nonetheless, the two-session format does require that the material and skills covered in the BFI remain highly streamlined. The goals of the intervention, as outlined above, are not nearly as extensive, nor are the skills introduced as complex, as those of standalone dyadic interventions for PTSD; this is appropriate given the BFI's intended use as an adjunct to individual treatment.

Only the family member attends the BFI sessions; the patient with PTSD is not present. This design choice was driven by several considerations: first, for practical purposes, it is much simpler to arrange a session with only one person (the FM) rather than two (FM and patient). The BFI is meant to be highly accessible and feasible, and thus focusing on coordinating sessions with just one attendee was preferred. Second, caring about and being in a close relationship with someone with PTSD is associated with a high degree of strain on FMs (Galovski & Lyons, 2004). Some FMs might feel constrained in speaking about the challenges and frustrations of daily life if the patient was present. FMs might also be hesitant to bring up sensitive topics like problematic substance use or suicidality if the patient is in the room. The BFI will be most useful to FMs if they can honestly describe their experiences, ask their questions, and share their concerns. Finally, I considered the comfort of the BFI providers. Specifically, many clinicians who specialize in PTSD treatment do not have a strong background in dyadic or family work. Thompson-Hollands et al. (2022) conducted interviews with a national sample of 31 VA-based clinicians and administrators. These providers regularly treat veterans with PTSD. When asked about barriers to family-inclusive work, 61% noted their own lack of training and supervision in couples or family work as a factor that reduced their likelihood of offering dyadic sessions. When establishing a novel intervention, it is critical that treatment developers consider the potential for future implementation of that treatment from its inception. The relative rarity of providers who are truly comfortable with and competent in dyadic work was another factor that weighed in favor of individual delivery of the BFI.

The BFI was developed for delivery to adult FMs (ages 18 or older). There is a great need for family work devoted to parenting and PTSD, and many veterans desire services that can help their child(ren) understand PTSD (Reuman & Thompson-Hollands, 2023). However, developmental considerations are paramount when designing services targeted to children. The same content cannot simply be delivered to younger audiences without significant revisions and expert input. Given that the BFI for PTSD has thus far been conducted exclusively within the VA system, child-focused programming or sessions are not a priority, nor are they particularly feasible in that setting. At times FMs participating in a BFI session will mention concerns related to children in the family; these may be specific to helping children understand PTSD/the parent's traumatic experience (e.g., what is appropriate in terms of sharing details about a trauma and what language to use) or the concerns may be around parenting skill deficits that the FM perceives on the part of the patient. Fortunately, a number of parenting- and child-focused materials have been developed by others (e.g., US Department of Veterans Affairs, 2015), and BFI participants receive lists of recommended evidence-based resources as needed.

The BFI is as accessible to FMs as possible, including the format in which FMs attend the sessions. The BFI can be delivered in person or through an appropriate (HIPAA-compliant) video platform. Phone-only sessions are an option if video sessions are impossible or highly burdensome, but a format in which the clinician and FM can see one another is strongly preferred. FMs may also wish to "mix-and-match" their format across the two sessions (e.g., attending the first session in person but the second session via video). As with any remotely delivered clinical intervention, it is important that the FM be in an environment that will allow them to fully participate in the session. This means both reducing distractions (e.g., not having the TV on in the room) and also ensuring privacy (e.g., being in a space where the FM cannot be overheard).

5.2.3 Relative Balance of Focus on Family Support for Treatment Versus Changing Accommodation

There may be times when the goal of reducing avoidance/accommodation may seem to be in conflict with maintaining a warm relationship within the dyad. For example, in some cases FM may be so overwhelmed or burnt out by the PTSD that by the time they arrive at the BFI session, it is clear that they are holding significant anger toward the patient. FMs in this state of profound depletion or resentment may interpret the psychoeducation around accommodation as clinical "permission" to immediately abandon any level of support for the patient. However, if FMs change their behavior in ways that strain the relationship with the patient, the ultimate impact on treatment outcomes may be negligible or potentially negative, as there is evidence that the quality of dyadic relationships influences the extent to which FM encouragement toward treatment is helpful. Meis and colleagues reported that the degree to which FMs encouraged veterans to approach distress (termed "social control" in their study) predicted lower dropout (Meis et al., 2019); however, follow-up analyses showed that this encouragement was most impactful in low-strain relationships, less impactful in moderate strain relationships, and nonsignificant in high strain relationships. The goal of reducing accommodation should not come at the expense of the dyadic connection.

Importantly, the patient and/or the FM may consider accommodation to be an act of love and care. Both the specific accommodative behaviors, as well as an overall stance of the FM making room for and not questioning the patient's preferences, may be highly valued within the dyad (Fernando et al., 2024; Renshaw et al., 2020). It is necessary to address the meaning that accommodation may have within the dyad while also trying to shift the behavior to better align with exposure-focused therapy.

During the BFI, the clinician attempts to optimize the process of reducing accommodation in several ways:

1. Describing the development and maintenance of PTSD such that FMs have a baseline of empathy for the patient's experience/behaviors. This empathy will hopefully allow the FM to move forward with changes to their own behavior that are motivated by a desire to support the patient's treatment goals rather than communicating exhaustion or resentment.
2. Acknowledging that accommodation is often driven by pragmatics and/or care for the individual, but highlighting its long-term function in the maintenance of the disorder. In this way, the clinician positions reductions in accommodation as the more caring, supportive response.

3. Conducting role-plays to help FMs practice implementing reductions in accommodation in the most empathic, effective manner.

These strategies can often result in a plan to reduce accommodation that is perceived as caring and gradual by both the patient and FM. As noted earlier, the clinician's observations with regard to the FM and the dyadic context more broadly are crucial in terms of how much emphasis is placed on particular behavioral changes. FMs who demonstrate a strong emotional connection to the patient, a high degree of skill in managing negative emotions (both in themselves and the patient), and comfort with emotional disclosure and vulnerability will be best able to manage more nuanced or potentially challenging behavioral shifts. *In cases where the clinician feels that the nature of the relationship or the relative lack of interpersonal skills on the part of the FM/patient preclude a successful plan to reduce accommodation, prioritize relationship-enhancing behaviors from the FM over reductions in accommodation.*

5.3 Research Evidence

5.3.1 The BFI in OCD

The BFI was originally developed for application with the FMs of patients undergoing individual treatment for obsessive-compulsive disorder (OCD; Thompson-Hollands et al., 2015). Much of the content of the protocol was similar to what has been described previously here, although there was relatively stronger emphasis on reducing accommodation and relatively less emphasis on preventing treatment dropout. The original study included 18 dyads of patients with OCD and their adult family members. Patients were recruited at the beginning of a course of individual exposure and response prevention (ERP). They identified an adult family member or significant other who they were interested in involving in their treatment. All patients went on to receive ERP, and the FMs were randomized to receive or not receive the BFI. Outcomes of interest were the feasibility/acceptability of the BFI, as well as changes in symptom accommodation and OCD severity. The comparison of a group of patients receiving the gold-standard individual treatment for OCD to another group of patients receiving that same gold-standard treatment with the addition of a brief family-inclusive intervention is a highly rigorous one; nonetheless, the BFI demonstrated large effects on both accommodation and OCD symptoms. FMs who received the BFI showed significantly greater reductions in accommodation compared to control group FMs; average accommodation scores in the control group at the final assessment point were 78% of their baseline scores, whereas average scores at the same point for FMs in the BFI group had decreased to 37% of baseline. Patients whose FMs had received the BFI had significantly lower levels of OCD symptoms at the end of ERP ($d = 1.27$). There was evidence that accommodation functioned as a key mechanism within the BFI; changes in accommodation significantly predicted patients' later symptom levels, but the reverse (symptom change predicting later accommodation) was not significant (Thompson-Hollands et al., 2015).

5.3.2 *The BFI in PTSD*

Based upon work showing that accommodation was a transdiagnostic phenomenon (e.g., Fredman et al., 2014; Thompson-Hollands et al., 2014), as well as data showing that veterans were highly interested in family involvement in their treatment (e.g., Meis et al., 2013), the BFI was adapted to be piloted among veterans with PTSD and their family members. The initial testing consisted of an open trial phase among 4 dyads (Thompson-Hollands et al., 2021c) followed by a small randomized controlled trial with 20 dyads (Thompson-Hollands et al., 2021b). The results from these early studies indicated that the BFI was feasible and acceptable to FMs and veterans.

Following the pilot trial, a larger study was funded to better establish the BFI's effects. This trial is currently ongoing and aims to recruit 100 veteran-FM dyads across 3 VA sites. The goal of the project is not only to test the impact of the BFI in an adequately powered sample but also to assess mechanisms and moderators of the intervention's impact. Mechanisms of interest include changes in accommodation, relationship satisfaction, and disclosure. Moderators of interest include the gender of the FM and/or veteran, PTSD symptom severity at baseline, accommodation at baseline, and individual treatment of the veteran (CPT or PE).

5.4 Clinical Considerations for Diverse Identities

5.4.1 *Gender*

The majority of the work on family-inclusive treatments for PTSD (especially among military and veteran samples, where the majority of such research has taken place) has been conducted among identified patients who are men and their romantic partners who are women. Considering veteran-focused studies alone, 96–100% of participating dyads in each sample have conformed to this structure (Fredman et al., 2020; Monson et al., 2004; Schumm et al., 2013; Thompson-Hollands et al., 2021b; Weissman et al., 2018). Even studies that have merely assessed openness to family-inclusive treatment have had heavily male samples (e.g., Meis et al., 2013). Comparatively little is known about the extent to which women patients with PTSD want FMs involved in their care and how to conduct such family-inclusive care most effectively for these patients. Reuman and Thompson-Hollands (2023) conducted a mixed-methods study that examined attitudes toward family-inclusive treatment among women veterans. The distribution of interest in family involvement in PTSD treatment was bimodally distributed among the women, with large numbers indicating both very high and very low interest. Interest was not significantly related to current PTSD symptom severity, but demographic factors were significantly associated with interest (specifically, women who were currently in a romantic relationship were more likely to express interest in family involvement, and women who identified as gay/lesbian were more likely than women who identified as straight to desire FM involvement). Women largely reported wishing to involve a romantic partner in their treatment, although there was also interest in involving children, parents, and friends. Participants indicated that their goals for family involvement included improving their relationship with the FM, having their FM learn about the PTSD diagnosis, and having their FM learn skills to help them. These findings, while arising from a single study, suggest that the BFI could be appealing to some women with PTSD. The BFI is appropriate for use with a range of FMs (although not for children younger than 18) and could address women's desires for psychoeducation and skill-building for their FMs.

It is important to note that many of the aspects of interests in and goals for family involvement in treatment that were identified by Reuman and Thompson-Hollands (2023) have never been examined among a sample of men with PTSD, so it is not clear whether such findings are unique to women or are broadly applicable across patients with PTSD. There are likely some differences in the ways that PTSD functions within the context of larger gender dynamics in relationships. While large portions of the BFI would be unchanged regardless of the gender of the patient/FM, it may be useful to consider the possible impact of gender socialization on how the patient and FM might express and receive support, or their levels of comfort with emotional vulnerability.

5.4.2 *Military Versus Civilian Status*

The BFI has been tested exclusively in veteran samples. Research indicates that patients with PTSD with military/veteran status differ in their interpersonal dynamics compared to civilians with PTSD. For example, military (versus civilian) samples show a stronger correlation between PTSD severity and relationship discord, as well as between PTSD severity and physical aggression (Taft et al., 2011). Additionally, FMs may respond differently to PTSD symptoms when the PTSD symptoms are attributed to military service. For example, Renshaw et al. (2020) developed a scale to assess the reasons that FMs of service members engaged in accommodation. In a study of female partners of male service members, partners who indicated that they accommodated in part because they felt that this behavior would serve the relationship or because they felt obligated to do so following their partners' military service were less distressed by accommodating. FMs of service members may therefore be less unhappy about accommodation behaviors if they see these actions as following naturally from their partner's military experiences, but they may also be less motivated to reduce their accommodation in such cases.

In earlier work, Renshaw and colleagues (Renshaw et al., 2008; Renshaw & Campbell, 2011) found that the association between service members' PTSD symptoms and their romantic partners' distress was weaker when the partners believed that the service members had experienced more traumatic events during their deployment. The perception of the extent of trauma exposure (and perhaps the "legitimacy" of that trauma exposure, with military service potentially being seen as a worthy/valid source) may therefore lead to somewhat less negative/strong reactions and greater support from FMs compared to trauma from events or settings that are viewed by the FM as less intense. When working with FMs of civilians it would therefore be especially important to be attuned to any suggestion by the FM that the patient's PTSD is an unwarranted response to their experiences or that the PTSD symptoms are due to an internal source (e.g., lack of effort and desire to remain impaired).

5.4.3 *Age*

Older dyads may present somewhat unique issues with regard to medical issues and how these can interact with and need to be differentiated from accommodation. Qualitative analyses by Reuman and Thompson-Hollands (2020) indicated that FMs can struggle to disentangle avoidance or functional challenges that are driven by a patient's pain or medical concerns from behaviors that are motivated more directly by PTSD-related avoidance. When general age-related declines or a specific medical condition are a factor, clinicians may need to spend extra time exploring the nuances of the patient's behavior/abilities in order to more clearly guide the FM toward any changes in their responses.

5.5 Case Vignette

5.5.1 *Background*

Christina and Jason were a couple living together in the Northeast United States. Jason was a 27-year-old white, non-Hispanic, heterosexual, cisgender man. Christina was a 26-year-old white, Latina, heterosexual, cisgender woman. Christina and Jason had grown up together in a nearby city and had kept in touch as friends when Jason deployed to Iraq as an infantry soldier in his early 20s. When he returned from the deployment, he and Christina began dating, and 2 years later Christina moved into the home Jason owned.

Jason had separated from the Army shortly after returning from deployment and had been hired as a firefighter in their town. He enjoyed the camaraderie of the fire station, where many of his coworkers were also veterans. Other than socializing at the station during his 24-hour shifts, Jason did not like to go out with friends or on dates with Christina. He spent most of his time working on his vehicles at home (he owned a truck and a sports car), playing video games, or sleeping to recover from long overnight shifts.

Christina worked as an office manager at a small construction company. She was a sociable and upbeat person and had a wide circle of friends, most of whom were also mutual friends or acquaintances of Jason's since they had known each other for so long. Christina had communicated with Jason during his deployment, but their conversations tended to center around lighthearted topics or updates from their hometown. She said "I knew he was going through a lot over there, and I didn't want to have him be focused on heavy things when he was talking to me." When Jason returned from deployment, he did not share much about his experiences, and Christina thought it was best not to "pry."

Christina had noticed that since Jason returned from deployment he had a shorter temper. As a high school student, Jason had been gregarious and easygoing, but after he separated from the Army he was quick to raise his voice and often seemed to be on the verge of an outburst. Recently, he had been out on a fire call and became frustrated with an onlooker at the scene. Jason had shouted at the man, repeatedly encroaching on his physical space and using foul language to order him to back up. His fellow firefighters ultimately had to step in to separate Jason from the bystander. Following the incident, the station chief, a man whom Jason highly respected, alerted Jason that he was close to being placed on probationary status. He urged Jason to speak to someone at the VA about treatment for his anger. During the course of Jason's evaluation at the VA, he was diagnosed with PTSD. The intake clinician recommended that Jason allow Christina to take part in the BFI so that she could be better prepared to support his work in treatment, and Jason agreed to this plan.

5.5.2 *Diagnostic and Functional Assessments*

As part of his clinical intake at the VA, Jason completed the PTSD Checklist for DSM-5 (PCL-5; Weathers et al., 2013). He anchored the PCL-5 to an incident in Iraq where a car approached a barricade that his unit was protecting. Jason shouted at the driver not to get any closer, but the car skidded to a halt nearby and the driver jumped from the vehicle and began racing toward the barricade. Jason again yelled at the man to stop, but when the man did not listen, Jason shot and killed him. Jason's PCL-5 score was 39, above the threshold of 31–33 for likely clinically significant PTSD symptoms (Bovin et al., 2016). After reviewing Jason's PCL-5 results, the intake clinician confirmed via an unstructured interview that Jason met the criteria for PTSD. The clinician also diagnosed Jason with Major Depressive Disorder.

As part of her intake into the BFI program, Christina completed the SORTS. The SORTS can be scored as two factors ("managing explosivity/conflict" and "avoidance/changing routine") or as a total score (Thompson-Hollands et al., 2024). Her score on the conflict factor was 35 and on the avoidance factor was 14, resulting in a total score of 49.

Both Jason and Christina completed the Conflict Tactics Scale Short Form (Straus & Douglas, 2004) to assess for intimate partner violence. Neither reported any physical or sexual aggression (mild or severe) although both endorsed frequent bidirectional verbal aggression in their relationship.

5.5.3 *BFI Sessions*

Christina chose to attend the BFI sessions in person. She met with Dr. Kelly Smith, a clinical psychologist within the VA's PTSD Clinical Team. Dr. Smith began by asking Christina to describe how she and Jason had met and become a couple, how much she knew about Jason's trauma history, and how she saw his PTSD symptoms manifesting at home. Christina described the trajectory of their relationship and said that she did not know much at all about what Jason had experienced during deployment. Regarding his symptoms, she said

> What I notice most is how touchy he is. He didn't used to be that way, but now the switch can just flip in an instant, over nothing! Over something so small. The other day I was thinking about rearranging our bedroom, just moving where the bed is in the space. So I had scooted it against another wall just to see, and he came home from work and I called him up to look. He started just yelling at me, saying it was a stupid idea and why would I do something like that without asking him about it. I told him it was just a small thing but he was really mad. Then other times I can tell he's in his head about stuff, like he'll just be quiet. And I don't really ask about that because I feel like if he wanted to talk to me about it he would.

Dr. Smith normalized that irritability is a common symptom that patients with PTSD experience, and that it can be quite impactful in their relationships. She also noted that Christina was noticing subtle symptoms that Jason was experiencing; when Christina could "tell he's in his head about stuff" even without him sharing details with her, it was possible that he was experiencing intrusive memories about a trauma.

Dr. Smith reviewed Christina's SORTS responses. Christina had rated anger-related items as much more frequent and bothersome than avoidance-related items, which is common and aligned with the symptoms she had described as being most impactful in her and Jason's relationship. Dr. Smith asked for clarification as to how the endorsed accommodation behaviors looked in daily life: for instance, Christina had rated item #1 ("Avoid [Jason] because of his/her irritable or angry mood") highly in terms of both frequency and distress.

Dr. Smith: "Can you describe what that looks like for you, avoiding Jason because of his irritable or angry mood?"

Christina: "I just know when to steer clear, like I can tell when he's got his little storm cloud over his head and it's not a good idea to get in his space. So if he comes downstairs in a mood like that, I'll just make sure I'm somewhere else in the house. If he's in the kitchen, I'm up in the bedroom. If he's in the TV room, I'm in the kitchen. I don't ask him questions, and I try to be super quiet because if I like bang a cabinet or something he's going to lose it. So I'm just trying to minimize anything with him, like no talking, kind of not even being where he can see or hear me, just let him do his thing."

In the review of SORTS items, Dr. Smith also relied on what she had learned from Christina earlier in the session about Jason's PTSD symptoms, as well as on her clinical expertise, to probe some possible areas of accommodation that Christina had not endorsed. For example, Christina had rated item #3 ("Cancel or rearrange plans or social activities because [Jason] did not want to do them?") as a 0 for frequency. Dr. Smith asked about this, and Christina replied "Well I said never because I never make those kinds of plans anymore, so there's nothing to cancel. I just know he's never going to do those things, and it ends up embarrassing me when I have to back out or show up alone. I think people have also stopped asking me because it was just never actually happening, my friends knew we'd never come."

Following the review of the SORTS, Dr. Smith segued into reviewing the different possible symptoms of PTSD, highlighting those that Christina had observed and noting that several symptoms (e.g., persistent negative emotions, detachment from others) can be less obviously trauma-related and therefore sometimes feel personal to FMs. Christina agreed that she has often felt hurt that Jason doesn't want to go on dates with her or go out with a group of their friends, stating that it sometimes felt like Jason was no longer interested in spending time with her.

Dr. Smith provided an overview of the rationale for and components of CPT, the treatment that Jason had selected. As part of the description of addressing "stuck points" (negative cognitions, which may be specific to the trauma event or more global), she provided examples to help illustrate the point.

Dr. Smith: "So after a trauma, a person might start thinking things like 'It's all my fault that this happened,' or 'I'm a bad person, I don't deserve to have good things in my life anymore.'"

Christina: "Jason wouldn't say things like that, he's super confident. Like, he's almost arrogant. He's kind of like, 'I'm the best, no one can touch me.' It's just hard to imagine him ever saying stuff like that, about being not awesome."

Dr. Smith: "So it sounds like Jason is someone who projects a lot of confidence in himself out in the world – when I'm mentioning these stuck points, they aren't things that the person necessarily would say aloud to someone else, and the person might not really even have fully realized they have this new way of looking at things. It's an internal process, and there can actually be a lot of shame around these thoughts, because if you think about it, 'I'm bad' or 'It's my fault' are pretty dark things to believe. And of course I don't know for sure what Jason's stuck points are – they might be different from the examples I gave! But we believe that these kinds of shifts in thinking are in play for pretty much everyone with PTSD."

After discussing CPT, Dr. Smith and Christina moved to talk about how Christina could provide practical and emotional support to Jason as he proceeded in treatment. Christina reported that Jason had plenty of space and privacy to complete his homework assignments, as she worked standard office hours during the week whereas he was frequently home during the day. She reported that he did not need help getting to appointments (he saw his provider virtually) or being on time for them. Therefore, the majority of this portion of the session was devoted to ways to demonstrate emotional support. Christina reported that she had been enthusiastic about Jason seeking care at the VA when he first shared that he was going to be seen but that she had not followed up or asked any questions since he had begun attending appointments regularly. Therefore, she and Dr. Smith role-played an interaction with Jason where Christina could mention the BFI session and also offer praise for Jason's choice to pursue treatment. Christina noted that she appreciated the opportunity to practice her wording prior to talking with Jason.

The session concluded with Dr. Smith returning to the topic of accommodation. She discussed with Christina the possible value of beginning to make more social plans as a couple; outings together had the potential to be intrinsically rewarding to Jason, and these experiences and situations would also provide natural exposure opportunities. They role-played how Christina might introduce the idea of making social plans and discussed what type of plan might be best to start with (i.e., a weeknight dinner at a familiar restaurant with one other couple, as opposed to attending a crowded sporting event in person). Dr. Smith also recommended that should Jason decline to attend at the last minute, Christina calmly attend without him.

5.5.4 Session Two

The following week, Christina returned for the second BFI session.

Dr. Smith: "Welcome back, it's very nice to see you again. How have things been over this past week? What have you been thinking about related to what we discussed in the last session?"

Christina: "It was so weird, you know how we were talking last time about how sometimes after trauma people can think 'I'm no good' or whatever? And I said that Jason would never feel that way, he's so overconfident? Well on Tuesday I got home from work and he wasn't in the living room, wasn't out in the garage. Finally I went up to the bedroom and he's in there lying in bed. And it was like 5pm! I said 'Hon, what are you doing, are you feeling okay?' And he just started talking about how he's feeling upset about some of the stuff that happened while he was in Iraq, just thinking about some of the things he did and it's weighing on him. And it was so surprising to me, I've definitely never seen him like that. At one point he got kind of teary."

Dr. Smith: "Wow, that sounds like a pretty new side of Jason for you to see. How did you react to what he was sharing with you?"

Christina: "Well I was thinking of what you'd said in the session, like I think I would have been way more freaked out if you hadn't told me about that stuff. So I just said 'I know you did the best you could over there. I'm here if you ever want to talk, but it's also really good that you're seeing someone at the VA and can be talking to them.' And he agreed with that."

Dr. Smith: "That's great, it sounds like you reacted with compassion and openness, and made it clear that it was okay to share those feelings with you. And you also reinforced his treatment-seeking! You did a fantastic job thinking on your feet."

Following this update, Dr. Smith asked if Christina had discussed the BFI session with Jason at any point during the prior week, and Christina replied that she had mentioned it to him right away when she got home after Session 1. Their discussion was brief but she conveyed to Jason that she had found the information useful and that she was happy to support him. Dr. Smith also asked if Christina had made any progress on the plan to reduce accommodation. Christina reported that, to her surprise, Jason had been willing to make plans to go out with their neighbors. The four of them had gone to a local diner for brunch over the weekend. Jason had seemed on edge as they were leaving the house and Christina had worried that he would back out at the last minute, but in the end, they made it and the group had a nice meal. Christina reported that it was the first such activity they'd done as a couple in months, and she was looking forward to planning another outing soon.

5.5.5 *Outcome*

Jason completed 12 sessions of CPT over approximately 16 weeks. His PCL-5 score decreased from a baseline of 39 to 20, a reliable reduction in PTSD symptoms.

Christina attended both BFI sessions in a timely manner. Approximately, 1 month after the second session, she completed the SORTS again. Her scores were 23 for the conflict factor and 3 for the avoidance factor, resulting in a total score of 26; this was a notable decrease from her baseline scores. During a follow-up phone call from Dr. Smith, Christina reported that she and Jason had continued to go out socially, both as a couple and in slightly larger groups. She also reported that his irritability had improved and that she, in turn, was speaking up more within their relationship. She had also entirely stopped arranging her schedule around Jason's moods and availability and was enjoying the freedom to participate in various hobbies. She thanked Dr. Smith for allowing her to attend the BFI sessions and expressed gratitude for the treatment that Jason had received at the VA.

5.6 Conclusion

The BFI is a brief, adjunctive family-inclusive intervention that is appropriate for combination with a range of TFTs. It has been designed to be highly feasible for FMs to attend and maybe a comfortable alternative to dyadic treatment for patients who desire more autonomy or privacy in their treatment sessions. The BFI is also likely an intervention that clinicians without extensive experience in couples or family treatments can comfortably deliver, thereby making family-inclusive treatment available to a greater number of patients and families. The BFI has preliminary evidence of benefit with regard to patients' retention in individual TFT and is grounded in well-established theory and empirical work in PTSD. The intervention requires further testing to establish robust effect size estimates and clear evidence of moderators and mechanisms. Continued work on adjunctive family-inclusive interventions for PTSD and other disorders, as part of offering a range of family-inclusive services to meet the needs of diverse patients, FMs, and systems, is necessary.

References

Becker, C. B., Zayfert, C., & Anderson, E. (2004). A survey of psychologists' attitudes towards and utilization of exposure therapy for PTSD. *Behaviour Research and Therapy, 42*(3), 277–292. https://doi.org/10.1016/S0005-7967(03)00138-4

Bernardy, N. C., Hamblen, J. L., Friedman, M. J., Ruzek, J. I., & McFall, M. E. (2011). Implementation of a posttraumatic stress disorder mentoring program to improve treatment services. *Psychological Trauma: Theory, Research, Practice, and Policy, 3*(3), 292–299. https://doi.org/10.1037/a0024847

Bovin, M. J., Marx, B. P., Weathers, F. W., Gallagher, M. W., Rodriguez, P., Schnurr, P. P., & Keane, T. M. (2016). Psychometric properties of the PTSD Checklist for Diagnostic and Statistical Manual of Mental Disorders–Fifth Edition (PCL-5) in veterans. *Psychological Assessment, 28*(11), 1379–1391. https://doi.org/10.1037/pas0000254

Brewin, C. R., Andrews, B., & Valentine, J. D. (2000). Meta-analysis of risk factors for posttraumatic stress disorder in trauma-exposed adults. *Journal of Consulting and Clinical Psychology, 68*(5), 748–766. https://doi.org/10.1037/0022-006X.68.5.748

Evans, L., Cowlishaw, S., & Hopwood, M. (2009). Family functioning predicts outcomes for veterans in treatment for chronic posttraumatic stress disorder. *Journal of Family Psychology, 23*(4), 531–539. https://doi.org/10.1037/a0015877

Fernando, M., Fite, R., & Thompson-Hollands, J. (2024). Brief family involvement enhances veteran homework quality during trauma-focused psychotherapy. *Psychological Trauma: Theory Research, Practice, and Policy*. Advance online publication. https://doi.org/10.1037/tra0001678

Foa, E., Hembree, E. A., Rothbaum, B. O., & Rauch, S. (2019). *Prolonged exposure therapy for PTSD: Emotional processing of traumatic experiences – Therapist guide* (2nd ed.). Oxford University Press.

Fredman, S. J., Vorstenbosch, V., Wagner, A. C., Macdonald, A., & Monson, C. M. (2014). Partner accommodation in posttraumatic stress disorder: Initial testing of the Significant Others' Responses to Trauma Scale (SORTS). *Journal of Anxiety Disorders, 28*(4), 372–381. https://doi.org/10.1016/j.janxdis.2014.04.001

Fredman, S. J., Beck, J. G., Shnaider, P., Le, Y., Pukay-Martin, N. D., Pentel, K. Z., Monson, C. M., Simon, N. M., & Marques, L. (2017). Longitudinal associations between PTSD symptoms and dyadic conflict communication following a severe motor vehicle accident. *Behavior Therapy, 48*(2), 235–246. https://doi.org/10.1016/j.beth.2016.05.001

Fredman, S. J., Macdonald, A., Monson, C. M., Dondanville, K. A., Blount, T. H., Hall-Clark, B. N., Fina, B. A., Mintz, J., Litz, B. T., Young-McCaughan, S., Hancock, A. K., Rhoades, G. K., Yarvis, J. S., Resick, P. A., Roache, J. D., Le, Y., Wachen, J. S., Niles, B. L., McGeary, C. A., et al. (2020). Intensive, multi-couple group therapy for PTSD: A nonrandomized pilot study with military and veteran dyads. *Behavior Therapy, 51*(5), 700–714. https://doi.org/10.1016/j.beth.2019.10.003

Frueh, B. C., Cusack, K. J., Grubaugh, A. L., Sauvageot, J. A., & Wells, C. (2006). Clinicians' perspectives on cognitive-behavioral treatment for PTSD among persons with severe mental illness. *Psychiatric Services, 57*(7), 1027–1031. https://doi.org/10.1176/ps.2006.57.7.1027

Galovski, T., & Lyons, J. A. (2004). Psychological sequelae of combat violence: A review of the impact of PTSD on the veteran's family and possible interventions. *Aggression and Violent Behavior, 9*(5), 477–501. https://doi.org/10.1016/S1359-1789(03)00045-4

Gutner, C. A., Gallagher, M. W., Baker, A. S., Sloan, D. M., & Resick, P. A. (2016). Time course of treatment dropout in cognitive-behavioral therapies for posttraumatic stress disorder. *Psychological Trauma: Theory, Research, Practice, and Policy, 8*, 115–121. https://doi.org/10.1037/tra0000062

Harvey, A. G., & Gumport, N. B. (2015). Evidence-based psychological treatments for mental disorders: Modifiable barriers to access and possible solutions. *Behaviour Research and Therapy, 68*, 1–12. https://doi.org/10.1016/j.brat.2015.02.004

Howard, K. P., Spoont, M. R., Polusny, M. A., Eftekhari, A., Rosen, C. S., & Meis, L. A. (2023). The role of symptom accommodation in trauma-focused treatment engagement and response. *Journal of Traumatic Stress, 36*(3), 524–536. https://doi.org/10.1002/jts.22912

Johnson, S. M. (2002). *Emotionally focused couple therapy with trauma survivors: Strengthening attachment bonds*. Guilford.

Karlin, B. E., & Cross, G. (2014). From the laboratory to the therapy room: National dissemination and implementation of evidence-based psychotherapies in the U.S. Department of Veterans Affairs Health Care System. *American Psychologist, 69*(1), 19–33. https://doi.org/10.1037/a0033888

Lambert, J. E., Engh, R., Hasbun, A., & Holzer, J. (2012). Impact of posttraumatic stress disorder on the relationship quality and psychological distress of intimate partners: A meta-analytic review. *Journal of Family Psychology, 26*, 729–737. https://doi.org/10.1037/a0029341

Marshall, E. M., & Kuijer, R. G. (2017). Weathering the storm? The impact of trauma on romantic relationships. *Current Opinion in Psychology, 13*, 54–59. https://doi.org/10.1016/j.copsyc.2016.04.013

Meis, L. A., Schaaf, K. W., Erbes, C. R., Polusny, M. A., Miron, L. R., Schmitz, T. M., & Nugent, S. M. (2013). Interest in partner-involved services among veterans seeking mental health care from a VA PTSD clinic. *Psychological Trauma: Theory, Research, Practice, and Policy, 5*(4), 334–342. https://doi.org/10.1037/a0028366

Meis, L. A., Noorbaloochi, S., Hagel Campbell, E. M., Erbes, C. R., Polusny, M. A., Velasquez, T. L., Bangerter, A., Cutting, A., Eftekhari, A., Rosen, C. S., Tuerk, P. W., Burmeister, L. B., & Spoont, M. R. (2019). Sticking it out in trauma-focused treatment for PTSD: It takes a village. *Journal of Consulting and Clinical Psychology, 87*(3), 246–256. https://doi.org/10.1037/ccp0000386

Monson, C. M., & Fredman, S. J. (2012). *Cognitive-behavioral conjoint therapy for PTSD: Harnessing the healing power of relationships*. Guilford Press.

Monson, C. M., Schnurr, P. P., Stevens, S. P., & Guthrie, K. A. (2004). Cognitive–behavioral couple's treatment for posttraumatic stress disorder: Initial findings. *Journal of Traumatic Stress, 17*(4), 341–344. https://doi.org/10.1023/B:JOTS.0000038483.69570.5b

Monson, C. M., Fredman, S. J., & Dekel, R. (2010). Posttraumatic stress disorder in an interpersonal context. In J. G. Beck (Ed.), *Interpersonal processes in the anxiety disorders: Implications for understanding psychopathology and treatment* (pp. 179–208). American Psychological Association. https://doi.org/10.1037/12084-007

Morland, L. A., Macdonald, A., Grubbs, K. M., Mackintosh, M. A., Monson, C. M., Glassman, L. H., Becker, J., Sautter, F., Buzzella, B., Wrape, E., Wells, S. Y., Rooney, B. M., & Glynn, S. (2019). Design of a randomized superiority trial of a brief couple treatment for PTSD. *Contemporary Clinical Trials Communications, 15*, 100369. https://doi.org/10.1016/j.conctc.2019.100369

Nelson Goff, B. S., & Smith, D. B. (2005). Systemic traumatic stress: The couple adaptation to traumatic stress model. *Journal of Marital and Family Therapy, 31*(2), 145–157. https://doi.org/10.1111/j.1752-0606.2005.tb01552.x

Ozer, E. J., Best, S. R., Lipsey, T. L., & Weiss, D. S. (2008). Predictors of posttraumatic stress disorder and symptoms in adults: A meta-analysis. *Psychological Trauma: Theory, Research, Practice, and Policy, S*, 3–36. https://doi.org/10.1037/1942-9681.S.1.3

Renshaw, K. D., Rodrigues, C. S., & Jones, D. H. (2008). Psychological symptoms and marital satisfaction in spouses of Operation Iraqi Freedom veterans: Relationships with spouses' perceptions of veterans' experiences and symptoms. *Journal of Family Psychology, 22*(4), 586–594. https://doi.org/10.1037/0893-3200.22.3.586

Renshaw, K. D., & Campbell, S. B. (2011). Combat veterans' symptoms of PTSD and partners' distress: The role of partners' perceptions of veterans' deployment experiences. *Journal of Family Psychology, 25(6), 953–962.* https://doi.org/10.1037/a0025871

Renshaw, K. D., Allen, E. S., Carter, S. P., Markman, H. J., & Stanley, S. M. (2014). Partners' attributions for service members' symptoms of combat-related posttraumatic stress disorder. *Behavior Therapy, 45*(2), 187–198. https://doi.org/10.1016/j.beth.2013.10.005

Renshaw, K. D., Allen, E. S., Fredman, S. J., Giff, S. T., & Kern, C. (2020). Partners' motivations for accommodating posttraumatic stress disorder symptoms in service members: The reasons for accommodation of PTSD scale. *Journal of Anxiety Disorders, 71*, 102199. https://doi.org/10.1016/j.janxdis.2020.102199

Resick, P. A., Monson, C. M., & Chard, K. M. (2016). *Cognitive processing therapy for PTSD: A comprehensive manual*. Guilford Press.

Reuman, L., & Thompson-Hollands, J. (2020). Family accommodation in PTSD: Proposed considerations and distinctions from the established transdiagnostic literature. Clinical Psychology: Science and Practice, Advance online publication. https://doi.org/10.1111/cpsp.12375

Reuman, L., & Thompson-Hollands, J. (2023). Women veterans' attitudes toward family involvement in PTSD treatment: A mixed-methods examination. *Psychological Services, 20*(4), 770–779. https://doi.org/10.1037/ser0000707

Sautter, F. J., Glynn, S. M., Cretu, J. B., Senturk, D., & Vaught, A. S. (2015). Efficacy of structured approach therapy in reducing PTSD in returning veterans: A randomized clinical trial. *Psychological Services, 12*(3), 199–212. https://doi.org/10.1037/ser0000032

Sayer, N. A., Friedemann-Sanchez, G., Spoont, M., Murdoch, M., Parker, L. E., Chiros, C., & Rosenheck, R. (2009). A qualitative study of determinants of PTSD treatment initiation in veterans. *Psychiatry, 72*(3), 238–255. https://doi.org/10.1521/psyc.2009.72.3.238

Sayers, S. L., Farrow, V. A., Ross, J., & Oslin, D. W. (2009). Family problems among recently returned military veterans referred for a mental health evaluation. *Journal of Clinical Psychiatry, 70*(2), 163–170. https://doi.org/10.4088/JCP.07m03863

Schumm, J. A., Fredman, S. J., Monson, C. M., & Chard, K. M. (2013). Cognitive-behavioral conjoint therapy for PTSD: Initial findings for operations enduring and Iraqi Freedom male combat veterans and their partners. *The American Journal of Family Therapy, 41*, 277–287. https://doi.org/10.1080/01926187.2012.701592

Sippel, L. M., Watkins, L. E., Pietrzak, R. H., Hoff, R., & Harpaz-Rotem, I. (2019). Heterogeneity of posttraumatic stress symptomatology and social connectedness in treatment-seeking military veterans: A longitudinal examination. *European Journal of Psychotraumatology, 10*(1), 1–12. https://doi.org/10.1080/20008198.2019.1646091

Sloan, D. M., & Marx, B. P. (2019). *Written exposure therapy for PTSD: A brief treatment approach for mental health professionals* (1st ed.). American Psychological Association.

Straus, M. A., & Douglas, E. M. (2004). A short form of the revised conflict tactics scales, and typologies for severity and mutuality. *Violence and Victims, 19*(5), 507–520. https://doi.org/10.1891/vivi.19.5.507.63686

Taft, C. T., Watkins, L. E., Stafford, J., Street, A. E., & Monson, C. M. (2011). Posttraumatic stress disorder and intimate relationship problems: A meta-analysis. *Journal of Consulting and Clinical Psychology, 79(1), 22–33.* https://doi.org/10.1037/a0022196

Thompson-Hollands, J., Kerns, C. E., Pincus, D. B., & Comer, J. S. (2014). Parental accommodation of child anxiety and related symptoms: Range, impact, and correlates. *Journal of Anxiety Disorders, 28*(8), 765–773. https://doi.org/10.1016/j.janxdis.2014.09.007

Thompson-Hollands, J., Abramovitch, A., Tompson, M. C., & Barlow, D. H. (2015). A randomized clinical trial of a brief family intervention to reduce accommodation in obsessive-compulsive disorder: A preliminary study. *Behavior Therapy, 46*(2), 218–229. https://doi.org/10.1016/j.beth.2014.11.001

Thompson-Hollands, J., Burmeister, L. B., Rosen, C. S., O'Dougherty, M., Erickson, E. P. G., & Meis, L. A. (2021a). Veterans with poor PTSD treatment adherence: Exploring their loved ones' experience of PTSD and understanding of PTSD treatment. *Psychological Services, 18*(2), 216–226. https://doi.org/10.1037/ser0000389

Thompson-Hollands, J., Lee, D. J., & Sloan, D. M. (2021b). The use of a brief family intervention to reduce dropout among veterans in individual trauma-focused treatment: A randomized controlled trial. *Journal of Traumatic Stress, 34*(4), 829–839. https://doi.org/10.1002/jts.22680

Thompson-Hollands, J., Strage, M., DeVoe, E. R., Beidas, R. S., & Sloan, D. M. (2021c). Development of a brief adjunctive intervention for family members of veterans in individual PTSD treatment. *Cognitive and Behavioral Practice, 28*(2), 193–209. https://doi.org/10.1016/j.cbpra.2020.06.007

Thompson-Hollands, J., Rando, A. A., Stoycos, S. A., Meis, L. A., & Iverson, K. M. (2022). Family involvement in PTSD treatment: Perspectives from a nationwide sample of Veterans Health Administration clinicians. *Administration and Policy in Mental Health and Mental Health Services Research, 49*(6), 1019–1030. https://doi.org/10.1007/s10488-022-01214-1

Thompson-Hollands, J., Lunney, C. A., Sloan, D. M., Wiltsey Stirman, S., & Schnurr, P. P. (2023). Treatment length and symptom improvement in prolonged exposure and present-centered therapy for posttraumatic stress disorder: Comparing dose–response and good-enough level models in two manualized interventions. *Journal of Consulting and Clinical Psychology, 91*(10), 596–605. https://doi.org/10.1037/ccp0000834

Thompson-Hollands, J., Lee, D. J., Allen, E. S., Pukay-Martin, N. D., Campbell, S. B., Chard, K. M., Renshaw, K. D., Sprunger, J. G., Birkley, E., Dondanville, K. A., Litz, B. T., Riggs, D. S., Schobitz, R. P., Yarvis, J. S., Young-McCaughan, S., Keane, T. M., Peterson, A. L., Monson, C. M., & Fredman, S. J. (2024). The Significant Others' Responses to Trauma Scale (SORTS): Applying factor analysis and item response theory to a measure of PTSD symptom accommodation. *European Journal of Psychotraumatology, 15*(1), Article 2353530. https://doi.org/10.1080/20008066.2024.2353530.

US Department of Veterans Affairs. (2015). *A Veteran's guide to talking with kids about PTSD*. https://www.mirecc.va.gov/visn16/talking-with-kids-about-ptsd-guide.asp

Weathers, F. W., Litz, B. T., Keane, T. M., Palmieri, P. A., Marx, B. P., & Schnurr, P. P. (2013). *The PTSD Checklist for DSM-5 (PCL-5)*. www.ptsd.va.gov

Weissman, N., Batten, S. V., Rheem, K. D., Wiebe, S. A., Pasillas, R. M., Potts, W., Barone, M., Brown, C. H., & Dixon, L. B. (2018). The effectiveness of emotionally focused couples therapy with veterans with PTSD: A pilot study. *Journal of Couple & Relationship Therapy, 17*(1), 25–41. https://doi.org/10.1080/15332691.2017.1285261

Chapter 6
Community-Based Family-Inclusive Treatment

Kim T. Mueser and Cheryl Y. S. Foo

6.1 Introduction

Serious mental illness (SMI; also referred to as severe mental illness) is defined as a psychiatric disorder in adulthood that leads to significant and persistent impairment in the ability to function in areas such as social relationships, role functioning (e.g., work, school, parenting), and self-care/independent living (Ruggeri et al., 2000). In high-resource countries, the disability associated with SMI often makes individuals eligible for benefit programs, such as Social Security Supplemental Income and Social Security Disability Income in the United States. Estimates of the prevalence of SMI generally range between 3% and 6% of the adult population (Kessler et al., 2001; Ruggeri et al., 2000), with the most common disorders being schizophrenia (and schizoaffective disorder), bipolar disorder, and treatment-refractory major depression.

Prior to the discovery of psychotropic medications in the 1950s (e.g., antipsychotics, antidepressants, mood stabilizers), most individuals with SMI spent the rest of their lives in institutions following the onset of their disorder, receiving "custodial" care that often had iatrogenic effects (i.e., actually worsening their disorder) (Wing & Brown, 1979). Psychotropic medications were found to be remarkably effective at reducing prominent symptoms such as hallucinations, delusions, depression, and mood swings, with maintenance pharmacological treatment also useful for preventing relapses. Although these medications usually did not eliminate all

K. T. Mueser (✉)
Center for Psychiatric Rehabilitation, Boston University, Boston, MA, USA
e-mail: mueser@bu.edu

C. Y. S. Foo
Psychosis Clinical and Research Program, Department of Psychiatry, Massachusetts General Hospital/Harvard Medical School, Boston, MA, USA

L. Reuman, J. Thompson-Hollands (eds.), *Enhancing CBT Through Family and Peer Engagement*, CBT: Science Into Practice, https://doi.org/10.1007/978-3-031-74838-7_6

psychiatric symptoms and often had limited effects on improving psychosocial functioning, their widespread use in the 1960s enabled the vast majority of long-term institutionalized persons with SMI to be discharged and treated in the community (Johnson, 1990), and for the locus of treatment for those who subsequently developed SMI to shift to the local community mental health center, with psychiatric hospitalization required only during relatively brief periods of the disorder when the person presented a threat to oneself or others.

Following the deinstitutionalization movement, which began in the 1960s and continued for several decades thereafter, the daily life challenges of people with SMI in the community became readily apparent, such as difficulty coping with persistent symptoms, vulnerability to relapses and rehospitalizations, alcohol and drug use problems, housing instability and homelessness, limited social networks and support, and unemployment. Although pharmacological treatment has continued to be a mainstay in the treatment of SMI, a broad range of psychosocial interventions have been developed, tested, and shown to be effective at improving functioning in the decades that followed (Miklowitz et al., 2021; Solmi et al., 2023). Family intervention for SMI was one of the first psychosocial treatments to be developed, studied, and widely implemented because of the importance of the family. SMI frequently develops during early adulthood (and sometimes earlier, in late adolescence) (Kirkbride et al., 2006), when individuals are still living at home or in the process of establishing adult roles. Families play a critical role in getting a loved one into treatment and providing needed financial, practical, and emotional support (Oluwoye et al., 2020). Thus, with many persons with SMI living at home and many others dependent on family support, families are a natural potential ally for treatment providers at community mental health centers.

Collaboration with families is a crucial service component in the comprehensive community-based treatment of SMI. In the next section, we will provide the rationale for working with families of persons with SMI and the aims of family work. We will then describe the essential components of family collaboration and provide examples of family intervention programs.

6.2 Guide to Family Involvement in Community Mental Health Settings

This section begins with a brief discussion of the importance of families in the lives of people with SMI and the rationale for family intervention. The goals of family intervention are then considered, which are broadly aimed at developing a strong collaborative relationship between the family and treatment team. The remainder of the section provides practical guidance on engaging families in treatment and working with them, including strategies for ensuring that families feel welcomed and valued by clinicians at the mental health center, and family intervention methods and programs.

6.2.1 Why Is Family Work Important?

Family members provide vital emotional, financial, and practical help to their loved ones with SMI, and therefore, they are in an important position to play a role in their loved ones' treatment and to contribute to their long-term well-being. In addition to the deep concern families have about a member with SMI and their knowledge and understanding of how their relative is functioning, there are other reasons why treatment providers should strive to develop collaborative relationships with families. We describe several of these reasons below.

One important reason for family intervention is to reduce the stress and conflict among family members, which can have deleterious effects on the course of SMI. There is abundant evidence showing that stress is related to both the onset and course of schizophrenia and other SMIs, including the precipitation of symptom relapses and rehospitalizations (Lecomte et al., 2019; Nuechterlein & Dawson, 1984; Zubin & Spring, 1977). Stressful family relationships, as reflected by relatives' attitudes and behaviors such as criticism, hostility, and emotional overinvolvement toward a member (referred to as "expressed emotion"), have been found to be an especially potent predictor of symptom relapses in individuals living with or in frequent contact with family (Amaresha & Venkatasubramanian, 2012; Hooley, 2007). Reducing stressful communication styles in family members in order to improve the course of SMI is one of the first rationales for developing family intervention programs (Anderson et al., 1980; McFarlane, 2016), with evidence showing improvements in it mediate the benefits of family treatment (Miklowitz et al., 2009).

Stressful relationships can occur in any family, but the impact of SMI can take an extraordinarily high toll on the family. SMI frequently develops in late adolescence or early adulthood, challenging family members' expectations of the eventual independence of their offspring and thrusting them back into the role of caregivers and often treatment coordinators (Ferrara et al., 2021). When the mental illness develops somewhat later in life, such as between the ages of 25 and 45, the disruptive effects on the person's ability to fulfill role functions such as work or parenting, and the challenge to the partner's expectations of shared equity and responsibility, can be a major strain on even the strongest relationship (Häfner, 1986; Mueser & Brunette, 2003). The experience of having a family member with SMI can be extremely difficult as family members grapple to understand perplexing symptoms such as hallucinations or delusions, debilitating depression, the grandiosity and irresponsibility associated with mania, and the profound demotivation characteristic of negative symptoms (Lefley, 1996; Mueser et al., 1996). Aside from contributing to conflict among family members and negative communication styles, the net consequence of the financial and emotional burden of mental illness is a major reduction in the health and well-being of relatives (Dyck et al., 1999; Prasad et al., 2024), further increasing overall family stress. Family intervention can reduce the burden of caring for or having a close relationship with a member with SMI.

Related to the high stress experienced by relatives caring for a member with SMI is the lack of information most families have about major mental illnesses, often including information about their own family member's treatment. Families and clients alike have a strong desire for factual information about the nature of the mental illness in the affected member (e.g., diagnosis, characteristic symptoms, course), its treatment (e.g., medications, psychosocial interventions), and how to cope with it (Mueser et al., 1992; Sung et al., 2004). Yet historically, mental health professionals have been reluctant to engage and educate family members about mental illness, including providing basic information about a relative's treatment, preferring instead to invoke "patient confidentiality" as the reason for not providing information and leaving families in the dark. There is now compelling evidence that most people with SMI want their relatives involved in their treatment (Cohen et al., 2013), and mental health professionals have come to recognize that families are potentially important allies in the treatment of SMI, provided that they receive sufficient education about the disorder and have the opportunity for input into the treatment team. Thus, family education is critical to the ability of families to assist with monitoring the course of a relative's illness and supporting their adherence to treatment recommendations.

In addition to the important role of supporting a loved one's involvement in treatment for SMI, a final reason for working with families is that they know their relative better than anyone else. Instilling hope for change and setting and pursuing personal goals is recognized as crucial to engaging and motivating clients to learn about their disorder and becoming active participants in their own treatment (Mueser et al., 2002, 2015), including individual, group, and family formats. Families can be invaluable to the process of helping a relative identify personal goals and collaborating with them and the treatment team to pursue them.

6.2.2 The Goals of Family Work

Based on the importance of the family in the lives of people with SMI and their potential role as allies of treatment providers, family intervention is guided by several practical goals, including to:

- Develop a collaborative relationship with the family that includes providing members with easy access to the treatment team
- Provide education about the family member's mental illness, the principles of treatment, and treatment options
- Involve the family in shared decision-making about treatment options
- Facilitate the ability of the family to monitor the member's mental illness and support their adherence to treatment recommendations
- Reduce stress in the family
- Enlist the support of the family for the member's treatment and recovery goals, as well as a relapse prevention plan

6.2.3 *Family Intervention Approaches*

Over the past 40 years, numerous family intervention models for SMI have been developed, standardized, and empirically tested in community mental health centers and similar settings (Anderson et al., 1980; Barrowclough & Tarrier, 1992; Falloon et al., 1984; Kuipers et al., 2002; McFarlane, 2002; Miklowitz, 2010; Mueser & Glynn, 1999; Weisman de Mamani et al., 2021). Although there are differences between these (and other) programs in terms of format (single-family vs. multifamily groups), length (e.g., several months to 2 years or more), and specific techniques used (e.g., skills training, cognitive behavioral therapy, adapted family systems), they all share a common set of assumptions about working with families, employ many of the same methods, and are consistent with the goals of family work listed in the previous section. These commonalities across multiple empirically validated family programs for SMI more generally inform contemporary approaches to working with families that may not follow a specific family intervention model but are nevertheless effective. Common assumptions about family work are summarized in Table 6.1.

For treatment providers to work effectively with families, community mental health centers and clinicians need to be receptive and inviting to concerned family members. In the next section, we describe the characteristics of mental health agencies that foster collaboration with families. In the section following that, we review common therapeutic methods used in family intervention for SMI.

6.2.4 *Family-Friendly Agency*

Creating a "family-friendly agency" involves both establishing positive attitudes among staff about working with families and modifying policies and practices to facilitate engaging families. In some agencies with a history or culture of disparaging or pathologizing families or ignoring or discouraging families from trying to

Table 6.1 Important assumptions about working with families of people with serious mental illness

Families do not cause serious mental illness.
Living with or having frequent contact with a loved one with serious mental illness can be very stressful for family members.
Most people with serious mental illness want their family involved in their treatment, and most relatives are interested in meeting with and learning from treatment providers.
Family members have a right to basic information about their loved one's mental illness and treatment options.
True collaboration with families is a two-way street, with families learning from treatment providers and vice versa.
Family collaboration improves the course of serious mental illness, reduces stress in the family, and enhances the effectiveness of the treatment team.

learn more about their loved one's condition, significant changes from "usual practice" are required. Negative attitudes of mental health practitioners about families need to be countered with education that corrects common misconceptions, establishes the importance of families to clients, and reviews evidence of the beneficial effects of family intervention on the course of SMI. Outdated and unsupported beliefs of staff members about families causing SMI need to be corrected with more contemporary biopsychosocial models recognize the contribution of multiple factors to the onset and course of SMI (Mueser et al., 2013; Nuechterlein & Dawson, 1984). Staff members need to understand that the high levels of stress in families of people with SMI are more often the consequence of the SMI, not the cause. Finally, staff need to understand the high level of contact between clients and family members means that relatives are often in an ideal position to support a loved one's involvement in treatment and work toward their personal goals.

Education of staff members about the value and role of involving families should be complemented by direct exposure to family members with the "lived experience" of coping with a relative with SMI, such as through local advocacy organizations such as the National Alliance on Mental Illness (NAMI). Education and learning about the experiences of family members can begin to shift staff members toward more positive attitudes about families. However, the greatest change in attitude occurs gradually over time, when agencies become more receptive to engaging and working with families, and staff members are able to witness firsthand the benefits of collaborating with families.

Changes in routine practice and policy may also be needed to accommodate family involvement in treatment. At the most basic level, it is important that client contact with family members be inquired about as a standard part of the assessment. Clients who have regular contact with their families (e.g., 4 hours/week or more) should be engaged in a discussion with a clinician about the nature and benefits of involving their family members in their treatment, including different options for family involvement (e.g., family psychoeducation, involvement in treatment planning, etc.). The level of family involvement can be dynamic and changing, based on an ongoing process of shared decision-making and motivational enhancement with the client and the family, with a shared understanding and agreement of the bounds of confidentiality and the importance of family involvement during a crisis. When significant family stress is present, this stress should be normalized, and clients should be informed that reducing family stress is an important goal of family work.

To engage as many critical family members as possible, clinicians need to accommodate the availability of working members and have flexible schedules that permit some evening hours each week. It is also important that the mental health agency be welcoming and pleasant to family members who may accompany a loved one to treatment meetings or participate in family intervention. There should be convenient parking for families who drive. The waiting rooms should have ample and comfortable seating. Information brochures on display that are freely available to families can also be appealing, such as information about mental illness and family advocacy organizations (e.g., National Alliance on Mental Illness (USA)).

6.2.5 *Family Intervention Methods*

Who is considered "family" and who most often participates in family intervention? The word "family" is used loosely to refer to any person with a strong, enduring, caring (but non-professional) relationship with the client. Most often, family includes individuals who are related to the client, such as their family of origin (e.g., parents, siblings), spouse/partner, offspring, or extended family (e.g., grandparents). However, family can also include anyone else who has a close relationship with the client, such as a friend or community/religious leader (e.g., member of the clergy).

Individual meetings between the clinician and the client and family members are often useful for engaging families in family intervention. In such meetings, the clinician can explain the nature of family intervention (including issues related to confidentiality), explore possible individual goals for family work, and address any concerns the person might have. Following individual (or small family group) preparation for family work, most family sessions are conducted with both the client and other family members together for several reasons. First, by working with the whole family, the clinician can model effective communication skills for interacting with the client, which can be especially helpful for families with a member with schizophrenia, with whom communication can sometimes be especially challenging. Second, considering that both clients and relatives benefit from learning much of the same information and skills for managing a mental illness, conducting sessions with the whole family is more efficient than having separate sessions. Third, working with the whole family assuages concerns clients may have about being left out of family sessions and is consistent with respect for client autonomy, empowerment, and involvement in treatment decision-making, as reflected in the expression used among disability rights advocates, "Nothing about us without us."

A variety of different methods are commonly used in family intervention for SMI, including psychoeducation, relapse prevention planning, communication skills training, and treatment planning and review. Each of these methods is described briefly below.

6.2.5.1 Psychoeducation

Psychoeducation is the process of providing information to people about a psychiatric disorder and its treatment in a personally meaningful way that enables them to relate and apply it to their own experience. Educational handouts describing pertinent information are frequently employed when providing psychoeducation, with three to ten sessions devoted to covering the material (Glynn & Gingerich, 2020; Miklowitz, 2010; Mueser & Glynn, 1999). Table 6.2 provides an outline of common topics covered.

Psychoeducation is an interactive process with both the clinician and family members actively involved in talking about the information provided. A variety of different clinical methods are employed. One useful strategy early in the process is

Table 6.2 Common curriculum for family psychoeducation about psychiatric disorders

Name of psychiatric disorder and how diagnosis is established
Prevalence, onset, and possible courses of disorder
Characteristic symptoms and related problems
Theories about the etiology of the disorder (such as the stress-vulnerability model)
Challenging negative attitudes and beliefs about mental illness (stigma)
Pharmacological treatment: Names and types of medication Clinical effects (e.g., symptom reduction, relapse prevention) Side effects
Psychosocial treatment: Psychotherapy and counseling (e.g., cognitive behavioral therapy) Illness self-management programs Family psychoeducation Psychiatric rehabilitation (e.g., supported employment, cognitive remediation, social skills training)
The role of the family and other social supports Monitoring symptoms and supporting adherence to treatment recommendations Supporting and collaborating on personal recovery and treatment goals Practicing and reinforcing skills learnt at home
Peer support
Relapse prevention and crisis planning

for the clinician to connote the client and family members as "experts" in the experience of the mental illness and to tap that expertise when providing information about the disorder. For example:

Clinician: Today we are going to be talking about John's diagnosis, which is schizophrenia. While I know a lot about schizophrenia that I will be sharing with you, John, since you have been diagnosed with this disorder you are an expert in it. I was hoping that you would be willing to share some of your experiences with it when we are talking together today. Would that be OK?

John: Sure.

Connoting the client and family members as having expertise in the mental illness has the effect of "leveling the playing field" in terms of the special status and authority of the clinician, meaning that everyone in the family session has something of value to contribute and learn from everyone else.

The clinician frequently uses questions during psychoeducation to draw family members into the discussion, to get their perspectives, and to help them relate information to their own experiences. For example, continuing with the vignette above:

Clinician: I'd like to begin by learning a little about your understanding of the diagnosis of schizophrenia. John, what does schizophrenia mean to you?

To help family members relate information to their own lives, the clinician can ask specific questions. For example, continuing with the same session of the vignette, after eliciting family members' understanding of schizophrenia and then providing basic information (e.g., it is a relatively common psychiatric disorder diagnosed based on a clinical interview):

Clinician: One common symptom of schizophrenia is hallucinations. Hallucinations are hearing, seeing, feeling, smelling, or tasting something when nothing is actually present. The most common type of hallucinations are auditory hallucinations, frequently voices that are talking, which are often heard through the ears like ordinary voices of people. John, have you ever had auditory hallucinations or any other type of hallucinations?

Asking questions can also help the clinician check on family members' understanding of information or review previously covered information. For example, continuing with the vignette in the next family session:

Clinician: During our last meeting we talked about the diagnosis of schizophrenia. I'd like to spend a couple of minutes reviewing what we covered. What are some of the common symptoms of schizophrenia?

The clinician could then reinforce accurate answers, correct inaccurate ones, and provide supplementary information as needed.

During psychoeducation, it is useful to adopt language that is familiar and comfortable to family members to facilitate comprehension and integrate it into their understanding. For example, if family members referred to when the person developed the mental illness as when they had a "nervous breakdown," the clinician could adopt this term when referring to this time period.

When providing psychoeducation, the clinician should be direct, open, and honest in presenting information to the family while being respectful of differences members may have about certain points. Above all, the clinician should avoid arguments and attempts to persuade family members and instead seek common ground among all members that are the basis for working together. For example, many people with a diagnosis of schizophrenia do not believe they have the disorder (Amador & Johnson, 2000). However, in most cases, this is not an impediment to educating the family about schizophrenia (including the client) and teaching the rudiments of how to manage it collaboratively with the treatment team. Continuing the vignette with the client, John:

Clinician: John, you have been given a diagnosis of schizophrenia. What does the term schizophrenia mean to you?

John: Well, I don't believe I have schizophrenia. I believe I have a grave mental disability, but I don't think it's schizophrenia.

Clinician: Thank you for sharing that, John. Can you tell us what you think having a grave mental disability means to you?

Last, psychoeducation is a long-term process. Although basic information about mental illness and its treatment is generally provided over several psychoeducation sessions, not all the information can be completely absorbed and understood by family members. As family psychoeducation is ideally the beginning of a collaborative relationship with the family, the clinician should look for opportunities later when working together to review pertinent information that members may have forgotten or not fully understood.

6.2.5.2 Relapse Prevention Planning

This intervention method is frequently incorporated into family psychoeducation sessions following a basic introduction to mental illness and its treatment. Psychiatric disorders such as schizophrenia, bipolar disorder, and major depression usually have an episodic course, with the severity of symptoms varying over time and sometimes requiring hospitalization to protect the person from harm to self or others. A relapse is defined as the return of symptoms (in someone who was asymptomatic) or the worsening of symptoms (in someone with persistent symptoms) accompanied by a deterioration in functioning (e.g., social relationships, work/school, and self-care), which sometimes necessitate hospitalization. Because of the disruptive effects of relapses on both clients and relatives, the prevention of relapses is an important treatment priority.

Teaching families how to prevent relapses is based on the fact that relapses usually occur gradually over a period of several weeks, when symptoms begin to reappear or worsen, but before they have a major impact on functioning. This provides a "window of opportunity" for intervening early and preventing a full relapse. The small changes in symptoms and behavior that precede a full-blown relapse are called *early warning signs*. Although the early warning signs of relapse may include subtle changes such as a mild worsening of depression, increased avoidance of others, reduced personal hygiene, or attention difficulties, if family members are attuned to the client's specific signs, action can be taken to avoid a full relapse.

A relapse prevention plan can usually be completed in one family session. Standard worksheets for recording a relapse prevention plan are available (Glynn & Gingerich, 2020; Stanley & Brown, 2008). After the clinician explains the nature of relapses and the concept underlying a relapse prevention plan, they lead a discussion with the family about the most recent relapse the client had in order to pinpoint a few specific early warning signs of relapse, which are recorded on the worksheet. The clinician then leads a discussion aimed at developing a plan for responding to the early warning signs of a relapse. Although the plan may have several elements in it (e.g., how family members will talk with each other about their concerns), the most critical component is a specific plan to contact the treatment team and arrange a special appointment for the client with the prescribing clinician. Temporary increases in medication dosage in response to early warning signs are highly effective at preventing full-blown relapses and rehospitalizations. After the plan has been recorded on the worksheet, it is helpful for the clinician to lead the family in a role-play of using the plan to respond to the member's early warning signs of relapse.

6.2.5.3 Communication and Problem-Solving Skills Training

Psychoeducation about mental illness and its treatment is often effective at reducing family conflict and tension related to a lack of understanding of the disorder. Some families, however, continue to experience significant levels of stress and conflict, which may be evident in how they communicate with each other. For example, family members may be highly critical and negative, emotionally overinvolved and intrusive (Butzlaff & Hooley, 1998), talk in a vague and unclear way that is hard to follow, or have difficulty solving any problems together (Hoff et al., 2005; Sitskoorn et al., 2004). These families can benefit from training in communication skills.

Communication skills training is aimed at improving the clarity and effectiveness of verbal exchanges among family members (Miklowitz, 2010; Mueser & Glynn, 1999; Weisman de Mamani et al., 2021). Basic principles of effective communication include making clear "I" statements (as opposed to blaming "you" statements); behavioral specificity when referring to pleasing, upsetting, or desired behaviors; clear verbal feeling statements regarding positive and negative feelings; and keeping communications brief and to the point. Communication skills are taught using the principles of social skills training (modeling the skill, engaging family members in role-plays of the skill, providing positive and corrective feedback followed by additional role plays, and home assignments to practice skills outside of the session). Training over four to eight sessions usually focuses on teaching a core set of basic skills for improving communication, such as expressing positive feelings, making positive requests, expressing negative feelings, and active listening.

After bolstering communication skills, many families also benefit from five to ten sessions learning problem-solving skills. For example, families are often taught a six-step sequence for solving problems together, including (1) discuss and then define the problem to everyone's satisfaction, (2) brainstorm possible solutions, (3) identify advantages and disadvantages of each solution, (4) choose the best solution or combination of solutions, (5) make an action plan to implement the solution(s), and (6) set a date to carry out the plan and do additional problem-solving as needed (e.g., around potential obstacles to carrying out the plan).

6.2.5.4 Treatment Planning and Review

Many clients want and appreciate the involvement of their families in treatment planning and review of progress toward their goals. The nature and logistics of family involvement in treatment planning depend on the preferences of the client and the practicalities of family members' and the treatment team members' schedules. The most common way of involving the family is for the client and treatment team to draw up a draft of the treatment plan, which can then be reviewed with the family (with the client present) by the family clinician. Family members can then provide feedback and raise any questions or concerns they have. This approach maintains the primacy of the client in determining the treatment plan while allowing input from the family.

The most important objective of this collaboration with families is to obtain their support for the treatment plan, which can be critical to its success. Collaborative treatment planning can provide important opportunities to educate families about specific treatment goals and gain their support. For example, families may not understand the important role of medication in the treatment of SMI, and their lack of support for this can result in lower medication adherence, leading to more severe symptoms, relapses, and rehospitalizations.

For another example of the importance of family support for treatment goals, many clients want to work or resume their education (Westcott et al., 2015). Some families, however, are concerned that pursuing such goals may be too stressful and lead to relapses. These families often remember the onset of their relative's mental illness occurring during a hectic period in the person's life, such as in college or beginning a new job, and the ensuing chaos associated with understanding the problem and getting their relative into treatment. They are afraid that the challenges of a new job or returning to school will precipitate a relapse of symptoms and prefer to keep things as stable and unchanging as possible. The clinician can address these common concerns by first explaining that the client now has many relapse prevention tools in place that they did not previously have (e.g., medication, coping skills, relapse prevention plan). Second, the clinician can explain that having something meaningful and purposeful to do with one's time can actually reduce stress in people with SMI. For example, research shows that when people with SMI get a competitive job, their risk of rehospitalization is decreased (Hoffmann et al., 2014). This can both address family member's concerns about this important goal, get their support and help for the client's pursuit of it, and enlighten the family's understanding of the meaning and importance of personal recovery to people with SMI (Glynn et al., 2006).

Although having families weigh in on the tentative treatment plan is suitable for many clients, some may benefit from greater involvement by their family. Clients with more severe symptoms or cognitive impairments may have difficulty identifying and articulating treatment goals with the treatment team. As family members know their loved ones best (e.g., their past interests and talents, current strengths), their involvement in helping identify treatment goals can be invaluable. This can be accomplished by the family clinician conducting several meetings with the family aimed at exploring potential goals the client might benefit from working toward. These goals can then be communicated by the family clinician to the treatment team and incorporated into the treatment plan.

6.3 Research Evidence

Family intervention for people with SMI is one of the most widely studied psychosocial treatments for this population, with evidence supporting its effectiveness dating back over 40 years. Numerous meta-analyses have been conducted demonstrating the beneficial impact of family intervention on outcomes of SMI, with most research focusing on individuals with a psychotic disorder (Bighelli et al., 2021; Claxton et al., 2017; McDonagh et al., 2022; Rodolico et al., 2022; Solmi et al., 2023). The most widely studied outcome has been 1- to 2-year relapse (or rehospitalization) rates following treatment, with family intervention having a consistent effect on reducing relapses compared with usual care (e.g., medication, case management). For example, Rodolico et al. (2022) conducted a meta-analysis including 90 randomized controlled trials of 11 different family intervention models with 10,340 families and reported a significant effect on reducing relapse rates across the different treatment approaches, with minimal differences between models. In addition to reducing relapse rates, family intervention has also been shown to improve psychosocial functioning and quality of life (Claxton et al., 2017).

Meta-analyses focusing on family intervention for specific populations of people with SMI have shown similarly positive effects. Like research on psychotic disorders, meta-analyses have shown that family intervention is effective at reducing relapse rates in individuals with bipolar disorder (Baruch et al., 2018; Miklowitz et al., 2021). Also similar to findings from the broader population of psychotic disorders, meta-analyses have shown that family intervention is effective at reducing relapses and improving quality of life and functioning in people recovering from a first episode of non-affective psychosis (Camacho-Gomez & Castellvi, 2020).

Research on the effects of family intervention for SMI has not been limited to high-resource countries but has been extended to also include lower- and middle-income countries (LMICs), with adaptations made to the family treatment models as needed (e.g., task-shifting with psychoeducation provided by trained lay persons rather than mental health professionals). Considering the importance of the family for getting a loved one into treatment in general and the even greater centrality of the family in many LMICs, it is no surprise that family intervention approaches were among the first psychosocial interventions to be adapted and implemented in these countries. A recent review of 27 studies of family intervention in LMICs found that adaptations of family programs were associated with reductions in relapse rates and symptom severity and improvements in illness self-management, self-care, and social functioning (Morillo et al., 2022). Thus, the evidence base supporting the effectiveness of family intervention for SMI is strong.

6.4 Clinical Considerations for Diverse Identities

Individuals with SMI and their families from minoritized identities face inequalities in access to services, quality of care, and treatment outcomes. Generally, systematically disadvantaged groups such as racial-ethnic minorities and immigrant communities experience more complex and adverse pathways to care (e.g., involvement with police and involuntary hospital admissions) (Commander et al., 1999), poorer treatment engagement, and higher dropout rates (Oluwoye et al., 2018), and enhanced exposure to social stressors and systemic racism that are linked to worse recovery outcomes (DeLuca et al., 2022) compared with non-Hispanic white counterparts. In a study of community-based treatment settings for early psychosis in the United States, non-Hispanic Black families were less likely than non-Hispanic white families to receive family psychoeducation (Oluwoye et al., 2018, 2020). These concerning disparities underscore the need for culturally responsive family engagement and interventions to ensure that evidence-based SMI care is relevant and acceptable for diverse families.

Culture has a meaningful impact on the way individuals with SMI and their families understand their illness experience, how their symptoms present, and how they engage in help-seeking and ongoing care (Leavey et al., 2004; Lewis-Fernández et al., 2014). An individual's cultural orientation can be said to be made up of multiple intersecting aspects of their social backgrounds, including their age, class, race/ethnicity, gender, sexual orientation, faith, language, occupation, and, for some, immigration and acculturation. Cultural adaptations of evidence-based treatments accommodate and align language, cultural beliefs, norms, practices, and value systems, as well as context and access to resources to the client's cultural background and community (Bernal et al., 2009). Meta-analyses have found that cultural adaptations of psychosocial interventions for mental illness in general (Griner & Smith, 2006; Hall et al., 2016) and for schizophrenia specifically (Degnan et al., 2018) are effective, with moderate effect sizes for primary outcomes comparable with non-adapted interventions in Western populations. Furthermore, evidence shows that individuals with SMI are more likely to engage in and stay in treatment and have higher treatment satisfaction when cultural beliefs and explanatory models are considered (Naeem et al., 2023; Rathod et al., 2010).

There are several general principles for providing culturally competent care. First, given the important role of culture in making meaning of illness and treatment response, a cultural formulation in routine evaluation (e.g., using the standardized Diagnostic and Statistical Manual of Mental Disorders, 5th Edition: Cultural Formulation Interview) (Aggarwal & Lewis-Fernández, 2020) (www.psychiatry.org/practice/dsm/dsm5/online-assessment-measures) could be a best practice in identifying the role of culture in a person's and family's experience of illness and care.

Second, providers should maintain a stance of "cultural humility" that demonstrates genuine respect and appreciation for the family and client's role as experts on their own experience and its interpretation, as well as how it might be influenced by and interact with the perceptions of their cultural community. Inherent in practicing cultural humility is recognizing, understanding, and challenging personal biases that may affect service delivery or lead to therapeutic misattunement. For instance, instead of legitimizing the medical approach as "truth" or "knowledge," it is important that providers cultivate a view that it is one of many ways of understanding mental illness and recovery. Differing views within families and between family and the treatment team can be approached with respect and curiosity while simultaneously presenting empirical evidence for clinical care as an alternative explanation.

Finally, providers should consider culturally acceptable ways of delivering information, including using the client's and family's preferred language. In the United States, federally funded health services are mandated to provide free, competent interpretation to individuals with limited English proficiency to ensure that care is of the same quality and availability as those of English-language services. Other reviews/guidelines outline best practices for integrating and working with qualified interpreters in SMI care (OnTrack New York, 2019). Where stigma toward receiving mental health care is high for some racial minorities, agencies can consider supplementing regular services with more community outreach and education congruent with the social structures of certain cultures and conducting services such as group meetings/educational workshops for families in non-stigmatizing and accessible community spaces (Chien & Lee, 2010). Multifamily group formats can also be used to benefit multicultural communities (Lefley, 1988; McFarlane, 2002). For instance, in a psychoeducational support group for families with SMI (Lefley, 1988), the long-standing program brought together mostly ethnic minority families with immigrant histories who shared common stressors (e.g., intergenerational conflict, stigma toward mental health) that affected caring for their loved ones with SMI. A group format can be advantageous to sharing mutual experiences, information, and strategies, as well as providing longer term community orinter-family support (McFarlane, 2002).

6.4.1 Family Psychoeducation in Diverse Populations

This section discusses the robustness of family psychoeducation across various cultures and contexts, highlighting considerations such as different cultures' role in the family and how they might affect shared decision-making in SMI treatment. We will focus primarily on clinical considerations for racial-ethnic minorities, with special attention to the role of religion and spirituality within family work for SMI, while acknowledging that other intersectional and diverse families exist and require nuanced, tailored approaches.

Psychoeducational interventions for families with a relative with SMI have been the most frequently employed with valuable culturally appropriate adaptations, demonstrating effectiveness in diverse populations and a broad range of contexts (Degnan et al., 2018; Lefley, 2012; Maura & Weisman de Mamani, 2017; Stuart & Schlosser, 2009). For example, Culturally Informed Therapy for Schizophrenia

(Weisman de Mamani et al., 2021), based on behavioral family therapy (Falloon et al., 1984; Miklowitz, 2010), is effective in reducing patient symptom severity (Weisman de Mamani et al., 2014) and decreasing caregiver burden (Weisman de Mamani & Suro, 2016). Multifamily group therapy (MFGT) based on a psychoeducational model has been frequently adapted for families of Asian, Hispanic/Latine, and African-American descent (Maura & Weisman de Mamani, 2017). One randomized controlled trial of MFGT culturally adapted for Mexican Americans found it to be more effective than standard MFGT or usual treatment in reducing rates of medication nonadherence and hospitalization (Kopelowicz et al., 2012). In these culturally adapted family psychoeducation interventions, the core principles of family psychoeducation as described earlier remain operative, where families gain basic knowledge of SMI and their treatment, skills to identify and solve problems that arise while caring for a relative with SMI and collaborate on how to support the relative's mental health and psychosocial rehabilitation.

Crucially, in family-oriented, collectivistic cultures commonly present in racial-ethnic minorities, the important role of the family can be capitalized on, aligning the goals of family psychoeducation with the strengths and values of the family. In several cultural groups, "family/relationship primacy" where interdependent social ties or family relationships are prioritized over individual needs (Schwartz et al., 2010), (e.g., "familism" among Hispanics/Latine communities (Campos et al., 2014); "communalism" among communities of African descent (Wallace & Constantine, 2005); filial piety in Asian communities (Yeh & Bedford, 2004)), are regarded as cultural values. These cultural priorities may come up against modern Western values of individual autonomy and individuation that are typically practiced in treatment decision-making, and which might be a source of conflict for families with intergenerational acculturation differences and culture-specific expectations (e.g., expecting younger members not to question their elders) (Chien & Chan, 2004). In these cases, it is important to clarify the client's and family's views and expectations of individuation and autonomy, especially with regard to treatment decision-making and recovery, and to negotiate differences to find shared concerns or goals (e.g., client's well-being, gaining employment). For traditional families, an eye toward preserving and strengthening family cohesion is important, with consideration of how to respect both the family hierarchy of decision-making and patient autonomy. Extended family members (e.g., grandparents) and community leaders can also be important figures to involve in family psychoeducation as they may be part of the client and family's support system and crucial to establishing trust with, as well as have the power to influence decision-making about recovery and treatment.

Additionally, providers can consider adaptations to the content and delivery of family psychoeducation depending on cultural groups; we discuss the role of religion and spirituality as an example of a key cultural construct that influences how families make sense of and cope with the SMI experience. Strong religious interpretations of mental illness can be normative in some cultures, such as viewing psychosis as a spiritual experience or having mental illness as a "possession," fulfillment of ancestral curses, or punishment for past sins. Families may also be inclined to use traditional healing or religious practices/systems as a solution to mental health difficulties. These interpretations should be elicited and discussed respectfully within the context of current scientific information (e.g., biopsychosocial model and explanations of evidence-based treatment approaches). Finding a "common ground" with "folk concepts" of mental illness and traditional and spiritual healing practices may look like building on a common desire to support the client and the family. These beliefs and practices are not necessarily in conflict, but can complement psychiatric treatment, where providers can highlight the ways in which they can be a strength, effective coping strategy, and support system for the family. Family psychoeducation can purposefully incorporate and reinforce spiritual or religious practices and coping methods, such as the use of traditional healers, religious texts, prayer, or worship (Habib et al., 2015). Engaging with religious and spiritual communities as a way of developing culturally competent care, as well as involving spiritual advisors or religious leaders, could bridge knowledge gaps and find points of convergence between clinical and faith-based/spiritual goals.

6.5 Case Vignette

The following case vignette provides an illustration of family psychoeducation for psychotic disorders in an outpatient community mental health setting, incorporating discussions on key goals of family work and cultural considerations. Names and identifying details have been modified to preserve anonymity.

During her second year of college, Jenn, a 19-year-old Chinese American woman, began having difficulties with her coursework and spending less time with friends and more time alone. She became paranoid that her classmates and teachers were gossiping about her behind her back and spreading rumors that she had done "bad things," which worsened and gradually led to suicidal ideation. Jenn was hospitalized after describing some of her concerns to her mother and diagnosed with schizoaffective disorder.

Following her hospitalization, she began participating in a coordinated specialty care (CSC) program for first-episode psychosis (Heinssen et al., 2014), including pharmacotherapy and weekly cognitive behavioral-based psychotherapy, which helped her better manage and cope with her psychotic symptoms, depression, and suicidal ideation over time. Although family psychoeducation was a recommended component of Jenn's CSC program, her father, Tony, and her mother, Ling, both immigrants from China more than two decades ago, were initially ambivalent about having "family therapy" as they felt Jenn was already getting better and that they did not need "mental health treatment" themselves. This ambivalence and their beliefs about family intervention are common in many families across cultures, and it is important for the family clinician (or program director) to dispel any misperceptions about the nature and goals of family work early when engaging them in treatment. The clinician explained to Tony and Ling how their involvement could help support Jenn's recovery and prevent hospitalizations and oriented them to what would be covered in family sessions (see Table 6.2).

The first few family sessions, which included Jenn and her parents, focused on helping Tony and Ling have a better understanding of psychosis, Jenn's symptoms, the role of antipsychotic medication in treatment, and how to support Jenn's personal recovery goals. After her hospitalization, Jenn moved back from her college dormitory to live with her parents and attended classes virtually. As her symptoms improved with treatment, she felt more confident and ready to go back to live independently at college and have more frequent, in-person interactions with her friends at school.

Jenn's parents were not supportive of her plan to return to college, as they were worried about her having a relapse and its impact on her academic goals, considering that she first developed her psychotic disorder while away at college. Tony expressed concerns to Jenn in a session in a harsh tone, saying, "You are not thinking clearly, and as parents, we know what is best for you," and made clear their expectations that Jenn would continue to live at home. Jenn was silent but tearful. The clinician first validated and normalized Tony and Ling's fears about relapse and Jenn's ability to be independent as common concerns families of people with psychosis experience and acknowledged their desire for Jenn to stay well and succeed in school. The clinician then explained to her parents that Jenn was in a much better place to prevent a relapse of symptoms and rehospitalization and identified the tools that she now had for managing her mental illness, including taking medications, working hard in individual therapy to learn coping strategies for symptoms and stress, and having the support of her family and the treatment team. With the goal of getting Jenn's parents to support her goals of building independence and her friendships at school, the clinician guided the family in weighing the pros and cons of her staying at home versus returning to the college dormitory. With prompting from the clinician, Tony said he could understand that keeping Jenn "safe at home" also impeded her from moving on with her life and achieving independence, something which both parents hoped for Jenn in the long term.

After talking it over, Jenn and her family agreed that she would try living at the college for the next semester, but at the suggestion of the clinician, they also decided to develop a relapse prevention ("wellness") plan. The clinician explained the importance of developing this plan, including Jenn's anticipating stressors and how to prevent and cope with them, and how her parents could help her monitor early warning signs of relapse and take action to prevent a relapse (e.g., reaching out to the treatment team) if needed. Jenn identified common stressors that made her symptoms worse, such as during exams and when she is in a large group of people, and the strategies she could use to prevent and cope with these stressors. Jenn and her parents identified her early warning signs of her symptoms or mood worsening, including behaviors that her parents could observe. Jenn listed effective coping strategies she could use in the event of worsening symptoms and mood, and her parents found it helpful to know how they could remind her to practice using her coping skills without "nagging." Tony and Ling felt more comfortable with Jenn's decision to go back to live at college after they had developed the relapse prevention plan, which was printed out or saved on their phones by all three of them.

As this family conflict unfolded and resolved, the clinician noted how Jenn's father took over decision-making and had a strong opinion on what was best care for her in a way that conflicted with her personal recovery goals. This could be influenced by broader cultural considerations of gender roles, parenting behaviors, and parent-child dynamics. While still prioritizing key goals of family work and covering the core content of family psychoeducation (individualized to Jenn and her family's experiences), future work with the family could support more positive and effective communication, such as coaching Tony and Ling on how to express validation and support for Jenn's recovery goals, as well as coaching Jenn on assertive communication and how to express her needs and wants effectively. Multifamily group therapy and support could also be introduced in tandem with individual family psychoeducation to provide Jenn and her family with an opportunity to learn problem-solving skills and feel supported by other families with similar experiences of a loved one recovering from psychosis.

6.6 Conclusion

Family involvement and support are critical in the treatment and recovery of persons with SMI. Family support improves family members' and their relatives' understanding of SMI and shared decision-making about treatment options, reduces family stress, and equips families with knowledge and ways to support their relative's involvement in treatment progress toward personal goals. We outlined key considerations for community mental health centers to be open and engaging in involving families in the treatment of a loved one with SMI, as well as the "active ingredients" and core components of evidence-based family interventions, including family psychoeducation, communication and problem-solving skills training, relapse prevention planning, and treatment collaboration and review. We underscored the importance of practicing cultural competency and humility when working with diverse families to promote engagement and to enhance the effectiveness of family interventions. Recognizing the unique cultural understandings of mental illness and recovery, as well as culturally distinct family structures and processes, can inform modifications to the content, delivery, and therapeutic stance of family interventions for SMI. These strands were brought together in the final case vignette, which illustrated how family members can be effectively engaged and leveraged to support their loved ones' recovery.

References

Aggarwal, N. K., & Lewis-Fernández, R. (2020). An introduction to the cultural formulation interview. *Focus, 18*(1), 77–82. https://doi.org/10.1176/appi.focus.18103

Amador, X., & Johnson, A.-L. (2000). *I'm not sick, I don't need help! Helping the seriously mentally ill accept treatment: A practical guide for families and therapists*. Vida Press.

Amaresha, A. C., & Venkatasubramanian, G. (2012). Expressed emotion in schizophrenia: An overview. *Indian Journal of Psychological Medicine, 34*, 12–20. https://doi.org/10.4103/0253-7176.96149

Anderson, C. M., Hogarty, G. E., & Reiss, D. J. (1980). Family treatment of adult schizophrenic patients: A psycho-educational approach. *Schizophrenia Bulletin, 6*, 490–505. https://doi.org/10.1093/schbul/6.3.490

Barrowclough, C., & Tarrier, N. (1992). *Families of schizophrenic patients: Cognitive behavioural intervention*. Chapman & Hall.

Baruch, E., Pistrang, N., & Barker, C. (2018). Psychological interventions for caregivers of people with bipolar disorder: A systematic review and meta-analysis. *Journal of Affective Disorders, 236*, 187–198. https://doi.org/10.1016/j.jad.2018.04.077

Bernal, G., Jimenez-Chafey, M., & Domenech Rodriguez, M. M. (2009). Cultural adaptation of treatments: A resource for considering culture in evidence-based practice. *Professional Psychology: Research and Practice, 40*, 361–368. https://doi.org/10.1037/a0016401

Bighelli, I., Rodolico, A., García-Mieres, H., Pitschel-Walz, G., Hansen, W. P., Schneider-Thoma, J., Siafis, S., Wu, H., Wang, D., Salanti, G., Furukawa, T. A., Barbui, C., & Leucht, S. (2021). Psychosocial and psychological interventions for relapse prevention in schizophrenia: A systematic review and network meta-analysis. *Lancet Psychiatry, 8*, 969–980. https://doi.org/10.1016/S2215-0366(21)00243-1

Butzlaff, R. L., & Hooley, J. M. (1998). Expressed emotion and psychiatric relapse. *Archives of General Psychiatry, 55*, 547–552. https://doi.org/10.1001/archpsyc.55.6.547

Camacho-Gomez, M., & Castellvi, P. (2020). Effectiveness of family intervention for preventing relapse in first-episode psychosis until 24 months of follow-up: A systematic review with meta-analysis of randomized controlled trials. *Schizophrenia Bulletin, 46*, 98–109. https://doi.org/10.1093/schbul/sbz038

Campos, B., Ullman, J. B., Aguilera, A., & Schetter, C. D. (2014). Familism and psychological health: The intervening role of closeness and social support. *Cultural Diversity & Ethnic Minority Psychology, 20*, 191–201. https://doi.org/10.1037/a0034094

Chien, W.-T., & Chan, S. W. C. (2004). One-year follow-up of a multiple-family-group intervention for Chinese families of patients with schizophrenia. *Psychiatric Services, 55*, 1276–1284. https://doi.org/10.1176/appi.ps.55.11.1276

Chien, W. T., & Lee, I. Y. M. (2010). The schizophrenia care management program for family caregivers of Chinese patients with schizophrenia. *Psychiatric Services, 61*, 317–320.

Claxton, M., Onwumere, J., & Fornells-Ambrojo, M. (2017). Do family interventions improve outcomes in early psychosis? A systematic review and meta-analysis. *Frontiers in Psychology, 8*, 371. https://doi.org/10.3389/fpsyg.2017.00371

Cohen, A. N., Drapalski, A. L., Glynn, S. M., Medoff, D., Fang, L. J., & Dixon, L. B. (2013). Preferences for family involvement in care among consumers with serious mental illness. *Psychiatric Services, 64*, 257–263. https://doi.org/10.1176/appi.ps.201200176

Commander, M. J., Cochrane, R., Sashidharan, S. P., Akilu, F., & Wildsmith, E. (1999). Mental health care for Asian, black and white patients with non-affective psychoses: Pathways to the psychiatric hospital, in-patient and after-care. *Social Psychiatry and Psychiatric Epidemiology, 34*, 484–491. https://doi.org/10.1007/s001270050224

Degnan, A., Baker, S., Edge, D., Nottidge, W., Noke, M., Press, C. J., Husain, N., Rathod, S., & Drake, R. J. (2018). The nature and efficacy of culturally-adapted psychosocial interventions for schizophrenia: A systematic review and meta-analysis. *Psychological Medicine, 48*, 714–727. https://doi.org/10.1017/S0033291717002264

DeLuca, J. S., Novacek, D. M., Adery, L. H., Herrera, S. N., Landa, Y., Corcoran, C. M., & Walker, E. F. (2022). Equity in mental health services for youth at clinical high risk for psychosis: Considering marginalized identities and stressors. *Evidence-Based Practice in Child and Adolescent Mental Health, 7*, 176–197. https://doi.org/10.1080/23794925.2022.2042874

Dyck, D. G., Short, R. A., & Vitaliano, P. P. (1999). Predictors of burden and infectious illness in schizophrenia caregivers. *Psychosomatic Medicine, 61*, 411–419. https://doi.org/10.1097/00006842-199907000-00001

Falloon, I. R. H., Boyd, J. L., & McGill, C. W. (1984). *Family care of schizophrenia: A problem-solving approach to the treatment of mental illness*. Guilford Press.

Ferrara, M., Guloksuz, S., Mathis, W. S., Li, F., Lin, I.-H., Syed, S., Gallagher, K., Shah, J., Kline, E., Tek, C., Keshavan, M., & Srihari, V. H. (2021). First help-seeking attempt before and after psychosis onset: Measures of delay and aversive pathways to care. *Social Psychiatry and Psychiatric Epidemiology, 56*, 1359–1369. https://doi.org/10.1007/s00127-021-02090-0

Glynn, S. M., & Gingerich, S. (2020). *NAVIGATE family education manual* (Rev. ed.). http://navigateconsultants.org/2020manuals/family_2020.pdf

Glynn, S. M., Cohen, A. N., Dixon, L. B., & Niv, N. (2006). The potential impact of the recovery movement on family interventions for schizophrenia: Opportunities and obstacles. *Schizophrenia Bulletin, 32*, 451–463.

Griner, D., & Smith, T. B. (2006). Culturally adapted mental health intervention: A meta-analytic review. *Psychotherapy, 43*, 531–548. https://doi.org/10.1037/0033-3204.43.4.531

Habib, N., Dawood, S., Kingdon, D., & Naeem, F. (2015). Preliminary evaluation of culturally adapted CBT for psychosis (CA-CBTp): Findings from developing culturally-sensitive CBT project (DCCP). *Behavioural and Cognitive Psychotherapy, 43*, 200–208. https://doi.org/10.1017/S1352465813000829

Häfner, R. J. (1986). *Marriage and mental illness: A sex roles perspective*. Guilford Publications.

Hall, G. C. N., Ibaraki, A. Y., Huang, E. R., Marti, C. N., & Stice, E. (2016). A meta-analysis of cultural adaptations of psychological interventions. *Behavior Therapy, 47*, 993–1014. https://doi.org/10.1016/j.beth.2016.09.005

Heinssen, R. K., Goldstein, A. B., & Azrin, S. T. (2014). *Evidence-based treatments for first episode psychosis: Components of coordinated specialty care* [White paper]. National Institute of Mental Health. https://www.nimh.nih.gov/health/topics/schizophrenia/raise/evidence-based-treatments-for-first-episode-psychosis-components-of-coordinated-specialty-care

Hoff, A. L., Svetina, C., Maurizio, A. M., Crow, T. J., Spokes, K., & DeLisi, L. E. (2005). Familial cognitive deficits in schizophrenia. *American Journal of Medical Genetics Part B: Neuropsychiatric Genetics, 133B*, 43–49. https://doi.org/10.1002/ajmg.b.30120

Hoffmann, H., Jäckel, D., Glauser, S., Mueser, K. T., & Kupper, Z. (2014). Long-term effectiveness of supported employment: Five-year follow-up of a randomized controlled trial. *American Journal of Psychiatry, 171*, 1183–1190. https://doi.org/10.1176/appi.ajp.2014.13070857

Hooley, J. M. (2007). Expressed emotion and relapse of psychopathology. *Annual Review of Clinical Psychology, 3*, 329–352. https://doi.org/10.1146/annurev.clinpsy.2.022305.095236

Johnson, A. B. (1990). *Out of bedlam: The truth about deinstitutionalization*. Basic Books.

Kessler, R. C., Berglund, P. A., Bruce, M. L., Koch, J. R., Laska, E. M., Leaf, P. J., Manderscheid, R. W., Rosenheck, R. A., Walters, E. E., & Wang, P. S. (2001). The prevalence and correlates of untreated serious mental illness. *Health Services Research, 36*, 987–1007.

Kirkbride, J. B., Fearon, P., Morgan, C., Dazzan, P., Morgan, K., Tarrant, J., Lloyd, T., Holloway, J., Hutchinson, G., Leff, J. P., Mallett, R. M., Harrison, G. L., Murray, R. M., & Jones, P. B. (2006). Heterogeneity in incidence rates of schizophrenia and other psychotic syndromes: Findings from the 3-center AeSOP study. Archives of General Psychiatry, 63, 250–258. https://doi.org/10.1001/archpsyc.63.3.250.

Kopelowicz, A., Zarate, R., Wallace, C. J., Liberman, R. P., Lopez, S. R., & Mintz, J. (2012). The ability of multifamily groups to improve treatment adherence in Mexican Americans with schizophrenia. *Archives of General Psychiatry, 69*, 265–273. https://doi.org/10.1001/archgenpsychiatry.2011.135

Kuipers, L., Leff, J., & Lam, D. (2002). *Family work for schizophrenia: A practical guide* (2nd ed.). Gaskell.

Leavey, G., Gulamhussein, S., Papadopoulos, C., Johnson-Sabine, E., Blizard, B., & King, M. (2004). A randomized controlled trial of a brief intervention for families of patients with a first episode of psychosis. *Psychological Medicine, 34*, 423–431. https://doi.org/10.1017/s0033291703001594

Lecomte, T., Potvin, S., Samson, C., Francoeur, A., Hache-Labelle, C., Boucher, J., Bouchard, M., Gagné, S., & Mueser, K. T. (2019). Predicting and preventing symptom onset in schizophrenia-A metareview of current empirical evidence. *Journal of Abnormal Psychology, 128*, 840–854. https://doi.org/10.1037/abn0000447

Lefley, H. P. (1988). Training professionals to work with families of chronic patient. *Community Mental Health Journal, 24*, 338–357. https://doi.org/10.1007/BF00752476

Lefley, H. P. (1996). *Family caregiving in mental illness*. Sage.

Lefley, H. P. (2012). Cross-cultural perspective of family psychoeducation. *Psychiatric Annals, 42*, 236–240. https://doi.org/10.3928/00485713-20120606-07

Lewis-Fernández, R., Aggarwal, N. K., Bäärnhielm, S., Rohlof, H., Kirmayer, L. J., Weiss, M. G., Jadhav, S., Hinton, L., Alarcón, R. D., Bhugra, D., Groen, S., van Dijk, R., Qureshi, A., Collazos, F., Rousseau, C., Caballero, L., Ramos, M., & Lu, F. (2014). Culture and psychiatric evaluation: Operationalizing cultural formulation for DSM-5. *Psychiatry, 77*, 130–154. https://doi.org/10.1521/psyc.2014.77.2.130

Maura, J., & Weisman de Mamani, A. (2017). Culturally adapted psychosocial interventions for schizophrenia: A review. *Cognitive and Behavioral Practice, 24*, 445–458. https://doi.org/10.1016/j.cbpra.2017.01.004

McDonagh, M. S., Dana, T., Kopelovich, S. L., Monroe-DeVita, M., Blazina, I., Bougatsos, C., Grusing, S., & Selph, S. S. (2022). Psychosocial interventions for adults with schizophrenia: An overview and update of systematic reviews. *Psychiatric Services, 73*, 299–312. https://doi.org/10.1176/appi.ps.202000649

McFarlane, W. R. (2002). *Multifamily groups in the treatment of severe psychiatric disorders*. Guilford Press.

McFarlane, W. R. (2016). Family interventions for schizophrenia and the psychoses: A review. *Family Process, 55*, 460–482. https://doi.org/10.1111/famp.12235

Miklowitz, D. J. (2010). *Bipolar disorder: A family-focused treatment approach* (2nd ed.). Guilford Press.

Miklowitz, D. J., Axelson, D. A., George, E. L., Taylor, D. O., Schneck, C. D., Sullivan, A. E., Dickinson, L. M., & Birmaher, B. (2009). Expressed emotion moderates the effects of family-focused treatment for bipolar adolescents. *Journal of the American Academy of Child & Adolescent Psychiatry, 48*, 643–651. https://doi.org/10.1097/CHI.0b013e3181a0ab9d

Miklowitz, D. J., Efthimiou, O., Furukawa, T. A., Scott, J., McLaren, R., Geddes, J. R., & Cipriani, A. (2021). Adjunctive psychotherapy for bipolar disorder: A systematic review and component network meta-analysis. *JAMA Psychiatry, 78*, 141–150. https://doi.org/10.1001/jamapsychiatry.2020.2993

Morillo, H., Lowry, S., & Henderson, C. (2022). Exploring the effectiveness of family-based interventions for psychosis in low- and middle-income countries: A systematic review. *Social Psychiatry and Psychiatric Epidemiology, 57*, 1749–1769. https://doi.org/10.1007/s00127-022-02309-8

Mueser, K. T., & Brunette, M. F. (2003). Schizophrenia-spectrum disorders. In D. K. Snyder & M. A. Whisman (Eds.), *Treating difficult couples* (pp. 137–158). Guilford Press.

Mueser, K. T., & Glynn, S. M. (1999). *Behavioral family therapy for psychiatric disorders* (2nd ed.). New Harbinger.

Mueser, K. T., Bellack, A. S., Wade, J. H., Sayers, S. L., & Rosenthal, C. K. (1992). An assessment of the educational needs of chronic psychiatric patients and their relatives. *British Journal of Psychiatry, 160*, 674–680. https://doi.org/10.1192/bjp.160.5.674

Mueser, K. T., Webb, C., Pfeiffer, M., Gladis, M., & Levinson, D. F. (1996). Family burden of schizophrenia and bipolar disorder: Perceptions of relatives and professionals. *Psychiatric Services, 47*, 507–511. https://doi.org/10.1176/ps.47.5.507

Mueser, K. T., Corrigan, P. W., Hilton, D., Tanzman, B., Schaub, A., Gingerich, S., Essock, S. M., Tarrier, N., Morey, B., Vogel-Scibilia, S., & Herz, M. I. (2002). Illness management and recovery: A review of the research. *Psychiatric Services, 53*, 1272–1284. https://doi.org/10.1176/appi.ps.53.10.1272

Mueser, K. T., Deavers, F., Penn, D. L., & Cassisi, J. (2013). Psychosocial treatments for schizophrenia. *Annual Review of Clinical Psychology, 9*, 465–497. https://doi.org/10.1146/annurev-clinpsy-050212-185620

Mueser, K. T., Penn, D. L., Addington, J., Brunette, M. F., Gingerich, S., Glynn, S. M., Lynde, D. W., Gottlieb, J. D., Meyer-Kalos, P., Cather, C., McGurk, S. R., Saade, S., Robinson, D. G., Schooler, N. R., Rosenheck, R. A., & Kane, J. M. (2015). The NAVIGATE program for first episode psychosis: Rationale, overview, and description of psychosocial components. *Psychiatric Services, 66*, 680–690. https://doi.org/10.1176/appi.ps.201400413

Naeem, F., Naz, S., & Phiri, P. (2023). Culturally adapted CBT for psychosis. In J. A. Díaz-Garrido, R. Zúñiga, H. Laffite, & E. Morris (Eds.), *Psychological interventions for psychosis: Towards a paradigm shift* (pp. 125–139). Springer Nature. https://doi.org/10.1007/978-3-031-27003-1_7

Nuechterlein, K. H., & Dawson, M. E. (1984). A heuristic vulnerability/stress model of schizophrenic episodes. *Schizophrenia Bulletin, 10*, 300–312. https://doi.org/10.1093/schbul/10.2.300

Oluwoye, O., Stiles, B., Monroe-DeVita, M., Chwasiak, L., McClellan, J. M., Dyck, D. G., Cabassa, L. J., & McDonell, M. G. (2018). Racial-ethnic disparities in first-episode psychosis treatment outcomes from the RAISE-ETP study. *Psychiatric Services, 69*, 1138–1145. https://doi.org/10.1176/appi.ps.201800067

Oluwoye, O., Stokes, B., Stiles, B., Monroe-DeVita, M., & McDonnell, M. G. (2020). Understanding differences in family engagement and provider outreach in New Journeys: A coordinated specialty care program for first episode psychosis. *Psychiatry Research, 291*, 113286. https://doi.org/10.1016/j.psychres.2020.113286

OnTrack New York. (2019). *Delivering culturally competent care: OnTrackNY guide*. Retrieved September 26 from http://nyculturalcompetence.org/what-matters-most/delivering-culturally-competent-care-ontrackny-guide/

Prasad, F., Hahn, M. K., Chintoh, A. F., Remington, G., Foussias, G., Rotenberg, M., & Agarwal, S. M. (2024). Depression in caregivers of patients with schizophrenia: A scoping review. *Social Psychiatry and Psychiatric Epidemiology, 59*, 1–23. https://doi.org/10.1007/s00127-023-02504-1

Rathod, S., Phiri, P., Kingdon, D., & Gobbi, M. (2010). Developing culturally sensitive cognitive behaviour therapy for psychosis for ethnic minority patients by exploration and incorporation of service users' and health professionals' views and opinions. *Behavioural and Cognitive Psychotherapy, 38*, 511–533. https://doi.org/10.1017/S1352465810000378

Rodolico, A., Bighelli, I., Avanzato, C., Concerto, C., Cutrufelli, P., Mineo, L., Siafis, S., Signorelli, M. S., Wu, H., Wang, D., Furukawa, T. A., Pitschel-Walz, G., Aguglia, E., & Leucht, S. (2022). Family interventions for relapse prevention in schizophrenia: A systematic review and network meta-analysis. *Lancet Psychiatry, 9*, 211–221. https://doi.org/10.1016/S2215-0366(21)00437-5

Ruggeri, M., Leese, M., Thornicroft, G., Bisoffi, G., & Tansella, M. (2000). Definition and prevalence of severe and persistent mental illness. *British Journal of Psychiatry, 176*, 149–155. https://doi.org/10.1192/bjp.177.2.149

Schwartz, S. J., Unger, J. B., Zamboanga, B. L., & Szapocznik, J. (2010). Rethinking the concept of acculturation: Implications for theory and research. *The American Psychologist, 65*, 237–251. https://doi.org/10.1037/a0019330

Sitskoorn, M. M., Aleman, A., Ebisch, S. J. H., Appels, M. C. M., & Kahn, R. S. (2004). Cognitive deficits in relatives of patients with schizophrenia: A meta-analysis. *Schizophrenia Research, 71*, 285–295. https://doi.org/10.1016/j.schres.2004.03.007

Solmi, M., Piva, G., Rosson, S., Fusar-Poli, P., Rubio, J., Carvalho, A. F., Vieta, E., Arango, C., DeTore, N., Eberlin, E., Mueser, K. T., & Correll, C. (2023). Efficacy and acceptability of psychosocial interventions in schizophrenia: Systematic overview and quality appraisal of the meta-analytic evidence. *Molecular Psychiatry, 28*, 354–368. https://doi.org/10.1038/s41380-022-01727-z

Stanley, B., & Brown, G. K. (2008). *The safety plan treatment manual to reduce suicide risk: Veteran version*. United States Department of Veterans Affairs.

Stuart, B. K., & Schlosser, D. A. (2009). Multifamily group treatment for schizophrenia. *International Journal of Group Psychotherapy, 59*, 435–440. https://doi.org/10.1521/ijgp.2009.59.3.435

Sung, S.-C., Hixson, A., & Yorker, B. C. (2004). Predischarge psychoeducational needs in Taiwan: Comparisons of psychiatric patients, relatives, and professionals. *Issues in Mental Health Nursing, 25*, 579–588. https://doi.org/10.1080/01612840490472110

Wallace, B. C., & Constantine, M. G. (2005). Africentric cultural values, psychological help-seeking attitudes, and self-concealment in African American college students. *Journal of Black Psychology, 31*, 369–385. https://doi.org/10.1177/0095798405281025

Weisman de Mamani, A., & Suro, G. (2016). The effect of a culturally informed therapy on self-conscious emotions and burden in caregivers of patients with schizophrenia: A randomized clinical trial. *Psychotherapy, 53*, 57–67. https://doi.org/10.1037/pst0000038

Weisman de Mamani, A., Weintraub, M. J., Gurak, K., & Maura, J. (2014). A randomized clinical trial to test the efficacy of a family-focused, culturally informed therapy for schizophrenia. *Journal of Family Psychology, 28*, 800–810. https://doi.org/10.1037/fam0000021

Weisman de Mamani, A., McLaughlin, M., Altamirano, O., Lopez, D., & Ahmad, S. S. (2021). *Culturally informed therapy for schizophrenia: A family-focused cognitive behavioral approach, clinician guide*. Oxford University Press.

Westcott, C., Waghorn, G., McLean, D., Statham, D., & Mowry, B. (2015). Interest in employment among people with schizophrenia. *American Journal of Psychiatric Rehabilitation, 18*, 187–207. https://doi.org/10.1080/15487768.2014.954162

Wing, J. K., & Brown, G. W. (1979). *Institutionalism and schizophrenia: A comparative study of three mental hospitals*. Cambridge University Press.

Yeh, K.-H., & Bedford, O. (2004). Filial belief and parent-child conflict. *International Journal of Psychology, 39*, 132–144. https://doi.org/10.1080/00207590344000312

Zubin, J., & Spring, B. (1977). Vulnerability: A new view of schizophrenia. *Journal of Abnormal Psychology, 86*, 103–126. https://doi.org/10.1037/0021-843X.86.2.103

Chapter 7
Dyadic Treatment in the Context of Medical Concerns

Sacha McBain and Andrew T. Schramm

7.1 Introduction

Undisputed is the statement that the effects of serious physical illness or injury extend beyond physical pathologies to include an individual's existential, emotional, and social worlds. The biopsychosocial model, now prominent in medical education, speaks to the interrelatedness of multiple aspects of an individual's context in influencing well-being. As psychopathology impacts medical illness (e.g., depression contributing to decreased adherence with diabetes management; Gonzalez et al., 2008), so too does medical illness impact risk of psychopathology, an association that is thought to be mediated by social and psychological factors. A patient with cardiovascular disease requiring hospitalization, for example, may now feel socially isolated—a known risk factor for depression. Treatment of the biological pathology in this case has impacted the patient's social context, leading to depression, which in turn contributes to poorer behavioral compliance with treatment recommendations and, ultimately, compromises medical outcomes. In this case, depression has been linked with a poorer prognosis, demonstrating the interconnectedness of these areas of functioning.

Recognition of the interrelatedness of each of these domains has led to the development of behavioral health interventions designed to promote patient and family adjustment to illness or injury and medical outcomes. The targets of these interventions often include the promotion of protective factors such as social support. Involving patients' family members in such interventions has the potential to

S. McBain (✉)
Department of Psychiatry & Behavioral Sciences, Rush University, Chicago, IL, USA
e-mail: Sacha_mcbain@rush.edu

A. T. Schramm
Medical College of Wisconsin, Milwaukee, WI, USA

L. Reuman, J. Thompson-Hollands (eds.), *Enhancing CBT Through Family and Peer Engagement*, CBT: Science Into Practice, https://doi.org/10.1007/978-3-031-74838-7_7

increase their efficacy. Our focus in this chapter is the theoretical and empirical basis for involving family members or romantic partners in psychosocial interventions for patients being medically treated for illness or injury. We provide an in-depth review of one intervention involving family members/romantic partners that has shown promise in this population called Promotion of Emotional Disclosure (PED). The goal of this chapter is to highlight the current state of the field, identify theoretical bases for the inclusion of family members or romantic partners in these interventions, and detail an example of treatment using a specific intervention approach.

7.2 Psychosocial Impact of Medical Conditions and Injury

Understanding the psychosocial nature of medical conditions and injuries is integral to the analysis of cognitive behavioral interventions in healthcare settings and—more specifically—the benefit of involving family members in these interventions. Over the last several decades, medical education and practice has evolved to increasingly recognize the psychological and social aspects of illness and injury (Jaini & Lee, 2015). Shifting away from a one-dimensional medical model toward a more holistic conceptualization of patients recognizes that illness does not occur in a vacuum. Rather, an individual's experience and context are interrelated with the individual's biomedical functioning. This is the very premise of the biopsychosocial model proposed by Engel (1977, 1981) at the end of the twentieth century and now widespread in its reach (Wade & Halligan, 2017).

Support for the link between physical illness or injury and psychological functioning comes from a burgeoning body of research demonstrating a heightened risk for psychopathology among patients being treated for a wide range of medical conditions. Examples of this include heightened rates of depression and anxiety among oncology patients (Pitman et al., 2018; Rhondali et al., 2012), patients with diabetes (Roy & Lloyd, 2012; Smith et al., 2013), and those with cardiovascular disease (Hare et al., 2014). Significant research efforts have sought to disentangle the longitudinal nature of and mechanisms explaining these associations. There is an indication that underlying physiological factors may contribute risk to both physical and mental health issues, with many researchers emphasizing a bidirectional association between the two (Katon, 2011). In a systematic review and meta-analysis of longitudinal research on associations between depression and diabetes, Nouwen et al. (2019) found that baseline diabetes complications were associated with subsequent depression. At the same time, depression was associated with greater rates of later medical complications of diabetes. This and other studies raise the possibility of shared etiologies contributing to physical and psychological disease.

The effect of psychopathology on physical disease outcomes may be mediated by behavioral changes associated with mental illness and their impact on health-related behavior. A meta-analysis showed that, in comparison to nondepressed patients, the odds of noncompliance with medical recommendations are three times greater among patients with depression (DiMatteo et al., 2000). More specifically, other studies have found that in individuals with diabetes, the presence of depression is associated with significantly less adherence to medical recommendations (Gonzalez et al., 2008). Depression, in addition to being an established risk factor for the development of cardiovascular disease, is also a predictor of poor prognosis following a cardiac event (e.g., heart failure; Joynt et al., 2003). In an especially striking finding, Halawi et al. (2019) found that psychological distress following total hip and knee arthroplasty (i.e., joint replacement) independently predicted prolonged hospitalization.

Adding to the web of these interrelated factors is the finding that medical treatments and hospitalizations may themselves be stressors that contribute to the risk for psychopathology (Mundy & Baum, 2004; Birk et al., 2019). A review by Tedstone and Tarrier (2003) found that patients treated in an intensive care unit had the highest prevalence rates of medical-related posttraumatic stress in comparison to patients with medical illness treated in less acute settings. Patients treated for traumatic injury have also been shown to be at significant risk for depression and posttraumatic stress reactions (Anderson et al., 2011; deRoon-Cassini et al., 2010). These studies make it clear that the promotion of healthy adjustment to illness or injury is an important endeavor.

7.3 Social Support and Dyadic Coping

Recognition of the biopsychosocial aspects of medical illness and injury has led researchers to investigate risk and protective factors for adjustment following illness or injury. Across many studies, findings have converged upon the potent protective role of social support. Social support has been defined as "the amount of practical and emotional support that patients perceive" (Rosland et al., 2012, p. 1). Increasingly, social support has been identified as a public health priority by researchers and policymakers who cite the finding that the impact of social support on well-being is of similar or greater magnitude as many other social determinants of health (Holt-Lunstad et al., 2017). Holt-Lunstad and colleagues (2017), referring to social support, state "There are perhaps no other factors that can have such a large impact on both length and quality of life–from cradle to the grave" (p. 13). Indeed, the World Health Organization now lists social support networks among the most critical determinants of health (WHO, n.d.), and in 2023, the United States Surgeon General released an advisory on the "epidemic of loneliness and isolation" (Surgeon General of the United States, 2023).

We posit that the vulnerable and stressful context of treatment for medical illness or injury—which our patients often describe as among the most difficult experiences of their lives—makes the presence of caring others especially powerful. Broadly speaking, social psychological research has shown that the helpful presence of others is especially impactful in times of stress (Fiske, 2014). More specifically, however, several mechanisms have been proposed to explain the pathway through which social support exerts its protective influence on medical outcomes and psychological functioning among medical patients. A 2012 meta-analysis by Rosland and colleagues examined studies on the impact of family behavior and communication on the outcomes of patients with chronic illness. Patient populations included in the review spanned from arthritis, chronic cardiovascular disease, diabetes, and end-stage renal disease. Across the 30 studies reviewed, positive medical outcomes were associated with "family emphasis on self-reliance and personal achievement, family cohesion, and attentive responses to symptoms" (Rosland et al., 2012, p. 221).

A theoretical model of dyadic coping with chronic illness developed by Badr and Acitelli (2017) emphasizes each member of the couple's illness-related cognitions. The authors describe appraisals, a form of cognition, as "subjective interpretations of an event as harmful or beneficial and include assessments of the coping strategies and resources needed to deal with the situation" (p. 44). As proposed by Badr and Acitelli, individual appraisals of the illness (e.g., "How bad is this and what can I do about it" [p. 46]) lead to individual coping strategies which, when ineffective, are communicated to the individual's partner. This, in turn, gives rise to dyadic/shared illness appraisals (e.g., "How bad is this and what can we do about it?" (p. 46), dyadic approaches to coping, and both individual (e.g., psychological adjustment) and relationship outcomes (e.g., relationship satisfaction).

This model (i.e., Badr & Acitelli, 2017) highlights a critical point in our discussion of social support and adjustment to illness or injury: Although social support is a protective factor, family members' responses can, in fact, be harmful to patient adjustment. There is potential, in fact, for well-intentioned family members to model or inadvertently reinforce maladaptive cognitive, behavioral, and emotional coping. This may take the form of engaging in avoidant coping by avoiding discussion of illness-related topics (Badr & Acitelli, 2017). Work in psycho-oncology identified social constraints to the disclosure of cancer-related thoughts and feelings to loved ones as having a negative impact on coping and adjustment (Lepore & Revenson, 2007). Additionally, Rosland et al. (2012) found in their review of family behaviors and communication patterns on illness outcomes that "critical, overprotective, controlling, and distancing family responses to illness management were associated with negative patient outcomes" (p. 221) such as poor self-management and worse illness trajectory. In the context of exposure to potentially traumatic events (e.g., injury), family member responses characterized by hostility or blame have been shown to increase the risk for negative psychological outcomes such as posttraumatic stress disorder (PTSD; Guay et al., 2006).

7.4 Psychosocial Interventions Including Family Members in Medical Contexts

Thus far, we have highlighted the interrelatedness of biopsychosocial factors among patients being treated for medical illness or injury, the role of social support in promoting good medical and psychological outcomes in this population, and the power of unhelpful family responses to negatively influence medical and psychological trajectories. Recognition of the psychosocial toll of medical illness and the importance of family member involvement in medical care has given rise to the development of approaches to psychosocial interventions to promote the protective role of social support and to guide family members in how to support their loved one's psychological adjustment to illness/injury. Such approaches highlight the importance of considering the interpersonal context of injury recovery (Bannon et al., 2022a, b, c). Indeed, guidelines for psychologists working in medical and rehabilitation settings identify engaging family members in psychosocial interventions as a best practice (American Psychological Association, 2013; Cox et al., 2013). Other disciplines, such as nursing, have also explicitly emphasized models of care that emphasize the relational aspect of recovery (Porter et al., 2014).

Despite this, the involvement of family members in cognitive behavioral interventions for patients in medical settings is relatively understudied. Medical family therapy is a discipline within family therapy that highlights the multiple spheres of factors that impact recovery from medical illness or injury (Hodgson et al., 2014). However, specific operationalization and empirical testing of this treatment approach is in need of further development. Additionally, many interventions designed for medical settings target either the patient (e.g., depression) or family members (e.g., caregiving stress); less often are family members integrated into the psychosocial treatment provided to the patient (Martire et al., 2004). This gap was noted in a meta-analysis of studies testing the benefit of family member involvement in psychosocial interventions for chronic illness (Martire et al., 2004). Evidence is building, however, for the efficacy of interventions that include both family members and patients. For example, the *Recovery Together* intervention to promote dyadic resilience (Bannon et al., 2022, b, c) has been shown to positively affect both individual's level of distress (Bannon et al., 2022, b, c).

While additional research is needed to further test the role of involving family members in treatments delivered to patients with illness/injury in healthcare settings, we also draw upon studies related to clinical conditions often found in these settings. This is particularly true in research examining the role of family member involvement in the treatment of PTSD. Meuleman et al. (2023) completed a systematic review of studies on PTSD treatments that involved a significant other in the treatment process. The authors found that interventions that actively involve a support person were most effective in reducing PTSD symptoms in comparison to those that passively involve or do not involve a support person. Research from Shnaider and colleagues suggests that in cognitive behavioral conjoint therapy for PTSD, level of social support moderated treatment effects such that higher levels of social support were associated with greatest decreases in PTSD symptom severity (Shnaider et al., 2017). In the text that follows, we describe in greater depth a specific psychosocial intervention—Promotion of Emotional Disclosure—which has shown promising results as a brief intervention following medical stressors.

7.5 Promotion of Emotional Disclosure Intervention: Addressing Psychosocial Consequences of Illness and Injury

Promotion of Emotional Disclosure (PED) was initially conceptualized by Cordova et al. (2003) as a brief dyadic cognitive-behavioral intervention designed to leverage patients' social networks to promote recovery following exposure to an acute traumatic event. PED's efficacy was evaluated in a randomized control trial with patients who presented to one of two emergency departments in Montreal following a life-threatening event (Brunet et al., 2013). Participants were recruited within 10 days of experiencing a life-threatening event that elicited a peritraumatic response (i.e., fear, helplessness, or horror) and were randomized to receive PED (administered by a trained social worker or nurse) or symptom monitoring. Participants received the intervention at the hospital on average 26 days after the traumatic event with the second session occurring 2 weeks later. Intervention and control groups were administered questionnaires 21 days post-trauma (pretreatment), 35 days post-trauma (mid-intervention), and 3 months post-trauma (posttreatment). In an intent-to-treat analysis, a time-by-group interaction was found, whereby participants who received the intervention had less PTSD symptoms at the posttreatment but not at the pretreatment compared with controls.

In a two-year follow-up study of PED, a significant mean decrease in PTSD symptoms persisted for participants randomized to the intervention group. Among those who received the intervention, none met the criteria for PTSD at the 2-year mark compared with five participants in the control group (Des Groseilliers et al., 2013). These findings demonstrated the promise of PED as a public health intervention to mitigate the impact of acute trauma within a hospital setting.

PED has also been featured as a preventative intervention with emerging evidence in the International Society for Traumatic Stress Studies' (ISTSS) Posttraumatic Stress Disorder Prevention and Treatment Guidelines (Bisson et al., 2019; O'Donnell et al., 2020) due to its promise as a multi-session selective intervention for prevention of PTSD. Despite these initial findings and endorsement by ISTSS, there has been minimal examination of PED in clinical research or implementation into routine clinical practice. Although further evidence is needed to support PED's efficacy, its interventional components are grounded in foundational cognitive-behavioral theories of trauma recovery as discussed in the following sections.

7.5.1 Theoretical Basis

The PED protocol is designed to specifically address the traumatic experiences (e.g., a motor vehicle collision) and traumatic stress reactions that may arise following illness or injury (i.e., medical trauma). If left unaddressed, medical trauma can lead to significant negative psychosocial consequences for both patients and their families including emotional distress and impaired social functioning as previously discussed in this chapter. These psychosocial outcomes have important implications for physical functioning, medical service utilization, treatment adherence, morbidity, and mortality (Birk et al., 2019; Edmondson et al., 2012; Holbrook et al., 1999; O'Donnell et al., 2003; Rosenberg et al., 2018). Family members are also at greater risk of experiencing anxiety, low mood, and reduced quality of life (Green et al., 1998; Rolland, 1994).

Many existing hospital-based psychosocial interventions address clinical outcomes that may be mediated by traumatic stress but do not address traumatic stress reactions explicitly, instead focusing on health-related quality of life (HRQoL) or generalized anxiety or depression as previously discussed. Unlike many types of trauma exposure, the characteristics of medical trauma offer a unique opportunity to provide preventative, early interventions due to the context the trauma is occurring in. Healthcare systems can more readily identify when potentially traumatic medical events (e.g., life-threatening diagnoses, painful procedures) are likely to occur and employ appropriate brief interventions to mitigate its impacts (McBain et al., 2023). However, the opportunity to employ trauma-informed psychosocial interventions in the acute phase of illness and injury recovery is often underutilized.

PED has a dual focus on both the impacts of medical trauma and its interaction with health-related psychosocial outcomes (e.g., HRQoL, adjustment). PED is grounded in the social-cognitive processing theory of adjustment to stressors that seeks to explain the impact of the social context of recovery on emotional adjustment (Lepore et al., 2001). Given many illness and injury experiences are life-threatening and potentially traumatic events (Birk et al., 2019), PED also draws on the social-cognitive theory of PTSD and the associations between perceived social support and traumatic stress to inform components of the intervention.

7.5.1.1 Cognitive Processing

Exposure to potentially traumatic medical events can dramatically impact patients' and families' perception of themselves, their relationships, and the world around them. As a result, individuals can experience fundamental, sometimes conflicting, changes in their mental models and schemas resulting in emotional distress (Horowitz, 1986; Lepore et al., 2001). Following a trauma, individuals are compelled to seek understanding of the event and to integrate its meaning into their larger mental model. Adaptive confrontation, contemplation, and revaluation (i.e., accommodation) in the context of supportive or benign social support can facilitate natural recovery through the integration of balanced meaning-making of the event (e.g., "it's not my fault I got sick"; Resick & Schnicke, 1992). However, reinterpreting trauma-related information to fit preexisting negative beliefs (i.e., assimilation; i.e., "If I didn't work so hard I wouldn't have gotten cancer") or drastic negative changes in schemas to account for trauma-related information (i.e., overaccommodation; e.g., "I'm not capable of taking care of my health") can block adaptive emotional processing and contribute to the development of medical traumatic stress. This process is further compounded by individuals' attempts to avoid distressing trauma-related content (e.g., thoughts, images, feelings), ultimately impeding adaptive cognitive processing and accommodation of trauma-related material.

7.5.1.2 Social Processing

As previously discussed, perceived social support has been consistently found to be a significant contributor to the development and maintenance of PTSD symptoms (Simon et al., 2019). However, the exact mechanism through which social support modulates the development of PTSD continues to be explored. Increased losses and obstacles following trauma exposure can negatively impact an individual's ability to mitigate the psychosocial consequences of the trauma and engage in adaptive emotional processing. An individual's access to positive social support may help to protect against PTSD by bolstering access to psychosocial resources and functional support to overcome the material consequences of the trauma (Platt et al., 2014). This may be especially crucial in the context of medical trauma, which is often characterized by an acute need for support from others to meet activities of daily living (e.g., meal preparation), manage components of the illness/injury (e.g., wound care), and navigate complexities of the healthcare system (e.g., maintaining appointments).

Positive social connectedness can also help to facilitate cognitive and emotional processing. Discussing trauma-related content enables individuals to contemplate and reframe trauma-related thoughts and feelings while increasing a sense of rapport and esteem with trusted others. Often trauma survivors hold unchallenged negative cognitions and meanings regarding the event that may increase perceived social isolation or lead to avoidance behaviors. However, when discussed openly, these negative assumptions can be appropriately challenged by supportive others (e.g., "I'm a burden on the family") and help the trauma survivor to adopt more balanced beliefs regarding the event and its impacts (Lepore, 2001). Further, adaptive emotional disclosure may serve to consolidate trauma memories and increase distress tolerance when discussing trauma-related content, therefore increasing an individual's sense of mastery over trauma-related content and emotional responses (Lepore, 2001).

Although positive perceived social support has been demonstrated to be a protective factor against PTSD development, absent or poor-quality social support (i.e., "social constraints") may increase the risk for PTSD and other negative psychosocial outcomes following medical stressors (Lepore & Helgeson, 1998). Just as positive social support may facilitate processing, absent or poor-quality social support may impede cognitive processing and subsequent adjustment, therefore increasing psychological distress. When individuals are exposed to negative social interactions regarding the trauma, they may react by avoiding future conversations regarding the trauma with others. Negative social interactions may also serve to reinforce negative meaning-making and secondary emotions in response to the event such as self-blame, guilt, and shame. A chronic lack of opportunity to process trauma-related content may in turn limit access to new information that may challenge trauma-related beliefs that are contributing to difficulty with mood, coping, and/or adjustment (Lepore, 2001; Lepore & Revenson, 2007). Importantly, this external avoidance may also contribute to increased internal avoidance (e.g., avoiding thoughts, feelings, sensations) further limiting opportunities to reconsolidate trauma-related material and to increase tolerance for uncomfortable emotions and sensations (e.g., pain).

The presence of social constraints may contribute to elevated psychological distress and negatively impact adjustment following chronic illness (Lepore & Revenson, 2007). In the context of medical stressors, social constraints can be elicited by any member of a patient's social network including family, friends, colleagues, and medical personnel. Socially constraining behaviors are often characterized by social contacts who minimize a patient's experience, become uncomfortable with emotional disclosure, or engage in invalidation or critical behavior.

Existing literature demonstrates that patients consistently identify interactions with medical personnel as a significant source of distress. Further, negative interactions with medical personnel have been shown to increase the risk for the development of medically induced PTSD following potentially traumatic medical events (Taft et al., 2022). These negative interactions are often compounded by experiences of bias, discrimination, and the perpetuation of power differentials that are often enacted at the individual (e.g., patient-provider communication) and organizational levels (e.g., discriminatory policies or procedures; Benjamins & Whitman, 2014). Social constraints enacted within the healthcare system can reinforce negative meaning-making and may constrain adaptive emotional processing within the social network more generally (Lepore & Revenson, 2007).

7.5.2 Treatment Overview

The PED protocol is a two-session dyadic intervention designed to reduce the long-term negative psychosocial consequences of illness and injury. The intervention is intended to be delivered in 45–60 minute visits with patients and a supporter of their choice (e.g., romantic partner, adult child, friend) soon after discharge from an inpatient hospital stay. The protocol provides trauma-informed education to patients and supporters about interpersonal obstacles to emotional and interpersonal processing of their medical experiences. PED is primarily a psychoeducational intervention with components of motivational interviewing and problem-solving designed to increase confidence, skill, and willingness to engage in emotional processing.

PED's strength is in its ability to flexibly apply several strategies to meet these objectives. Each strategy can be uniquely tailored to each dyad to facilitate meaningful engagement. The protocol begins with psychoeducation regarding the process of adjustment to illness and injury which includes comparisons to expectations regarding physical recovery (e.g., "just as you would clean a wound…"). The protocol also emphasizes the importance of normalization and validation of negative affect associated with illness and injury. For some patients and supporters, this may be the first time that difficult emotions are discussed and contextualized as a normative part of the adjustment process. The significant silos between mental health and physical health are often reinforced by multidisciplinary clinicians in medical settings (Scott et al., 2023). PED seeks to bridge these gaps by prioritizing discussion about illness/injury-related concerns and their relationship with emotional distress. After psychoeducation, skills to facilitate supportive communication are reviewed and discussed followed by motivational interviewing to explore readiness to engage in emotional processing regarding the illness or injury. As necessary, problem-solving techniques are used to identify and overcome practical and interpersonal barriers to engagement in adaptive processing. Finally, a brief review of effective coping strategies to support the process of recovery are discussed.

7.5.2.1 Objectives of the Intervention

PED consists of five core objectives that are conceptualized to facilitate socioemotional processing and natural recovery following a potentially traumatic experience. The first objective is to enhance knowledge of adjustment processes following an illness/injury. The intervention's initial focus on psychoeducation serves as a foundation for an introduction to adaptive coping and emotional processing. The second objective of the intervention is to increase patients' and their supporters' ability and willingness to tolerate negative emotions (e.g., anxiety, fear, anger) that may have arisen as a result of the event. The intervention seeks to bolster the capacity to adaptively manage these negative emotions in order to mitigate the emotional impacts of the event. The core objectives of the intervention are focused on increasing the quality and frequency of discussions about the illness/injury while instilling a sense of motivation and self-efficacy around emotional disclosure. Given socially constraining behaviors can greatly impact both the quality and frequency of these conversations, the intervention specifically focuses on addressing behaviors (e.g., changing the subject, criticizing, minimizing) that may discourage meaningful emotional processing. The final objective of the intervention aims to equip patients and their supporters with effective coping strategies while concurrently reducing problematic coping.

7.5.2.2 Clinical Components of the Intervention

Each component of the intervention is designed to meet one or more of its aforementioned objectives while flexibly applying the clinical strategies. The components are designed to build on one another and so should be delivered in the described order. However, the amount of time spent on each component will be determined by the needs of the patient and their supporter. Importantly, the goal of the intervention is *not* to engage in trauma-focused processing in the session, but rather to equip the dyad with the knowledge, skills, and confidence to independently engage in meaningful social-emotional processing throughout the recovery process.

The intervention begins with the *orientation* component in which patients and their chosen supporter are oriented to the purpose of the intervention (i.e., to learn about common reactions to illness/injury; to anticipate potential problems and solutions during recovery; and to promote adaptive communication and coping). The orientation to the purpose and goals of the intervention is followed by a psychoeducational component specifically focused on *common reactions* following illness/injury. Depending on the clinical setting, this section may have common reactions specific to one illness/injury experience (e.g., cancer, traumatic injury) or provide general information about common reactions that may arise across a wide range of medical experiences. These reactions are then normalized and contextualized for the patient and their supporter. Following psychoeducation regarding common reactions, the patient and their supporter are provided information about natural recovery and the *importance of processing* in promoting recovery and adjustment following a medical experience. This component reinforces the idea that disclosing illness/injury-related thoughts and feelings with trusted others is a core aspect of the recovery process. The intervention then preempts patients' and supporters' possible ambivalence or concerns regarding emotional disclosure by proactively discussing *social constraints* and the tendency to avoid uncomfortable thoughts, feelings, and experiences which inhibit engagement in disclosure.

The remainder of the intervention focuses on the introduction of practical strategies to improve the quality of emotional disclosure and adaptive coping as well as motivational interviewing to generate motivation and efficacy in adopting these strategies. This process begins with a review of the *dos and don'ts in communicating about feelings*, a component of the intervention focused on effective and ineffective ways of initiating disclosure, providing support to others, and effectively responding to social constraints. This component acknowledges that both patients and supporters may be engaging in ineffective communication and so is focused on strategies that both members of the dyad can utilize to improve communication and facilitate emotional disclosure. After the introduction of the strategies, a *motivational interview* is utilized to assess the dyad's motivation to engage in emotional disclosure and their confidence in adopting these skills. This includes a review of the pros and cons of discussing illness/injury-related thoughts and further coaching and/or problem-solving on how to improve the quality and/or frequency of emotional processing. The subsequent component focuses on the *dos and don'ts in coping* which reviews potentially adaptive and maladaptive coping responses and explores the dyad's use of positive coping behaviors. The intervention concludes with a *discussion* of what the patient and their supporter have learned from the session as well as any disagreements or concerns that may have arisen and a *recap* of the major points of the intervention and the discussion. The patient and their supporter are provided *written support materials* including handouts reviewing the core messages of the intervention: common reactions, likely and unlikely outcomes of talking about feelings, dos and don'ts in communicating about feelings and coping, when to seek professional help, and how to contact professional help. These materials also include handouts to facilitate retaining the information and recording/monitoring of coping and disclosure behaviors between sessions. Finally, the second session of the intervention is scheduled for approximately 2 weeks later and the dyad is provided with a booster session reminder card.

The second session of the intervention serves as a booster session functioning as a review of the components of session one and as a coaching session. Following a similar outline, the session briefly summarizes the purpose of the intervention and information discussed in the first session. Immediately following a brief review, the clinician facilitates a discussion about experiences related to each component including the dyad's experiences between sessions, motivation and engagement in emotional processing, and utilization of the strategies introduced in session one.

7.5.3 Implementation Considerations

7.5.3.1 Identifying Appropriate Patients

PED is designed as a population-based intervention appropriate for almost all patients as a component of routine clinical practice, analogous to brief physician-delivered public health advice (Cordova et al., 2003). The intervention is optimally designed to be completed with a patient and a supportive other of their choice. While patients are encouraged to identify their support person, clinicians may have to discern the appropriateness of the presumed support person. For example, additional screening may be warranted in cases of known domestic violence or ongoing abuse (Karakurt et al., 2016). Clinicians administering PED should be trained to recognize signs of domestic violence, provide appropriate resources, and create a safe environment for disclosure if necessary (Crasta et al., 2022). Patients without an identified support person need not be automatically ineligible for the intervention, as they may still find some benefit in the introduction of the concepts and strategies. In these cases, PED can help to explore opportunities to establish meaningful social connections and elicit positive social support.

Although PED may be appropriate for most patients, organizations may opt to take a more targeted approach due to resource and/or time restraints. In these cases, organizations can look to the Institute of Medicine's (IOM) Committee on Prevention of Mental Disorders for guidance on implementation (Muñoz et al., 1996). The IOM outlines three tiers of preventative intervention: universal interventions which are offered to all patients regardless of risk for the development of negative mental health outcomes; selective interventions which are offered to patients determined to be at an increased risk of developing negative outcomes; and indicated interventions which focus on providing interventions to those who are demonstrating early signs of distress (Compton & Shim, 2020).

As a universal intervention, organizations could consider the implementation of a protocol that would allow PED to be offered to all patients. Given that PED does not emphasize trauma processing but rather focuses on psychoeducation, skill building, and motivation to utilize skills, PED could be appropriately offered to most patients and may reduce the implementation burden associated with the development of screening and referral protocols. However, PED has not been empirically tested as a universal intervention and should be further evaluated. Should an organization prefer to implement PED as a selective intervention for those determined to be at elevated risk to develop negative mental health outcomes, settings may opt to utilize a predictive risk screener (either self- or clinician-administered) or predictive risk algorithms that can be embedded within an organization's electronic medical record (Richmond et al., 2011) to identify patients who may benefit from PED. For those interested in providing PED to only patients demonstrating symptoms as an indicated preventive intervention, settings should consider implementation of a brief symptom screener in order to identify patients who are demonstrating early signs of distress (Brunet et al., 2013). The type of risk screener and symptom measure may vary depending on the patient population and may necessitate the inclusion of tools that have been validated and/or adapted for the target population (e.g., specific disease experience or a general medical population; see Hunt et al. (2021) as an example).

7.5.3.2 Identifying Interventionists

PED is intended to be delivered by a healthcare provider and can be provided in any location where clinical care typically occurs. PED may be most helpful when embedded within a healthcare setting where patients are already accessing components of their primary medical care (e.g., clinic, hospital, other care facility). Integration of PED in these settings may serve to increase access to care, while also demonstrating that psychosocial health is prioritized by the treatment team.

The clinician providing the intervention should have some knowledge regarding emotional adjustment following a stressful or traumatic medical experience and mental health intervention. Although social workers, psychologists, psychiatrists, and chaplains embedded within hospital systems will be equipped to provide the intervention; nurses, physician assistants, physicians, and others are also well positioned to provide the intervention with appropriate orientation and training (Brunet et al., 2013). The ability of a wide range of professionals to facilitate this intervention can greatly increase its feasibility in settings with limited access to psychosocial support team members as demonstrated with other brief interventions in medical settings (Darnell et al., 2019). To facilitate implementation, organizations should consider how the intervention may align with the role of clinicians within the system as well as opportunities to augment existing family education or psychosocial resourcing practices.

7.5.4 *Timing*

The intervention is designed to be provided within 1 month following discharge from an inpatient hospital stay with the second session occurring approximately 2 weeks later. The authors emphasize the potential utility of the intervention being delivered when illness/injury-related distress appears to be likely (e.g., at the time of diagnosis). Although PED is designed to be delivered in two 45–60 minute sessions, staffing and/or time constraints may require flexibility in delivery. To this end, the authors also identify reasonable alternatives in delivery such as implementing the intervention in 5-minute segments over a period of a few days (in the inpatient setting), or delivering it separately to patients and significant others (Cordova et al., 2003). Although not yet empirically validated, PED may be effectively delivered via telehealth. Research on other forms of mental health treatment suggests that intervention delivered by telehealth is comparable to in person (McGeary et al., 2023). Administration of PED via telehealth may increase access for patients living significant distances from where they receive their medical care and may help to ensure patients are receiving services within the suggested timeframe of the intervention.

Navigating chronic illness is likely to expose patients and their support systems to many stressors that may elicit emotional reactions. Given patients are likely to be exposed to numerous medical stressors, clinicians may need to consider the appropriate timing to administer PED. For instance, clinicians must discern what constitutes an appropriate index event to initiate engagement in PED such as initial hospitalization, diagnosis, readmission, or another disease-specific stressor or milestone. Given the often layered and compounding stressors associated with medical events, organizations are encouraged to offer PED early in the course of the patient establishing care within the setting in order to leverage the preventative nature of this intervention. Introducing PED shortly after a patient is introduced to the healthcare setting can optimize PED's ability to mitigate the emotional impact of ongoing stressors associated with patients' health concerns and disease management (Cordova et al., 2003). Implementation of this approach soon after diagnosis is also consistent with prior research on the promotion of adaptive dyadic coping (Badr & Acitelli, 2017).

7.6 Clinical Considerations for Diverse Identities

Providing a trauma-focused intervention, like PED, within a trauma-informed care framework is paramount for ensuring the holistic well-being of patients who have experienced trauma (Raja et al., 2015). The Substance Abuse and Mental Health Services Administration (SAMHSA) offers a framework for the implementation of trauma-informed healthcare including the adoption of several principles including safety, trustworthiness, collaboration, empowerment, and cultural humility (SAMHSA, 2014).

When addressing the emotional and psychological needs of patients and their supporters, it is essential to recognize the diverse cultural backgrounds and identities that may impact their experiences of medical events. PED's flexible approach allows the intervention to be delivered to fidelity while allowing for cultural adaptations as indicated. As acknowledged by the authors, PED is primarily grounded within Western cultural values and requires a culturally humble stance when offered to diverse patients and supporters, especially those who may have different values or norms regarding emotional disclosure. The authors encourage a flexible approach to delivering PED in order to respect variation in emotional expression and coping across patients and their social networks. A version of the PED protocol was recently adapted and underwent cultural adaptations to better serve the needs of diverse sexual assault survivors. This included adding culturally relevant content, prompts to share relevant aspects of their identity, and prompts to help patients tailor skills to their needs and values (Dworkin et al., 2022). These cultural adaptations have not been evaluated with patients following medical stressors. This section outlines cultural considerations that may be relevant to medical patients and their families. Evaluation of the acceptability and effectiveness of these proposed cultural adaptations to PED is necessary.

7.6.1 Communication and Language

Language and communication barriers may arise and contribute to difficulty with adjustment or healthcare navigation following a medical stressor (Guttman et al., 2021). Further research is needed to evaluate cultural adaptations to PED including provision of the intervention in languages other than English or French. Clinicians should still consider strategies to minimize the reenactment of communication and language barriers while administering PED. Should patients necessitate or prefer services to be provided in a language other than English, ensure that PED materials have been appropriately translated by a medical translation service and that the intervention is conducted with appropriate interpreter services. Organizations may consider training the organization's interpreters in PED and/or orient interpreters to the goals and objectives of the intervention prior to initiating contact with the patient and their supporter.

Given the characteristics of the target population, patients may also need other communication-based accommodations or adaptations to ensure PED's accessibility. For example, PED allows for multimodal administration of information (e.g., written and verbal) by including written handouts summarizing key concepts to be discussed. Clinicians may consider other accessibility adaptations to content such as increasing the text size of handouts, adjusting the organization of handouts for readability (e.g., breaking up paragraphs), or seeking additional review by health literacy services to facilitate comprehension. Clinicians may consider accessibility-focused process adaptations such as shortening the length of the initial session or utilizing teach-back approaches (i.e., clinician teaches, patient repeats back) for patients experiencing neurocognitive symptoms as a means to support attention, retention, and comprehension of the content.

7.6.2 Family Structure

PED recognizes and respects the diversity of family structures and support systems by empowering patients to select their support person, irrespective of traditional family norms. Notably, the presence of socially constraining behavior from a spouse has been found to contribute to greater distress than socially constraining behavior from friends or other family members among patients with cancer (Lepore & Revenson, 2007). Clinicians may need to explore with patients the pros and cons of including a supporter who may be more primed to naturally provide adaptive support (e.g., an emotionally supportive sibling) versus a supporter who is eliciting more emotional distress (e.g., a critical spouse). In the case of more challenging patient-supporter dynamics, PED may offer patients a structured environment to address these concerns in a non-defensive way with the support of a clinician.

In some instances, patients may want to identify more than one support person to participate in PED. If feasible, clinicians could consider spaces where PED may take place and its ability to accommodate additional support people (e.g., size, seating). Alternatively, clinicians can discuss identifying a support person who will act as a "point person" to participate in PED who can help the patient disseminate key information to the larger support network. Printing multiple copies of intervention materials to disseminate among supporters may also help to validate patients who want to include a number of support people without increasing the number of support persons who directly participate.

7.6.3 Gender-Affirming Care

Transgender and gender-diverse patients are likely to experience discrimination and bias within the context of their healthcare (Casanova-Perez et al., 2021). Clinicians need to pay special attention to their own engagement in gender-affirming practices (e.g., respecting pronouns and names; creating safe spaces). Further, the educational component of PED allows the opportunity to validate patients' experiences of their healthcare. Patients may choose to explore how gender-based discrimination can be a medical stressor and contribute to difficulties with coping, adjustment, and willingness or ability to engage in emotional disclosure.

7.6.4 Gender Norms

Gender norms and roles can influence how individuals express and cope with emotions. Men, in particular, may face societal expectations related to stoicism and the inhibition of emotional expression. As a result, men may engage in more socially constraining behaviors in their relationships (Lepore & Revenson, 2007). Women often have a wider support network compared to men (Harrison et al., 1995), which may or may not involve their spouse. Therefore, women are more likely than men to seek (and access) additional, nonrestrictive channels for emotional disclosure. Generally, women engage in less socially constraining behaviors than men (Lepore & Revenson, 2007). Because men primarily turn to their spouses for discussing their concerns and feelings, when socially constraining behaviors are present in the romantic relationship, they may become more susceptible to emotional distress and have less established means for accessing adaptive emotional support. Clinicians can explore the impact of gender norms and expectations on readiness to engage in emotional disclosure.

7.6.5 *Income and Insurance*

Socioeconomic factors, including income and insurance status, can affect a patient's access to support and care (Allen et al., 2017). Organizations should consider these factors when addressing barriers to engagement and provide resources or referrals to help patients overcome financial obstacles. Patients' financial barriers may also inform how the intervention is implemented including considerations for setting (e.g., providing inpatient so visit is subsumed under inpatient charges), method (e.g., telehealth to reduce transportation cost), interventionist (e.g., trainees who can offer free or low cost services), or funding source (e.g., grant support; deRoon-Cassini et al., 2019). Ultimately, providing PED can also help to increase access to mental health support that may not otherwise be accessed due to financial barriers.

7.6.6 *Medical Racism*

Medical racism has a profound impact on individuals' access to care, quality of care, and adjustment to illness (Liu et al., 2023). Systemic disparities in healthcare can lead to mistrust, delayed diagnosis, inadequate treatment, and unequal access to resources, all of which significantly hinder adjustment to illness (Liu et al., 2023). Experiences of medical racism, including encountering bias and discrimination (Bailey et al., 2017), can engender feelings of frustration, anger, and helplessness, further complicating the emotional processing and coping mechanisms necessary for recovery. Research suggests that social connectedness may help to buffer against the negative health impacts of racial discrimination (Ransome et al., 2023). Clinicians can acknowledge and create space for patients to discuss experiences of medical racism in the psychoeducational phase of PED, discuss skills to support patients impacted by medical racism, and promote emotional processing regarding experiences of medical racism.

7.6.7 *Prognostic Awareness*

Different cultural backgrounds may influence how individuals perceive and communicate about prognosis. Some cultures may have a more open approach to discussing potential outcomes, while others may prefer to avoid such discussions (Sutar & Chaudhary, 2022). Clinicians are encouraged to engage patients and supporters in conversation about their individual preferences. Relational strain around prognostic awareness such as denial, avoidance, and conflict on the part of patients or their supporters may also contribute to socially constraining behaviors (Lepore & Revenson, 2007). PED can be leveraged to promote discussion and introduce effective communication skills when patients and their supporters have different or conflicting values regarding their communication about prognosis.

7.6.8 *Religious Coping*

Patients from different religious backgrounds may rely on religious coping strategies when dealing with illness or injury (e.g., praying for a miracle, confiding in religious leaders). Clinicians should respect and incorporate these beliefs into the intervention (Martins et al., 2021). This may involve discussing how religious coping can coexist with the strategies introduced in the intervention and ensuring that patients feel comfortable discussing their faith-related concerns.

In this section, we have provided a non-exhaustive list of potential cultural considerations when implementing PED. These recommendations are based on existing literature when available and clinical experience and have not yet been empirically tested as adaptations of PED. Therefore, clinicians should utilize their clinical judgment when applying these recommendations. Incorporating cultural considerations into PED demonstrates a commitment to cultural humility and patient-centered care. By adapting PED to the diverse needs and identities of patients and their supporters, clinicians may enhance its effectiveness and ensure that it is truly inclusive and supportive. This approach not only respects cultural differences, but also empowers patients and their supporters to actively engage in the process of emotional healing and recovery. Clinicians may consider integrating tools to assess the need for cultural adaptations such as screening tools (e.g., Discrimination in Medical Settings Scale; Peek et al., 2011) or clinical interviews (e.g., Cultural Formulation Interview (CFI); Aggarwal & Lewis-Fernandez, 2020).

7.7 Case Vignette

The following case vignette represents a fictional patient, Brandon, and his wife, Alyssa, who are each a composite of patients designed to characterize common presenting concerns and clinical symptoms seen by the authors in their clinical practice in medical settings.

7.7.1 Case Overview

Brandon is a 38-year-old Black American man who sustained multiple injuries when a scaffolding structure on which he was standing unexpectedly collapsed. In addition to bilateral lower extremity fractures, Brandon suffered multiple vertebral fractures, resulting in a spinal cord injury (SCI). His spinal cord was partially severed, resulting in an unclear initial prognostic outlook. He retained some sensory capabilities and was able to sense touch on his feet but was unable to move his legs or feet.

Brandon described having a high level of social support. During his hospitalization, multiple members of Brandon's family were always present during visiting hours. His wife, Alyssa, was the main family point of contact and would go on to take over much of his caregiving needs after discharge. He and Alyssa had two daughters, ages 3 and 6. Brandon and Alyssa described themselves as Christians and identified prayer and their religious beliefs about the presence of God as a major source of comfort. The inpatient trauma psychology service was consulted due to concern for Brandon's limited engagement in physical therapy. Alyssa was present for the initial exam, which was notable for significant depressive and acute stress symptoms.

When Brandon spoke about the incident, which he did only when absolutely necessary (e.g., an interview with his lawyer), he became visibly upset including crying, sweating, and expressing a feeling of panic. In response to this, his family discouraged him from speaking about the event because they did not want him to get upset. In these circumstances, or when Brandon expressed anger about his circumstances, Alyssa often told him to rely on God by praying and to think more positively. His family encouraged him to speak about other topics. Brandon expressed that he felt this was helpful. After exhausting all surgical options, his medical providers met with the family to provide an update on his likely functional prognosis. They stated that Brandon would not regain motor functioning of his lower extremities. His team aimed to discuss a plan for inpatient physical rehabilitation and began emphasizing the need to learn how to live with his new abilities in order to maximize his independence.

Brandon and his wife vehemently disagreed with the medical providers' statements and took offense to their approach, feeling that the providers no longer maintained hope for Brandon's recovery. They indicated that they would continue praying and waiting for a miracle. The physical therapists struggled to engage Brandon in therapy. When meeting individually with Brandon, he expressed a strong sense of shame due to his family members seeing him require significant assistance to complete activities of daily living. He also shared that he felt intense anger toward his employer, who had ignored his and his co-workers' complaints about the condition of safety equipment, and expressed a sense of fear that he would not be able to raise his young daughters if the paraplegia of his legs persisted.

Over the course of several days, Brandon, his wife, and his care team continued to discuss expectations regarding recovery and the role of acute rehabilitation in facilitating Brandon's goals. Ultimately, Brandon and his wife were agreeable to discharge to an acute rehabilitation facility where he completed 25 days of acute rehabilitation.

7.7.2 Diagnostic and Functional Assessments

As a component of routine clinical care, Brandon was administered the Injured Trauma Survivor Screen (ITSS) during his inpatient admission prior to the trauma psychology service being consulted (Hunt et al., 2018). The ITSS is a predictive risk screener used to determine risk for the development of post-injury PTSD and depression by evaluating pre-, peri-, and post-trauma risk factors. Brandon did not endorse any pre-injury risk factors (e.g., history of mental health concerns). He endorsed one peritraumatic risk factor that he believed he was going to die at the time of injury (i.e., perceived life threat) and several post-injury risk factors including emotional numbing, increased restlessness, worry, and belief that other people cannot be trusted. His results on the ITSS suggested that Brandon was at an elevated risk of experiencing post-injury PTSD and depression.

During the initial assessment with the inpatient trauma psychology consult service, Brandon completed the Patient Health Questionnaire-9 (PHQ-9; Kroenke et al., 1999) and the PTSD Checklist-5 (PCL-5; Weathers et al., 2013). Brandon scored a 10 on the PHQ-9 suggesting moderate depressive symptoms and a 31 on the PCL-5 indicating the presence of significant traumatic stress reactions. Given the timeframe (within 1 month of trauma exposure), the PCL-5 was utilized to monitor traumatic stress symptoms and not to determine a diagnosis of PTSD. Following feedback on his self-report symptom measures, Brandon was offered referrals to outpatient mental health treatment for further evaluation and intervention. He declined mental health services citing his family and church community as adequate sources of support.

Following discharge from acute SCI rehabilitation, Brandon was seen for follow-up in the outpatient surgery clinic visit. During his visit, a member of the trauma psychology team met with Brandon to assess his mood, coping, and adjustment since discharge. He was asked to complete the PHQ-9 and the PCL-5 to reassess post-injury mental health symptoms. A slight increase in his PHQ-9 was noted with a score of 12 suggesting continued moderate depressive symptoms. His PCL-5 score suggested a significant increase in traumatic stress symptoms with a total score of 52, now indicating a likely diagnosis of PTSD.

Brandon was once again offered psychoeducation regarding PTSD treatment and possible referrals. He continued to express ambivalence regarding outpatient mental health therapy, however, acknowledged that his current coping strategies were not sufficiently addressing his ongoing mental health symptoms. Although technically outside of the 30 days from inpatient discharge that is recommended for PED, his psychologist believed that PED might still be an appropriate intervention. First, it was conceptualized that acute rehabilitation was an extension of the original medical stressor, and therefore, it would still be appropriate to provide PED shortly after discharge from the rehab facility as Brandon was beginning to be expected to return to "normal" life and likely to encounter new stressors and barriers. Second, despite significant PTSD symptoms and acknowledged difficulties, Brandon continued to express hesitation to engage in formal mental health services. PED was, therefore, introduced as a means to begin to address his clinically significant PTSD symptoms by "coaching" his social support network on how to facilitate adaptive emotional disclosure. This approach respected Brandon's hesitancy to establish outpatient therapy services and aligned with Brandon's values of utilizing his social network while offering an evidence-based intervention to address PTSD symptoms in a familiar environment (e.g., the intervention was administered by the psychologist who worked with Brandon and his family during admission and in the surgery clinic). Brandon identified his wife, Alyssa, as his supporter for PED.

Prior to initiating PED, the Cultural Formulation Interview (CFI) for DSM-5 was used to establish rapport and enhance clinical understanding of Brandon and his family's experiences of his injuries and hospitalization. This included understanding their cultural definition of the problem, meaning-making regarding his injuries and prognosis, stressors and supports, and cultural factors affecting self-coping and help-seeking. Supplementary modules relevant to Brandon's adjustment to injury were also included such as the Level of Functioning module which was used to assess the impact of his injuries on multiple domains of functioning (e.g., occupational, financial, social, enjoyment).

7.7.3 Case Formulation

After an initial assessment, the trauma psychologist conceptualized much of Brandon's adjustment difficulties as the result of avoidance of processing emotions related to his injury. He had significant traumatic stress symptoms, including nightmares, intrusive thoughts, and marked physiological arousal and emotional upset when reminded of the incident or his injuries. Brandon presented with notable dysphoria and expressed a deep sense of despair and hopelessness. He repeatedly raised existential questions surrounding his worth as a father and husband if he were no longer able to provide for and protect his family. Brandon was viewed as not having been able to express his warranted anger or to speak about the incident due to avoidant coping on the part of himself and his family. Given his ambivalence toward mental health intervention, PED offered a more accessible framework to begin exploring his thoughts and feelings surrounding the event. Given the recency of the event and ongoing focus on adjustment to injury, it was possible that Brandon could continue to be on a recovery trajectory and that administration of PED could help to facilitate his natural recovery process.

7.7.4 Sessions Overview

The intervention began with the *orientation* component in which Brandon and Alyssa were oriented to the purpose of the intervention. The orientation to the purpose and goals of the intervention was followed by a psychoeducational component specifically focused on *common reactions* following injury. This included common reactions to SCI and negative experiences within the healthcare setting (e.g., medical racism) that Brandon and his family may have experienced. These reactions were then normalized and contextualized for Brandon and Alyssa. Initially, Alyssa demonstrated difficulty trusting the psychologist due to viewing them as a member of the surgical team that she believed gave up on her husband. By directly addressing the types of conflict, mistrust, and disappointment that can arise for patients and families following serious injuries, Alyssa was able to see the psychologist as someone who was able to accept their concerns as credible and valid.

Following psychoeducation regarding common reactions, Brandon and Alyssa were provided information about natural recovery and the *importance of processing* in promoting recovery and adjustment following a medical experience. This component reinforces the idea that disclosing injury-related thoughts and feelings with trusted others is a core aspect of the recovery process. Brandon and Alyssa endorsed ongoing avoidance of their injury-related thoughts and feelings. Although Brandon had begun to develop insight into the detriment of continued emotional avoidance, Alyssa continued to emphasize the importance of "focusing on the good" and limiting discussion of difficult topics. As these interpersonal dynamics are not uncommon, the intervention then preempted possible ambivalence or concerns regarding emotional disclosure by proactively discussing *social constraints* and the tendency to avoid uncomfortable thoughts, feelings, and experiences which inhibit engagement in disclosure. Brandon disclosed fears that he would be seen as "weak" by Alyssa if he were to discuss his emotions and shared his attempts to hide his feelings in order to reduce Alyssa's burden as a caregiver. Alyssa reported concerns that Brandon was losing his faith in God when he focused on the negative, and struggling with envy (and resulting shame) herself when seeing others who were not juggling the multiple roles that she was as a mother, wife, and now caregiver. Both reported that they had never shared these thoughts with each other as most of their communications had been focused on problem-solving (e.g., scheduling multiple appointments, navigating child care) and addressing practical matters (e.g., hospital bills, daily tasks):

Alyssa [A]: Sometimes I see you struggling and it is too much for me to see you in pain. I just wish we could just be back to normal again. I just don't know how to fix it for you.

Therapist [T]: Alyssa, I want to first acknowledge your vulnerability in sharing this with us. It is so normal to grieve what life was like before and to want to take your husband's pain away. I can tell that you care for him deeply. You have been such a source of support throughout his recovery. I also want to discuss what can happen when we focus so much on "fixing" a situation. Sometimes our attempts to fix can actually make it more difficult for our loved one to truly process their feelings. This is called a "social constraint." Our desire to fix, even with the best intentions, can be our attempt to avoid our own uncomfortable thoughts and feelings. As a result, we can constrain or limit our partner's normal processing that leads to emotional recovery. Perhaps the thing that might be most helpful, is releasing the pressure to fix and to focus on being present with each other. Brandon, is there anything you'd like to respond to?

Brandon [B]: I see how hard you have been working to support me since the accident. I couldn't have done any of this without you. I'm sorry this happened, I wish we could go back too. I've been trying to stay strong for you and sometimes I worry I am failing you.

T: You are both working to process a life changing event. What you're doing right now—connecting with each other and sharing how you're feeling, is going to be what supports both of your healing. We have some skills that we can discuss that will help you both with getting more comfortable asking for and receiving emotional support. Is there anything else you'd like to discuss before I introduce those skills?

Following psychoeducation and normalization regarding common reactions to the trauma, the importance of processing, and barriers to emotional processing, the remainder of the intervention focuses on the introduction of practical strategies to improve the quality of emotional disclosure and adaptive coping as well as motivational interviewing to generate motivation and efficacy in adopting these strategies. This process begins with a review of *dos and don'ts in communicating about feelings*, a component of the intervention focused on effective and ineffective ways of initiating disclosure, providing support to others, and effectively responding to social constraints. Brandon and Alyssa both acknowledged their tendencies to make assumptions about what other were feeling, which ultimately limited their engagement in emotional disclosure. Gender norms within their marriage were also explored such as their expectations of how a husband and wife "should" interact with each other and its impact on their communication style. Alyssa expressed her value of "giving it to God" and her concern that expressing negative emotions could "lead them away from God."

After the introduction of the strategies, a *motivational interview* was utilized to assess and promote the dyad's motivation to engage in emotional disclosure and their confidence in adopting these skills. This includes a review of the pros and cons of discussing injury-related thoughts and further coaching and/or problem-solving on how to improve the quality and/or quality of emotional processing. Alyssa began to examine her belief that God may give many ways of making sense of the world, including through the expression of emotions. She expressed motivation to continue processing these beliefs with spiritual guidance and to create space for Brandon to share his emotions. Brandon acknowledged that his worries of how he would be perceived were often a significant barrier to emotional disclosure and that he could operate at the emotional extremes—acting as if everything was okay to lashing out in seemingly unrelated situations (e.g., panic and irritability in response to minor inconveniences), which further worried Alyssa and his family and consequently led them to avoid sharing their concerns with Brandon. As demonstrated in this excerpt:

T: That's a thoughtful perspective, Alyssa. Creating that safe space is crucial. Brandon, you also mentioned some barriers to talking, including concerns about how you might be perceived and how you handle your emotions when they come up. Can you share more about this?

B: Well, it's not that easy for me. I've always been taught to be strong and not show vulnerability. I worry that if I share my emotions, Alyssa might see me differently, and not in a good way. I've seen how my emotions can confuse and worry her, and that makes me even more hesitant to open up.

T: Thank you for sharing, Brandon. You've been through immense stress over the last few months and it makes sense you're wrestling with some strong emotions that you may not have a lot of practice processing yet. Your willingness to talk about them now and your worries is an important milestone. Alyssa, what do you notice when it comes to seeing Brandon struggle with these things?

A: Brandon, I want you to know that your behavior, the emotional swings and bottling things up, it worries me because it feels like I'm not getting the chance to truly know how you're feeling. It makes me hesitant to share my own emotions because I don't want to overwhelm you or add to your burden. I know we both have a lot to process, and I'd like us to find a way to support each other through this, without fear or judgment.

T: What are you noticing coming up for you, Brandon?

B: I'm trying to be more open, but it's not easy for me, and I'm still hesitant. I want you to know that I value your emotions and your thoughts, but it's going to take time for me to fully open up. I'm working on not letting my fears hold me back, and I promise to support you as well. We can go forward together, one day at a time, and trust in God to take care of us.

T: At the beginning of our visit today, you both shared a lot of hesitancy to talk about your feelings. How did this conversation compare to your expectations?

A: It actually felt better than I expected. I think we've both had some idea that we've been feeling this way. We just didn't say it out loud to each other. [Brandon nodding in agreement].

T: Your willingness to communicate about these challenges is an important step forward. Recognizing each other's concerns is a vital part of building a supportive and open dynamic. How can you work together to encourage open and honest emotional sharing?

The subsequent component focused on the *dos and don'ts in coping* and reviewed potentially adaptive and maladaptive coping responses. Brandon and Alyssa's use of positive coping behaviors was explored and reinforced. The intervention concluded with a *discussion* of what Brandon and Alyssa learned from the session as well as any disagreements or concerns that may have arisen and a *recap* of the major points of the intervention and the discussion. Brandon and Alyssa were then provided *written support materials,* including handouts reviewing the core messages of the intervention: common reactions, likely and unlikely outcomes of talking about feelings, do's and don'ts in communicating about feelings and coping, when to seek professional help, and how to contact professional help. These materials also include handouts to facilitate retaining the information and recording/monitoring of coping and disclosure behaviors between sessions.

7.7.5 Outcomes

The second and final session of the intervention was scheduled for approximately 2 weeks later, and Brandon and Alyssa were provided with a booster session reminder card. In the booster session, Brandon and Alyssa both reported increased motivation to engage in emotional disclosure while also acknowledging their ongoing need to build habits around processing with each other. It was determined that they continue to have trouble initiating conversations, but are able to have meaningful conversations once they begin talking. The psychologist reviewed the strategies on how to initiate communication and conducted additional motivational interviewing to explore barriers to initiating disclosure. Brandon reported that he was able to open up to his friend and former co-worker. He learned that his concerns that he would be seen as weak were unfounded and that many of his co-workers shared Brandon's safety concerns and frustrations. Alyssa reported increasing comfort with her own emotions. She reported that she had been journaling as a way to process her feelings. She expressed she was beginning to prioritize time for herself and delegating more tasks to Brandon (e.g., calling in prescriptions) to increase his sense of agency and alleviate her stress. Brandon and Alyssa also came to conceptualize the physical therapists and other members of the care team as "agents of God" who were meant to convey God's healing abilities and continued to rely on their faith to support their coping and adjustment.

On symptom assessment, Brandon experienced a meaningful drop in depression symptoms on the PHQ-9 with a total score of 6 at the final session. On the PCL-5, Brandon experienced a mild improvement in symptoms with a total score of 45 representing a 7-point reduction. Brandon continued to decline outpatient mental health therapy referrals, however, noted satisfaction with PED and an overall sense of improvement in his mood and coping despite ongoing PTSD symptoms. He was encouraged to contact a trusted care provider for appropriate referrals should any urgent concerns arise regarding his mood, coping, or adjustment.

Brandon and Alyssa represent the role that PED can play in facilitating natural recovery and adjustment to injury. Although Brandon was hesitant to engage in mental health services, and that was not changed by PED, he and his wife were able to access an evidence-based brief intervention due to the integration of PED within the existing care structures that Brandon came into contact with. The characteristics and framing of PED as a very brief set of two educational or "coaching" sessions likely increased the acceptability and accessibility of this potent mental health intervention. Although Brandon may go on to experience clinically significant PTSD symptoms, he has been equipped with knowledge, a set of tools, and resources to support his recovery in a way that is aligned with his values and current priorities.

Acknowledgments The authors wish to thank Kerry Short, RN, MSN, ACNP-BC, from the Medical College of Wisconsin for reviewing the case vignette for medical accuracy.

References

Aggarwal, N. K., & Lewis-Fernandez, R. (2020). An introduction to the cultural formulation interview. *Diversity, Equity and Inclusion in Psychiatry, 18*(1), 77–82. https://doi.org/10.1176/appi.focus.18103

Allen, E. M., Call, K. T., Beebe, T. J., McAlpine, D. D., & Johnson, P. J. (2017). Barriers to care and health care utilization among the publicly insured. *Medical Care, 55*(3), 207–214. https://doi.org/10.1097/MLR.0000000000000644

American Psychological Association. (2013). Guidelines for psychological practice in health care delivery systems. *American Psychologist, 68*(1), 1–6. https://doi.org/10.1037/a0029890

Anderson, J. L., Brasel, K. J., & DeRoon-Cassini, T. (2011). Predicting six-month posttraumatic stress disorder symptoms and quality of life in an injured trauma population. *Journal of Surgical Research, 165*(2), 244. https://doi.org/10.1016/j.jss.2010.11.499

Badr, H., & Acitelli, L. K. (2017). Re-thinking dyadic coping in the context of chronic illness. *Current Opinion in Psychology, 13*, 44–48. https://doi.org/10.1016/j.copsyc.2016.03.001

Bailey, Z. D., Krieger, N., Agénor, M., Graves, J., Linos, N., & Bassett, M. T. (2017). Structural racism and health inequities in the USA: Evidence and interventions. *Lancet, 389*(10077), 1453–1463. https://doi.org/10.1016/S0140-6736(17)30569-X

Bannon, S. M., Cornelius, T., Gates, M. V., Lester, E., Mace, R. A., Popok, P., et al. (2022a). Emotional distress in neuro-ICU survivor–caregiver dyads: The recovering together randomized clinical trial. *Health Psychology, 41*(4), 268–277. https://doi.org/10.1037/hea0001102

Bannon, S. M., Fishbein, N. S., Lovette, B. C., Wang, K., Waterhouse, C., Rajala, C. E., et al. (2022b). A meta-synthesis of individual, interpersonal, and systemic factors impacting resilience after traumatic brain injury. *Rehabilitation Psychology, 67*(4), 535–545. https://doi.org/10.1037/rep0000462

Bannon, S. M., Grunberg, V. A., Manglani, H. R., Lester, E. G., Ritchie, C., & Vranceanu, A. M. (2022c). Together from the start: A transdiagnostic framework for early dyadic interventions for neurodegenerative diseases. *Journal of the American Geriatrics Society, 70*(6), 1850–1862. https://doi.org/10.1111/jgs.17801

Benjamins, M. R., & Whitman, S. (2014). Relationships between discrimination in health care and health care outcomes among four race/ethnic groups. *Journal of Behavioral Medicine, 37*, 402–413. https://doi.org/10.1007/s10865-013-9496-7

Birk, J. L., Sumner, J. A., Haerizadeh, M., Heyman-Kantor, R., Falzon, L., Gonzalez, C., Gershengoren, L., Shapiro, P., Edmondson, D., & Kronish, I. M. (2019). Early interventions to prevent posttraumatic stress disorder symptoms in survivors of life-threatening medical events: A systematic review. *Journal of Anxiety Disorders, 64*, 24–39. https://doi.org/10.1016/j.janxdis.2019.03.003

Bisson, J. I., Berliner, L., Cloitre, M., Forbes, D., Jensen, T. K., Lewis, C., Monson, C. M., Olff, M., Pilling, S., Riggs, D. S., Roberts, N. P., & Shapiro, F. (2019). The International Society for Traumatic Stress Studies new guidelines for the prevention and treatment of PTSD:

Methodology and development process. *Journal of Traumatic Stress, 32*(4), 475–483. https://doi.org/10.1002/jts.22421

Brunet, A., Des Groseilliers, I. B., Cordova, M. J., & Ruzek, J. I. (2013). Randomized controlled trial of a brief dyadic cognitive-behavioral intervention designed to prevent PTSD. *European Journal of Psychotraumatology, 4*. https://doi.org/10.3402/ejpt.v4i0.21572

Casanova-Perez, R., Apodaca, C., Bascom, E., Mohanraj, D., Lane, C., Vidyarthi, D., et al. (2021). Broken down by bias: Healthcare biases experienced by BIPOC and LGBTQ+ patients. In *AMIA annual symposium proceedings* (Vol. 2021, p. 275). American Medical Informatics Association.

Compton, M. T., & Shim, R. S. (2020). Mental illness prevention and mental health promotion: When, who, and how. *Psychiatric Services, 71*(9), 981–983. https://doi.org/10.1176/appi.ps.201900374

Cordova, M. J., Ruzek, J. I., Benoi, M., & Brunet, A. (2003). Promotion of emotional disclosure following illness and injury: A brief intervention for medical patients and their families. *Cognitive and Behavioral Practice, 10*(4), 358–371. https://doi.org/10.1016/S1077-7229(03)80053-6

Cox, D. R., Cox, R. H., & Caplan, B. (2013). *Specialty competencies in rehabilitation psychology*. Oxford University Press.

Crasta, D., Crane, C. A., Trabold, N., Shepardson, R. L., Possemato, K., & Funderburk, J. S. (2022). Relationship health and intimate partner violence in integrated primary care: Individual characteristics and preferences for relationship support across risk levels. *International Journal of Environmental Research and Public Health, 19*(21), 13984. https://doi.org/10.3390/ijerph192113984

Darnell, D. A., Parker, L. E., Wagner, A. W., Dunn, C. W., Atkins, D. C., Dorsey, S., & Zatzick, D. F. (2019). Task-shifting to improve the reach of mental health interventions for trauma patients: Findings from a pilot study of trauma nurse training in patient-centered activity scheduling for PTSD and depression. *Cognitive Behaviour Therapy, 48*(6), 482–496. https://doi.org/10.1080/16506073.2018.1541928

deRoon-Cassini, T. A., Mancini, A. D., Rusch, M. D., & Bonanno, G. A. (2010). Psychopathology and resilience following traumatic injury: A latent growth mixture model analysis. *Rehabilitation Psychology, 55*(1), 1–11. https://doi.org/10.1037/a0018601

deRoon-Cassini, T. A., Hunt, J. C., Geier, T. J., Warren, A. M., Ruggiero, K. J., Scott, K., George, J., Halling, M., Jurkovich, G., Fakhry, S. M., Zatzick, D., & Brasel, K. J. (2019). Screening and treating hospitalized trauma survivors for posttraumatic stress disorder and depression. *The Journal of Trauma and Acute Care Surgery, 87*(2), 440–450. https://doi.org/10.1097/TA.0000000000002370

Des Groseilliers, I. B., Marchand, A., Cordova, M. J., Ruzek, J. I., & Brunet, A. (2013). Two-year follow-up of a brief dyadic cognitive-behavioral intervention designed to prevent PTSD. *Psychological Trauma: Theory, Research, Practice, and Policy, 5*(5), 462–469. https://doi.org/10.1037/a0031967

DiMatteo, M. R., Lepper, H. S., & Croghan, T. W. (2000). Depression is a risk factor for noncompliance with medical treatment: Meta-analysis of the effects of anxiety and depression on patient adherence. *Archives of Internal Medicine, 160*(14), 2101–2107. https://doi.org/10.1001/archinte.160.14.2101

Dworkin, E. R., Ruzek, J. I., Cordova, M. J., Fitzpatrick, S., Merchant, L., Stewart, T., Santos, J. P., Mohr, J., & Bedard-Gilligan, M. (2022). Supporter-focused early intervention for recent sexual assault survivors: Study protocol for a pilot randomized clinical trial. *Contemporary Clinical Trials, 119*, 106848. https://doi.org/10.1016/j.cct.2022.106848

Edmondson, D., Richardson, S., Falzon, L., Davidson, K., Mills, M., & Neria, Y. (2012). Posttraumatic stress disorder prevalence and risk of recurrence in acute coronary syndrome patients: A meta-analytic review. *PLoS One, 7*(6), e38915. https://doi.org/10.1371/journal.pone.0038915

Engel, G. L. (1977). The need for a new medical model: A challenge for biomedicine. *Science, 196*(4286), 129–136. https://doi.org/10.1126/science.847460

Engel, G. L. (1981). The clinical application of the biopsychosocial model. *The Journal of Medicine and Philosophy, 6*(2), 101–124. https://doi.org/10.1176/ajp.137.5.535
Fiske, S. T. (2014). *Social beings: Core motives in social psychology*. Wiley.
Gonzalez, J. S., Peyrot, M., McCarl, L. A., Collins, E. M., Serpa, L., Mimiaga, M. J., & Safren, S. A. (2008). Depression and diabetes treatment nonadherence: A meta-analysis. *Diabetes Care, 31*(12), 2398–2403. https://doi.org/10.2337/dc08-1341
Green, B. L., Epstein, S. A., Krupnick, J. L., & Rowland, J. H. (1998). Trauma and medical illness: Assessing trauma-related disorders in medical settings. In J. P. Wilson & T. M. Keane (Eds.), *Assessing psychological trauma and PTSD* (pp. 160–191). Guilford Press.
Guay, S., Billette, V., & Marchand, A. (2006). Exploring the links between posttraumatic stress disorder and social support: Processes and potential research avenues. *Journal of Traumatic Stress, 19*(3), 327–338. https://doi.org/10.1002/jts.20124
Guttman, O. T., Lazzara, E. H., Keebler, J. R., Webster, K. L. W., Gisick, L. M., & Baker, A. L. (2021). Dissecting communication barriers in healthcare: A path to enhancing communication resiliency, reliability, and patient safety. *Journal of Patient Safety, 17*(8), e1465–e1471. https://doi.org/10.1097/PTS.0000000000000541
Halawi, M. J., Chiu, D., Gronbeck, C., Savoy, L., Williams, V. J., & Cote, M. P. (2019). Psychological distress independently predicts prolonged hospitalization after primary total hip and knee arthroplasty. *The Journal of Arthroplasty, 34*(8), 1598–1601. https://doi.org/10.1016/j.arth.2019.03.063
Hare, D. L., Toukhsati, S. R., Johansson, P., & Jaarsma, T. (2014). Depression and cardiovascular disease: A clinical review. *European Heart Journal, 35*(21), 1365–1372. https://doi.org/10.1093/eurheartj/eht462
Harrison, J., Maguire, P., & Pitceathly, C. (1995). Confiding in crisis: Gender differences in pattern of confiding among cancer patients. *Social Science and Medicine, 41*(9), 1255–1260. https://doi.org/10.1016/0277-9536(94)00411-L
Hodgson, J., Lamson, A., Mendenhall, T., & Tyndall, L. (Eds.). (2014). *Medical family therapy: Advanced applications*. Springer International Publishing.
Holbrook, T. L., Anderson, J. P., Sieber, W. J., Browner, D., & Hoyt, D. B. (1999). Outcome after major trauma: 12-month and 18-month follow-up results from the trauma recovery project. *The Journal of Trauma: Injury, Infection, and Critical Care, 46*(5), 765–773. https://doi.org/10.1097/00005373-199905000-00003
Holt-Lunstad, J. (2017) The potential public health relevance of social isolation and loneliness: Prevalence, epidemiology, and risk factors, *Public Policy & Aging Report, 27*(4), 127–130. https://doi.org/10.1093/ppar/prx030
Horowitz, M. J. (1986). Stress-response syndromes: A review of posttraumatic and adjustment disorders. *Hospital & Community Psychiatry, 37*(3), 241–249. https://doi.org/10.1176/ps.37.3.241
Hunt, J. C., Herrera-Hernandez, E., Brandolino, A., Jazinski-Chambers, K., Maher, K., Jackson, B., Smith, R. N., Lape, D., Cook, M., Bergner, C., Schramm, A. T., Brasel, K. J., de Moya, M. A., & deRoon-Cassini, T. A. (2021). Validation of the injured trauma survivor screen: An American Association for the Surgery of Trauma multi-institutional trial. *The Journal of Trauma and Acute Care Surgery, 90*(5), 797–806. https://doi.org/10.1097/TA.0000000000003079
Hunt, J. C., Chesney, S. A., Brasel, K., & deRoon-Cassini, T. A. (2018). Six-month follow-up of the injured trauma survivor screen: Clinical implications and future directions. *The journal of trauma and acute care surgery, 85*(2), 263–270. https://doi.org/10.1097/TA.0000000000001944
Jaini, P. A., & Lee, J. S. H. (2015). A review of 21st-century utility of a biopsychosocial model in United States medical school education. *Journal of Lifestyle Medicine, 5*(2), 49–55. https://doi.org/10.15280/jlm.2015.5.2.49
Joynt, K. E., Whellan, D. J., & O'Connor, C. M. (2003). Depression and cardiovascular disease: Mechanisms of interaction. *Biological Psychiatry, 54*(3), 248–261. https://doi.org/10.1016/s0006-3223(03)00568-7

Karakurt, G., Whiting, K., van Esch, C., Bolen, S. D., & Calabrese, J. R. (2016). Couples therapy for intimate partner violence: A systematic review and meta-analysis. *Journal of Marital and Family Therapy, 42*(4), 567–583. https://doi.org/10.1111/jmft.12178

Katon, W. J. (2011). Epidemiology and treatment of depression in patients with chronic medical illness. *Dialogues in Clinical Neuroscience, 13*(1), 7–23. https://doi.org/10.31887/DCNS.2011.13.1/wkaton

Kroenke, K., Spitzer, R. L., & Williams, J. B. W. (1999). *Patient Health Questionnaire-9 (PHQ-9)* [Database record].

Lepore, S. J. (2001). A social–cognitive processing model of emotional adjustment to cancer. In A. Baum & B. L. Andersen (Eds.), *Psychosocial interventions for cancer* (pp. 99–116). American Psychological Association. https://doi.org/10.1037/10402-006

Lepore S. (2001). A social–cognitive processing model of emotional adjustment to cancer. In: Baum A, Andersen BL, editors. *Psychosocial interventions for cancer*. American Psychological Association (pp. 99–118). Washington, DC.

Lepore, S. J., & Helgeson, V. S. (1998). Social constraints, intrusive thoughts, and mental health after prostate cancer. *Journal of Social and Clinical Psychology, 17*(1), 89–106. https://doi.org/10.1521/jscp.1998.17.1.89

Lepore, S. J., & Revenson, T. A. (2007). Social constraints on disclosure and adjustment to cancer. *Social and Personality Psychology Compass, 1*(1), 313–333. https://doi.org/10.1111/j.1751-9004.2007.00013.x

Liu, J. J., DeCuir, N., Kia, L., Peterson, J., Miller, C., & Issaka, R. B. (2023). Tools to measure the impact of structural racism and discrimination on gastrointestinal and hepatology disease outcomes: A scoping review. *Clinical Gastroenterology and Hepatology, 21*(11), 2759–2788.e6. https://doi.org/10.1016/j.cgh.2022.12.002

Martins, D. A., Coêlho, P. D. L. P., Becker, S. G., Ferreira, A. A., Oliveira, M. L. C., & Monteiro, L. B. (2021). Religiosity and mental health as aspects of comprehensiveness in care. *Revista Brasileira de Enfermagem, 75*(1), e20201011. https://doi.org/10.1590/0034-7167-2020-1011

Martire, L. M., Lustig, A. P., Schulz, R., Miller, G. E., & Helgeson, V. S. (2004). Is it beneficial to involve a family member? A meta-analysis of psychosocial interventions for chronic illness. *Health psychology: official journal of the Division of Health Psychology, American Psychological Association, 23*(6), 599–611. https://doi.org/10.1037/0278-6133.23.6.599

McBain, S. A., Stoycos, S., & Doenges, T. (2023). Breaking silos to address medical trauma: The need for integration of trauma and health psychology training. *Journal of Clinical Psychology in Medical Settings, 30*(2), 380–386. https://doi.org/10.1007/s10880-022-09897-2

McGeary, C. A., Morland, L. A., Resick, P. A., Straud, C. L., Moring, J. C., Sohn, M. J., Mackintosh, M. A., Young-McCaughan, S., Acierno, R., Rauch, S. A. M., Mintz, J., McGeary, D. D., Wells, S. Y., Grubbs, K., Nabity, P. S., McMahon, C. J., Litz, B. T., Velligan, D. I., Macdonald, A., Mata-Galan, E., et al. (2023). Impact and efficiency of treatment across two PTSD clinical trials comparing in-person and telehealth service delivery formats. *Psychological Services, 21*(1), 73–81. https://doi.org/10.1037/ser0000774

Meuleman, E., Sloover, M., & van Ee, E. (2023). Involving a significant other in treatment of patients with PTSD symptoms: A systematic review of treatment interventions. *Trauma, Violence, & Abuse, 24*(3), 2034–2044. https://doi.org/10.1177/15248380221082939

Mundy, E., & Baum, A. (2004). Medical disorders as a cause of psychological trauma and posttraumatic stress disorder [Editorial]. *Current Opinion in Psychiatry, 17*(2), 123–127. https://doi.org/10.1097/00001504-200403000-00009

Muñoz, R. F., Mrazek, P. J., & Haggerty, R. J. (1996). Institute of Medicine report on prevention of mental disorders: Summary and commentary. *American Psychologist, 51*(11), 1116–1122. https://doi.org/10.1037/0003-066X.51.11.1116

Nouwen, A., Adriaanse, M. C., van Dam, K., Iversen, M. M., Viechtbauer, W., Peyrot, M., Caramlau, I., Kokoszka, A., Kanc, K., de Groot, M., Nefs, G., Pouwer, F., & European Depression in Diabetes (EDID) Research Consortium. (2019). Longitudinal associations between depression and diabetes complications: A systematic review and meta-analysis. *Diabetic Medicine, 36*(12), 1562–1572. https://doi.org/10.1111/dme.14054

O'Donnell, M. L., Creamer, M., Bryant, R. A., Schnyder, U., & Shalev, A. (2003). Posttraumatic disorders following injury: An empirical and methodological review. *Clinical Psychology Review, 23*(4), 587–603. https://doi.org/10.1016/S0272-7358(03)00036-9

O'Donnell, M. L., Pacella, B. J., Bryant, R. A., Olff, M., & Forbes, D. (2020). Early intervention for trauma-related psychopathology. In D. Forbes, J. I. Bisson, C. M. Monson, & L. Berliner (Eds.), *Effective treatments for PTSD: Practice guidelines from the International Society for Traumatic Stress Studies* (pp. 117–131). Guilford Press.

Peek, M. E., Nunez-Smith, M., Drum, M., & Lewis, T. T. (2011). Adapting the everyday discrimination scale to medical settings: Reliability and validity testing in a sample of African American patients. *Ethnicity & Disease, 21*(4), 502–509.

Pitman, A., Suleman, S., Hyde, N., & Hodgkiss, A. (2018). Depression and anxiety in patients with cancer. *BMJ (Clinical research ed.), 361*, 1415. https://doi.org/10.1136/bmj.k1415

Platt, J., Keyes, K. M., & Koenen, K. C. (2014). Size of the social network versus quality of social support: Which is more protective against PTSD? *Social Psychiatry and Psychiatric Epidemiology, 49*(8), 1279–1286. https://doi.org/10.1007/s00127-013-0798-4

Porter, C. A., Cortese, M., Vezina, M., & Fitzpatrick, J. J. (2014). Nurse caring behaviors following implementation of a relationship centered care professional practice model. *International Journal of Caring Sciences, 7*(3), 818–822.

Raja, S., Hasnain, M., Hoersch, M., Gove-Yin, S., & Rajagopalan, C. (2015). Trauma informed care in medicine: Current knowledge and future research directions. *Family & Community Health, 38*(3), 216–226. https://doi.org/10.1097/FCH.0000000000000071

Ransome, Y., Valido, A. D., Espelage, D. L., Clements, G. L., Harrell, C., Eckel, C., Price, N., Nassau, R., Nyhan, K., & Taggar, T. L. (2023). A systematic review of how social connectedness impacts associations between racism and discrimination on health outcomes. *Epidemiologic Reviews*. https://doi.org/10.1093/epirev/mxad009

Resick, P. A., & Schnicke, M. K. (1992). Cognitive processing therapy for sexual assault victims. *Journal of Consulting and Clinical Psychology, 60*(5), 748–756. https://doi.org/10.1037/0022-006X.60.5.748

Rhondali, W., Perceau, E., Berthiller, J., Saltel, P., Trillet-Lenoir, V., Tredan, O., Coulon, J. P., Bruera, E., & Filbet, M. (2012). Frequency of depression among oncology outpatients and association with other symptoms. *Supportive Care in Cancer, 20*(11), 2795–2802. https://doi.org/10.1007/s00520-012-1401-3

Richmond, T. S., Ruzek, J., Ackerson, T., Wiebe, D. J., Winston, F., & Kassam-Adams, N. (2011). Predicting the future development of depression or PTSD after injury. *General Hospital Psychiatry, 33*(4), 327–335. https://doi.org/10.1016/j.genhosppsych.2011.05.003

Rolland, J. S. (1994). In sickness and in health: The impact of illness on couples' relationships. *Journal of Marital and Family Therapy, 20*(4), 327–347. https://doi.org/10.1111/j.1752-0606.1994.tb00125.x

Roy, T., & Lloyd, C. E. (2012). Epidemiology of depression and diabetes: a systematic review. *Journal of affective disorders, 142 Suppl*, S8–S21. https://doi.org/10.1016/S0165-0327(12)70004-6

Rosenberg, G. M., Stave, C., Spain, D. A., & Weiser, T. G. (2018). Patient-reported outcomes in trauma: A scoping study of published research. *Trauma Surgery & Acute Care Open, 3*(1), e000202. https://doi.org/10.1136/tsaco-2018-000202

Rosland, A.-M., Heisler, M., & Piette, J. D. (2012). The impact of family behaviors and communication patterns on chronic illness outcomes: A systematic review. *Journal of Behavioral Medicine, 35*(2), 221–239. https://doi.org/10.1007/s10865-011-9354-4

Scott, J., Yellowlees, P., Becker, D. F., & Chen, C. (2023). Virtual care and mental health: Dismantling silos to strengthen care delivery. *Telemedicine Reports, 4*(1), 174–179. https://doi.org/10.1089/tmr.2023.0016

Shnaider, P., Sijercic, I., Wanklyn, S. G., Suvak, M. K., & Monson, C. M. (2017). The role of social support in cognitive-behavioral conjoint therapy for posttraumatic stress disorder. *Behavior Therapy, 48*(3), 285–294. https://doi.org/10.1016/j.beth.2016.05.003

Simon, N., Roberts, N. P., Lewis, C. E., van Gelderen, M. J., & Bisson, J. I. (2019). Associations between perceived social support, posttraumatic stress disorder (PTSD) and complex PTSD

(CPTSD): Implications for treatment. *European Journal of Psychotraumatology, 10*(1), 1573129. https://doi.org/10.1080/20008198.2019.1573129

Smith, K. J., Béland, M., Clyde, M., Gariépy, G., Pagé, V., Badawi, G., Rabasa-Lhoret, R., & Schmitz, N. (2013). Association of diabetes with anxiety: A systematic review and meta-analysis. *Journal of Psychosomatic Research, 74*(2), 89–99. https://doi.org/10.1016/j.jpsychores.2012.11.013

Substance Abuse and Mental Health Services Administration. (2014). *SAMHSA's Concept of trauma and guidance for a trauma-informed approach*. Retrieved from: https://store.samhsa.gov/product/SAMHSA-s-Concept-of-Trauma-and-Guidance-for-a-Trauma-Informed-Approach/SMA14-4884

Surgeon General of the United States. (2023). Our epidemic of loneliness and isolation: The U.S. Surgeon General's advisory on the healing effects of social connection and community. *United States Public Health Service*. Accessed 21 October 2023 at https://www.hhs.gov/sites/default/files/surgeon-general-social-connection-advisory.pdf

Sutar, R., & Chaudhary, P. (2022). Prognostic disclosure in cancer care: A systematic literature review. *Palliative Care and Social Practice, 16*, 1–24. https://doi.org/10.1177/26323524221101077

Taft, T. H., Quinton, S., Jedel, S., Simons, M., Mutlu, E. A., & Hanauer, S. B. (2022). Posttraumatic stress in patients with inflammatory bowel disease: Prevalence and relationships to patient-reported outcomes. *Inflammatory Bowel Diseases, 28*(5), 710–719. https://doi.org/10.1093/ibd/izab152

Tedstone, J. E., & Tarrier, N. (2003). Posttraumatic stress disorder following medical illness and treatment. *Clinical psychology review, 23*(3), 409–448. https://doi.org/10.1016/s0272-7358(03)00031-x

Wade, D. T., & Halligan, P. W. (2017). The biopsychosocial model of illness: A model whose time has come. *Clinical Rehabilitation, 31*(8), 995–1004. https://doi.org/10.1177/0269215517709890

Weathers, F. W., Litz, B. T., Keane, T. M., Palmieri, P. A., Marx, B. P., & Schnurr, P. P. (2013). *The PTSD Checklist for DSM-5 (PCL-5)*. Scale available from the National Center for PTSD at www.ptsd.va.gov.

World Health Organization. (n.d.). *The determinants of health*. Retrieved from http://www.who.int/hia/evidence/doh/en/

Part III
Interventions with Children and Adolescents

Chapter 8
Parent Involvement in Weekly Outpatient Treatment

Amy E. West and Bridgid M. Conn

8.1 Introduction

Family involvement has been demonstrated to be a crucial component of successful cognitive-behavioral intervention in addressing a range of internalizing and externalizing youth mental health issues. Indeed, it has often been observed as a mechanism of therapeutic change for youth, highlighting the importance of leveraging parental influence to improve treatment outcomes (e.g., Weinstein & West, 2021). Of note, the term "parent" is used throughout this chapter; however, this does not solely refer to biological parents and may include extended family members, guardians, and other caregivers who are in a parental role for the youth. In treatment research, biological mothers have been historically overrepresented as participants. However, there have been more recent efforts to increase the engagement of fathers and other caregivers/family members and to understand the unique contributions of these other caregivers to pediatric anxiety and treatment outcomes (Bögels & Phares, 2008; Duhig et al., 2002; Podell & Kendall, 2011; Reuman et al., 2021; Smith et al., 2018).

A scoping review by Carr (2019) updated prior literature reviews including recent meta-analyses, systematic and narrative literature reviews, and clinical trials evaluating the effectiveness of family-based treatment for a range of developmental psychopathology. In general, family-focused cognitive-behavioral interventions are

A. E. West (✉) · B. M. Conn
Children's Hospital Los Angeles, Keck School of Medicine, University of Southern California, Los Angeles, CA, USA
e-mail: amwest@chla.usc.edu; bconn@chla.usc.edu

L. Reuman, J. Thompson-Hollands (eds.), *Enhancing CBT Through Family and Peer Engagement*, CBT: Science Into Practice, https://doi.org/10.1007/978-3-031-74838-7_8

associated with better mental health outcomes for youth, especially for both anxiety and depression. For example, a plethora of meta-analyses and narrative reviews indicate that family-based, trauma-focused cognitive-behavioral therapy (TF-CBT) had the strongest evidence base for the treatment of post-traumatic stress disorder (PTSD) in youth (Dorsey et al., 2014; Kowalik et al., 2011; Lenz & Hollenbaugh, 2015). Maric et al. (2018) found better long-term anxiety outcomes for those in family-based CBT compared with child-only cognitive-behavioral therapy (CBT), especially for children with high attention-deficit/hyperactivity disorder (ADHD) symptoms. More recently, the use of the transdiagnostic family-based CBT protocol was significantly associated with decreased anxiety and depression and increased tolerance for distressing sounds for youth with misophonia (Lewin et al., 2021). In their recent study, Tompson et al. (2020) found that compared with individual supportive therapy, family-focused CBT was associated with reduced depression and fewer suicide attempts. Similarly, in studies of dialectical behavior therapy (DBT; see Chap. 11), a "third wave" CBT that incorporates mindfulness and other Zen Buddhism-related practices, interventions that incorporated family therapy were associated with reductions in suicide attempts and nonsuicidal self-harm behavior compared with treatment as usual (Asarnow et al., 2017). Freeman et al. (2016) concluded that DBT with family therapy was an effective intervention for adolescents who had attempted suicide, leading to significant reductions in nonsuicidal self-harming behavior, suicidal ideation, and depressive symptoms. Overall, there is a robust theoretical and evidence base to suggest that parent and family involvement in CBT for childhood disorders is a crucial component of treatment and deserving of further empirical attention.

8.2 Treatment Overview: Guide to Parental Involvement in CBT

Child clinical mental health professionals generally affirm that parent involvement is a critical component of effective child therapy. However, parental involvement can take many forms and different kinds of parental involvement may be needed based on the type of CBT, the condition being treated, the age of the child, individual characteristics of the child, the parent-child relationship, and other potential contributing factors. The spectrum of parent involvement may span from infrequent check-ins to apprise the parent of what is being covered in the primarily individual child treatment all the way to intensive parental involvement in weekly family-based CBT. In this section, we briefly describe the different roles that parents can have in child treatment. These roles are not mutually exclusive; parent involvement may shift depending on the target of treatment, the phase of treatment, parent and/or child desire, and many other variables.

8.2.1 Parents as Informants About Treatment Targets and Outcomes

Parents almost always serve as informants on child history and behavior, both at the outset of treatment and as treatment progresses. Parents are generally involved in the initial assessment and treatment planning as a primary reporter on the child's reason for presenting to treatment as well as pertinent psychiatric, medical, developmental, social, academic, and family history. This is an important role for parents as they often hold more detailed and accurate information about their child's development, particularly with respect to historical events and chronology. Parents can also serve as critical informants of treatment progress. CBT is an outcomes-oriented treatment that generally involves careful monitoring and measuring of particular symptoms or behaviors over time. While children are key reporters of their behavioral and emotional experiences, parents can add additional information about what they observe to provide a more holistic and comprehensive perspective (see Chap. 2). Therefore, CBT often involves parent reports of both symptoms and other key functional outcomes, such as peer relationships and school functioning.

8.2.2 Parents as Practical Support

One of the critical roles that parents play in weekly outpatient CBT is that of providing practical support in the form of transportation to and from sessions, scheduling, providing resources and materials at home, advocacy at school, etc. Parents are often the conduit to receiving services in the first place by following up on a referral or self-referring based on concerns about their child. Even if not actively involved in treatment, CBT therapists often "check-in" frequently with parents to explain what is being covered and what their children are being asked to do. This can be important because CBT often requires at-home tasks which may need parental support to complete. For example, in exposure-based CBT for anxiety, a child may need access to a phone to make a call to a store as an assigned exposure homework assignment and thus, parents may need to grant access to a phone. This kind of instrumental support can be especially important with CBT since it often requires both homework and shifts in the child's routines or structured environment, which parents would have to help support and facilitate.

8.2.3 Parents as Coaches/Guides

Parents might also be integrated into treatment as coaches or guides. In this scenario, the CBT may involve providing psychoeducation and skills to the parents to support, scaffold, and reinforce the child's behavior at home. For example, in CBT for mood dysregulation, children often work with their clinicians to develop methods for anticipating and recognizing triggers and enacting coping strategies to manage dysregulation more effectively. It is important for parents to be aware of triggers, reactivity, and coping plans, and to understand the conceptualization of their connection so that they can support their child's adaptive coping. They may need to help escort their child to their "cool down corner" or safe space or encourage their child to use mantras or cognitive restructuring, depending on the situation. In this case, the CBT therapist is likely incorporating parent sessions or having the parent attend parts of each session so that they can learn the material and be involved in planning and problem-solving to help the child be successful at applying skills in their environment outside of therapy.

8.2.4 Parents as Active Treatment Participants

In certain cases, the role of the parent may extend beyond that of a coach or facilitator, and parents may actively participate in CBT in a way that requires more active investment and involvement. This type of involvement goes beyond mere parental involvement and is more appropriately thought of as "family-based CBT" where the treatment is really focused on the family system and not solely the individual child. In family-based CBT, parents participate alongside their children, learning from psychoeducation, helping identify patterns, engaging in problem-solving, setting goals, and generating ideas and solutions. Their work may focus not only on supporting these processes targeting their children, but also on examining their own role in perpetuating and/or potentially intervening through their own cognitive and behavioral choices. For example, in exposure-based CBT, clinicians often have to work with parents around their tendency to accommodate their child's anxiety. In this case, a parent may be unknowingly facilitating their child's avoidance (and thus increasing their anxiety) in the interest of minimizing their immediate distress. A parent would have to work alongside their child, and with the help of the clinician, to actively identify situations where they are accommodating their child's avoidance and work to alter their own behavioral responses. In family-based CBT, the parents are typically receiving a similar dosage of treatment as their child—with alternating family and individual sessions or mostly family sessions with parent and individual sessions alternating intermittently. This decision will depend on the nature of the problem and how extensively the issues are conceptualized as being embedded within the family system versus parallel work for the child and parent; most commonly there is a mix of family-based patterns along with individual foci for both the child and parent.

8.2.5 Parents as Treatment Recipients

There are some cases where parents become the equal or primary treatment target, or when treatment may need to shift to primarily parent work because of significant challenges at the parent or family level. This may be because parents have their own psychopathology, or impairing symptoms, or they demonstrate functional impairment that must be addressed before intervention with the child will be effective. For example, a child may be in treatment for behavioral and emotional dysregulation, and eventually, it becomes evident that the parent is also very dysregulated, reactive, and engages in patterns of communication and behavioral management that are rooted in their own regulation challenges and counterproductive to effective parenting. In this case, it may become important for a clinician to either first, or alongside the child, work directly with the parent to identify their own patterns of dysregulation and how those come to bear in their interactions with their child. In this case, the clinician may target the majority of treatment sessions to the parent only or the family together in order to provide the intensive level of intervention required at the parent as well as the child level.

8.2.6 Complexities of Parent Involvement

Most effective child therapy will entail some level of parental involvement. Although parent involvement likely increases engagement and effectiveness, it is not without complexities. Whenever multiple parties are involved in treatment, particularly parties that may be in conflict, boundaries and role clarification become critically important. One of the most challenging aspects for a clinician to navigate when working with a child and parent in CBT is confidentiality. Depending on the age of the patient and the nature of the presenting problem and treatment goals, parent(s) may need to be involved in ways that require them to have some degree of knowledge about the child's course in therapy. For instance, clients in early and middle childhood may require more parental involvement around exposures, such as transportation to a social setting or having access to a phone to make a call to a store. Parents may also need to be aware of the exposures and practices in order to best help their children and support around minimizing avoidance. It is beneficial to the therapeutic process to manage this such that, to the greatest degree possible, the child still feels a sense of agency and control over what is shared and how and understand the limits of confidentiality and plan for sharing information. Privacy and confidentiality can be further complicated when a child reports symptoms such as suicidal ideation or risky behaviors, or if suicidality with imminent risk meets the threshold of mandatory disclosure described in the limits of confidentiality but there may be various levels of suicidality and self-harm that do not meet this threshold and the child requests to keep private. The extent to which these factors are related to the child's symptoms, functioning, or capacity to cope with these issues may present a challenge to parental involvement or family-based CBT. For example, an adolescent whose triggers for suicidality may not be known or understood by their parents may be hesitant to share their safety plan. In cases where clinicians are balancing confidentiality and safety monitoring, it may be helpful for the client to develop a more in-depth safety plan with relevant details and numbers for close friends or crisis lines. If a youth identifies as part of the LGBTQ+ community, there may be specific resources and contacts on this plan that they may keep private. The therapist can then help them develop another safety plan to be shared with parents(s) that allows caregivers to support the youth in communicating about risk and potential coping skills and resources to tap into.

Another circumstance in which a child may express a particular desire for privacy is related to sensitive aspects of the child's identity, such as gender identity or sexual orientation. Ultimately, the child's desire for privacy and confidentiality is core to the maintenance of a productive therapeutic relationship and must be respected, even if it means parents cannot support or scaffold them in a way that might be helpful to the overall treatment progress. However, there also may be a role for the clinician to educate and encourage disclosure and communication when it might be consistent with the child's goals for treatment and/or the clinician's judgment about what would be therapeutically beneficial. In the end, the CBT clinician must manage these complexities with confidentiality in an individualized way as each case will call for a novel approach and perspective.

Parental involvement can also introduce complexities with respect to managing family conflict and the dynamics of the family system. It can be difficult to manage alliances, maintain a neutral stance, and build and sustain rapport with families where there are high levels of conflict and contrasting perspectives about the issues being targeted in CBT. When parents are actively and intensively involved in treatment, there are multiple avenues for communication and relationship, which can be helpful for achieving treatment goals, but also can require a large amount of effort on the part of the clinician to balance transparency, objectivity, and conflict-resolution within such a complicated system. Most seasoned CBT clinicians who have engaged in family-based CBT approaches have experience and expertise from which to draw in managing these complexities with respect to parent and family involvement, yet it is also the case that each child and parent(s) will introduce a unique set of circumstances and relationships that will need to be assessed and integrated effectively into a productive and meaningful therapeutic process.

8.3 Research Evidence on Parental Involvement in CBT

There is a burgeoning research base from which to draw conclusions about the importance of each of these roles that parents might play in their child's CBT treatment. Evidence points to core factors associated with improved treatment prognosis due to family involvement, namely, improved treatment attendance and engagement, use of behavioral management strategies, facilitation of skills practice and generalization, and addressing of co-occurring parental mental health challenges and problems of family functioning.

8.3.1 Treatment Attendance and Engagement

First and foremost, parents are key facilitators for treatment engagement, as they are often the primary referral source for youth treatment. Parents and caregivers are likely referring their children to services due to observed challenges in youths' quality of life and functioning in multiple domains, such as school, home, and social settings. Thus, they are likely to be motivated to not only bring their children to treatment but also to provide support around engagement. In one study focused on pediatric bipolar disorder (West et al., 2014), child- and family-focused CBT was associated with increased attendance, lower dropout rates, and greater treatment satisfaction compared with the control group (i.e., psychotherapy-as-usual). For youth in foster care, Dorsey et al. (2014) found that parental engagement strategies for foster parents improved retention and lower dropout in TF-CBT treatment, with important implications for improving treatment outcomes for these vulnerable youth. Positive treatment gains were observed at 3-month follow-up with family-based CBT delivered via videoconferencing with high treatment retention, high client satisfaction, strong therapeutic alliance, and low barriers to participation reported by families (Carpenter et al., 2018). Thus, it may be that family involvement may support attendance and engagement for youth participating in CBT via telehealth.

8.3.2 Behavioral Management

Extant research, including an excess of 100 studies, has identified that parent behavioral management training is particularly effective in addressing the impact of childhood behavior problems, resulting in behavior improvement in the majority of children (Brestan & Eyberg, 1998; Furlong et al., 2012; Helander et al., 2022; Tarver et al., 2019). Further, such research has also noted treatment gains in parental behavioral management training observed up to 1 year at follow-up, especially when booster sessions were provided (e.g., Brestan & Eyberg, 1998; Furlong et al., 2012; Leijten et al., 2013; Michelson et al., 2013). A core component of this intervention is contingency management, which is an evidence-based intervention where motivational incentives (e.g., praise, playtime) are provided to increase desired behavior in an individual (e.g., taking turns, speaking aloud). Manassis et al. (2014) found that cognitive-behavioral family therapy was particularly effective in helping young people maintain treatment gains a year after treatment had ended. More specifically, in family-based CBT, parents were coached in using contingency management to reinforce children's coping with exposure to anxiety-provoking stimuli or situations. Such approaches were significantly more effective in the long term compared with interventions where parents had limited involvement, or where there was more parental involvement, but which did not involve using contingency management.

8.3.3 Skills Practice and Generalization

Similarly, within anxiety-focused CBT treatment, parents can be taught the same skills as their youth to support skills practice in different settings and encourage generalization (i.e., applying new skills or behaviors in settings outside of therapy, such as school, home, or in social situations). For example, the family-based component of the FRIENDS program teaches parents to reward their children's use of anxiety management skills when facing feared stimuli, ignore their children's avoidant or anxious behavior, and manage their own anxiety (Barrett & Shortt, 2003; Pahl & Barrett, 2010). These strategies have been linked to more successful outcomes, including reduction in anxiety and avoidance behaviors, and longer-term maintenance of treatment gains. The Coping Cat Program is a widely used, evidence-based treatment for anxiety among children (with its adaptation, The C.A.T. Project for adolescents) that integrates parental or caregiver involvement specifically to support generalization and skills practice through targeted homework assignments (Kendall, 1994; Kendall et al., 1997; Podell et al., 2010). Parental support has been identified as a crucial component in supporting youth around CBT homework completion, as parents can act as coaches and sources of support, as well as holding youth accountable for achieving their weekly goals (Selles et al., 2018).

In CBT treatment that requires exposure-based practices, such as with social anxiety or obsessive-compulsive disorder (OCD), parental or caregiver support is often quite necessary to help youth with completing their exposure activities. Several studies, including meta-analyses, have shown that family-based exposure and response prevention treatment was effective in alleviating symptoms in the majority of cases of pediatric OCD and that family-based CBT is more effective than psychotropic treatment alone (Marien et al., 2009; Pediatric OCD Treatment Study (POTS) Team, 2004; Thompson-Hollands et al., 2014; Watson & Rees, 2008). In their review, Kose et al. (2018) found that parental involvement most often enhanced outcomes for youth with co-occurring autism spectrum disorder and OCD. In one study, Reynolds et al. (2013) found that parental involvement in treatment for OCD was associated with larger reductions in anxiety symptoms, though there was no difference in low compared with high parental involvement, suggesting that even lower levels of parental engagement may be beneficial in helping youth to achieve their goals.

With separation anxiety disorder, where children experience intense anxiety in response to separation from parents, school refusal is often observed as a means of avoiding such anxiety. Systematic reviews have identified that behavioral family therapy contributes to remission of symptoms and improvement in school attendance for most youth compared with youth in individual treatment (Elliott, 1999; Heyne et al., 2014; King et al., 2000; King & Bernstein, 2001). In the treatment of school refusal, parental involvement is key as parents' own anxiety and enabling may facilitate avoidance as they do not wish to see their children in distress and wish to accommodate and avoid panic attacks or tantrums. Thus, the intervention also focuses on reducing parental accommodation and supporting parents in using behavioral strategies to coach their youth in using coping skills, reducing avoidance, and returning to school successfully (Heyne et al., 2014). While research supports the additive benefit of parental involvement in treatment, there are no studies to date examining family-engaged CBT for school refusal compared with individual therapy; thus, this remains an important area for future research (Maynard et al., 2018).

8.3.4 Addressing Parental Mental Health and Improving Family Functioning

A secondary benefit of family involvement in CBT is exposure for parents and other family members (e.g., siblings) to treatment content and processes that may also improve parental mental health and overall family functioning. For instance, the inclusion of family members in CBT is highlighted as an important component of effective pediatric anxiety treatment. More specifically, family involvement allows clinicians to address common family-level barriers to symptom reduction (e.g., parental accommodation, conflict, or challenging family dynamics; Selles et al., 2018). For example, Selles et al. (2018) found that group family-based CBT showed significant improvement in parental accommodation and overall family functioning and that homework was a core predictor for symptom improvement. Homework, or treatment-based assignments or practices that are conducted by the youth often with family support outside of therapy sessions, is likely to be a key mechanism of change in parental or other family members given its ability to transmit key treatment content to others. Homework also supports others in practicing the same skills that youth are learning and practicing. More recently, in their study of family-centered CBT for anxiety for young children with ASD, Driscoll et al. (2020) found improvement in both child and parental anxiety, as well as improved family functioning and coping. In a study examining treatment mechanisms in peer-involvement group CBT (GCBT) and parent-involvement CBT (PCBT), parental psychological control was identified as a significant mediator of change for PCBT while positive peer relationship was the mediator for youth in GCBT (Silverman et al., 2019).

Finally, a recent controlled trial of child- and family-focused CBT (CFF-CBT) for pediatric bipolar disorder demonstrated that the key mediators of child symptom improvement over the course of CBT were all parent and family-level factors—parent coping, parenting efficacy, family functioning, and parent cognitive restructuring—suggesting a critical role for changes at the parent and family level in contributing to child outcomes (West et al., 2014).

In TF-CBT, the involvement of a nonoffending parent is a key component of treatment. Prior research has found that TF-CBT for both abused young people and their nonabusing parents has been shown to reduce symptoms of post-traumatic stress disorder and improve overall adjustment (Deblinger et al., 2016). A recent review found that inclusion of nonoffending caregivers is associated with TF-CBT outcomes, and that this may occur through enhancing caregiver support of the child and/or reducing caregivers' trauma-related maladaptive cognitions (Brown et al., 2020). Another study found support for family-based CBT family therapy reducing future abuse and supporting youth emotional regulation (Kolko et al., 2018).

A recent large effectiveness trial found that individual family therapy in combination with intensive multifamily therapy was significantly more effective than single family therapy in the treatment of adolescent anorexia nervosa, a condition with a significant impact on family functioning (Eisler et al., 2016). Sparse research has evaluated whether the use of multifamily group settings confers additional benefit over single family therapy, though it may be hypothesized that the additional benefits of peer support, empathy, and accountability within group settings would only serve to improve outcomes, especially where addressing parenting skills and family dynamics may play a key role in improving mental health outcomes for youth.

8.3.5 Considerations for Future Directions

Many studies have demonstrated that parents may play a key role in achieving better treatment outcomes for youth, but there have been studies that have not found such associations (e.g., Thulin et al., 2014). In their review of CBT for pediatric anxiety, Breinholst et al. (2012) recommend greater consistency in methodology to assess the role of parents in treatment outcomes, particularly in assessing factors that may shape youth mental health and maintenance of treatment gains, such as changes in parental behaviors and family functioning, rather than focusing on youth mental health symptoms as the sole indicator of treatment success. Further, they recommend continued clinical trials examining the additive effect of parental involvement in CBT. Some studies have found no difference between CBT with or without parental involvement, and other research suggests trends toward better outcomes if parents are engaged in treatment; thus, continued studies are needed to support this assertion more fully (e.g., Reuman et al., 2021; Spence et al., 2000).

8.4 Clinical Considerations for Diverse Identities

8.4.1 Clinical Considerations in Working with Families Identifying as Black, Indigenous, and People of Color

As noted, family involvement is a crucial part of pediatric mental health treatment. Prior research supports family involvement in treatment as a particularly important mechanism for enhancing outcomes for ethnically and racially minoritized youth (Campos & Kim, 2017; Pina et al., 2009). This may be particularly impactful within cultures that emphasize family involvement and hold values and beliefs that consider the self as interdependent with others in one's community or family (Campos & Kim, 2017). Holding such perspectives may lead to better outcomes when treatment actively involves family and other community members. Family-oriented interventions have been found efficacious for communities where family relationships are prioritized, interrelatedness is highly valued, and family involvement is integral to treatment success (Mehta, 1990). In their review of parenting style and its relationship with pediatric anxiety, Wei and Kendall (2014) noted that cultural differences in parenting, such as parental control, parental warmth or rejection, and parental involvement, were associated with child anxiety in several cross-cultural studies. Associations that were observed for White or European American families were not observed in families reflecting the global majority (i.e., Latin and South America, Asia). More specifically, one study found that only European American youths' negative cognitive styles of disconnection and rejection mediated the relationship between perceived maternal control and anxiety compared with their Latin American and African American peers. The authors posit that this finding may support that maternal control may be more normative in some cultures and not necessarily associated with negative cognitive styles and greater anxiety in BIPOC youth (Creveling et al., 2010). Such research supports a culturally informed approach to treatment development for BIPOC families as initial models for treatment were developed with predominantly White or European populations and likely do not reflect the nuances, values, beliefs, and practices that would impact the successful treatment of pediatric mental health conditions within diverse communities.

8.4.2 Considerations for Addressing Barriers to Treatment

Historically, research has suggested that communities of diverse racial/ethnic and cultural backgrounds experience greater barriers to treatment and more attrition from treatment associated with a lack of time, resources, and culturally responsive and linguistically accessible intervention. In their qualitative study on delivering CBT to Latino children in a rural setting, Chavira and colleagues (2017) found that both bilingual Latino mental health providers and Latino parents identified language and literacy, time and availability, and cultural fit as barriers in the CBT-based treatment, though it was viewed as preferable to medication to treat children's anxiety. In a recent study that found that CBT was effective in treating anxiety among Latino youth, acculturation of parents was identified as a significant moderator (Patriarca et al., 2022). Specifically, the authors found that when parental acculturation was low, intervention that targeted reducing the use of negative reinforcement was associated with better anxiety outcomes; whereas when parental acculturation was high, intervention that targeted decreasing parental psychological control was associated with better anxiety outcomes for youth. These findings support parental involvement as best practice in working with Latino youth with anxiety. Further, the authors suggest clinical flexibility in targeting parental use of negative reinforcement or psychological control in treatment, such that positive outcomes with this focus may be dependent upon parental acculturation status.

In research examining outcomes of family-based CBT for pediatric OCD, there were no differences between racial/ethnic groups, such that all youth experienced improvement following treatment. However, findings indicated that race/ethnicity was a moderator between two types of family-based CBT. Compared with non-White youth who received standard family-based CBT (ST) consisting of weekly family check-ins, systematic psychoeducation, and support, non-White youth appeared to benefit more from enhanced family therapy (EFT), which included sessions focused on emotion regulation skills training, collaborative problem-solving, and behavioral parent training, in addition to the support included in ST (Peris et al., 2020). The authors posit that EFT's emphasis on collaborative family problem-solving, systematically and collaboratively reducing symptom accommodation as a team, and practicing distress tolerance skills as a family may be well-aligned with the needs and values of BIPOC families.

With youth of various racial/ethnic cultures, family involvement has also been shown to be particularly beneficial in improving treatment engagement, ensuring completion of treatment homework assignments, and even improving longer-term outcomes. In a study of parental perspectives of cognitive-behavioral intervention for trauma in schools among Latiné families, parents reported high satisfaction and perceived benefit in a culturally adapted family component, highlighting the importance of parental involvement and culturally relevant treatment content (Santiago et al., 2016). In their study with Southeast Asian Muslim families, assessing cultural congruence or normativity of dysfunctional beliefs was identified as a core component of CBT. The authors note that as some of these beliefs might be shared by the family and may be culturally accepted, there is a need to assess with the client, family, or other community members whether these are culturally accepted beliefs or not. Further, they recommend exploring the role of stigma within culture and/or family. Further, they shared that family may also be a resource in therapy for skills practice and addressing or modifying thoughts (Naeem et al., 2015). Finally, Rathod and colleagues (2010) explored how CBT for psychosis may be culturally adapted for Black and other racial/ethnic minority groups to include addressing culturally bound beliefs, stigma, and support symptom reduction.

Finally, research has also supported providing intervention in the client and family's first language, if possible, as this may help to reduce barriers to treatment attendance and support greater engagement and processing in treatment (Nicasio et al., 2022). In their study implementing TF-CBT among trauma-exposed Puerto Rican youth and their caregivers, Orengo-Aguayo and colleagues (2022) found a significant reduction in post-traumatic stress, depression, and anxiety symptoms posttreatment, and posited that the cultural value of *familismo* (i.e., family support and social connections are highly valued and encouraged) played a large role in treatment engagement. Further, these efforts highlight the importance of ensuring sufficient resources and effort (including services in primary language, case management, and psychoeducation) to engage families from under-resources or marginalized communities, including immigrant families, to ensure connection and engagement in evidence-based treatment (Beehler et al., 2012).

8.4.3 Clinical Considerations for LGBTQ+ Youth and Families

Family rejection is a major contributor to psychological distress among LGBTQ+ (i.e., lesbian, gay, bisexual, transgender, queer, and other sexual and gender minorities) youth and may exacerbate ongoing mental health issues (Taylor & Neppl, 2023). In general, family involvement around rejection and nonaffirmation can help to change unhelpful family dynamics, reduce rejection and isolation, and reduce the risk of future trauma for youth. For LQBTQ youth in particular, family involvement is extremely beneficial, even more so with targeted focus on addressing stigma and discrimination and increasing support at home (Parker et al., 2018). For instance, a study of Chinese sexual minority adults found that family support and resilience mediated the path between sexual minority stigma and depression. The authors identified both as potential intervenable factors and targets for intervention to mitigate the negative impact of such stigma on mental health among Chinese sexual minority individuals (Wang et al., 2022).

The Family Acceptance Project (FAP), a longstanding program founded in 2002 by Drs Caitlin Ryan and Rafael Diaz, aims to address gaps in the field by providing psychoeducation, healthcare and policy-related advocacy, and adapted interventions to assist diverse families in supporting their LGBTQ+ youth (https://lgbtqfamilyacceptance.org). One effort focuses on providing adapted TF-CBT to include parental involvement, even among youth with rejecting parents or caregivers. Typically, in TF-CBT, participation by parents or caregivers who have been involved in youths' trauma is not generally advisable; however, when the goal may be to repair and address the rejection as part of the trauma more specifically, parental involvement has been recommended and even encouraged, such as with FAP-TF-CBT (Ryan et al., 2023). Likewise, attachment-based family therapy (ABFT) has growing evidence for reducing depression and suicidality among LGBTQ+ youth. It aims to support positive communication, relational repair, collaborative problem-solving, and shifting adolescents' thoughts and beliefs associated with experiences of parental rejection and conflict, leading to improved trust and increased self-competency for youth. Although grounded in attachment theory and rooted in structural and multidimensional family therapy, as well as emotion-focused family therapy (G. Diamond et al., 2016), the treatment targets and processes of ABFT are aligned with family-focused CBT approaches and offer much in the way of potential aims and mechanisms for treatment for ongoing CBT development for LGBTQ+ families. Similar to evidence with family-engaged CBT, treatment mechanisms for ABFT have been found to include reduced parental control and criticism and increased parental warmth and autonomy-granting, leading to improvements in parent-child relationship and reductions in youth anxiety and depression symptoms (G. Diamond et al., 2016). Moreover, ABFT facilitates change toward acceptance and shifting fears and beliefs, including internalized stigma and homophobia/transphobia, shame, and feelings of grief or loss associated with expectations for their child's future and concerns or worries about victimization or oppression that their children may experience as a result of their minoritized gender and/or sexual identities (G. M. Diamond et al., 2012). These targets for intervention appear key in improving family relationships, are well-aligned with goals for family-based CBT, and are amenable to integration within CBT approaches.

8.4.4 Future Directions for Research

Given the dynamic complexities of these clinical considerations for working with families of myriad socioeconomic, linguistic, national or immigrant experience, cultural, religious, and sexual or gender minority status, additional work is needed to understand how to best apply cognitive-behavioral interventions and whether culturally adapted or tailored interventions are needed. In their scoping review, Parker and colleagues (2018) noted very little peer-reviewed research on family-engaged interventions for LGBTQ+ youth and highlighted the crucial need for such interventions to address stigma and discrimination and help foster supportive environments within families. Moreover, a substantial amount of research asserts that youth with intersecting minoritized identities experience significantly greater effects of minority stress and mental health challenges (Murphy & Hardaway, 2017). Intersectionality, a term first coined by scholar Kimberlé Crenshaw to describe the compounding stressors and challenges experienced by Black women has increasingly been used to understand the complex and nuanced experiences of racialized individuals who also experience additional stressors associated with other minoritized identities (e.g., sexual, gender, religious/spiritual, ability status identities; Crenshaw, 2017). Additional efforts are much needed to identify CBT treatment approaches and mechanisms of treatment to improve outcomes specifically for LGBTQ+ BIPOC youth and their families.

8.5 Case Vignette

8.5.1 Presenting Problem and History of Presenting Problem

Molly H. was a 13-year-old bisexual, cisgender Mexican-American female who lived at home with her biological mother, stepfather, and biological 17-year-old sister. She was referred to receive child- and family-focused cognitive-behavioral therapy (CFF-CBT/RAINBOW therapy), an evidence-based CBT program for youth with mood disorders, delivered in her local children's hospital behavioral health program. Initial assessment via structured interview and mood symptom rating scales (parent, child, and clinician report) indicated that Molly met the diagnostic criteria for Bipolar I Disorder. Molly was experiencing moderate to severe symptoms of depression, including suicidal ideation, and moderate symptoms of mania, including frequent irritability, mood lability, and intense periods of anger or "rage episodes." When depressed, Molly demonstrated intense sadness, hopelessness, low energy, sleep disruption, social withdrawal, and thoughts of death, occasionally expressing suicidal ideation (e.g., stating "*I wish I was never born*" and "*I want to kill myself*"). During periods of mania, Molly was irritable and highly reactive, displaying verbal aggression, and becoming easily frustrated. She also had a history of experiencing periods of elated and giddy moods with increased energy, increased activity in several areas (e.g., working on several projects or playing for hours without being able to transition to other activities), motor hyperactivity, reduced sleep, and mild flight of ideas. During periods of mania, about one to two times per week, Molly would experience what her mother, Ms. H., called a "meltdown" during which she would "lose control of her emotions," scream at her family, and then cry for hours. Mrs H. reported that she had difficulty containing or consoling Molly during her meltdowns. These episodes of extreme dysregulation only occurred at home, whereas Molly had minimal behavioral difficulties at school, where she was in the eighth grade. The periods of elated moods and agitation were typically followed by a period of increased irritability and then cycling into a depressed mood and feelings of worthlessness. At times, Molly would cycle between euphoric, angry/irritable, and depressed states within the same day, and other times these episodes would last for days to weeks. At the evaluation, Molly's parents reported that her mood difficulties were negatively impacting all family members as well as Molly's interpersonal relationships with peers.

Molly attended a local public school and had a history of strong academic performance. Despite having several friends, Molly had difficulties maintaining friendships and was very worried about social rejection. In addition, she experienced bullying at school. Her parents shared that her worries about rejection and bullying occurred after she disclosed to a friend that she had a crush on a female peer, which ended up being spread around her school last year. Molly shared feeling hurt by her friend sharing this personal information and feeling shame about her romantic interest and attraction to both boys and girls. Her parents stated that they were initially surprised when the school informed them of this incident and have tried to be supportive while questioning whether Molly is old enough to know her sexual identity yet. They reported that they haven't really talked about this incident much or her interests in her peers since.

At the start of therapy, Molly had recently initiated treatment with a mood stabilizer and the family had attended two medication management sessions with the child psychiatrist. She had never been hospitalized for psychiatric reasons.

8.5.2 Goals for Treatment

Initial goals for Molly's treatment focused on (1) improved mood stability and mood regulation; (2) improved understanding for Molly and her parents about pediatric bipolar disorder; (3) improved self-esteem and self-efficacy in youth and family; and (4) improved interpersonal functioning with family and peers.

8.5.3 Course of Treatment

Molly attended sessions with her mother, and her stepfather and older sister participated in the family session and intermittent maintenance sessions. Table 8.1 provides an outline of the content and format of the acute 12-session treatment phase.

Treatment initially focused on engaging the family in the treatment process, addressing expectations of and barriers to treatment, and identifying key treatment goals (Sessions 1 and 2). Mrs H. identified anger management, suicidal statements, and transitions as key targets for treatment, and Molly added "bullies" as her goal and addressed her worries related to rejection about her bisexuality. In addition, Molly and Mrs H. were provided with psychoeducation regarding pediatric bipolar disorder. Molly's core symptoms were discussed in the context of documented differences in brain functioning during periods of excessive emotions to reduce blame and negative attributions surrounding her mood dysregulation and anger episodes. Molly and her mother also developed a common language for her symptoms and talked about her "mood changes." This process allowed Molly to distance herself from her symptoms, thereby increasing her comfort and ability to discuss these difficulties. Lastly, Molly's mood fluctuations were monitored on a Daily Mood Calendar app where Molly was able to rate her moods at different times of the day using a mood thermometer and label potential triggers, which she shared with her mother to help with monitoring. Mornings were identified as a particularly difficult time for her.

At the outset of treatment, Mrs H. expressed significant doubt about Molly's diagnosis, questioning whether this was a "phase" related to diet or the manifestation of her anxiety. However, after Session 2, she reported increased acceptance of the diagnosis given Molly's family history and her experience of the key symptoms of bipolar disorder. The initial phase of treatment also focused on assessing Molly's

Table 8.1 Outline of child- and family-focused RAINBOW session content and format

Session	Participants	Topics covered
1	Child and parents together	Orientation to treatment/goal-setting Engagement and relationship-building with child and parents
2	Child and parents together	Psychoeducation about PBD Mood charting via Daily Mood Calendar
3	Parents only	Affect regulation skills: establishing routines and anger management Identifying and acknowledging parents' difficult feelings
4	Child only; parent check-in	Affect regulation skills Labeling emotions; recognizing difficult feelings; triggers of anger and sadness
5	Child only; parent check-in	Cognitive and behavioral ("think" and "do") coping skills Problem-solving and positive thinking
6	Parents only	Identifying and promoting positive qualities in child Positive thinking and mantras; reframing negative thoughts; mindfulness strategies
7	Child only; parent check-in	Communication skills and interpersonal problem-solving
8	Parents only	Promoting child's social competence Behavior management strategies Balanced lifestyle for parents and enhancing self-care
9	Parents, child, siblings	Psychoeducation about PBD providing to siblings Family coping and problem-solving
10	Child and parents together	Identifying and enhancing access of social support networks
11	Child and parents together	Reflection on RAINBOW experience Review of RAINBOW skills, creation of RAINBOW binder to internalize and consolidate therapy tools
12	Child and parents together	Celebration; follow-up/maintenance plan

history of suicidality and whether there was an intent to die or plans or means for killing herself. Molly reported that she infrequently had thoughts about a suicidal plan, but that when she was feeling "really down" she sometimes felt like "disappearing" or that she wished she would "fall asleep and not wake up again." Molly agreed that the therapist would bring her mother into session if Molly disclosed having any active thoughts of wanting to hurt herself or if she was having difficulty coping with her "loud and pushy" passive suicidal thoughts, where she was struggling to distract herself or push the thoughts away. Molly agreed that they would talk about the thoughts together as a team and problem-solve what kind of support she needed, whether it was more monitoring at home or whether she needed to be evaluated at the hospital.

Molly was coached in identifying triggers for these thoughts and together with her therapist, she identified a list of soothing and distraction tools that she could use when having these thoughts to help take her mind off them and give her time to start to feel better. With her mother's support, she created a coping box where she put her favorite coping tools, like pictures of her dog, close friends, and her favorite childhood stuffed animal that she loved to hug when she was sad. The therapist helped Molly to learn about "Five Senses" coping where she could focus on self-soothing by focusing her attention on pleasant things that she could see (e.g., happy pictures or funny videos on social media), hear (e.g., calming music), taste (e.g., ice cream, comfort snack), smell (e.g., favorite lotion), and touch (e.g., petting her dog, hugging her stuffed animal). Molly was also supported in using a visual rating scale to help communicate with her therapist and mother about how strong and distressing her suicidal thoughts were. Mrs H. also participated in this discussion after the therapist talked with Molly about the importance of having a shared language and communication system with her mother in order to keep her safe. Molly stated that it was easier to talk about her suicidal thoughts through this rating scale as it made her feel less anxious about how to share her feelings as she was worried about triggering her family's worries and answering a lot of questions about her thoughts. Mrs H. agreed to this plan and identified a plan for securing any access to lethal means in the home, such as locking away access to medications.

The next phase of treatment (Sessions 3 through 6) focused on affect dysregulation and the prevention and management of Molly's mood changes. Parent sessions dealt with the implementation of consistent, predictable routines to improve two identified areas of difficulty: sleep and unanticipated transitions. Specific methods for improving Molly's sleep routine were implemented at home (e.g., the use of a sleep schedule to ensure the same bedtime and wake-up every day as well as good sleep hygiene practices). To minimize Molly's experience of transitions, Mrs H. began to provide ample warnings prior to transitions and posted reminders of the day's schedule. With additional problem-solving and fine-tuning across sessions, Mrs H. reported an improvement in Molly's sleep and mood in the mornings. Parent sessions also focused on helping Molly manage her mood changes as a family. The analogy of "putting out a fire" was used to facilitate Mrs H.'s ability to remain neutral and calm while defusing the situation versus engaging in the episode and exacerbating Molly's distress. Coping plans for the prevention and acute management of Molly's mood changes were developed with Mrs H., including ways Mrs H. could remain calm (e.g., using a mantra, "I need to put out the fire, she is not in control"), using a code word with Molly's stepfather and sister to enlist their support, and implementing a soothing "cool-down" area to help Molly de-escalate her anger. Coping plans also involved how and when to enforce appropriate consequences for target negative behaviors (e.g., physical or verbal aggression), such that consequences would be enforced only after Molly and others' elevated emotions had stabilized.

Additionally, parent sessions during this phase focused on Mrs H.'s range of emotions regarding parenting a child with bipolar disorder and identifying ways to both accept and cope with the inevitable feelings of anger, helplessness, and guilt. Sessions included instruction in cognitive techniques to use during difficult situations (e.g., reframing Molly's behavior in the context of her neurocircuitry versus deliberate attempts to hurt others), as well as mindfulness techniques to help Mrs H. focus on the present moment to manage feeling overwhelmed. Mrs H. expressed immense relief after disclosing her difficult emotions and reported greater effectiveness in helping defuse tense situations with Molly when she used coping techniques.

Sessions with Molly focused on feelings identification, her physiological manifestations of anger, and increasing Molly's insight into the triggers of her negative moods. Molly's triggers included household chores and her bullies at school. Molly was often reluctant to describe any difficulties she experienced during the week but appeared more engaged in skill-building activities focused on affect regulation, like coloring and practicing deep breathing. Worksheets and role-play were used to help Molly practice cognitive and behavioral skills for coping with future triggers and her resulting rising anger. Yet, despite Molly's enthusiasm during the session, she often resisted using her identified coping skills when triggered at home. Thus, it was important to normalize the experience of anger and sadness as acceptable emotions as well as the difficulty of learning new skills. Mrs H. was encouraged to provide Molly with reassurance and support when prompting Molly's use of coping skills (e.g., "*I love you and I want to help you feel better by trying [this tool]*"). Lastly, Molly's experiences of mood changes were discussed as one small part of her identity, and family sessions focused on the promotion of Molly's strengths and competencies. Across sessions, Molly gradually increased her ability to recognize her triggers and warning signs, appropriately seek help (e.g., asking for a hug), and use positive statements to cope with her anger. Mrs H. also became increasingly confident in her ability to comfort and redirect Molly to use her skills.

As Molly's family improved in their ability to prevent and manage Molly's affect dysregulation, the focus widened to the management of family and environmental stressors during the third phase of treatment (Sessions 7 through 10). Molly's sessions centered on improving her communication and interpersonal problem-solving skills. For example, Molly developed various ways of dealing with bullying at her school and practiced these in session (e.g., direct and respectful expression of feelings, seeking help from school personnel, and use of coping mantras to help Molly manage her sadness and anger in response to bullying). Molly was also supported in discussing the impact of bullying on triggering her moods and was provided information about stigma and shame about bisexuality. Parent sessions focused on incorporating elements of affirming and attachment-based interventions focused on helping Molly's parents to process and accept Molly's bisexual identity, including space to ask questions about sexual identity development and address misconceptions and stigma around nonheterosexual identities. Her parents were open to learning more through online resources for understanding sexual diversity within the Catholic faith, and they ultimately agreed that they wanted to work on accepting and supporting Molly so that they did not further injure their relationship with her. Her parents also discussed concerns about how to address bullying in school and worked with the school counselor to identify how Molly could reach out for support at school and acknowledge the ways her mood might interfere with her school performance. An essential component of this phase was also an emphasis on Mrs H.'s well-being and balance between self-care and parenting responsibilities. Mrs H. recognized that her parenting abilities suffered when she felt "burned out." She thus identified important self-care activities to pursue, including outings with a friend, joining a local book club, organizing a church social club, and seeking help with dinner from the family.

Lastly, a family session was held with Molly, her older sister, and her parents. This session was used to provide an update on the course of therapy and to improve family interactions via family problem-solving. With assistance from the therapist, family members identified their strengths as well as family conflict, practiced using feeling statements, and developed coping plans for managing their conflict as a team. It was important to maintain an atmosphere of acceptance, nonjudgment, and teamwork to manage the difficulties that *all* family members experience. Molly reported some relief about having her family better understand her PBD diagnosis and that everyone was on the same page on how to help her manage her mood symptoms, including her anger, as well as her safety plan for addressing her chronic suicidality.

The final sessions of the acute phase (Sessions 11 and 12) focused on preparing for the shift from weekly therapy to monthly maintenance sessions. Molly created a RAINBOW book of therapy exercises to help her remember and use these therapy tools. Mrs H. and Molly also discussed ways to continually use therapy strategies at home, such as weekly dinner meetings to discuss family conflict and plan family outings. Positive family changes across treatment were reviewed and celebrated, including Molly's increased awareness of her moods and triggers, a reduction in Molly's anger episodes from larger outbursts several times a week to milder episodes occurring one to two times per month, improved relationships with her mother and her sister, and less stress with her peers at school.

During the maintenance phase (six monthly sessions), Molly and her mother remained engaged in treatment. Sessions included teen, parent, and family components and focused on continued practice of skills and problem-solving difficulties. In addition, an Individualized Education Plan (IEP) was developed by the school personnel to provide accommodation for her bipolar diagnosis. Accommodations included a sanctioned cool-down area outside of the classroom, greater supervision during unstructured periods to minimize bullying, and the use of a private cue system between Molly and her teachers to prompt Molly's use of her coping strategies.

8.5.4 Outcomes

Across treatment, Molly demonstrated greater insight into her symptoms, improved self-esteem, and acceptance of her diagnosis as only "one small part of me." She improved in her ability to reframe angry thoughts (e.g., "Mom doesn't love me") and use relaxation to manage distress. An essential component of Molly's treatment success was the presentation of therapy material in a nonthreatening, creative, and engaging manner, as well as helping her recognize her many positive qualities. Mrs H.'s success in treatment was driven by her active engagement in the process, her willingness and dedication to implement novel strategies at home, and recognition of her own emotions, thoughts, and needs.

Consistent with the episodic nature of bipolar disorder, Molly's relative stability was punctuated by periods of greater difficulties (e.g., depression, anger, aggression, feelings of worthlessness) but these had decreased in intensity, frequency, and duration across treatment. Moreover, these challenging periods were now accompanied by a mobilization of resources at the individual and family level to prevent further escalation. Molly's parents became increasingly proficient in their ability to recognize warning signs of distress and redirect Molly, and Molly was increasingly able to use coping skills independently at less intense levels of anger. Objective measures at the conclusion of the acute phase indicated significant improvement in mania and depression symptoms, family cohesion, and global functioning, and these treatment gains were maintained on objective measures at the final treatment session.

Finally, Molly and her family appeared to greatly benefit from the incorporation of support around understanding and accepting her bisexual identity. As this was a focus of her bullying and social rejection, it became clear that family acceptance would be a crucial component to buffering her mental health against the deleterious impact of peer rejection and social isolation. Thus, helping Molly's parents to navigate their own feelings and concerns while centering their value of loving and caring for Molly was crucial in repairing any relational injury and protecting trust in the parent-teen relationship. Molly reported feeling supported by her parents in exploring her sexuality without shame or fear of rejection from her family.

8.6 Conclusion

Significant research has supported family-focused or family-engaged CBT for a wide range of pediatric mental health conditions. Youth presenting with internalizing and externalizing symptoms experience significant difficulties in social, emotional, and academic functioning, and while individual therapy has been found efficacious, the inclusion of parents and other significant family members has been shown to bolster treatment effects and support generalization of skills to home, school, and community settings. As noted, the previous decades of research indicate that family engagement in CBT is linked with greater treatment attendance, homework and practice completion, greater skills generalization, and improvements in family functioning and overall well-being. To date, these efforts have often focused on White/European youth and families of middle or upper socioeconomic status in the Western hemisphere, rather than communities reflecting the global majority, those with fewer socioeconomic resources, and families of minoritized and marginalized identities (e.g., LGBTQ+ families, non-Judeo-Christian families). Ongoing research is needed to examine additional interventions for diverse, under-researched populations, as well as predictors, moderators, and mediators of treatment that answer the question of which treatment works best for which youth and why.

References

Asarnow, J. R., Hughes, J. L., Babeva, K. N., & Sugar, C. A. (2017). Cognitive-behavioral family treatment for suicide attempt prevention: A randomized controlled trial. *Journal of the American Academy of Child and Adolescent Psychiatry, 56*(6), 506–514. https://doi.org/10.1016/j.jaac.2017.03.015

Barrett, P. M., & Shortt, A. L. (2003). Parental involvement in the treatment of anxious children. In A. E. Kazdin & J. R. Weisz (Eds.), *Evidence-based psychotherapies for children and adolescents* (pp. 101–119). The Guilford Press.

Beehler, S., Birman, D., & Campbell, R. (2012). The effectiveness of Cultural Adjustment and Trauma Services (CATS): Generating practice-based evidence on a comprehensive, school-based mental health intervention for immigrant youth. *American Journal of Community Psychology, 50*(1), 155–168. https://doi.org/10.1007/s10464-011-9486-2

Bögels, S., & Phares, V. (2008). Fathers' role in the etiology, prevention and treatment of child anxiety: A review and new model. *Clinical Psychology Review, 28*(4), 539–558. https://doi.org/10.1016/j.cpr.2007.07.011

Breinholst, S., Esbjørn, B. H., Reinholdt-Dunne, M. L., & Stallard, P. (2012). CBT for the treatment of child anxiety disorders: A review of why parental involvement has not enhanced outcomes. *Journal of Anxiety Disorders, 26*(3), 416–424. https://doi.org/10.1016/j.janxdis.2011.12.014

Brestan, E. V., & Eyberg, S. M. (1998). Effective psychosocial treatments of conduct-disordered children and adolescents: 29 years, 82 studies, and 5,272 kids. *Journal of Clinical Child Psychology, 27*(2), 180–189. https://doi.org/10.1207/s15374424jccp2702_5

Brown, E. J., Cohen, J. A., & Mannarino, A. P. (2020). Trauma-focused cognitive-behavioral therapy: The role of caregivers. *Journal of Affective Disorders, 277*, 39–45. https://doi.org/10.1016/j.jad.2020.07.123

Campos, B., & Kim, H. S. (2017). Incorporating the cultural diversity of family and close relationships into the study of health. *The American Psychologist, 72*(6), 543–554. https://doi.org/10.1037/amp0000122

Carpenter, A. L., Pincus, D. B., Furr, J. M., & Comer, J. S. (2018). Working from home: An initial pilot examination of videoconferencing-based cognitive behavioral therapy for anxious youth delivered to the home setting. *Behavior Therapy, 49*(6), 917–930. https://doi.org/10.1016/j.beth.2018.01.007

Carr, A. (2019). Family therapy and systemic interventions for child-focused problems: The current evidence base. *Journal of Family Therapy, 41*(2), 153–213. https://doi.org/10.1111/1467-6427.12226

Chavira, D. A., Bustos, C. E., Garcia, M. S., Ng, B., & Camacho, A. (2017). Delivering CBT to rural Latino children with anxiety disorders: A qualitative study. *Community Mental Health Journal, 53*(1), 53–61. https://doi.org/10.1007/s10597-015-9903-3

Crenshaw, K. (2017). *On intersectionality: Essential writings*. Faculty Books. https://scholarship.law.columbia.edu/books/255

Creveling, C. C., Varela, R. E., Weems, C. F., & Corey, D. M. (2010). Maternal control, cognitive style, and childhood anxiety: A test of a theoretical model in a multi-ethnic sample. *Journal of Family Psychology, 24*(4), 439–448. https://doi.org/10.1037/a0020388

Deblinger, E., Pollio, E., & Dorsey, S. (2016). Applying trauma-focused cognitive-behavioral therapy in group format. *Child Maltreatment, 21*(1), 59–73. https://doi.org/10.1177/1077559515620668

Diamond, G. M., Diamond, G. S., Levy, S., Closs, C., Ladipo, T., & Siqueland, L. (2012). Attachment-based family therapy for suicidal lesbian, gay, and bisexual adolescents: A treatment development study and open trial with preliminary findings. *Psychotherapy (Chicago, Ill.), 49*(1), 62–71. https://doi.org/10.1037/a0026247

Diamond, G., Russon, J., & Levy, S. (2016). Attachment-based family therapy: A review of the empirical support. *Family Process, 55*(3), 595–610. https://doi.org/10.1111/famp.12241

Dorsey, S., Pullmann, M. D., Berliner, L., Koschmann, E., McKay, M., & Deblinger, E. (2014). Engaging foster parents in treatment: A randomized trial of supplementing trauma-focused cognitive behavioral therapy with evidence-based engagement strategies. *Child Abuse & Neglect, 38*(9), 1508–1520. https://doi.org/10.1016/j.chiabu.2014.03.020

Driscoll, K., Schonberg, M., Stark, M. F., Carter, A. S., & Hirshfeld-Becker, D. (2020). Family-centered cognitive behavioral therapy for anxiety in very young children with autism spectrum disorder. *Journal of Autism and Developmental Disorders, 50*(11), 3905–3920. https://doi.org/10.1007/s10803-020-04446-y

Duhig, A. M., Phares, V., & Birkeland, R. W. (2002). Involvement of fathers in therapy: A survey of clinicians. *Professional Psychology: Research and Practice, 33*(4), 389–395. https://doi.org/10.1037/0735-7028.33.4.389

Eisler, I., Simic, M., Hodsoll, J., Asen, E., Berelowitz, M., Connan, F., Ellis, G., Hugo, P., Schmidt, U., Treasure, J., Yi, I., & Landau, S. (2016). A pragmatic randomised multi-centre trial of multifamily and single family therapy for adolescent anorexia nervosa. *BMC Psychiatry, 16*(1), 422. https://doi.org/10.1186/s12888-016-1129-6

Elliott, J. G. (1999). School refusal: Issues of conceptualisation, assessment, and treatment. *Journal of Child Psychology and Psychiatry, and Allied Disciplines, 40*(7), 1001–1012. https://doi.org/10.1111/1469-7610.00519

Freeman, K. R., James, S., Klein, K. P., Mayo, D., & Montgomery, S. (2016). Outpatient dialectical behavior therapy for adolescents engaged in deliberate self-harm: Conceptual and methodological considerations. *Child & Adolescent Social Work Journal, 33*(2), 123–135. https://doi.org/10.1007/s10560-015-0412-6

Furlong, M., McGilloway, S., Bywater, T., Hutchings, J., Smith, S. M., & Donnelly, M. (2012). Behavioural and cognitive-behavioural group-based parenting programmes for early-onset conduct problems in children aged 3 to 12 years. *Cochrane Database of Systematic Reviews, 2*, CD008225. https://doi.org/10.1002/14651858.CD008225.pub2

Helander, M., Asperholm, M., Wetterborg, D., Öst, L.-G., Hellner, C., Herlitz, A., & Enebrink, P. (2022). The efficacy of parent management training with or without involving the child in the treatment among children with clinical levels of disruptive behavior: A meta-analysis. *Child Psychiatry & Human Development, 55*, 164–181. https://doi.org/10.1007/s10578-022-01367-y

Heyne, D., Sauter, F. M., Ollendick, T. H., Van Widenfelt, B. M., & Westenberg, P. M. (2014). Developmentally sensitive cognitive behavioral therapy for adolescent school refusal: Rationale and case illustration. *Clinical Child and Family Psychology Review, 17*(2), 191–215. https://doi.org/10.1007/s10567-013-0160-0

Kendall, P. C. (1994). Treating anxiety disorders in children: Results of a randomized clinical trial. *Journal of Consulting and Clinical Psychology, 62*(1), 100–110. https://doi.org/10.1037/0022-006x.62.1.100

Kendall, P. C., Flannery-Schroeder, E., Panichelli-Mindel, S. M., Southam-Gerow, M., Henin, A., & Warman, M. (1997). Therapy for youths with anxiety disorders: A second randomized clinical trial. *Journal of Consulting and Clinical Psychology, 65*(3), 366–380. https://doi.org/10.1037/0022-006x.65.3.366

King, N. J., & Bernstein, G. A. (2001). School refusal in children and adolescents: A review of the past 10 years. *Journal of the American Academy of Child & Adolescent Psychiatry, 40*(2), 197–205. https://doi.org/10.1097/00004583-200102000-00014

King, N., Tonge, B. J., Heyne, D., & Ollendick, T. H. (2000). Research on the cognitive-behavioral treatment of school refusal: A review and recommendations. *Clinical Psychology Review, 20*(4), 495–507. https://doi.org/10.1016/S0272-7358(99)00039-2

Kolko, D. J., Herschell, A. D., Baumann, B. L., Hart, J. A., & Wisniewski, S. R. (2018). AF-CBT for families experiencing physical aggression or abuse served by the mental health or child welfare system: An effectiveness trial. *Child Maltreatment, 23*(4), 319–333. https://doi.org/10.1177/1077559518781068

Kose, L. K., Fox, L., & Storch, E. A. (2018). Effectiveness of cognitive behavioral therapy for individuals with autism spectrum disorders and comorbid obsessive-compulsive disorder: A review of the research. *Journal of Developmental and Physical Disabilities, 30*(1), 69–87. https://doi.org/10.1007/s10882-017-9559-8

Kowalik, J., Weller, J., Venter, J., & Drachman, D. (2011). Cognitive behavioral therapy for the treatment of pediatric posttraumatic stress disorder: A review and meta-analysis. *Journal of Behavior Therapy and Experimental Psychiatry, 42*(3), 405–413. https://doi.org/10.1016/j.jbtep.2011.02.002

Leijten, P., Raaijmakers, M. A. J., de Castro, B. O., & Matthys, W. (2013). Does socioeconomic status matter? A meta-analysis on parent training effectiveness for disruptive child behavior. *Journal of Clinical Child and Adolescent Psychology, 42*(3), 384–392. https://doi.org/10.1080/15374416.2013.769169

Lenz, A. S., & Hollenbaugh, K. M. (2015). Meta-analysis of trauma-focused cognitive behavioral therapy for treating PTSD and co-occurring depression among children and adolescents. *Counseling Outcome Research and Evaluation, 6*(1), 18–32. https://doi.org/10.1177/2150137815573790

Lewin, A. B., Dickinson, S., Kudryk, K., Karlovich, A. R., Harmon, S. L., Phillips, D. A., Tonarely, N. A., Gruen, R., Small, B., & Ehrenreich-May, J. (2021). Transdiagnostic cognitive behavioral therapy for misophonia in youth: Methods for a clinical trial and four pilot cases. *Journal of Affective Disorders, 291*, 400–408. https://doi.org/10.1016/j.jad.2021.04.027

Manassis, K., Lee, T. C., Bennett, K., Zhao, X. Y., Mendlowitz, S., Duda, S., Saini, M., Wilansky, P., Baer, S., Barrett, P., Bodden, D., Cobham, V. E., Dadds, M. R., Flannery-Schroeder, E., Ginsburg, G., Heyne, D., Hudson, J. L., Kendall, P. C., Liber, J., et al. (2014). Types of parental involvement in CBT with anxious youth: A preliminary meta-analysis. *Journal of Consulting and Clinical Psychology, 82*(6), 1163–1172. https://doi.org/10.1037/a0036969

Maric, M., Van Steensel, F. J. A., & Bögels, S. M. (2018). Parental involvement in CBT for anxiety-disordered youth revisited: Family CBT outperforms child CBT in the long term for children with comorbid ADHD symptoms. *Journal of Attention Disorders, 22*(5), 506–514. https://doi.org/10.1177/1087054715573991

Marien, W. E., Storch, E. A., Geffken, G. R., & Murphy, T. K. (2009). Intensive family-based cognitive-behavioral therapy for pediatric obsessive-compulsive disorder: Applications for treatment of medication partial- or nonresponders. *Cognitive and Behavioral Practice, 16*(3), 304–316. https://doi.org/10.1016/j.cbpra.2008.12.006

Maynard, B. R., Heyne, D., Brendel, K. E., Bulanda, J. J., Thompson, A. M., & Pigott, T. D. (2018). Treatment for school refusal among children and adolescents: A systematic review and meta-analysis. *Research on Social Work Practice, 28*(1), 56–67. https://doi.org/10.1177/1049731515598619

Mehta, M. (1990). A comparative study of family-based and patient-based behavioural management in obsessive-compulsive disorder. *The British Journal of Psychiatry, 157*(1), 133–135. https://doi.org/10.1192/bjp.157.1.133

Michelson, D., Davenport, C., Dretzke, J., Barlow, J., & Day, C. (2013). Do evidence-based interventions work when tested in the "real world?" A systematic review and meta-analysis of parent management training for the treatment of child disruptive behavior. *Clinical Child and Family Psychology Review, 16*(1), 18–34. https://doi.org/10.1007/s10567-013-0128-0

Murphy, J., & Hardaway, R. (2017). LGBTQ adolescents of color: Considerations for working with youth and their families. *Journal of Gay & Lesbian Mental Health, 21*(3), 221–227. https://doi.org/10.1080/19359705.2017.1320741

Naeem, F., Phiri, P., Munshi, T., Rathod, S., Ayub, M., Gobbi, M., & Kingdon, D. (2015). Using cognitive behaviour therapy with South Asian Muslims: Findings from the culturally sensitive CBT project. *International Review of Psychiatry, 27*(3), 233–246. https://doi.org/10.3109/09540261.2015.1067598

Nicasio, A. V., Hernandez Rodriguez, J., Villalobos, B. T., Dueweke, A. R., de Arellano, M. A., & Stewart, R. W. (2022). Cultural and telehealth considerations for trauma-focused treatment among Latinx youth: Case reports and clinical recommendations to enhance treatment engagement. *Cognitive and Behavioral Practice, 29*(4), 816–830. https://doi.org/10.1016/j.cbpra.2022.06.007

Orengo-Aguayo, R., Dueweke, A. R., Nicasio, A., de Arellano, M. A., Rivera, S., Cohen, J. A., Mannarino, A. P., & Stewart, R. W. (2022). Trauma-focused cognitive behavioral therapy with Puerto Rican youth in a post-disaster context: Tailoring, implementation, and program evaluation outcomes. *Child Abuse & Neglect, 129*, 105671. https://doi.org/10.1016/j.chiabu.2022.105671

Pahl, K. M., & Barrett, P. M. (2010). Preventing anxiety and promoting social and emotional strength in preschool children: A universal evaluation of the fun FRIENDS program. *Advances in School Mental Health Promotion, 3*(3), 14–25. https://doi.org/10.1080/1754730X.2010.9715683

Parker, C. M., Hirsch, J. S., Philbin, M. M., & Parker, R. G. (2018). The urgent need for research and interventions to address family-based stigma and discrimination against lesbian, gay, bisexual, transgender, and queer youth. *Journal of Adolescent Health, 63*(4), 383–393. https://doi.org/10.1016/j.jadohealth.2018.05.018

Patriarca, G. C., Rey, Y., Marin, C. E., Yeguez, C. E., Pettit, J. W., & Silverman, W. K. (2022). Parent involvement enhances CBTs for anxiety disorders in Hispanic/Latino youth: Acculturation as a moderator. *Journal of Consulting and Clinical Psychology, 90*(10), 827–836. https://doi.org/10.1037/ccp0000770

Pediatric OCD Treatment Study (POTS) Team. (2004). Cognitive-behavior therapy, sertraline, and their combination for children and adolescents with obsessive-compulsive disorder: The Pediatric OCD Treatment Study (POTS) randomized controlled trial. *JAMA, 292*(16), 1969–1976. https://doi.org/10.1001/jama.292.16.1969

Peris, T. S., Rozenman, M. S., Bai, S., Perez, J., Thamrin, H., & Piacentini, J. (2020). Ethnicity moderates outcome in family focused treatment for pediatric obsessive compulsive disorder. *Journal of Anxiety Disorders, 73*, 102229. https://doi.org/10.1016/j.janxdis.2020.102229

Pina, A. A., Villalta, I. K., & Zerr, A. A. (2009). Exposure-based cognitive behavioral treatment of anxiety in youth: An emerging culturally-prescriptive framework. *Behavioral Psychology, 17*(1), 111–135.

Podell, J. L., & Kendall, P. C. (2011). Mothers and fathers in family cognitive-behavioral therapy for anxious youth. *Journal of Child and Family Studies, 20*(2), 182–195. https://doi.org/10.1007/s10826-010-9420-5

Podell, J. L., Mychailyszyn, M., Edmunds, J., Puleo, C. M., & Kendall, P. C. (2010). The coping cat program for anxious youth: The FEAR plan comes to life. *Cognitive and Behavioral Practice, 17*(2), 132–141. https://doi.org/10.1016/j.cbpra.2009.11.001

Rathod, S., Kingdon, D., Phiri, P., & Gobbi, M. (2010). Developing culturally sensitive cognitive behaviour therapy for psychosis for ethnic minority patients by exploration and incorporation of service users' and health professionals' views and opinions. *Behavioural and Cognitive Psychotherapy, 38*(5), 511–533. https://doi.org/10.1017/S1352465810000378

Reuman, L., Thompson-Hollands, J., & Abramowitz, J. S. (2021). Better together: A review and recommendations to optimize research on family involvement in CBT for anxiety and related disorders. *Behavior Therapy, 52*(3), 594–606. https://doi.org/10.1016/j.beth.2020.07.008

Reynolds, S. A., Clark, S., Smith, H., Langdon, P. E., Payne, R., Bowers, G., Norton, E., & McIlwham, H. (2013). Randomized controlled trial of parent-enhanced CBT compared with individual CBT for obsessive-compulsive disorder in young people. *Journal of Consulting and Clinical Psychology, 81*(6), 1021–1026. https://doi.org/10.1037/a0034429

Ryan, C., Barba, A., & Cohen, J. A. (2023). Family-based psychosocial care for transgender and gender-diverse children and youth who experience trauma. *Child and Adolescent Psychiatric Clinics of North America, 32*(4), 775–788. https://doi.org/10.1016/j.chc.2023.03.002

Santiago, C. D., Fuller, A. K., Lennon, J. M., & Kataoka, S. H. (2016). Parent perspectives from participating in a family component for CBITS: Acceptability of a culturally informed school-based program. *Psychological Trauma: Theory, Research, Practice, and Policy, 8*(3), 325–333. https://doi.org/10.1037/tra0000076

Selles, R. R., Belschner, L., Negreiros, J., Lin, S., Schuberth, D., McKenney, K., Gregorowski, N., Simpson, A., Bliss, A., & Stewart, S. E. (2018). Group family-based cognitive behavioral therapy for pediatric obsessive compulsive disorder: Global outcomes and predictors of improvement. *Psychiatry Research, 260*, 116–122. https://doi.org/10.1016/j.psychres.2017.11.041

Silverman, W. K., Marin, C. E., Rey, Y., Kurtines, W. M., Jaccard, J., & Pettit, J. W. (2019). Group-versus parent-involvement CBT for childhood anxiety disorders: Treatment specificity and long-term recovery mediation. *Clinical Psychological Science, 7*(4), 840–855. https://doi.org/10.1177/2167702619830404

Smith, G. C., Hayslip, B., Jr., Hancock, G. R., Strieder, F. H., & Montoro-Rodriguez, J. (2018). A randomized clinical trial of interventions for improving well-being in custodial grandfamilies. *Journal of Family Psychology, 32*(6), 816–827. https://doi.org/10.1037/fam0000457

Spence, S. H., Donovan, C., & Brechman-Toussaint, M. (2000). The treatment of childhood social phobia: The effectiveness of a social skills training-based, cognitive-behavioural intervention, with and without parental involvement. *The Journal of Child Psychology and Psychiatry and Allied Disciplines, 41*(6), 713–726. https://doi.org/10.1111/1469-7610.00659

Tarver, J., Palmer, M., Webb, S., Scott, S., Slonims, V., Simonoff, E., & Charman, T. (2019). Child and parent outcomes following parent interventions for child emotional and behavioral problems in autism spectrum disorders: A systematic review and meta-analysis. *Autism, 23*(7), 1630–1644. https://doi.org/10.1177/1362361319830042

Taylor, A. B., & Neppl, T. K. (2023). Sexual identity in lesbian, gay, bisexual, transgender, and queer or questioning emerging adults: The role of parental rejection, and sexuality specific family support. *Journal of Family Issues, 44*(2), 409–428. https://doi.org/10.1177/0192513X211050063

Thompson-Hollands, J., Edson, A., Tompson, M. C., & Comer, J. S. (2014). Family involvement in the psychological treatment of obsessive–compulsive disorder: A meta-analysis. *Journal of Family Psychology, 28*(3), 287–298. https://doi.org/10.1037/a0036709

Thulin, U., Svirsky, L., Serlachius, E., Andersson, G., & Öst, L.-G. (2014). The effect of parent involvement in the treatment of anxiety disorders in children: A meta-analysis. *Cognitive Behaviour Therapy, 43*(3), 185–200. https://doi.org/10.1080/16506073.2014.923928

Tompson, M. C., Langer, D. A., & Asarnow, J. R. (2020). Development and efficacy of a family-focused treatment for depression in childhood. *Journal of Affective Disorders, 276*, 686–695. https://doi.org/10.1016/j.jad.2020.06.057

Wang, Y., Lao, C. K., Wang, Q., & Zhou, G. (2022). The impact of sexual minority stigma on depression: The roles of resilience and family support. *Sexuality Research and Social Policy, 19*(2), 442–452. https://doi.org/10.1007/s13178-021-00558-x

Watson, H. J., & Rees, C. S. (2008). Meta-analysis of randomized, controlled treatment trials for pediatric obsessive-compulsive disorder. *Journal of Child Psychology and Psychiatry, and Allied Disciplines, 49*(5), 489–498. https://doi.org/10.1111/j.1469-7610.2007.01875.x

Wei, C., & Kendall, P. C. (2014). Parental involvement: Contribution to childhood anxiety and its treatment. *Clinical Child and Family Psychology Review, 17*(4), 319–339. https://doi.org/10.1007/s10567-014-0170-6

Weinstein, S. M., & West, A. E. (2021). Psychosocial interventions for childhood affective disorders: Is the family the key to success? *Journal of Affective Disorders, 294*, 447. https://doi.org/10.1016/j.jad.2021.07.089

West, A. E., Weinstein, S. M., Peters, A. T., Katz, A., Henry, D., Cruz, R., & Pavuluri, M. (2014). Child- and family-focused cognitive-behavioral therapy for pediatric bipolar disorder: A randomized clinical trial. *Journal of the American Academy of Child and Adolescent Psychiatry, 53*(11), 1168–1178.e1. https://doi.org/10.1016/j.jaac.2014.08.013

Chapter 9
Parent-Only Treatment of Children and Adolescents

Rebecca G. Etkin, Yaara Shimshoni, and Eli R. Lebowitz

9.1 Introduction

Parents play an important role in the etiology of child and adolescent obsessive-compulsive disorder (OCD) and anxiety disorders (i.e., anxiety-related disorders; ARDs), suggesting the utility of involving parents in their treatment (Silverman & Kurtines, 1996). Over the last 30 years, numerous randomized controlled trials (RCTs) of youth ARD treatment have involved parents in various ways. Parents either were trained in cognitive-behavioral therapy (CBT) strategies to implement with their child, were provided general parenting techniques (e.g., communication, positive reinforcement), or received treatment for their own anxiety (e.g., Barrett et al., 1996; Kendall et al., 2008; Nauta et al., 2003). Yet, evidence from these trials has not consistently shown that involving parents in these ways improves treatment efficacy over and above the child participating in treatment alone (Peris et al., 2021; Wei & Kendall, 2014). This raises questions about how best to include parents in youth ARD treatment, and what aspects of parenting to target.

In the last 10 years, a specific aspect of parenting behavior has garnered considerable theoretical, empirical, and clinical attention for its role in child and adolescent ARDs: *family accommodation*. Family accommodation is defined as behavior intended to prevent or alleviate a child's symptom-related distress (Calvocoressi et al., 1995; Lebowitz et al., 2013). Children naturally turn to parents for help escaping or avoiding anxiety-provoking stimuli and anxiety symptoms themselves. Parents, in turn, may feel compelled to respond in ways that mitigate or facilitate avoidance of feared situations or distressing symptoms. As a result, parents and children are often stuck in a repeated cycle of child anxiety symptoms, direct or

R. G. Etkin (✉) · Y. Shimshoni · E. R. Lebowitz
Yale Child Study Center, Yale University School of Medicine, New Haven, CT, USA
e-mail: rebecca.etkin@yale.edu; yaara.shimshoni@yale.edu; eli.lebowitz@yale.edu

L. Reuman, J. Thompson-Hollands (eds.), *Enhancing CBT Through Family and Peer Engagement*, CBT: Science Into Practice, https://doi.org/10.1007/978-3-031-74838-7_9

indirect child solicitations of parental help, and family accommodation. The accommodation leads to short-term distress reduction until the anxiety appears again and the cycle repeats (Shimshoni et al., 2019). Empirically, research shows that higher levels of accommodation are associated with greater child ARD severity and related impairment (Iniesta-Sepúlveda et al., 2020).

Clinically, accommodation has been identified as an important treatment target (Kendall et al., 2020). Because accommodation is directly related to a key maintaining feature of ARDs—behavioral and experiential avoidance—high levels of accommodation may interfere with a child's treatment progress. Indeed, treatment studies show that lower pretreatment levels of family accommodation tend to predict better outcomes (i.e., lower posttreatment youth anxiety symptom severity, greater treatment response), whereas higher pretreatment levels of family accommodation predict worse outcomes for children and adolescents with ARDs. These findings are consistent across different treatment types and modalities (e.g., medication, CBT; Garcia et al., 2010; Kagan et al., 2016; Merlo et al., 2009; Salloum et al., 2018).

Targeting family accommodation, therefore, represents a promising direction for improving treatment efficacy for children and adolescents with ARDs. Further, targeting family accommodation has high clinical utility, as it is fully within the parents' purview and does not necessitate any child participation or cooperation. When children are unwilling or unable to engage in treatment or work on their anxiety, it poses a clear and significant barrier to them receiving the help they need. Parents and therapists alike may find themselves in the difficult, if not impossible, position of trying to *make* the child engage in therapy. Yet, therapeutic approaches for other clinical presentations (e.g., attention-deficit/hyperactivity disorder (ADHD), oppositional defiant disorder) demonstrate that child improvement is not contingent on their direct participation in treatment. Rather, this change can be achieved solely through working with parents and modifying parent behavior. Until recently, this therapeutic model had not been applied to internalizing disorders, including ARDs (Forehand et al., 2013). In the following sections, we describe a treatment that, therefore, represents a significant departure from other youth ARD treatment approaches (including with parent involvement) by working *exclusively* with parents to target accommodation: SPACE (Supportive Parenting for Anxious Childhood Emotions; Lebowitz 2013).

9.2 Treatment Overview

9.2.1 Background

SPACE adopts an interpersonal, systemic perspective on childhood anxiety and is informed by theoretical frameworks including attachment theory (Bowlby, 1969) and nonviolent resistance (NVR; Omer, 2001). Attachment theory provides a basis for understanding how children's reactions to fear and anxiety differ meaningfully from those of adults. In adults, activation of the threat detection system triggers responses centered primarily around confrontation or avoidance. In children, the response includes a more prominent social aspect: seeking protection and emotional regulation from caregivers. When there is an actual threat to the child, this response to fear is adaptive (e.g., a child who reaches for their parent's hand when facing a busy street of cars). When a child has an ARD and repeatedly perceives benign stimuli and situations as threatening, this response to fear can become maladaptive (e.g., a child who demands their parent lays next to them to fall asleep every night). Children "activate" the interpersonal system for managing anxiety by displaying fear to their parents (e.g., crying, clinging, seeking reassurance). When this system is activated, parents will naturally respond by providing protection and emotional regulation to alleviate the child's anxiety, such as offering reassurance, soothing, and removing anxiety-provoking stimuli. In other words, parents *accommodate*. Yet, when parents continuously accommodate their child's anxiety, the child has few opportunities to face their fears and independently regulate their emotions. Reducing accommodation, therefore, increases these opportunities for the child, ultimately helping them overcome their anxiety.

SPACE also incorporates the principles of NVR. NVR emphasizes changing one's own behavior to promote a process of change rather than attempting to directly impose change on others, which is often ineffective and can lead to escalating conflict. NVR as a philosophy has guided important political movements, such as those led by Gandhi and Martin Luther King, Jr. NVR as a therapeutic approach has been used primarily to help parents manage youth aggressive and destructive behaviors (Omer & Lebowitz, 2016). SPACE effectively applies this principle to the process of reducing family accommodation and promoting more independent child coping. This is important because children who are highly anxious and reliant on parents for accommodation may initially resist or oppose reductions in accommodation, sometimes in aggressive or destructive ways (Lebowitz et al., 2011a, b, c). To help these children without contributing to additional resistance and escalation, parents focus on modifying their own behavior, without demanding changes from the child. This eliminates the need for unhelpful conflict and power struggles, allowing the parents to follow through with their goal of reducing accommodation.

By integrating these frameworks, SPACE represents a conceptual shift in parent-based treatment for child and adolescent ARDs. Namely, SPACE does not conceptualize the role of parents as teaching their child particular skills or making their child engage in or disengage from certain behaviors. Instead, SPACE conceptualizes the role of parents as changing their own behavior. It does this by targeting the attachment-driven process whereby children rely on and elicit accommodation from their parents, and parents provide these accommodations. Focusing on family accommodation means that SPACE does not rely on the child's direct participation in treatment. Many anxious children and adolescents decline or have difficulty meaningfully engaging in treatment (e.g., Sauter et al., 2009); a fully parent-based approach enables youth to receive the intervention they need regardless of these factors. In addition, an approach that is not contingent on child-based change frees parents from the often-impossible task of making their child follow directives, including engaging in therapeutic tasks.

9.2.2 Treatment Components

SPACE is a structured, manualized treatment that can be tailored and individualized for different families. It has eight parts that are delivered sequentially. It also has four modules addressing challenges that may arise in particular cases and can be implemented as needed, at any point in the course of treatment. The total number of sessions can vary for each case, but SPACE is designed to be a short-term treatment. In clinical trials, SPACE is typically completed in 10–12 sessions (Lebowitz et al., 2014, 2019).

Part I of SPACE focuses on setting the stage for the treatment. This entails discussing why parents are involved in treatment instead of the child, with an emphasis on dispelling misconceptions about parents' blame for the child's anxiety. Rather, the discussion focuses on how it is natural for parents to be drawn into their child's anxiety in various ways. To illustrate this, the concept of anxiety blurring boundaries in the family is introduced. Parents are asked to reflect on how their child's anxiety has blurred boundaries between them and their child. For example, a parent of a child with separation anxiety disorder (SAD) might find that they cannot go to the bathroom without their child right next to them or spend time alone with their partner. A parent of a child with OCD might find themselves engaging in excessive handwashing or nightly rituals due to the child's symptoms. Or, a parent of a child with severe anxiety may find their own anxiety is triggered by the child's distress and may struggle to regulate their own emotions.

These discussions segue into a description of how treatment will focus on changing only what parents can control: their own behavior. It is made explicit that parents will not be asked to directly demand that their child do or not do something. Parents can reflect on how attempts to make such demands have gone in the past (e.g., telling their child to take deep breaths when anxious, convincing their child that they don't need to worry). It is explained that in SPACE such demands are irrelevant and that instead the parents will work hard between sessions (ideally with both parents, if applicable) to change their own behavior. The therapist also provides an overview of the steps of treatment and describes how working through these steps in a systematic manner will help the child overcome their anxiety.

Part II of SPACE focuses on increasing supportive parental responses. Support is defined as integrating expressions of acceptance with expressions of confidence in response to the child's anxiety. Acceptance entails conveying judgment-free validation of the child's distress. Confidence entails conveying the belief that the child can handle or tolerate anxiety-related distress. Parents are trained on the use of supportive statements that integrate both messages and are instructed to consistently use them between sessions. An example of a supportive statement is: "I see you are very worried, and I know you can handle those feelings!" The therapist engages parents in a discussion of how they typically respond to their child's anxiety. Many parents describe responding with either protective statements (e.g., "It's too hard, you don't have to do it") or demanding statements (e.g., "it's not hard, don't worry about it!"). Many also describe vacillating between these two types of responses depending on contextual factors, such as how much time or patience they have, or how anxious the child is. Children with ARDs have reduced beliefs they can cope with anxiety and help themselves (Landon et al., 2007); starting to believe that they can tolerate anxiety is important to achieving remission and also sets the stage for them to be able to tolerate and understand the other changes parents will make in the course of SPACE.

It is important that the therapist sets expectations with parents about what might happen when they respond to their child supportively. For some children, supportive language can have an immediate downregulating effect, leading to reduced expression of distress. For others, it will take time for this message to "sink in." Using supportive statements is, therefore, the first exercise in unilateral action and self-control. Parents' only job is to say the supportive statements; they are not responsible for making their child accept or agree with the statements.

Some parents will experience challenges responding in a supportive manner. These challenges can include the parent not feeling confident that their child actually can handle anxiety, not thinking their child "should" feel anxious, or worrying that acknowledging anxiety will actually make it worse. These barriers are addressed during this stage of treatment, and role-play is used to practice the supportive statements. A focus on support and the use of supportive statements is maintained throughout all of SPACE, even as the focus shifts more to accommodation reduction in the next stages of treatment.

Part III of SPACE focuses on introducing and charting accommodation. The therapist may have briefly mentioned the concept of accommodation in Part I, or some parents may have come to treatment already familiar with it. In Part III, the therapist provides more in-depth psychoeducation about accommodation. Parents learn how a "cycle of accommodation" drives them to behave in ways that reduce their child's distress in the short term but ultimately maintain anxiety and reliance on them for regulation in the long term. Parents provide examples of how they accommodate, and the therapist can highlight important themes, such as how negative short-term consequences of not accommodating have led them to feel as though accommodation is their only option. For example, parents may worry that not accommodating a child's request to be driven to school in the morning (rather than taking the bus) will lead to the child not attending school or them being late for work. Such challenges can be used to illustrate why almost all parents of children with ARDs accommodate their child.

This discussion sets the stage for the remainder of treatment to focus on parents reducing accommodation in supportive, practical, and systematic ways. The first step in doing so is charting the various accommodation behaviors parents presently engage in. The therapist guides parents through thinking over their typical day and identifying all the accommodations they provide, including estimating the frequency of each accommodation. Culture is an important consideration (see section below) in determining what parent behaviors constitute accommodations. A certain behavior may be typical and normative in one culture, but less so in another, and therefore, more likely to be a form of accommodation.

Part IV of SPACE focuses on selecting a target accommodation to reduce. In making this choice, the therapist will prefer to focus on an accommodation that occurs frequently and that parents consider to be important and are motivated to change. Choosing to target an accommodation that occurs infrequently will cause parents to not have sufficient opportunities to practice changing their behavior, whereas choosing a target they are not motivated to address will likely result in lower adherence to the treatment plan. It is also important to ensure that the target accommodation is a parent-enacted behavior that they are in direct control over and that it is related primarily to the child's anxiety.

Part V of SPACE focuses on developing a detailed plan for reducing the target accommodation. This process may take an entire treatment session or more, as it involves a high level of detail such that parents feel confident and prepared to implement the plan, even in light of challenges or barriers that might arise. A detailed plan will ensure that parents know precisely what is expected of them for the coming week. Since not all children will be amenable to the idea of their parent reducing accommodation, ample time is spent discussing how to cope with potentially difficult reactions from the child. These can include, for example, anxiety, sadness, anger, or aggression. Role-play is especially helpful for preparing parents for these scenarios. Responses involving serious aggression or threats of self-harm require an additional level of intervention; if these responses are anticipated, the therapist will draw on relevant treatment modules (described below). Developing a plan often necessitates the help of other individuals aside from parents, referred to as "supporters." Supporters and their various roles are also described in the module below. An example of a detailed plan to reduce accommodation is also provided in the case vignette that follows.

Part VI of SPACE focuses on preparing parents to inform the child of their plan to reduce the target accommodation. It is important that children not only have information about the nature of the changes that they can expect from parents but also context and rationale for why the changes are occurring. The *announcement* is a way for parents to communicate the details of the plan as well as why they are enacting it. In the announcement, parents explicitly acknowledge the child's anxiety problem and their realization that continuing to accommodate is not the best way to help. Parents describe to the child the plan to change their own behavior, without making any demands that the child change their behavior, or even cooperate with the plan at all. Overall, the announcement is concise, specific, developmentally appropriate, and parent-focused and is delivered in a loving and supportive tone. The therapist also helps parents anticipate the different ways the child might react, from happiness and gratitude to ignoring or indifference to sadness, worry, or anger, and provides guidance on how the parents are to manage these reactions.

Part VII of SPACE focuses on parents implementing the plan they developed to reduce accommodation. Parents are encouraged to begin doing so soon after making the announcement and close to their next therapy session. As parents implement their plans, they are encouraged to monitor their progress. Taking notes on when they implemented the plan and how it went (e.g., what made it easy or difficult) makes for a productive review with the therapist and aids in identifying patterns or areas for improvement.

In this phase of treatment, emphasis is placed on praise for both the child and the parents. The therapist will emphasize that because no demand was placed on the child, the child earns praise simply by coping with the parents following their plan, even if the child expressed distress or anger. Likewise, parents are worthy and deserving of praise from the therapist for their hard work in reducing accommodation. Sessions will also include a review of the child's progress, both in regard to the specific target and their anxiety more generally. Expectations are clearly set that parents likely will not see an immediate improvement in their child's anxiety but that symptoms should improve within a few weeks of consistent implementation. When parents are able to implement their plan relatively consistently and without great difficulty, they are ready to consider introducing additional targets.

Part VIII of SPACE focuses on selecting additional targets and developing additional plans to reduce accommodation. A typical course of SPACE will target two to three different accommodations, though this is variable. This sometimes surprises families, who may have generated a list of many accommodations they provide. The relatively low number of targets is due to generalization that occurs over the course of treatment. Increasing support and targeting even one accommodation treats anxiety more broadly by teaching the child that they can handle and cope with anxiety. In choosing subsequent targets, the accommodation chart is consulted and updated, often demonstrating how much generalization has occurred. Parts V through VII are then repeated until sufficient improvement has been achieved to consider ending treatment.

Termination, similar to most other therapies, involves reviewing progress and planning for relapse prevention. To review progress, the therapist may once again consult the accommodation chart to highlight how much has changed. The therapist may also have parents rate their perceived level of accommodation and support and compare them to ratings from the start of treatment. The therapist highlights the changes they observed in parents' attitudes and skills across the course of treatment, as well as the changes in the child. A useful exercise is to walk parents through how they may identify increases in their child's anxiety and their own accommodation in the future. A related useful exercise involves engaging parents in brainstorming about how they might approach a future anxiety problem that arises for the child, including how they would select a target accommodation and develop a plan to reduce it.

Modules are introduced throughout treatment on an as-needed basis. A module on supporters is used in almost every SPACE case (90% in Lebowitz et al., 2014). This is because supporters can assume a variety of different roles and, therefore, are helpful for most families. Supporters can be extended family members, coaches, teachers, religious leaders, neighbors, friends of the family, and others. In some cases, they will help to facilitate a plan to reduce accommodation (e.g., serving as "backup" to pick a child up from school if they do not get on the bus). In other cases, they may provide more emotional support for the child or parent. For instance, a supporter may send the child encouraging messages about their ability to cope with anxiety or be available to talk to parents during a difficult time.

Another module helps the parents to effectively respond to and reduce violent or destructive child behaviors in response to accommodation reduction. The module includes strategies for the prevention of aggressive/disruptive behaviors and for de-escalating and maintaining safety during explosive outbursts. Parents also learn effective responses that can reduce the likelihood of such behaviors recurring in the future. This module too makes use of supporters by encouraging the parents to have a supporter present when announcing or implementing a plan, and by encouraging supporters to communicate to the child that violent or destructive behaviors are serious and unacceptable actions.

Another module is utilized when children react to reductions in parental accommodation by threatening to harm themselves. A child's suicidal threat places parents in a frightening position and they may feel compelled to resume an accommodation to prevent risk to the child. The module helps parents to navigate this situation by providing tools for maintaining the child's safety and reducing the risk of self-harm, while simultaneously allowing the parent to continue following the treatment plan, reducing their accommodation, and treating the child's ARD.

A final module focuses on improving the collaboration between parents whose difficulty working together poses a barrier to successful treatment. Many factors contribute to difficulties in parent collaboration, ranging from differences in parenting styles and understanding of child anxiety to marital issues that spill over into treatment. When these issues are impeding progress, the therapist can implement strategies aimed at finding common ground between the parents, improving communication, reducing guilt and blame between parents, and highlighting the complementary strengths each parent brings to the table. For instance, if one parent tends to be more validating toward the child while the other is more confident, the therapist can help parents recognize the utility in each approach and how they are both part of the necessary components of support as defined in SPACE.

Participation of two parents is not critical for implementing SPACE, however, treatment can be conducted with any of the child's parents or guardians who choose to be a part of the process. If parents live in separate homes, modifications can be made such that a plan to reduce accommodation only takes place in one parent's home while the other parent plays a supportive role, or the plan is enacted in both homes with adjustments as needed.

9.3 Research Evidence

SPACE's acceptability, feasibility, and efficacy have been tested in several clinical trials. The first two open trials of SPACE were conducted in youth with OCD and anxiety disorders, respectively (Lebowitz, 2013; Lebowitz et al., 2014). Lebowitz (2013) tested ten sessions of SPACE with parents of six 10–13-year-old children with OCD who declined to participate in CBT. All parents completed treatment with reports of high satisfaction. Children showed significant decreases in parent-rated measures of OCD symptoms, accommodation, and coercive-disruptive behavior from pre- to posttreatment. Lebowitz et al. (2014) likewise tested ten sessions of SPACE with parents of ten 9–13-year-old children with diagnoses of generalized anxiety disorder (GAD), social anxiety disorder (SoAD), SAD, or OCD. All children either refused to attend the assessment or to participate in CBT. All parents completed all treatment sessions with high satisfaction ratings. Sixty percent of children were treatment responders (based on clinician-rated improvement), and parent ratings of child anxiety symptoms and accommodation decreased significantly from pre- to posttreatment.

SPACE was also compared with CBT in a randomized noninferiority trial involving parents of $N = 124$ 7–14-year-old children with primary GAD, SAD, or SoAD (Lebowitz et al., 2019). Ninety-six families completed the trial, with no significant differences in attrition for SPACE and CBT. Treatment credibility and satisfaction were high for SPACE and also did not significantly differ from CBT. There were reductions in parenting stress and accommodation from pre- to posttreatment in both arms, although the reduction in accommodation was significantly greater following SPACE than CBT. SPACE was noninferior to CBT on primary and secondary child anxiety outcomes rated by independent evaluators, parents, and children.

Given the evidence that SPACE and CBT have comparable efficacy, Lebowitz and colleagues (2021) examined moderators of treatment efficacy for the youth in the non-inferiority trial to shed light on which youth and families may benefit most from which treatment. They examined a range of demographic (e.g., age, sex), child socioemotional (e.g., anxiety diagnosis and severity), parenting (e.g., acceptance, negativity), parent socioemotional (e.g., anxiety, depression), and biological (i.e., child and parent salivary oxytocin levels) variables as potential moderators, using a machine learning approach. Parent-reported child anxiety outcomes were moderated by parent negativity and child oxytocin levels. Child-reported outcomes were moderated by baseline anxiety, parent negativity, and parent oxytocin levels. Independent-evaluator-reported outcomes were moderated by baseline anxiety. Children assigned to their optimal treatment condition based on the identified moderators had a significantly greater reduction in anxiety symptoms compared with children assigned to their nonoptimal treatment. For children with higher parent negativity and higher child oxytocin, SPACE led to greater parent-rated child anxiety symptom reduction than CBT. For children with lower parent negativity, CBT led to greater parent-rated child anxiety symptom reduction than SPACE. For children with higher baseline anxiety severity, CBT led to more child-rated anxiety symptom reduction than SPACE.

There is also evidence that SPACE and CBT can be used concurrently to treat ARDs in childhood through young adulthood. One published case study documents an 18-year-old young woman with severe agoraphobia treated simultaneously with CBT and SPACE. There were substantial reductions in her anxiety symptoms, anxiety sensitivity, and family accommodation from pre- to posttreatment with additional gains 8 months later (Raila et al., 2021). However, clinical trial data are needed to test the efficacy of this combined approach.

9.3.1 Treatment Adaptations

SPACE was developed as an individual treatment but has since been adapted for delivery in a group format. In the one published trial testing this approach, Dekel et al. (2021) offered a SPACE group intervention to parents of 30 children (M_{age} = 11.14 years) with an anxiety disorder or OCD who were either on a waitlist for individual CBT or previously refused or did not respond to CBT. Groups (mostly mothers) met for 10–12-hour-long sessions that followed the parts of SPACE described above (e.g., increasing support, developing and implementing specific plans to reduce accommodation). As the group progressed, parents were encouraged to increasingly take the lead in choosing targets and formulating plans. Regarding outcomes, 84% of participants completed the group, mean attendance was 77%, and average treatment satisfaction was high. There were significant decreases in parent-rated family accommodation, family power struggles, and parental sense of helplessness from pre- to posttreatment. Results also revealed significant decreases in the severity of clinician-rated child anxiety/OCD symptoms, with clinically significant symptom improvement for 79.1% of children.

SPACE has also been tested for the treatment of anxiety in youth with autism spectrum disorders (ASD). Rozenblat et al. (2023) conducted a pilot trial of this approach in parents of children (ages 6–10 years old) with ASD, at least average cognitive abilities, and high levels of anxiety. Parents participated in 13 weekly sessions of SPACE. The treatment protocol was the same as described above but with additional introductory focus and psychoeducation on ASD in addition to anxiety. Of the 26 eligible families, 22 (84.62%) elected to participate and 15 (68.18%) completed treatment, with high ratings of satisfaction. Child anxiety symptom severity and family accommodation significantly decreased from pre- to posttreatment, and gains were maintained at 2-month follow-up. This trial provides preliminary evidence that SPACE is feasible, acceptable, and satisfactory and produces improvement in anxiety in youth with ASD.

SPACE has also been adapted for the treatment of other clinical disorders in youth. Shimshoni et al. (2020) adapted and tested SPACE for the treatment of avoidant/restrictive food intake disorder (ARFID). ARFID shares several key features with youth ARDs, including anxiety, avoidance, and accommodation. As family accommodation can contribute to food-related rigidity and ARFID symptom maintenance, SPACE-ARFID helps parents systematically reduce their accommodations, reduce food-related stress, and increase supportive responses. In an open trial of this approach, parents of 15 children (6–14 years old) with ARFID participated in 12 sessions of SPACE-ARFID. The overall parts of treatment are the same as those described above but with a focus on improving children's food-related flexibility through the modification of parents' responses to symptoms. There is also an increased focus on psychoeducation about ARFID, discussing family food habits and attitudes, reducing stress and conflict about food, and additional tools to increase children's exposure to nonpreferred foods and food-related situations. Regarding outcomes, 14 of the 15 families completed all treatment sessions and rated treatment satisfaction as high. Child ARFID symptom severity and impairment, as well as family accommodation, significantly decreased from pre- to posttreatment. There were also increases in children's food-related flexibility.

Another clinical presentation defined by high levels of anxiety and family accommodation is that of highly dependent adult children, often termed "failure to launch" (FTL) (Lebowitz, 2016). Adults with FTL are able (i.e., have not suffered a major injury or disease) but are not engaged in higher education or gainful employment and remain highly dependent on their parents. This leads to significant concern, frustration, and burden for parents and to negative sequelae for the adult child. SPACE-FTL (Berger & Lebowitz, 2022) follows the general structure and strategies of SPACE described above but focuses on reducing parental accommodation of the adult child's lack of function and on developing and implementing plans for increasing their functional independence. Accommodations for adults with FTL often look different than those for youth with ARDs. For example, accommodations include letting the adult live at the parents' house, paying for goods or services, acting as a go-between for other people, and maintaining secrecy. SPACE-FTL helps parents determine whether these accommodations are promoting or impeding progress toward more adaptive functioning and develop plans to reduce unhelpful accommodations. As in SPACE, de-escalation and engaging supporters play a particularly important role in this work. A clinical trial of SPACE-FTL is complete, and data are forthcoming.

9.4 Clinical Considerations for Diverse Identities

There is a strong indication that a treatment for youth ARDs focused on reducing family accommodation is applicable across cultures and diverse identities. Although cross-cultural research is still needed, accommodation is a worldwide phenomenon with similar rates across countries and similar associations with youth anxiety (e.g., Bipeta et al., 2013; Iniesta-Sepúlveda et al., 2020; Ishikawa et al., 2022; Zamani et al., 2019). To date, clinical trials of SPACE have included relatively homogeneous samples in terms of racial/ethnic and socioeconomic diversity; however, SPACE is taught and implemented all over the world and in a variety of clinical contexts and settings. Some research has been conducted in international samples (Dekel et al., 2021; Rozenblat et al., 2023).

One consideration relating to the diversity of families receiving SPACE is how specific accommodations may vary by culture, even when *rates* of accommodation remain similar. For example, sleeping in a child's bed may be an anxiety-driven accommodating behavior in one cultural context, but not in another in which the same behavior is in accordance with cultural norms (Barrett, 2000). This is essential to consider when charting accommodations and selecting a target accommodation to reduce. Parents can help a therapist disentangle what may be a cultural custom from what may be an accommodation by answering questions about their rationale and motivations for engaging in different behaviors and what the consequences would be if they did not engage in said behavior. Therapists can self-reflect on their own identity and maintain a curious and open attitude that values the differences of others, avoids uninformed assumptions about clients, and allows for treatment to be tailored and personalized to each individual circumstance.

Other considerations may relate to differences in family structures in different cultures and communities. For instance, in many cultures, larger families (i.e., >4 children) are common. Siblings in addition to parents often engage in accommodations, which may be especially pertinent to consider in larger families. Instead of focusing solely on parent accommodation, it is possible to modify the SPACE protocol to also identify and address sibling accommodation—especially for older adolescent or adult siblings (Dekel et al., 2021). For larger families, a greater focus on parents providing psychoeducation to siblings (of all ages) about accommodation and the importance of minimizing it may also have great utility (Dekel et al., 2021).

SPACE also relies strongly on the support of other individuals outside of the immediate, nuclear family. Leaning on a network of trusted individuals when raising a child is more normative in some cultures and communities than others. Therapeutic approaches designed for Black and African-American youth and families, for example, have long emphasized the importance of extended family patterns and kinship care (Boyd-Franklin, 2013). Engaging informal, noninstitutional sources of support may be preferable in these communities (Lindsey et al., 2013). As such, the importance of supporters in SPACE may be more intuitive and represent a significant strength during treatment. At the same time, concerns about mental health stigma and norms in terms of disclosing personal information (e.g., about one's family or challenges) vary across racial/ethnic and geographical groups in the United States (e.g., Abdullah & Brown, 2011). Therefore, in any case of SPACE, it is important to address parents' reservations about or barriers to involving supporters in the treatment process.

Ultimately, SPACE is designed to be highly flexible and tailorable to each family's unique needs and circumstances. All plans to reduce accommodation, for example, are individualized for every family with the feasibility of implementation as a foremost consideration. There is opportunity, and often necessity, throughout treatment to discuss how cultural factors may have influenced parents' way of responding to their anxious child. Parents often discuss their own upbringings, reflecting on the messages they received about their difficult emotions. Such reflections frequently lead to fruitful discussions about the utility of increasing supportive responses for their child. Also, in terms of flexibility and personalization, SPACE is well suited to families of different structures and parents of different sexual and gender identities (Lebowitz & Shimshoni, 2018). SPACE is also well suited for telehealth (Lebowitz et al., 2019), which may be particularly useful for families with lower access to services or barriers in terms of attending sessions (e.g., limited childcare or transportation resources). While additional research is needed on cross-cultural adaptations of SPACE, and on the acceptability, feasibility, and efficacy of SPACE among different diverse groups (e.g., racial/ethnic, socioeconomic), SPACE can be used broadly and adapted as needed to be culturally responsive.

9.5 Case Vignette

9.5.1 Background and Case Formulation

Conor was a 10-year-old, Hispanic, primarily English-speaking boy who lived with his single mother, Karrie, and his 6-year-old sister, Emma. Conor was referred for treatment by an occupational therapist who had been working with him since the beginning of second grade. Their work had centered around minor sensory sensitivity issues as well as organization skills, executive function, and social skills. Karrie described Conor as a sensitive, energetic, and sociable child, with a notable talent for athletics. She also noted an existing diagnosis of attention-deficit/hyperactivity disorder (ADHD; Combined Type) and a history of separation anxiety that emerged the year his sister was born but that seemed to have subsided mid-kindergarten without specialized intervention.

Conor's current symptoms began approximately 9 months prior to presenting for treatmen, following his sister experiencing a severe stomach bug that led to multiple episodes of vomiting and resulted in a visit to the emergency department due to dehydration. After this incident, Conor began expressing concerns about falling ill himself. Throughout the day, he would repeatedly ask Karrie whether various activities and foods could make him vomit. Initially, Karrie brushed off these questions with responses such as, "I've already told you, you won't get sick!" However, as Conor's questions persisted, she transitioned to addressing each one in detail, hoping that providing information would alleviate Conor's concerns. Unfortunately, this did not prove effective. Over the ensuing weeks and months, Conor's fear of becoming ill, particularly vomiting, persisted and began to have an increasingly adverse impact on various aspects of his life. He became hypervigilant about any discomfort in his stomach, interpreting these sensations as potential signs of an impending stomach bug that might lead to vomiting. This triggered a detrimental cycle wherein his fear of vomiting resulted in more frequent stomach aches, further intensifying his concerns about vomiting, and the cycle continued. Additionally, Conor became excessively watchful of the people around him, constantly on the lookout for any signs of illness.

This preoccupation led to increased distress, avoidance, and a growing decline in his daily functioning. Conor began avoiding people who appeared unwell to him. He refused to take the bus to and from school because the ride was "bumpy" and made him feel nauseous. Later this generalized to soccer carpools, where he worried that he would vomit in someone else's car. Throughout the day, Conor repeatedly expressed his worries to his mother, seeking reassurance that he would not vomit. His nighttime worries worsened, leaving him restless in bed. He would lie in bed thinking about all the different things he did that day that might have exposed him to a stomach bug or vomit and preferred that mom stay with him until he fell asleep. His worries were interfering with his ability to concentrate on his schoolwork and led to his avoidance of eating outside of the home.

In response to Conor's growing distress, Karrie engaged in many forms of accommodation. Throughout the day she would answer his worried questions, reassure him, and promise him that he would not vomit. She agreed to drive him to and from school so that he wouldn't have to take the bus. She also agreed to take on all the soccer carpool driving so Conor wouldn't have to ride in someone else's car. Before social engagements, she made sure that the people they were meeting were not sick, and she sat next to Conor's bed every night until he fell asleep. Despite her well-intentioned efforts to alleviate Conor's worries, Karrie realized that her behaviors were not proving effective. A conversation with the occupational therapist prompted her to take the next step: seeking treatment for Conor.

9.5.2 Diagnostic and Functional Assessment

The assessment was based on parent and child reports. Separately, Karrie and Conor were administered the Anxiety Disorders Interview Schedule (ADIS-C/P; Silverman & Albano, 1996) and several self-report rating scales. Based on the descriptions provided by Karrie and Conor, a diagnosis of emetophobia (vomit phobia) was confirmed. In addition, Conor exhibited some symptoms of generalized anxiety but did not meet the diagnostic criteria for the disorder. Karrie and Conor completed the Screen for Child Anxiety Related Emotional Disorders (SCARED; Birmaher et al., 1999) and scored 32 and 26, respectively, indicative of clinically significant anxiety. They also completed the Family Accommodation Scale—Anxiety (FAS-A; Lebowitz et al., 2013) and scored 30 and 16, respectively, indicating elevated levels of accommodation. Given these high levels of accommodation, as well as Conor's expressed hesitance to work on his anxiety, the therapist recommended SPACE as opposed to a child-focused intervention. The family agreed this approach would be a good fit for them.

9.5.3 Session-by-Session Overview

In the first SPACE session, the therapist introduced the systemic nature of child anxiety and laid the foundation for addressing child anxiety through working with parents. The therapist clarified that instead of attempting to directly modify Conor's behavior, the focus of treatment would be on Karrie's behavior, specifically her responses to Conor's anxiety symptoms. Karrie expressed her lack of confidence in the idea that changing her behavior could have a meaningful impact on Conor's anxiety. However, she acknowledged that her previous attempts to "get him to stop being anxious" had actually resulted in increased conflict between them without any improvement in his anxiety and, therefore, was open to exploring her reactions to Conor's anxiety. In addition to psychoeducation on child anxiety, an overview of treatment steps and goals was provided, and setting and expectations were discussed.

In the second session, Karrie and the therapist discussed the ways in which Conor's anxiety had blurred the boundaries between Karrie and Connor. Considering the different aspects of her identity as an independent person, Karrie was taken aback by the immense impact of Conor's anxiety on her life, affecting her physical space, her personal time, her thoughts, and her behavior. She said, "*His anxiety is always on my mind. When I wake up in the morning, I feel this dread…how will the day go? Will he see someone sick? Will he get upset and cry or be angry? Just thinking about the many questions and reassurances he'll ask for makes me tired and stressed. And this of course continues all day. Almost all of my time and energy is spent trying to manage his anxiety. You asked me, what would my life look like without the anxiety. To tell you the truth, I don't even know. It is tempting to think about it though….*" Later in the session, the therapist introduced a key component of treatment, *supportive responses*, as well as other not supportive, yet common, reactions parents have to their child's anxiety. Karrie described a tendency to fluctuate in her responses; sometimes she was overtaken by feelings of guilt about being the only parent, focusing on the ways she believed Conor was impacted by not having a second parent. This led her to feeling sorry for him and viewing him as disadvantaged in his abilities to overcome challenges, including anxiety. Other times she felt angry and frustrated with Conor for not "just dealing with it" and for draining all her time and energy, leaving nothing for her to give to Emma. She understood now how the supportive response, integrating acceptance and validation of Conor's fears and confidence in his abilities to tolerate them, could provide a positive and more consistent reaction to his behavior and agreed to practice responding with supportive messages such as, "*I know how nervous you get when you're not sure if something will make you vomit, and I know you can handle this worry.*"

The third session continued to focus on supportive responses. Karrie shared her experiences with using supportive statements and reflected on the challenges she faced in remembering to respond in this new way and managing Conor's sometimes unfavorable reactions to these statements. Discussing the barriers Karrie encountered helped clarify that the goal of the supportive messages was not to make Conor agree or act in a specific way. Instead, it aimed to gradually shift his perception of his ability to cope with anxiety. Although Conor's reactions were considered, they should not deter Karrie from conveying her perception of him as an anxious yet capable child. During role-play in the session, it became apparent that Karrie's apprehension about Conor's response led her to adopt an overly assertive, almost aggressive tone, which she was able to modify with practice.

In session four, Karrie and the therapist charted the accommodations Karrie had been making by conducting a thorough review of the family's daily routines and discussing any changes in Karrie's behavior aimed at reducing Conor's anxiety. This process helped Karrie break down what had appeared to be "complete chaos from morning to night," allowing her to distinguish between accommodations related to anxiety, which SPACE aims to address, and those associated with other issues, such as his ADHD. For example, it was clarified that while telling Conor several times that he will not be sick is an accommodation of his anxiety, telling him several times to put his shoes on is an accommodation of his inattentiveness. With the therapist, Karrie completed the Accommodation Chart (Table 9.1). She was asked to continue to add accommodations that she noticed herself doing throughout the week.

Table 9.1 Chart of family accommodation

	Accommodation provided	Frequency
Morning	Provides reassurance about not being ill Avoids talking about any illness	5–10 times per morning 1–2 times per morning Every morning
Going to school	Drives Conor to school Drives extra slowly so Connor will not feel nauseous Provides reassurance about illness	Every school day 3–4 times per drive
During the School Day	Picks Conor up early if a classmate becomes sick during the day Allows Conor to miss school trips or drives him instead of him taking the school bus	~ Once per month ~ Once per 2-3 months
Afternoon	Picks Conor up from school Drives extra slowly so Connor will not feel nauseous Drives Conor and friends to soccer Provides reassurance about not being ill	Every school day 3–4 times per week 5–10 times in the afternoon
Dinner	Avoids eating out Will provide replacements for dinner if Conor fears the food will make him sick	Never eat out, estimates that *would* eat out twice per week Once per week
Family time	Change the TV channel if any illness related content is on Before social engagements calls to verify that everyone is healthy	2–3 times per week Once per week
Bedtime	Lies next to Conor until he falls asleep Provides reassurance about his day, telling him that the things he did that day will not make him sick	Nightly 5–10 times per night
Nighttime	None	

Session five was dedicated to selecting an accommodation to change and creating a detailed, specific plan to implement this change. After careful consideration, Karrie chose to work on reducing the reassurance she provides to Conor, where she repeatedly promises him that he won't become sick. Since Karrie had been providing this reassurance multiple times throughout the day and was concerned about how her ability to cope with Conor's potential reaction to the change, it was decided that Karrie's plan would initially focus only on the hours after school and until dinner. During this time, if Conor asked for reassurance, Karrie planned to respond once with a supportive message, such as, "*I understand it's difficult not knowing for sure whether you'll be sick or not, and I'm confident you can handle it*," or "*I know you feel anxious when I don't promise you won't get sick, but I believe you can handle me not answering.*" After that initial response, Karrie would not engage with further reassurance-seeking questions but would continue to interact with Conor on other topics. Since Karrie was still concerned about her ability to remain calm if Conor persisted, she enlisted her brother, who was also her dearest friend, as a supporter. She informed him of her plan and asked that he be available every day during the specified hours in case she needed to talk to him. He willingly agreed to support her. With the plan formulated, the therapy session focused on how to communicate Karrie's plan to Conor. Together with the therapist, Karrie composed an announcement letter explaining the upcoming changes in her responses to his anxiety. Karrie planned to read Conor the announcement during the following week and begin implementing her plan. This was her announcement:

> My Special Conor,
>
> I love you so so much! You are a wonderful person, and I'm so proud to be the mother of the kind and sensitive boy that you are. I also see how you're so worried about becoming sick and vomiting, and I know that you can handle this worry. I've been trying to help you by promising you won't get sick so that you don't have to worry. I now understand that that was the wrong way to help. When I always promise you won't be sick, I'm not giving you the chance to see that you can handle your worries. That is why starting tomorrow, after school and until we eat dinner, I will not answer questions about getting sick or promise that you won't get sick.
>
> I want you to know that this is not a punishment! I really believe that this will help you to have less worry soon. I know this might sound hard, and I also know that you are strong, and you can handle this change.
>
> I love you! Mom

During session six, the therapist and Karrie reviewed the delivery of the announcement and the initial experiences of implementing the plan. Karrie shared that she had felt very nervous before reading the announcement to Conor, but his initial reaction was mild. Conor simply stated, "*Yeah, we're not doing that*," and returned to his video game. The following day, after school, Conor expressed concerns about an upcoming school trip to an amusement park and repeatedly asked his mother if he would vomit if he went. Karrie reminded him about her plan and offered a supportive statement. This led to Conor becoming visibly upset, crying, and insisting that she answer. As planned, Karrie went to the kitchen and started preparing dinner. Conor persisted, demanding a response. After what felt to Karrie like hours (though it was only a few minutes), she decided to go to the bathroom and call her brother for support. Conor followed her and knocked on the bathroom door. The conversation with her brother helped Karrie stay calm, and after a few minutes, Conor returned to his room, where he softly cried a little and then played his video game until dinner. The following day, Conor approached Karrie again during the after-school hours and became angry when she did not offer reassurance. He yelled at her, "*You are the worst mom in the world! You say you love me, but you don't!*" However, after that, he did not follow her around the house. During the therapy session, the therapist praised Karrie for her consistent implementation of the plan and helped her see the past week as significant progress. Karrie had made the unilateral decision to change how she responded to Conor's anxiety and had adhered to this decision despite Conor's challenging reactions. The discussion with the therapist helped Karrie to understand Conor's difficult responses as valid expressions of him feeling challenged by these changes. She told the therapist, "*Yes, of course what you're saying is true. If I take the longer view, I know I love him so much and that I am helping him. I need to remember that in the moment.*" She was encouraged to continue with the current plan and monitor her implementation closely to detect patterns of challenge and change. Special attention was given to helping her praise Conor for coping with these changes, especially given the apparent difficulty he was experiencing.

In session seven, Karrie was happy to report that it had become easier for her to not reassure Conor during the after-school hours and that Conor hardly asked for her reassurance anymore. She also noticed that he had reduced his worry questions in the morning as well and that it was taking him a shorter time to fall asleep at night. After reviewing progress and revisiting the use of supportive responses, the therapist encouraged Karrie to take another step forward in reducing her accommodations. A natural choice for Karrie was to expand her plan of not providing reassurance to other hours of the day. It was decided that she would provide one reassurance statement in the morning before school and one at bedtime. Aside from these, she would not respond to Conor's questions around vomit.

In session eight, Karrie and the therapist reviewed the implementation of the extended plan. Karrie was delighted to report that Conor had responded positively to this change. She also reflected on the improvement she had observed in the overall atmosphere at home recently. Specifically, she noticed that as she engaged less in reassurance, she engaged more with Conor around other topics (e.g., friends, hobbies). The session also revisited the accommodation map and updated accommodations that Karrie was no longer providing, even though they were not directly addressed. She observed that Conor had stopped discussing vomiting during meals and had not mentioned feeling nauseous in the car. During the discussion, Karrie felt it was time to address an accommodation that had been causing significant interference for her: the soccer carpool.

In session nine, Karrie and the therapist devised a plan to reduce Karrie's accommodations regarding the soccer carpool. Previously, Karrie had been hesitant to address this accommodation due to her fear that Conor might decide to quit soccer if she didn't drive him. However, at this point, Karrie had gained more confidence in Conor's ability to manage his anxiety overall, and she had come to see the potential outcome of him taking a break or quitting soccer as an acceptable risk. Karrie formulated a detailed plan for addressing this accommodation. It involved her returning to participating in the soccer carpool in a balanced manner, where she and the other parents would take turns driving on their designated days. She also decided to have a conversation with the other parents and request their support if Conor resisted joining them. Karrie and the therapist composed a second announcement, and Karrie was enthusiastic about taking on this next step.

Session 10 focused on reviewing the implementation of the new plan. On the first day of the carpool, Conor initially refused to come out to the car. The parent who was driving (and the other kids) entered the house and cheered Conor on until he agreed to join them. After that day, Conor continued to express worries about vomiting in the car but did not refuse to join the carpool. Karrie made sure to praise Conor and asked her brother to do the same. Conor appeared very pleased with this positive attention and praise.

The final session was dedicated to reviewing the treatment process and discussing relapse prevention. The therapist encouraged Karrie to be vigilant for any signs of recurring anxiety symptoms or the emergence of new accommodations. The therapist emphasized the importance of maintaining a supportive attitude and not hesitating to address any accommodations when noticed, rather than hoping that minor accommodations would resolve the issue. Karrie reflected on the significant changes that had occurred over the past few weeks. Conor's anxiety appeared to be significantly reduced, with fewer symptoms and less interference in his daily life. She had successfully followed unilateral plans and systematically reduced her accommodations. She observed how these plans had made it easier for her to create stable changes in her behavior and within the family system. She was astonished to see the generalization of the impact of these specific changes on Conor's overall anxiety levels. Most importantly, she noticed a shift in her perception of Conor's ability to manage his anxiety and reflected on her sense that he had also internalized this perception. As the treatment concluded, Karrie drafted a plan to stop driving Conor to and from school. The therapist helped her refine this plan, and Karrie felt confident that she could implement it independently.

9.5.4 Treatment Outcomes

Following the last session, a posttreatment evaluation was conducted. Conor and Karrie were separately administered the ADIS with results indicating subclinical levels of emetophobia and generalized anxiety disorder. Karrie and Conor completed the SCARED and scored 17 and 10, respectively, indicating some anxiety symptoms, though not clinically significant. Scores on the FAS-A decreased to eight per both Karrie and Conor's report.

References

Abdullah, T., & Brown, T. L. (2011). Mental illness stigma and ethnocultural beliefs, values, and norms: An integrative review. *Clinical Psychology Review, 31*(6), 934–948. https://doi.org/10.1016/j.cpr.2011.05.003

Barrett, P. M. (2000). Treatment of childhood anxiety: Developmental aspects. *Clinical Psychology Review, 20*(4), 479–494. https://doi.org/10.1016/S0272-7358(99)00038-0

Barrett, P. M., Dadds, M. R., & Rapee, R. M. (1996). Family treatment of childhood anxiety: A controlled trial. *Journal of Consulting and Clinical Psychology, 64*(2), 333–342. https://doi.org/10.1037/0022-006X.64.2.333

Berger, U., & Lebowitz, E. (2022). Parent training for dependent, yet abled, young adults. *Bulletin of the Menninger Clinic, 86*(3), 249–281

Bipeta, R., Yerramilli, S. S., Pingali, S., Karredla, A. R., & Ali, M. O. (2013). A cross-sectional study of insight and family accommodation in pediatric obsessive-compulsive disorder. *Child and Adolescent Psychiatry and Mental Health, 7*, 1–11. https://doi.org/10.1186/1753-2000-7-20

Birmaher, B., Brent, D. A., Chiappetta, L., Bridge, J., Monga, S., & Baugher, M. (1999). Psychometric properties of the Screen for Child Anxiety Related Emotional Disorders (SCARED): A replication study. *Journal of the American Academy of Child & Adolescent Psychiatry, 38*(10), 1230–1236. https://doi.org/10.1097/00004583-199910000-00011

Bowlby, J. (1969). Attachment and Loss, Volume 1, Attachment. New York: Basic Books.

Boyd-Franklin, N. (2013). *Black families in therapy: Understanding the African American experience*. Guilford Publications.

Calvocoressi, L., Lewis, B., Harris, M., Trufan, S. J., Goodman, W. K., McDougle, C. J., & Price, L. H. (1995). Family accommodation in obsessive-compulsive disorder. *The American Journal of Psychiatry, 152*(3), 441–443. https://doi.org/10.1176/ajp.152.3.441

Dekel, I., Dorman-Ilan, S., Lang, C., Bar-David, E., Zilka, H., Shilton, T., Lebowitz, E. R., & Gothelf, D. (2021). The feasibility of a parent group treatment for youth with anxiety disorders and obsessive compulsive disorder. *Child Psychiatry & Human Development, 52*, 1044–1049. https://doi.org/10.1007/s10578-020-01082-6

Forehand, R., Jones, D. J., & Parent, J. (2013). Behavioral parenting interventions for child disruptive behaviors and anxiety: What's different and what's the same. *Clinical Psychology Review, 33*(1), 133–145. https://doi.org/10.1016/j.cpr.2012.10.010

Garcia, A. M., Sapyta, J. J., Moore, P. S., Freeman, J. B., Franklin, M. E., March, J. S., & Foa, E. B. (2010). Predictors and moderators of treatment outcome in the Pediatric Obsessive Compulsive Treatment Study (POTS I). *Journal of the American Academy of Child & Adolescent Psychiatry, 49*(10), 1024–1033. https://doi.org/10.1016/j.jaac.2010.06.013

Iniesta-Sepúlveda, M., Rodríguez-Jiménez, T., Lebowitz, E. R., Goodman, W. K., & Storch, E. A. (2020). The relationship of family accommodation with pediatric anxiety severity: Meta-analytic findings and child, family and methodological moderators. *Child Psychiatry and Human Development, 52*, 1–14. https://doi.org/10.1007/s10578-020-00987-6

Ishikawa, S.-I., Romano, M., & Hudson, J. L. (2022). A comparison of interactions among children, parents, and therapists in cognitive behavior therapy for anxiety disorders in Australia and Japan. *Behavior Therapy, 53*(1), 34–48. https://doi.org/10.1016/j.beth.2021.05.008

Kagan, E. R., Peterman, J. S., Carper, M. M., & Kendall, P. C. (2016). Accommodation and treatment of anxious youth. *Depression and Anxiety, 33*(9), 840–847. https://doi.org/10.1002/da.22520

Kendall, P. C., Hudson, J. L., Gosch, E., Flannery-Schroeder, E., & Suveg, C. (2008). Cognitive-behavioral therapy for anxiety disordered youth: A randomized clinical trial evaluating child and family modalities. *Journal of Consulting and Clinical Psychology, 76*(2), 282–297. https://doi.org/10.1037/0022-006X.76.2.282

Kendall, P. C., Norris, L. A., Rabner, J. C., Crane, M. E., & Rifkin, L. S. (2020). Intolerance of uncertainty and parental accommodation: Promising targets for personalized intervention for youth anxiety. *Current Psychiatry Reports, 22*(9), 1–8. https://doi.org/10.1007/s11920-020-01170-3

Landon, T. M., Ehrenreich, J. T., & Pincus, D. B. (2007). Self-efficacy: A comparison between clinically anxious and non-referred youth. *Child Psychiatry and Human Development, 38*, 31–45. https://doi.org/10.1007/s10578-006-0038-1

Lebowitz, E. R. (2013). Parent-based treatment for childhood and adolescent OCD. *Journal of Obsessive-Compulsive and Related Disorders, 2*(4), 425–431. https://doi.org/10.1016/j.jocrd.2013.08.004

Lebowitz, E. R. (2016). "Failure to launch": Shaping intervention for highly dependent adult children. *Journal of the American Academy of Child and Adolescent Psychiatry, 55*(2), 89–90. https://doi.org/10.1016/j.jaac.2015.10.014

Lebowitz, E. R., & Shimshoni, Y. (2018). The SPACE program, a parent-based treatment for childhood and adolescent OCD: The case of Jasmine. *Bulletin of the Menninger Clinic, 82*(4), 266–287. https://doi.org/10.1521/bumc.2018.82.4.266

Lebowitz, E. R., Omer, H., & Leckman, J. F. (2011a). Coercive and disruptive behaviors in pediatric obsessive-compulsive disorder. *Depression and Anxiety, 28*(10), 899–905. https://doi.org/10.1002/da.20858

Lebowitz, E. R., Vitulano, L. A., Mataix-Cols, D., & Leckman, J. F. (2011b). When OCD takes over…the family! Coercive and disruptive behaviours in paediatric obsessive compulsive disorder. *Journal of Child Psychology and Psychiatry, 52*(12), 1249–1250. https://doi.org/10.1111/j.1469-7610.2011.02480.x

Lebowitz, E. R., Vitulano, L. A., & Omer, H. (2011c). Coercive and disruptive behaviors in pediatric obsessive compulsive disorder: A qualitative analysis. *Psychiatry: Interpersonal and Biological Processes, 74*(4), 362–371. https://doi.org/10.1521/psyc.2011.74.4.362

Lebowitz, E. R., Woolston, J., Bar-Haim, Y., Calvocoressi, L., Dauser, C., Warnick, E., Scahill, L., Chakir, A. R., Shechner, T., Hermes, H., Vitulano, L. A., King, R. A., & Leckman, J. F. (2013). Family accommodation in pediatric anxiety disorders. *Depression and Anxiety, 30*(1), 47–54. https://doi.org/10.1002/da.21998

Lebowitz, E. R., Omer, H., Hermes, H., & Scahill, L. (2014). Parent training for childhood anxiety disorders: The SPACE program. *Cognitive and Behavioral Practice, 21*(4), 456–469. https://doi.org/10.1016/j.cbpra.2013.10.004

Lebowitz, E. R., Marin, C., Martino, A., Shimshoni, Y., & Silverman, W. K. (2019). Parent-based treatment as efficacious as cognitive-behavioral therapy for childhood anxiety: A randomized noninferiority study of supportive parenting for anxious childhood emotions. *Journal of the American Academy of Child & Adolescent Psychiatry, 59*(3), 362–372. https://doi.org/10.1016/j.jaac.2019.02.014

Lebowitz, E. R., Zilcha-Mano, S., Orbach, M., Shimshoni, Y., & Silverman, W. K. (2021). Moderators of response to child-based and parent-based child anxiety treatment: A machine learning-based analysis. *Journal of Child Psychology and Psychiatry, 62*(10), 1175–1182.

Lindsey, M. A., Chambers, K., Pohle, C., Beall, P., & Lucksted, A. (2013). Understanding the behavioral determinants of mental health service use by urban, under-resourced Black youth: Adolescent and caregiver perspectives. *Journal of Child and Family Studies, 22*(1), 107–121. https://doi.org/10.1007/s10826-012-9668-z

Merlo, L. J., Lehmkuhl, H. D., Geffken, G. R., & Storch, E. A. (2009). Decreased family accommodation associated with improved therapy outcome in pediatric obsessive–compulsive disorder. *Journal of Consulting and Clinical Psychology, 77*(2), 355–360. https://doi.org/10.1037/a0012652

Nauta, M. H., Scholing, A., Emmelkamp, P. M., & Minderaa, R. B. (2003). Cognitive-behavioral therapy for children with anxiety disorders in a clinical setting: No additional effect of a cognitive parent training. *Journal of the American Academy of Child & Adolescent Psychiatry, 42*(11), 1270–1278. https://doi.org/10.1097/01.chi.0000085752.71002.93

Omer, H. (2001). Helping parents deal with children's acute disciplinary problems without escalation: The principle of nonviolent resistance. *Family Process, 40*(1), 53–66. https://doi.org/10.1111/j.1545-5300.2001.4010100053.x

Omer, H., & Lebowitz, E. R. (2016). Nonviolent resistance: Helping caregivers reduce problematic behaviors in children and adolescents. *Journal of Marital and Family Therapy, 42*(4), 688–700. https://doi.org/10.1111/jmft.12168

Peris, T. S., Thamrin, H., & Rozenman, M. S. (2021). Family intervention for child and adolescent anxiety: A meta-analytic review of therapy targets, techniques, and outcomes. *Journal of Affective Disorders, 286*, 282–295. https://doi.org/10.1016/j.jad.2021.02.053

Raila, H. E., Julian, M. M., Lebowitz, E. R., & Silverman, W. K. (2021). Separating from the mothership: A coordinated individual and parent-based approach to severe agoraphobia in a young adult. *Cognitive and Behavioral Practice, 28*(3), 422–434. https://doi.org/10.1016/j.cbpra.2020.06.004

Rozenblat, S., Shimshoni, Y., Lebowitz, E. R., Perez, M., & Koller, J. (2023). A pilot trial of SPACE (Supportive Parenting for Anxious Childhood Emotions) in autism. *Child Psychiatry & Human Development*, 1–15. https://doi.org/10.1007/s10578-023-01555-4

Salloum, A., Andel, R., Lewin, A. B., Johnco, C., McBride, N. M., & Storch, E. A. (2018). Family accommodation as a predictor of cognitive-behavioral treatment outcome for childhood anxiety. *Families in Society, 99*(1), 45–55. https://doi.org/10.1177/1044389418756326

Sauter, F. M., Heyne, D., & Michiel Westenberg, P. (2009). Cognitive behavior therapy for anxious adolescents: Developmental influences on treatment design and delivery. *Clinical Child and Family Psychology Review, 12*(4), 310–335. https://doi.org/10.1007/s10567-009-0058-z

Shimshoni, Y., Shrinivasa, B., Cherian, A. V., & Lebowitz, E. R. (2019). Family accommodation in psychopathology: A synthesized review. *Indian Journal of Psychiatry, 61*(Suppl 1), S93. https://doi.org/10.4103/psychiatry.IndianJPsychiatry_530_18

Shimshoni, Y., Silverman, W. K., & Lebowitz, E. R. (2020). SPACE-ARFID: A pilot trial of a novel parent-based treatment for avoidant/restrictive food intake disorder. *International Journal of Eating Disorders, 53*(10), 1623–1635. https://doi.org/10.1002/eat.23341

Silverman, W. K., & Albano, A. M. (1996). *Anxiety disorders interview schedule: ADIS-IV child interview schedule* (Vol. 2). Graywind Publications.

Silverman, W. K., & Kurtines, W. M. (1996). *Anxiety and phobic disorders: A pragmatic approach.* Springer Science & Business Media.

Wei, C., & Kendall, P. C. (2014). Parental involvement: Contribution to childhood anxiety and its treatment. *Clinical Child and Family Psychology Review, 17*, 319–339. https://doi.org/10.1007/s10567-014-0170-6

Zamani, M., Jalali, M., & Pourahmadi, E. (2019). Role of family accommodation of child symptoms, parenting style and parental stress in prediction of anxiety disorder in 6-10 years old children in Northern Iran. *Journal of Gorgan University of Medical Sciences, 21*(2), 89–98.

Chapter 10
Technology-Enabled Behavioral Parent Training

Margaret T. Anton

10.1 Introduction

Early-onset disruptive behavior disorders, including oppositional defiant disorder, conduct disorder, and attention deficit hyperactivity disorder, are some of the most common child mental health disorders (Merikangas et al., 2022). If left untreated, disruptive behavior disorders can be associated with later antisocial behavior, substance use, academic challenges, and employment instability (Piquero et al., 2016).

Behavioral parent training (BPT) programs are the gold standard intervention for disruptive behavior disorders and associated impairments (see Rodriguez et al., 2023 for a review). BPT can be delivered in a range of formats, including individual therapy with the parent–child dyad (e.g., *Helping the Noncompliant Child* or *Parent–Child Interaction Therapy*), concurrent parent/child groups (e.g., *Incredible Years Parent Training*), or parent-only groups (e.g., *Parent Management Training-Oregon Model*). Despite being distinct programs with different delivery formats and scope, BPT programs share common features, including a focus on improving the quality of the parent–child relationship, increasing positive reinforcement for desired behaviors, and using effective alternatives to physical punishment. These common features are a result of similar theoretical underpinnings and understanding of the mechanisms involved in problematic child behavior, including social learning theory and the coercive cycle in parent–child interactions (Kaehler et al., 2016; Leijten et al., 2019).

The evidence for BPT is robust, yet access to and engagement in these interventions is often challenging for families. Like all evidence-based interventions, few families in need of these services receive them. In fact, only about 20% of children

M. T. Anton (✉)
Two Chairs, San Francisco, CA, USA
e-mail: manton@twochairs.com

L. Reuman, J. Thompson-Hollands (eds.), *Enhancing CBT Through Family and Peer Engagement*, CBT: Science Into Practice, https://doi.org/10.1007/978-3-031-74838-7_10

in need of BPT services access them (McGoron & Ondersma, 2015). Additionally, even when families can access BPT programs, attrition rates are approximately 50% (Chacko et al., 2016). Many families drop out before receiving an adequate dose of treatment and, therefore, experience no or limited benefit from these interventions (Pearl et al., 2012). Even when families complete the full course of treatment, BPT is time and cost intensive for parents and families. Parents are expected to attend weekly sessions with their child, practice skills daily with their child for at least 15 min a day, and, in some treatment models, complete a brief check-in with the therapist between sessions. This can make BPT particularly hard to access and complete for some of the most at-risk families, including families with low incomes who are more likely to have a child with a disruptive behavior disorder compared to families with relatively higher incomes (Chacko et al., 2016; Shaw & Taraban, 2017).

Technology has been proposed as a mechanism to enhance family access to and engagement in BPT (Jones et al., 2013; McGoron & Ondersma, 2015). There is a long history of the use of technology to enhance BPT programs with increasingly robust evidence for the effectiveness of these interventions. This chapter focuses on the research regarding using technology to deliver and enhance BPT with a specific focus on the role of parents in care. Throughout this chapter the term "parent" is used to refer to any caregiver in the parenting role for children. First, I provide an overview of BPT programs and common challenges families experience accessing and engaging in BPT programs. Then, I describe the diverse ways technology is being used to address these barriers to care, including an overview of the evidence for the effectiveness of these approaches. Finally, cultural considerations and a case example are provided.

10.2 Overview of Technology-Enabled Behavioral Parent Training

Unlike other common child interventions where the parents' role in treatment is to support the child and reinforce skill use outside of session (e.g., practicing communication strategies, engaging in a feared activity), parents are considered the primary agent of change in BPT programs. This means that all therapeutic content is directed at the parent rather than the child. Therapists work with parents to teach them a set of skills that, when implemented correctly and consistently, should improve child behavior and enhance the parent–child relationship. These skills are designed to disrupt the coercive cycle between parents and children. The coercive cycle is a maladaptive pattern of parent–child interactions in which the child learns that escalations in problematic behavior (e.g., whining, yelling, tantrums) result in parents acquiescing. During these times, both the parent and child are reinforced. The child stops the problematic behavior, and the parent allows the child to either get out of an undesired task (e.g., cleaning) or get something important to them (e.g., more screen time). Over time, as the child learns that problem behavior is functional, their behavior worsens, and parents become increasingly frustrated and hopeless. BPT programs are based on similar theoretical underpinnings and target this coercive cycle.

There are several different BPT programs ranging from self-help interventions to individual therapy with the parent–child dyad to group therapy, including concurrent parent–child groups and parent-only groups. The individual therapy programs include but are not limited to *Helping the Noncompliant Child* (HNC; McMahon & Forehand, 2003) and *Parent–Child Interaction Therapy* (PCIT; Eyberg & Robinson, 1982). These programs are two-phase, mastery-based programs. Weekly sessions (60 min) are active and include psychoeducation for parents, modeling and coaching by the therapist, and in vivo skill practice with the parent and child. During in vivo skills practice, therapists assess and code parents' skill acquisition. Parents need to meet pre-set criteria (i.e., specified skill use per minute) to demonstrate skill mastery before they progress to the next skill.

During the first phase of treatment, parents learn a set of skills designed to orient their attention to children's desired behaviors, such as compliance or quiet play. Parents are taught to attend to this behavior by narrating the child's play (like a sportscaster) and offering verbal or physical praise (e.g., a high five). Parents are also instructed to avoid giving commands, directing the child's play, or asking questions to decrease demands on the child's behavior. If undesired behaviors occur, parents are instructed to ignore undesired behavior that is not harmful to the child or others, such as whining, arguing, or bossy play. Parents are expected to practice daily for 10–15 min outside of the session by organizing special time with child-directed play. This time serves two primary functions: (1) it provides parents an opportunity to practice these skills, and (2) it helps re-establish a positive relationship between the parent and child.

During the second phase of treatment, parents learn effective discipline strategies designed to enhance child compliance. These include giving the child clear instructions and consistently using time out for non-compliance and more serious and potentially dangerous undesired behaviors, like hitting or kicking. These skills are practiced in session in the context of parent-directed activities. For example, parents may initiate a cleanup task in which they issue a command. If the child complies with the parent's command, the parent is instructed to issue verbal praise. If the child does not comply, the parent issues a warning and time out is initiated if the child continues to not comply. Once time out is completed, the child is expected to comply with the initial command. If they do not, the time out sequence starts again. This continues until the child complies.

Group interventions like *Incredible Years Parent Training* (IYPT; Webster-Stratton, 1981), *GenerationPMTO (formerly known as Parent Management Training-Oregon Model*; Forgatch & Patterson, 2010), and *Positive Parenting Program* (*Triple P; Sanders,* 1999) also target parenting practices, child behavior, and aim to enhance the parent–child relationship. Like the individual format interventions, IYPT is attended by both parent and child, and includes skills such as teaching parents positive parenting practices, using child-directed play to promote the parent–child relationship, socio-emotional learning, improving verbal skills, decreasing negative or harsh discipline (e.g., hitting, spanking, and yelling) and promoting positive discipline. They also have the unique benefits of improving parents' support networks, promoting social learning among parents, and improving access to evidence-based care.

Families enrolled in IYPT learn these new parenting skills via a series of brief video vignettes modeling skill use, including praise, limit setting, and behavior management (Menting et al., 2013). Parents then work with trained group leaders to practice these skills through role-plays, discuss strategies for implementation and reflect on how these skills can be used outside of session, and engage in problem-solving. There are several different versions of IYPT that are based on child developmental stage: babies (0–12 months); toddlers (1–3 years); preschoolers (3–6 years); and school age (6–12 years).

GenerationPMTO and Triple P are also group format BPT programs. Unlike IYPT where parents and children attend together, in GenerationPMTO and Triple P parents attend sessions alone. Like the individual BPT programs and IYPT, weekly sessions in GenerationPMTO focus on introducing and practicing skills, including limit setting, monitoring/supervision, problem-solving, and positive involvement (Forgatch & Kjøbli, 2016). Group facilitators use an active approach where skills are introduced, role played, and problem-solving occurs. Triple P differs from the other programs in that it is a multilevel program that has a different group curriculum depending on severity of problem behaviors, including a universal program aimed at prevention and more targeted interventions for specific behavioral needs and development stages. Similar to Generation PTMO, Triple P focuses on teaching parents a set of skills aimed at enhancing positive parenting, consistent discipline, and improving the parent–child relationship.

10.2.1 Common Challenges in Behavioral Parent Training

Despite there being several evidence-based BPT programs available, there are multiple shared challenges that limit families' access to and engagement in these programs. Fifty percent of the families who need BPT are unable to access it, or enroll in the program but never attend, or drop out prematurely (Chacko et al., 2012). Barriers to access and engagement range from systemic to family level barriers, including delivery locations, availability of trained providers, time and financial constraints, and stigma (Forehand & Kotchick, 2002; Weisenmuller & Hilton, 2021). Like other child mental health services, there are far fewer providers available than needed. There are even fewer providers available who have been intensively trained and deliver BPT programs with fidelity, and these providers are not evenly dispersed throughout the country—leaving many areas without any access to adequate or appropriate care.

Even when caregivers can access care, barriers and challenges to engagement remain. Session attendance, homework compliance, and treatment completion are a persistent challenge in children's mental health; paradoxically, BPT may exacerbate some of these challenges due to key characteristics of these interventions. First, the benefits of BPT depend on parent engagement and adherence (Ros et al., 2016), and BPT programs place high demands on parents. Most BPT programs require the parent and, in many cases, both the parent and child to attend weekly sessions, practice skills outside of session daily, and complete weekly phone check-ins. Second, parents are often expected to teach other caregivers in the child's life (e.g., coparents, teachers, grandparents) their newly acquired skills and ensure that they are being implemented consistently across caregivers. Finally, parents are also expected to implement these skills in a setting that is often quite different than the therapy room where the skills are learned and practiced.

In terms of attendance, parents are expected to attend weekly sessions for approximately 10–14 weeks, depending on the BPT program and skill progression. This often requires finding childcare for other children in the home, missing work, and driving long distances to access care. This is difficult for many families and may be particularly challenging for families with fewer economic resources, single parents, and those in more rural areas. In addition to weekly session attendance, parents are expected to complete daily home practice, use skills in between sessions, complete worksheets, and read materials.

BPT programs' effectiveness is also contingent on the consistency with which the skills are delivered outside of session. Typically, only one parent consistently attends sessions. This means that the onus of including other parents and/or caregivers (e.g., grandparents or teachers) in treatment typically falls on the parent engaged in care. They are often responsible for providing psychoeducation, modeling skills use, and coaching other caregivers to deliver these skills. This is a challenge for most parents but may be particularly difficult when there is conflict between caregivers, different expectations, norms, and values around parenting, and communication challenges (Weeland et al., 2021).

An additional challenge is that the therapy room is often highly controlled relative to the home environment where skills need to be implemented. For example, it is often hard for families to find an appropriate and safe time out space in their home. This means that even when skills are adequately learned and mastered in session, it is often hard to implement them effectively outside of session. Despite attempts to make the therapy room more ecologically valid, it is often hard to replicate the home environment where there are often siblings, pets, and other distraction. Given these challenges, even when caregivers can engage in and complete BPT programs, as many as a quarter to a third of families receive only limited or no benefit from these programs (Shelleby & Shaw, 2014).

10.2.2 The Promise of Technology

Over the past decade, there has been substantial excitement surrounding the promise of technology to improve access to and engagement in BPT programs (see Jones et al., 2013; McGoron & Ondersma, 2015 for reviews). Telehealth, digital interventions, and technology enhancements to BPT programs can address some of the key barriers to access and engagement by diversifying the ways families access care.

Although the ways in which technology are being incorporated have become increasingly sophisticated as technological capabilities advance, there is a long history of using technology to deliver components of BPT. In the 1970s, researchers began to test the efficacy of technology-enabled BPT relative to standard face-to-face treatment. O'Dell et al. (1979) developed a series of video-based training materials to teach caregivers proper administration of time out. These videos provided psychoeducation and modeled skill use. Parents were randomized to six different treatment groups: (1) a control group; (2) reading materials; (3) the video series alone; (4) the video series and brief checkout with a therapist; (5) individual trainings; and (6) brief training. In this randomized trial, the video series alone outperformed all other treatment modalities. Additionally, radio transmitters were used in interventions with parents and children for the therapist to communicate with the parent without disrupting the interaction between parent and child (Wolfe et al., 1988). These technology enhancements improved the ecological validity of these interventions, made it easier to deliver care to groups of families, and set the stage for later technological advances.

Many of the contemporary BPT programs expanded on this early innovation and leveraged technology even before the technology revolution of the last decade. For example, IYPT has a long history of using videos to deliver intervention components. These videos provide psychoeducation, skill demonstration, and case vignettes that group facilitators use to structure the content of sessions and generate group discussion (Webster-Stratton, 1981). Similarly, in Triple P's prevention program, many treatment components are delivered via video. These videos depict how to apply behavioral management strategies to common behavior problems and model positive parenting strategies (Sanders, 1999). Although these videos are a core part of the prevention level of the program, they are also leveraged in the intervention programs. Triple P also uses other novel approaches that leverage technology and mass media, like television, to expand the reach of BPT. This approach includes six-episode, weekly television series called "Families" and "Driving Mum and Dad Mad" that parents watch independently (Calam et al., 2008; Sanders et al., 2008). The series features the experiences of multiple families who are enrolled in group Triple P and demonstrate the use of different parenting skills. In addition to the television series, parents also have access to psychoeducational materials and a website with additional resources and videos.

The "bug in the ear" technique that is a hallmark of PCIT is a different use of technology that also stems directly from these early technology enhancements. In PCIT, therapists monitor family interactions from an observation room via a one-way mirror and provide live, personalized, and unobstructive coaching through a parent-worn ear device (e.g., Bluetooth earpiece). Research suggests that parents prefer this model of coaching to in-room coaching, and that it is linked to positive treatment outcomes (Lieneman et al., 2017).

10.2.3 Novel Approaches to BPT Care Delivery

Despite this early innovation, challenges persist in making BPT programs available to everyone who needs them. As new technological capabilities and devices emerged and became widely available researchers leveraged these advances to continue to address some of the most common barriers to BPT programs. Although some of these approaches are in the relatively nascent stage of development, others have become more widely accepted and available—their uptake accelerated at least in part by the COVID-19 pandemic. These technology-enabled BPT programs fall into three broad categories that will be explored in more detail below: (1) self-guided digital interventions, (2) adjunctive digital technologies, and (3) telehealth delivery.

10.2.3.1 Self-Guided Digital Interventions

Like its long history with technology, BPT also has a long history of self-help or self-directed intervention models. Self-guided digital interventions are the technology-based version of these early self-directed interventions. They require no therapist support, rather, parents access and progress through training material on their own. The flexible nature of these interventions overcomes many barriers to traditional face-to-face BPT interventions. They are cost-effective, convenient, and allow families to engage with materials from their own home at times that work best for them and their family.

Some examples of early self-guided digital interventions were described earlier in this chapter, including Triple P's universal prevention program that is all video delivered. Although these videos were previously accessible through CD-ROM and DVD, they are now easily accessible on the web. Triple P Online (TPOL; www2.tripleponline.net) can be accessed for $79.95 for a one-year subscription (at the time of publication). TPOL is highly structured and leads parents through a set program with eight sequential modules. Modules include topics such as positive parenting, encouraging desired behaviors, managing misbehavior, and preventing problems and planning. Modules are designed to take about 20–30 min to complete and include videos, interactive activities, and homework assignments. Between modules parents can access additional activities and exercises to practice skills between sessions. Parents can also opt into text-based tips and reminders and emails with additional resources such as blog posts and podcasts (Baumel & Faber, 2018).

Although these interventions mitigate several barriers to access, engagement remains a significant concern. Engagement with these interventions is relatively high and consistent in randomized trials, yet engagement in real-world settings is much lower and less consistent. For self-guided digital interventions more broadly, the median use of these tools is just one day (Baumel et al., 2019). The interventions also cannot easily be tailored or adapted to individual families' needs. Although these interventions are highly flexible in terms of when and where they are accessed and used, content is fixed. The static nature of the content makes it challenging to address cultural considerations or meet the needs of all families.

10.2.3.2 Adjunctive Digital Interventions

Adjunctive digital technologies or guided digital interventions are enhancements to either traditional face-to-face or telehealth services or digital interventions supported by a therapist or coach. These interventions tend to have better engagement and lower dropout rates than the self-guided digital intervention due at least in part to the supportive accountability provided by the therapist or coach. Although these interventions include human support, the amount of support varies drastically from intervention to intervention. For example, some programs include full face-to-face delivery of care with digital add-ons, while others include only brief check-ins (5–10 min per week) with a coach or therapist.

Jones et al. (2014), developed a mobile application, Tantrum Tamers©, to enhance standard delivery of a BPT program, *Helping the Noncompliant Child* (HNC). In this intervention model, parents attend weekly HNC sessions but also have access to a mobile application to support care. The app was designed for families with limited financial resources to enhance engagement and improve the efficiency of care. Tantrum Tamers© has several interactive and passive features, including daily surveys to assess skill practice, capabilities to record weekly home practice for the therapist to review, daily text message reminders, a weekly video call with the therapist consistent with the HNC model, and a series of skills videos to help model new parenting skills. Similarly, a multi-media eBook was designed to supplement standard PCIT (Jent et al., 2021). The eBook consists of chapters that reinforce skills taught in the first phase of PCIT. Each chapter consists of reading materials and videos (e.g., therapist explanations and parent testimonials) that reinforce and demonstrate skills taught in session, normalize treatment, and provide tips for problem-solving.

Guided digital interventions may offer similar benefits while allowing more flexibility for families and requiring less therapist time. For example, a blended intervention to improve behavior in children with ADHD uses online modules to deliver most of the intervention content and uses brief face-to-face therapist interactions to tailor the intervention and reinforce skill use (Breider et al., 2019). The online content included six modules, such as psychoeducation, communication strategies, limit setting, rewards, and discipline strategies. Before starting the online program, parents attended a 90-min orientation session to select target behaviors and receive a program orientation. There were four subsequent face-to-face evaluation sessions lasting about 45 min. During these, therapists reinforced progress in the online program. Therapists also provided online feedback on practice exercises and gave parents access to new training once the parent was ready to progress to the next module.

These interventions are more easily adapted to families' needs and may boost engagement with the technology. If families have challenges using the technology, the therapist and/or coach can troubleshoot. They are also able to reinforce use of the technology. Additionally, therapists can guide use of the technology in a way that tailors these interventions to specific family needs. For example, families can be assigned specific videos or activities based on the therapist or coaches' assessment of their needs.

10.2.3.3 Telehealth-Delivered Interventions

Telehealth refers to the remote delivery of interventions through videoconferencing software, like Zoom and Google Meet. Telehealth delivery of BPT has the potential to overcome many of the traditional barriers to care, including availability (e.g., lack of trained providers in certain geographic regions), accessibility (e.g., transportation challenges and childcare constraints), and acceptability (e.g., stigma). Before the COVID-19 pandemic, there was early work to establish the efficacy of telehealth-delivered BPT programs. Comer et al. (2015) conducted a proof-of-concept trial of Internet-delivered PCIT (IPCIT). PCIT was particularly well-suited for this format because providers were already separated from the family (via a one-way mirror) during treatment and coaching could still happen in an unobtrusive way through headphones or other widely available earpieces. The authors found that this approach was acceptable to caregivers and led to fewer parent-perceived barriers to care. These early telehealth services, however, required expensive equipment that over time has become more ubiquitous, including webcams, videoconferencing platforms, and Bluetooth earpieces, making it easier for providers and families to engage in these methods. Yet policies limiting reimbursement for home-based services continued to present challenges to families accessing telehealth services.

Group BPT models have also been delivered remotely via videoconferencing technology (Reese et al., 2012). Unlike IPCIT, this intervention was not delivered in families' homes. Rather, families attended sessions at a remote regional medical center. Providers were located at a different location and provided sessions synchronously via videoconferencing software. This allowed families in rural areas to access evidence-based care that either would not have been accessible or would have been time or cost prohibitive for families in remote areas.

This foundational work allowed for the rapid transition to telehealth when then the COVID-19 pandemic hit. Closure of in-person services coupled with sweeping policy changes that reimbursed home-based telehealth appointments for mental health led to huge expansion of telehealth BPT services. In fact, provider surveys suggest that more than 8 out of 10 (82%) providers delivering PCIT transitioned to IPCIT early in the pandemic, with almost half (48%) reporting that they made the transition in less than one week after the closure of their clinics (Rosas et al., 2022). Despite this rapid uptake, additional research is needed to understand which families are best served by telehealth, to better understand associated challenges, and to improve efficacy.

10.3 Research Evidence for Technology-Enabled Behavioral Parent Training

10.3.1 Self-Guided Interventions

Overall, systematic review and meta-analytic data suggest that self-guided digital interventions have a medium to large effect on child behavior relative to no treatment controls and a small to moderate effect relative to active controls, such as traditional face-to-face BPT programs (Baumel et al., 2017; Bausback & Bunge, 2021; Spencer et al., 2020). All self-guided digital interventions included in these analyses demonstrated positive posttreatment effects on child problem behavior. For example, TPOL, which includes a combination of both passive and interactive components, has been evaluated in three randomized controlled trials. In studies comparing TPOL to a no treatment control, researchers found that after 3 months of engagement with the self-guided digital intervention parents experienced significant improvements in child behavior relative to the no treatment control group. These effects were maintained in a 6-month follow-up period. Similar findings were observed in a briefer TPOL intervention that took place over 8 weeks and included five modules. Small to moderate effect sizes were observed. In addition to improvements in child behavior, research suggests that self-guided digital interventions improve positive parenting, reduce negative parent–child interactions, reduce physical discipline, and improve parental stress (Spencer et al., 2020).

Given the varying design and functionality of these interventions, researchers are interested in understanding if different components or functionality are related to outcomes. Some research suggests that interactive self-guided interventions (e.g., activities and exercises) are more engaging and effective than passive interventions (e.g., reading materials, videos, podcasts; Baumel et al., 2017), while other research suggests that interactive and passive interventions have similar effectiveness (Bausback & Bunge, 2021). Additional research is needed to better understand which intervention features are most effective and for which families. Interventions that include both passive and interactive components may be most effective in that they offer a variety of options and parents canselect interventions that best fit their learning style, preferences, and needs. Despite these promising findings, the benefits of these interventions need to be considered in the context of engagement. In the broader literature, engagement with self-guided digital intervention outside of the context of research is very low with 30-day retention of only 3.9% (Baumel et al., 2019). Few studies have directly evaluated real-world uptake and engagement with self-guided digital BPT programs. Day and Sanders (2018) found that more than a quarter of parents (28%) assigned to self-guided TPOL either did not log-in to the program or did not complete the module. Additionally, parents completed on average less than half of the eight modules (3.3 modules). As such, additional research is needed to better understand predictors of engagement.

10.3.2 Adjunctive Digital Technologies

Meta-analytic and systematic review data also suggest that adjunctive digital technologies, including guided digital interventions and face-to-face delivery of BPT supplemented with digital technology are associated with significant improvements in child behavior (Baumel et al., 2017; Bausback & Bunge, 2021; Spencer et al., 2020). There was a moderate to large effect on child behavior, as well as parenting changes, including increased positive parenting and encouragement and reductions in physical punishment and parental stress (Spencer et al., 2020). In fact, effect sizes for these interventions are similar to those observed in traditional face-to-face BPT programs (Bausback & Bunge, 2021; Spencer et al., 2020).

In addition to symptom reduction and improvements in parenting, adjunctive digital interventions are associated with additional benefits, including improved engagement, improved efficiency of care, and reduced therapist time relative to traditional delivery. In a randomized trial, Jones et al. (2021) found that a standard BPT program enhanced with a mobile application improved family engagement, including homework completion and coaching call participation. They also found that the mobile app led to faster skill acquisition for parents and, in turn, improved care efficiency by reducing the number of sessions required to complete treatment (Anton et al., 2016; Jones et al., 2021). Rabbitt and colleagues (Rabbitt et al., 2016) tested a reduced contact parent management training program in which there was no direct face-to-face interaction between the therapist and the parent. Therapists emailed a link to a pre-recorded treatment session and called families (15–20 min) to address questions and concerns after the parent viewed the session. They found that children and parents had similar treatment outcomes relative to traditional face-to-face delivery and that therapist time was reduced approximately 80%.

Despite these exciting findings, there is mixed evidence as to whether human support increases engagement in and efficacy of these interventions. For example, Spencer and colleagues (2020) did not observe significant differences in the strength of effects between interventions that included some level of human support and those that did not. Other studies, however, have found that additional human support significantly enhanced engagement and outcomes for digital interventions (Day & Sanders, 2018). The effect of human support likely depends on the amount and type of support offered. The role of therapists and coaches varies from intervention to intervention making it difficult to draw definitive conclusions (Baumel et al., 2017). Additional research is needed to understand the optimal ways to incorporate human support in these digital interventions, and studies comparing the same digital intervention with and without support are needed.

10.3.3 Telehealth Delivery

There is evidence to suggest that telehealth-delivered BPT interventions are as effective as standard face-to-face delivery (Bausback & Bunge, 2021). Several randomized trials tested the effectiveness of IPCIT relative to standard PCIT and demonstrated the efficacy of IPCIT in reducing child problem behavior and improving parent skill use. Additionally, parents in the IPCIT group reported fewer treatment barriers (Comer et al., 2017). In fact, some studies suggested that outcomes may be better in IPCIT relative to standard care. For example, Comer et al. (2017) found that 70% of children treated with IPCIT responded to treatment relative to 50% of children treated with traditional PCIT. Although more research is needed to better understand the unique mechanisms of telehealth-delivered interventions, IPCIT and other telehealth-delivered interventions may enhance the ecological validity of the intervention and make it easier for parents to transfer skills from session into the home environment.

Telehealth-delivered BPT makes it easier for families, especially those living in rural areas, underserved communities, and families with limited transportation options to access evidence-based care. The format also may increase session attendance by minimizing time and cost constraints related to traveling to in-person sessions (Monzon et al., 2021). Despite these findings and telehealth's rapid uptake during the COVID-19 pandemic, additional research is needed to understand for whom and when to use this approach. Some studies have noted some potential limitations of these approaches. For example, Peskin et al. (2023) found that although children had similar outcomes, parents in the telehealth group used fewer positive parenting behaviors and more coercive statements, and meta-analytic data suggested that in half of the studies the active control outperformed the telehealth-delivered intervention (Bausback & Bunge, 2021). This may be due to challenges with delivering care in the home environment, including parental distraction in the home environment, less control over the types and quantity of toys in the home, and technological challenges that interfere with comprehensive coaching.

10.3.4 Conclusions

Taken together, this growing body of research suggests that there are now several efficacious, convenient, and cost-effective alternatives to traditional BPT delivery that may make it easier for families experiencing systematic barriers and challenges to accessing and engaging in traditional care (Baumel et al., 2017; Bausback & Bunge, 2021). Although there are early promising findings demonstrating the efficacy and effectiveness of these interventions, more rigorous research is needed to compare these interventions to traditional, therapist-led, face-to-face interventions. Technology-enabled BPT has the potential to mitigate several barriers to care, but to date, few studies have directly explored how successful these alternative delivery methods are at improving access and engagement.

10.4 Clinical Considerations for Diverse Identities

Cultural norms affect how parents interact with—and discipline—their children. Differences between parenting practices (and cultural beliefs about parenting) and the skills taught in BPT programs can be a barrier to engagement in these interventions. One of the largest barriers to accessing and engaging in mental health treatment in general, and BPT specifically, is that the intervention is not acceptable to caregivers. For example, if certain parenting skills seem counterintuitive or misaligned with aspects of a given culture, parents are unlikely to adopt and implement these and may even discontinue treatment (Forehand & Kotchick, 2002; Weisenmuller & Hilton, 2021). Like most evidence-based practices, BPT has mostly been developed and tested with White families and individualistic communities. The positive parenting techniques presented in BPT programs may not be acceptable to other cultural groups, including cultures that tend to have more authoritarian parenting values emphasizing respect, and obedience.

Despite these potential challenges, research suggests that BPT outcomes are similar across cultural and socioeconomic groups (Leijten et al., 2019). For example, standard PCIT is effective across cultures and has been evaluated in Dutch, Norwegian, Chinese, and Puerto Rican populations (Rodriguez et al., 2023). Research, however, suggests that attrition rates may be higher and engagement is more challenging in some cultural groups than others, including historically marginalized families and families with fewer financial resources. As such, it is important to address cultural issues related to accessibility and barriers to treatment.

There are several cultural adaptations to BPT programs, as well as strategies to improve the acceptability and accessibility of BPT programs for historically marginalized groups. Cultural adaptations include, but are not limited to, ensuring all materials are translated, assessing parental cultural values and attempting to incorporate them into treatment, and modifying the treatment model. These adaptations can be simple, such as asking families how important it is to involve other caregivers in treatment. If this is important, attempts to accommodate other caregivers should be made, such as adjusting the timing of sessions to make it more feasible for other family members to attend, finding a space to hold sessions that fits more individuals, and video recording aspects of care so that it is easier for the parent to share with other family members. Other changes may include adapting or modifying key aspects of care. For example, when PCIT was delivered with American Indians and Alaska Natives, coding criteria for the child-directed interaction skills were adjusted to account for the slower speaking cadence of these cultures (BigFoot & Funderburk, 2011). Similarly, IYPT has also been adapted and tested in several different populations. For example, Lau et al. (2011) adapted IYPT to target risk factors for physical discipline in immigrant Chinese families. This intervention targeted unique stressors associated with immigration, acculturation, and minority status that may hinder positive parenting practices. The intervention included communication training to address conflict and frequent check-ins to address parental concerns about standard BPT skills like praise that may be inconsistent with cultural norms. Research findings suggested that this intervention was acceptable to parents and engaging and significantly decreased the use of physical punishment. Other adaptations include changing the length or structure of the program to make it easier for families to engage. For example, time-limited PCIT, which condenses the length and intensity of treatment, may be easier for historically marginalized or families with fewer financial resources to engage in by decreasing the time and cost of care (Peskin et al., 2023).

For technology-enabled BPT programs, it is also important to consider the unique ways in which the treatment format may introduce new cultural considerations to ensure that the technology itself does not exacerbate existing disparities. Although technology is more widely available now, there are still disparities in technological literacy and who can consistently access certain devices, capabilities, and the Internet. Recent polls suggest that most US households own a smartphone (85%) and/or desktop/laptop computer (77%). Although the rates of computer access vary to some extent by racial and ethnic groups, as well as socioeconomic status, the rates of smartphone ownership are relatively consistent. In fact, more than a quarter (27%) of households making less than $30,000 per year are dependent on their smartphone for online access. Trends are similar for Black and Latino families with 17% and 25% of households, respectively, relying solely on their mobile device for online access (Pew Research Center, 2021). Despite large federal investments to expand broadband Internet access to underserved areas, a quarter (25%) of the US population still does not have access to broadband Internet at home, and 30% report that they sometimes or often have problems connecting to the Internet at home. There are significant gaps in broadband Internet access between rural and suburban residents, as well as by race and ethnicity, with cost being the biggest barrier to access (Pew Research Center, 2021).

When developing technology-enabled services, it is important to consider which technologies will have the biggest impact on the systemic level challenges to accessing and engaging in care like geographical isolation and poverty. For example, although telehealth-delivered interventions can overcome some challenges related to geographical location, limited broadband access may limit the potential of these interventions due to connectivity challenges. Smartphone delivered or accessible interventions, like mobile apps or other adjunctive digital interventions, may offer the most potential to reach historically marginalized and underserved populations due to the ubiquity of these devices and families' preference for and reliance on them to access online information.

An additional challenge of some technology-enabled services, like self-guided digital interventions, is their inability to be easily tailored or adapted to specific family's needs. Much of the intervention content is fixed. Although they are designed to be universally applicable, the content is likely less relevant to certain cultural groups. These interventions are also rarely available in languages other than English, which limits the utility for non-English speaking caregivers or families. Despite these potential cultural challenges, recent meta-analytic data suggests that sociodemographic factors, including race, ethnicity, and socioeconomic status do not moderate the efficacy of technology-enabled BPT programs (Bausback & Bunge, 2021).

Additional research is needed to better understand how to develop these tools to be applicable to all families, particularly those who have been historically underserved.

10.5 Case Vignette

Mariah, age 4, and her mother, Jasmine, enrolled in *Helping the Noncompliant Child* (HNC). Jasmine reported that Mariah had begun acting out at age 3, and that her behavior had gotten significantly worse over the past year. Mariah is in preschool, and Jasmine often receives calls from Mariah's teachers indicating that she had acted out in class or was aggressive toward other children. Most recently, Mariah was sent home early from school for biting a peer who took a toy she was playing with. At home, Mariah engages in similar behaviors and often refuses to comply with parental instructions. Jasmine indicated that she and her husband, Mike, had resorted to spanking, because they "had no other choice." Jasmine indicated that she is seeking treatment because she is worried that Mariah will be unable to continue in preschool if she continues to behave aggressively toward other children. Her parents are also worried about her social development and want to ensure her behavior improves before starting kindergarten.

Prior to beginning treatment, the therapist completed a diagnostic interview and assessment. Mariah's mother completed the *Eyberg Child Behavior Inventory* (ECBI; Eyberg & Pincus, 1999), which measures the frequency of child disruptive behaviors and the extent to which the parent finds the child's behavior problematic. Based on the interview and assessment, Mariah met diagnostic criteria for Oppositional Defiant Disorder, Moderate. Mariah's disruptive behavior was occurring in at least two settings (i.e., home and school) and her ECBI scores were above the clinical cutoffs. She scored 200 on the Intensity Scale (range = 36–252; clinical cutoff ≥ 131) and 31 on the Problem scale (range = 0–36; clinical cutoff ≥ 15).

Mariah's mother, Jasmine, also completed the *Patient Health Questionnaire-9* (PHQ-9) to assess depression symptoms. Jasmine's score of 7 was below the clinical cutoff of 10 but indicated mild depression. Jasmine reported feeling at her "wits end." She noted that she and Mike had been having more frequent disagreements about how to manage Mariah's behavior and that they both were feeling helpless and frustrated. Jasmine described that they "try to pick their battles" with Mariah and work to avoid upsetting her. They often give into Mariah's "demands" and feel like she "gets away with everything."

Jasmine indicated that Mike's work schedule makes it "impossible" for him to also attend sessions. She noted that she feels like he could benefit from some guidance, because he often "resorts to spanking," and neither of them are comfortable with this type of discipline. Based on this assessment, the therapist believes that Mariah's behavior may be being inadvertently reinforced at home, and that inconsistent parenting between Jasmine and Mike is exacerbating the problematic behavior. Given this, the therapist believes this family could benefit from a standard BPT program. The therapist also would like to use Tantrum Tamers©, an adjunctive digital tool, to help reinforce skill use outside of session and make it easier for Jasmine to share what she learns with Mike.

The first session included an orientation to the HNC model and the suggested Tantrum Tamers addition. The therapist assessed Jasmine's openness to using the technology:

Therapist: Do you have a smartphone or tablet?

Jasmine: Yeah. I have a smartphone.

Therapist: I have an app in mind that I think would be great for us to use while we work together. Some parents find it's helpful for reminding them of what they've learned in session, and it may make it easier for you to show Mike what we are working on. It also helps me because it gives me a sense of how things are going at home. What are your thoughts?

Jasmine: That sounds nice in theory, but Mike and I are constantly getting on each other about spending too much time on our phones. I would hate to add another app that I am constantly looking at.

Therapist: I appreciate you sharing that. I know it can be a struggle to limit the amount of time we spend on our phones. I am happy to share some strategies about how to use this app, so that it doesn't add a lot of time to your day. Are you open to that?

Jasmine: Sure.

Therapist: Great! Part of what will make our time together most successful is if you consistently practice the skills we are learning at home. If we can pair the app use with that time, it should only add about 5 min to your practice sessions. If you are willing to try it, we can continue to chat about how it is going and adjust if needed. How does that sound?

Jasmine: Ok. I will give it a try.

Therapist: I would like to take a few minutes to show you the app. It's called Tantrum Tamers. Would you like me to show you it on my phone or would you like to download it on your phone or tablet, so that you can take a closer look?

Jasmine: We can use my phone. Wait, how much is this going to cost me?

Therapist: Part of what I like about this tool is that it is free to use. If you could please go to the app store, we can download the app. While it is downloading, I can tell you more about it.

Jasmine: Ok. It is downloading.

Therapist Great. Tantrum Tamers has several features for you to use. I will ask you to complete brief, less than a minute, surveys each day to help me get a sense of how things are going at home. Each week, I will also have you use the app to videorecord one of your home practices. I will review it and give you feedback during our mid-week check-in. You will also have access to a skills video series that you can use to show Mike the skills you are learning in session. Finally, you will also get text message reminders to help cue you to practice.

Sessions 2–5 focused on teaching Jasmine to implement differential attention, including learning to attend to—and reward—Mariah's desired behavior and ignore her undesired behavior. For each skill, the therapist first introduced and modeled the skill, and then practiced the skill with Jasmine using role-play. After practicing with the therapist, Jasmine was asked to practice the skill with Mariah as the therapist provided in vivo feedback and coaching. After coaching, the therapist stepped away to observe Mariah and Jasmine, and coded Jasmine's skill use. These skills are practiced in the context of Child's Game (i.e., child-directed play). Jasmine decided that she wanted to focus on reinforcing Mariah for using an "inside voice, using gentle hands, and having a calm body" by attending and rewarding these behaviors. Collaboratively with the therapist, Jasmine agreed to ignore (i.e., no look, no touch, no talk) all whining, tantrums, and yelling.

During session 2, Jasmine noted that attending to Mariah's behavior felt "really uncomfortable." Over the course of the session, Jasmine got more comfortable attending; however, when she used Tantrum Tamers to send the therapist a recording of home practice, the therapist noticed that Jasmine was struggling to implement the skills effectively. She continued to ask Mariah questions about her play and seemed to get distracted by other things going on in the home. During the mid-week check-in, the therapist provided feedback and helped Jasmine get back on track.

Therapist: I am so glad we are using the app. It gave me a clear picture of how challenging it is to implement these skills at home. You really are balancing a lot.

Jasmine: I know. It is harder than I expected.

Therapist: I know you will get the hang of it with some practice. I noticed that you were a bit distracted by work while you were practicing. Do you think it might work better to practice at a different time of day?

Jasmine: That's a good idea. Maybe while Mike is prepping dinner, I can take some time with Mariah to practice.

Therapist: That's a great idea. I will keep an eye on your surveys over the next few days to see how it is going.

Once Jasmine mastered the differential attention skills, she progressed to compliance training for sessions 6–8. During these sessions, Jasmine was taught to give Mariah clear instructions (e.g., one instruction at a time, attending to and rewarding compliance), an initial warning for non-compliance, and time out if non-compliance persists. These skills were practiced in session in the context of Parent's Game (i.e., parent-directed activities like cleanup tasks). Jasmine noted that she and Mike had tried time out before and that it "really didn't work." She noted that she was open to trying it, but that Mike might be resistant. She added that he believes that spanking has been "more effective." The therapist explained that there are different ways of implementing time out and encouraged Jasmine to use the skills videos to introduce the skill to Mike and point out ways in which this time out may be different than what they had previously tried. At the next session, the therapist checked-in to see how it went.

Therapist: Were you able to watch the skills videos with Mike?
Jasmine: Yeah! We actually watched them a few times.
Therapist: How did it go? Was he open to giving time out a try?
Jasmine: It went better than I expected. He noticed that we were giving Mariah a lot of attention in time out when we had tried to do it previously. Anytime she would whine or get out of her time out chair, we were negotiating with her and trying to get her to understand. The videos helped Mike see how different time out could look.
Therapist: That is great! I am so glad to hear it went better than you expected.

After meeting mastery criteria in the ninth session, the therapist did a final assessment. Mariah's ECBI scores were no longer in the clinically significant range (Intensity = 125; Problem = 10). Jasmine reported that it had been over a month since Mariah's preschool called her. She noted that she even showed some of the skills videos to Mariah's teacher to help her understand what they were learning in session and what was working at home. Jasmine indicated that she and Mike were feeling more in control. She noted that she was enjoying time with Mariah for the "first time in a long time." The therapist congratulated Jasmine and Mariah on the progress that they had made. She also encouraged Jasmine to continue to practice at home and use the skills videos to remind her of how to implement the skills effectively. The therapist also noted that the daily surveys could be a helpful way to monitor Mariah's behavior.

References

Anton, M. T., Jones, D. J., Cuellar, J., Forehand, R., Gonzalez, M., Honeycutt, A., Khavjou, O., Newey, G., Edwards, A., Jacobs, M., & Pitmman, S. (2016). Caregiver use of the core components of technology-enhanced helping the noncompliant child: A case series analysis of low-income families. *Cognitive and Behavioral Practice, 23*(2), 194–204. https://doi.org/10.1016/j.cbpra.2015.04.005

Baumel, A., & Faber, K. (2018). Evaluating triple P online: A digital parent training program for child behavior problems. *Cognitive and Behavioral Practice, 25*(4), 538–543. https://doi.org/10.1016/j.cbpra.2017.10.001

Baumel, A., Pawar, A., Mathur, N., Kane, J. M., & Correll, C. U. (2017). Technology-assisted parent training programs for children and adolescents with disruptive behaviors: A systematic review. *The Journal of Clinical Psychiatry, 78*(8), 20765. https://doi.org/10.4088/JCP.16r11063

Baumel, A., Muench, F., Edan, S., & Kane, J. M. (2019). Objective user engagement with mental health apps: Systematic search and panel-based usage analysis. *Journal of Medical Internet Research, 21*(9), e14567. https://doi.org/10.2196/14567

Bausback, K. B., & Bunge, E. L. (2021). Meta-analysis of parent training programs utilizing behavior intervention technologies. *Social Sciences, 10*(10), 367. https://doi.org/10.3390/socsci10100367

Breider, S., de Bildt, A., Nauta, M. H., Hoekstra, P. J., & van den Hoofdakker, B. J. (2019). Self directed or therapist-led parent training for children with attention deficit hyperactivity disorder? A randomized controlled non-inferiority pilot trial. *Internet Interventions, 18*, 100262. https://doi.org/10.1016/j.invent.2019.100262

Bigfoot, D. S., & Funderburk, B. W. (2011). Honoring children, making relatives: the cultural translation of parentchild interaction therapy for American Indian and Alaska Native families. *Journal of psychoactive drugs, 43*(4), 309–318. https://doi.org/10.1080/02791072.2011.628924

Calam, R., Sanders, M. R., Miller, C., Sadhnani, V., & Carmont, S. A. (2008). Can technology and the media help reduce dysfunctional parenting and increase engagement with preventative parenting interventions? *Child Maltreatment, 13*(4), 347–361. https://doi.org/10.1177/1077559508321272

Chacko, A., Wymbs, B. T., Chimiklis, A., Wymbs, F. A., & Pelham, W. E. (2012). Evaluating a comprehensive strategy to improve engagement to group-based behavioral parent training for high-risk families of children with ADHD. *Journal of Abnormal Child Psychology, 40*(8), 1351–1362. https://doi.org/10.1007/s10802-012-9666-z

Chacko, A., Jensen, S. A., Lowry, L. S., Cornwell, M., Chimklis, A., Chan, E., et al. (2016). Engagement in behavioral parent training: Review of the literature and implications for practice. *Clinical Child and Family Psychology Review, 19*, 204–215. https://doi.org/10.1007/s10567-016-0205-2

Comer, J. S., Furr, J. M., Cooper-Vince, C., Madigan, R. J., Chow, C., Chan, P., Idrobo, F., Chase, R. M., McNeil, C. B., & Eyberg, S. M. (2015). Rationale and considerations for the internet-based delivery of parent-child interaction therapy. *Cognitive and Behavioral Practice, 22*(3), 302–316. https://doi.org/10.1016/j.cbpra.2014.07.003

Comer, J. S., Furr, J. M., Kerns, C. E., Miguel, E., Coxe, S., Elkins, R. M., Carpenter, A. L., Cornacchio, D., Cooper-Vince, C. E., DeSerisy, M., Chou, T., Sanchez, A. L., Khanna, M., Franklin, M. E., Garcia, A. M., & Freeman, J. B. (2017). Internet-delivered, family-based treatment for early-onset OCD: A pilot randomized trial. *Journal of Consulting and Clinical Psychology, 85*(2), 178–186. https://doi.org/10.1037/ccp0000155

Day, J. J., & Sanders, M. R. (2018). Do parents benefit from help when completing a self-guided parenting program online? A randomized controlled trial comparing triple P online with and without telephone support. *Behavior Therapy, 49*(6), 1020–1038. https://doi.org/10.1016/j.beth.2018.03.002

Eyberg, S. M., & Robinson, E. A. (1982). Parent-child interaction training: Effects on family functioning. *Journal of Clinical Child & Adolescent Psychology, 11*(2), 130–137. https://doi.org/10.1080/15374418209533076

Eyberg, S., & Pincus, D. (1999). Eyberg Child Behavior Inventory & Sutter-Eyberg Student Behavior Inventory-Revised: Professional Manual. Odessa, FL: Psychological Assessment Resources.

Forehand, R., & Kotchick, B. A. (2002). Behavioral parent training: Current challenges and potential solutions. *Journal of Child and Family Studies, 11*(4), 377–384. https://doi.org/10.1023/A:1020913422609

Forgatch, M. S., & Kjøbli, J. (2016). Parent management training – Oregon model: Intervention with rigorous research. *Family Process, 55*(3), 500–513. https://doi.org/10.1111/famp.12224

Forgatch, M. S., & Patterson, G. R. (2010). Parent management training – Oregon model: Intervention for antisocial behavior in children and adolescents. In J. R. Weisz & A. E. Kazdin (Eds.), *Evidence-based psychotherapies for children and adolescents* (pp. 159–177). The Guilford Press.

Jent, J. F., Rothenberg, W. A., Weinstein, A., Stokes, J., Barnett, M., Srivatsa, N., et al. (2021). Comparing traditional and ebook-augmented Parent-Child Interaction Therapy (PCIT): A randomized control trial of pocket PCIT. *Behavior Therapy, 52*(6), 1311–1324. https://doi.org/10.1016/j.beth.2021.02.013

Jones, D. J., Forehand, R., Cuellar, J., Kincaid, C., Parent, J., Fenton, N., & Goodrum, N. (2013). Harnessing innovative technologies to advance children's mental health: Behavioral parent training as an example. *Clinical Psychology Review, 33*(2), 241–252. https://doi.org/10.1016/j.cpr.2012.11.003

Jones, D. J., Forehand, R., Cuellar, J., Parent, J., Honeycutt, A., Khavjou, O., et al. (2014). Technology-enhanced program for child disruptive behavior disorders: Development and pilot randomized control trial. *Journal of Clinical Child & Adolescent Psychology, 43*(1), 88–101. https://doi.org/10.1080/15374416.2013.822308

Jones, D. J., Loiselle, R., Zachary, C., Georgeson, A. R., Highlander, A., Turner, P., Youngstrom, J. K., Khavjou, O., Anton, M. T., Gonzalez, M., Bresland, N. L., & Forehand, R. (2021). Optimizing engagement in behavioral parent training: Progress toward a technology-enhanced treatment model. *Behavior Therapy, 52*(2), 508–521. https://doi.org/10.1016/j.beth.2020.07.001

Kaehler, L. A., Jacobs, M., & Jones, D. J. (2016). Distilling common history and practice elements to inform dissemination: Hanf-Model BPT programs as an example. *Clinical Child and Family Psychology Review, 19*(3), 236–258. https://doi.org/10.1007/s10567-016-0210-5

Lau, A. S., Fung, J. J., Ho, L. Y., Liu, L. L., & Gudiño, O. G. (2011). Parent training with high-risk immigrant Chinese families: A pilot group randomized trial yielding practice-based evidence. *Behavior Therapy, 42*(3), 413–426. https://doi.org/10.1016/j.beth.2010.11.001

Leijten, P., Gardner, F., Melendez-Torres, G. J., van Aar, J., Hutchings, J., Schulz, S., Knerr, W., & Overbeek, G. (2019). Meta-analyses: Key parenting program components for disruptive child behavior. *Journal of the American Academy of Child and Adolescent Psychiatry, 58*(2), 180–190. https://doi.org/10.1016/j.jaac.2018.07.900

Lieneman, C. C., Brabson, L. A., Highlander, A., Wallace, N. M., & McNeil, C. B. (2017). Parent-child interaction therapy: Current perspectives. *Psychology Research and Behavior Management, 10*, 239–256. https://doi.org/10.2147/PRBM.S91200

McGoron, L., & Ondersma, S. J. (2015). Reviewing the need for technological and other expansions of evidence-based parent training for young children. *Children and Youth Services Review, 59*, 71–83. https://doi.org/10.1016/j.childyouth.2015.10.012

McMahon, R. J., & Forehand, R. L. (2003). *Helping the noncompliant child: Family-based treatment for oppositional behavior* (2nd ed.). Guilford Press.

Menting, A. T., Orobio de Castro, B., & Matthys, W. (2013). Effectiveness of the incredible years parent training to modify disruptive and prosocial child behavior: A meta-analytic review. *Clinical Psychology Review, 33*(8), 901–913. https://doi.org/10.1016/j.cpr.2013.07.006

Merikangas, K. R., Nakamura, E. F., & Kessler, R. C. (2022). Epidemiology of mental disorders in children and adolescents. *Dialogues in Clinical Neuroscience, 11*(1), 7–20. https://doi.org/10.31887/DCNS.2009.11.1/krmerikangas

Monzon, A. D., Zhang, E., Marker, A. M., & Nelson, E. L. (2021). Overview of telebehavioral interventions using real-time videoconferencing. *Telemedicine, Telehealth and Telepresence: Principles, Strategies, Applications, and New Directions*, 347–364. https://doi.org/10.1007/978-3-030-56917-4_22

O'Dell, S. L., Mahoney, N. D., Horton, W. G., & Turner, P. E. (1979). Media-assisted parent training: Alternative models. *Behavior Therapy, 10*(1), 103–110. https://doi.org/10.1016/S0005-7894(79)80013-1

Pearl, E., Thieken, L., Olafson, E., Boat, B., Connelly, L., Barnes, J., & Putnam, F. (2012). Effectiveness of community dissemination of parent–child interaction therapy. *Psychological Trauma: Theory, Research, Practice, and Policy, 4*(2), 204–213. https://doi.org/10.1037/a0022948

Peskin, A., Barth, A., Rothenberg, W. A., Turzi, A., Formoso, D., Garcia, D., & Jent, J. (2023). New therapy for a new normal: Comparing telehealth and in-person time-limited parent-child interaction therapy. *Behavior Therapy, 55*(1), 106–121. https://doi.org/10.1016/j.beth.2023.05.002

Pew Research Center. (2021). *Demographics of mobile device ownership and adoption in the United States*. Pew Research Center: Internet, Science & Tech. Retrieved June 28, 2022, from https://www.pewresearch.org/internet/fact-sheet/mobile/

Piquero, A. R., Jennings, W. G., Diamond, B., Farrington, D. P., Tremblay, R. E., Welsh, B. C., & Gonzalez, J. M. R. (2016). A meta-analysis update on the effects of early family/parent training programs on antisocial behavior and delinquency. *Journal of Experimental Criminology, 12*, 229–248. https://doi.org/10.1007/s11292-016-9256-0

Rabbitt, S. M., Carrubba, E., Lecza, B., McWhinney, E., Pope, J., & Kazdin, A. E. (2016). Reducing therapist contact in parenting programs: Evaluation of internet-based treatments for child conduct problems. *Journal of Child and Family Studies, 25*(6), 2001–2020. https://doi.org/10.1007/s10826-016-0363-3

Reese, R. J., Slone, N. C., Soares, N., & Sprang, R. (2012). Telehealth for underserved families: An evidence-based parenting program. *Psychological Services, 9*(3), 320–322. https://doi.org/10.1037/a0026193

Rodriguez, B., Lynch, J. D., & Ciesielski, H. A. (2023). Parent training. In *Handbook of clinical child psychology: Integrating theory and research into practice* (pp. 507–525). Springer.

Ros, R., Hernandez, J., Graziano, P. A., & Bagner, D. M. (2016). Parent training for children with or at risk for developmental delay: The role of parental homework completion. *Behavior Therapy, 47*(1), 1–13. https://doi.org/10.1016/j.beth.2015.08.004

Rosas, Y. G., Sigal, M., Park, A., & Barnett, M. L. (2022). Predicting a rapid transition to telehealth-delivered parent-child interaction therapy amid COVID-19: A mixed methods study. *Global Implementation Research and Applications, 2*(4), 293–304. https://doi.org/10.1007/s43477-022-00057-0

Sanders, M. R. (1999). Triple P-Positive Parenting Program: Towards an empirically validated multilevel parenting and family support strategy for the prevention of behavior and emotional problems in children. *Clinical Child and Family Psychology Review, 2*(2), 71–90. https://doi.org/10.1023/a:1021843613840

Sanders, M., Calam, R., Durand, M., Liversidge, T., & Carmont, S. A. (2008). Does self-directed and web-based support for parents enhance the effects of viewing a reality television series based on the Triple P–Positive Parenting Programme? *Journal of Child Psychology and Psychiatry, 49*(9), 924–932. https://doi.org/10.1111/j.1469-7610.2008.01901.x

Shaw, D. S., & Taraban, L. E. (2017). New directions and challenges in preventing conduct problems in early childhood. *Child Development Perspectives, 11*(2), 85–89. https://doi.org/10.1111/cdep.12212

Shelleby, E. C., & Shaw, D. S. (2014). Outcomes of parenting interventions for child conduct problems: A review of differential effectiveness. *Child Psychiatry and Human Development, 45*(5), 628–645. https://doi.org/10.1007/s10578-013-0431-5

Spencer, C. M., Topham, G. L., & King, E. L. (2020). Do online parenting programs create change?: A meta-analysis. *Journal of Family Psychology, 34*(3), 364–374. https://doi.org/10.1037/fam0000605

Webster-Stratton, C. (1981). Modification of mothers' behaviors and attitudes through videotape modeling group discussion program. *Behavior Therapy, 12*, 634–643. https://doi.org/10.1016/S0005-7894(81)80135-9

Weeland, J., Helmerhorst, K. O., & Lucassen, N. (2021). Understanding differential effectiveness of behavioral parent training from a family systems perspective: Families are greater than "some of their parts". *Journal of Family Theory & Review, 13*(1), 34–57. https://doi.org/10.1111/jftr.12408

Weisenmuller, C., & Hilton, D. (2021). Barriers to access, implementation, and utilization of parenting interventions: Considerations for research and clinical applications. *American Psychologist, 76*(1), 104–115. https://doi.org/10.1037/amp0000613

Wolfe, D. A., Edwards, B., Manion, I., & Koverola, C. (1988). Early intervention for parents at risk of child abuse and neglect: A preliminary investigation. *Journal of Consulting and Clinical Psychology, 56*(1), 40–47. https://doi.org/10.1037/0022-006X.56.1.40

Chapter 11
Family Involvement in DBT for Adolescents Within a Partial Hospitalization Program Setting

Abigail M. Stark, Esther S. Tung, Kristen L. Batejan and Peg Worden

11.1 Introduction

Dialectical Behavior Therapy (DBT) treats pervasive emotion dysregulation (Koerner, 2013) and has been shown to be effective within a range of psychological disorders, most notably borderline personality disorder (BPD; Panos et al., 2014). DBT has been adapted for use with children (DBT-C; Perepletchikova et al., 2011) and adolescents (DBT-A; Miller et al., 2007). Although DBT-A began with a focus on adolescents who were self-harming or suicidal, it has been expanded to treat adolescents with a wide variety of emotional difficulties and corresponding behavioral challenges. There has been extensive research on the importance and increased treatment effectiveness of including family members, primarily caregivers, in DBT for children and adolescents (Miller et al., 2002; Hoffman et al., 1999). Some evidence points to family intervention and improvements in family functioning as a significant mediator of treatment outcomes for adolescents with BPD (Hoffman et al., 2007). Furthermore, research demonstrates the emotional toll that behaviors like suicide attempts or self-harm take on family members (Marshall et al., 2023; Rheinberger et al., 2023). For example, caregivers have reported

A. M. Stark (✉) · E. S. Tung · K. L. Batejan · P. Worden
McLean Hospital, Belmont, MA, USA
e-mail: amstark@mgh.harvard.edu; etung2@mgb.org; kbatejan@mgb.org; pworden@mgb.org

L. Reuman, J. Thompson-Hollands (eds.), *Enhancing CBT Through Family and Peer Engagement*, CBT: Science Into Practice, https://doi.org/10.1007/978-3-031-74838-7_11

profound anxiety after suicidal behaviors from their loved ones, as well as significant challenges with knowing how to provide interpersonal support (Marshall et al., 2023). Furthermore, given that difficulties with emotion dysregulation generally lead to interpersonal challenges, family work within DBT is particularly important (Lazarus et al., 2014).

Within the United States, the rates of suicidality, self-harm, and hospitalizations for adolescents have all exponentially increased within the past decade (Curtin, 2020). DBT-A has been implemented in differing levels of care (LOCs) with research support for its effectiveness, including inpatient (e.g., Tebbett-Mock et al., 2020), residential (e.g., Waitz et al., 2021), outpatient settings (e.g., Hiller & Hughes, 2022), and, perhaps the least researched, partial hospitalization programs (PHP; e.g., Del Conte et al., 2016). The use of DBT-A in higher LOCs has become increasingly common. Even within higher LOCs, research continues to support the importance of incorporating family members in DBT-A treatment, from assessment to conceptualization to intervention (Hoffman et al., 1999).

Most DBT research examines the efficacy of DBT treatment in traditional outpatient settings. However, some clients due to symptom severity, for example acute suicidality, benefit from higher LOCs. It is often helpful to step-down from inpatient or residential LOCs to a PHP (Neuhaus, 2006). For example, discharging from a hospital inpatient admission following a suicide attempt directly to once-a-week DBT can be an abrupt transition. Similarly, some clients may not thrive in an outpatient setting due to life-threatening behaviors (e.g., self-harm, suicidal ideation) yet may not require the intensity of an inpatient or residential level of care. Many clients benefit from entering PHPs after inpatient hospitalization where they can engage in intensive work while residing at home and experiencing typical situations and conflicts (for a review of general PHP effectiveness, see Moos, 2018; for a discussion of DBT PHP step-down care, see Mochrie et al., 2020). Another benefit of a DBT focused PHP is that clients will learn the entire DBT curriculum in a condensed period, compared to outpatient treatment (which can take upwards of 4–6 months to learn all skills modules; Miller et al., 2007). Thus, DBT treatment in a PHP can be an ideal setting to learn DBT skills in a rapid and comprehensive way while still residing at home (i.e., a familiar environment) to practice and generalize the skills.

This chapter aims to provide an overview of the main goals of incorporating families within DBT treatment in an adolescent PHP setting. As mentioned previously, this setting notably allows for adolescents to receive intensive DBT treatment while also returning home to a family setting to practice and enact these skills. Throughout the chapter, we will give examples of principles, skills, and techniques through the case example of "Mina," a 15-year-old Latinx, nonbinary (pronouns: she/they) individual with diagnoses of social anxiety disorder, major depressive disorder, and a history of several suicide attempts and self-harming behaviors via cutting resulting in multiple psychiatric hospitalizations. Mina also uses marijuana daily. Mina's parents are divorced and are both involved in her treatment. Mina and her family are representative of many of the clients seen within a DBT PHP setting.

11.2 Treatment Overview

Although there are several DBT PHPs around the country, the following descriptions focus on McLean Hospital's 3East Dialectic Behavior Therapy Partial Hospital Program located outside of Boston, MA. We use this PHP to illustrate how a DBT PHP can be structured and to provide a real example of family work in a DBT PHP setting.

The McLean 3East PHP is a four-to-six-week program for adolescents and young adults ranging in age from 14 to mid-twenties, presenting with significant emotion dysregulation and many impulsive and high-risk behaviors. We will use the term "adolescents" to refer to this population throughout the chapter. Standard DBT-A typically lasts 6 months to one year and involves weekly individual therapy, weekly family therapy, weekly multi-family skills group, 24-hour skills coaching access, and therapist consultation groups (Miller et al., 2007). Like other DBT PHPs (e.g., Del Conte et al., 2016), this program has adapted the outpatient DBT model into a "bootcamp" where adolescents learn DBT skills quickly and practice outside of therapy to generalize these skills in various settings. For a comprehensive review of this specific PHP including all aspects of programming, please reference Batejan et al. (2022).

This chapter aims to outline the following components within a DBT PHP: (1) initial intake, assessment, and conceptualization of the family system, (2) family-based components of treatment, (3) main skills used within DBT family work, (4) common challenges when working with families, and (5) discharge planning from a PHP.

11.2.1 Family-Based Intake: Assessment and Conceptualization

11.2.1.1 Assessment and Goal Setting

The PHP intake process begins with the adolescent and caregiver meeting with a clinician for a "commitment interview." These commitment interviews review the specifics and expectations of the program while also assessing the willingness and motivation for this treatment and this LOC (for a review of the DBT intake process and pre-treatment methods, see Linehan, 1993a). These meetings also offer an initial glimpse into what family sessions may look like if an admission is warranted. In these interviews, clinicians speak candidly about what can be accomplished in the short time frame and set expectations around caregivers' involvement. Although the adolescent is the identified client, the clinician nonjudgmentally frames problematic behaviors within an interactional and dynamic framework with the adolescent and caregiver (Miller et al., 2002). Clinicians work to nonjudgmentally increase caregiver insight into their own interactional role within the adolescent's challenging behaviors and help foster acceptance and willingness to change their own behaviors with new skills. In the interview, *both* the adolescents and caregivers are asked about their willingness to accept help, learn new skills, and approach potentially painful emotions to create long-term changes. Similarly, the ability for *both* the adolescent and caregivers to commit to this intensive level of treatment is assessed in the interview, and the commitment is made clear. Research evidence points to the importance of incorporating family members for effective DBT treatment (e.g., Hoffman et al., 2007; Wilks et al., 2017).

Additionally, the clinician will assess motivation around engaging in family therapy. Caregivers and adolescents alike may have concerns about discussing emotions and thoughts with one another. Exploring their fears around sharing as well as each family member's ability to remain regulated in session, are important initial components of assessing commitment to a family-based process. Due to the intensity of a PHP, this assessment around motivation, commitment, and willingness is vital to ensure that this is the appropriate level of care for a family system. In this way, these interviews function not only to gather information but also to generate commitment using motivational strategies from DBT (for a complete review of motivational strategies in DBT, see Linehan, 1993a) to help the adolescent and family prepare for the intensive DBT work ahead. Assessment and conceptualization of the family system begins at intake and continues throughout the PHP duration. Skills are interwoven from the start for families to begin implementing.

The clinician's formulation of the family system iteratively evolves as they gather data about the adolescent and overall family's functioning as well as continued observations of their interactions. There are several themes that clinicians attend to when first meeting with caregivers, including reframing judgmental language, pointing out examples of invalidation, and providing psychoeducation about emotions. In research on family-based interventions in DBT, letting go of judgmental language and assumptions as well as improving understanding of emotion dysregulation and BPD have been shown to improve family members' well-being and reduce depression and anxiety symptoms (Fruzzetti & Hoffman, 2004; Rajalin et al., 2009). Even during intake, the clinician will observe how the caregiver describes and conceptualizes the adolescent's challenges. For example, if a caregiver is describing their adolescent with judgmental language (e.g., "manipulative," "a problem," "dramatic," and "crazy"), the clinician may teach mindfulness skills such as using more descriptive, factual language while holding a nonjudgmental stance. In this way, the clinician is both teaching a skill while simultaneously gathering information by gently pointing out how pejorative language can impact both caregivers' and clinicians' abilities to hold compassion for the adolescent.

At the beginning of treatment, each family member, including the adolescent, is asked about their goals for these meetings. Individual DBT goals fall into four main behavioral "targets" that are hierarchical in order of importance. They include targeting: (1) life-threatening behaviors (inclusive of self-harm), (2) treatment-interfering behaviors, (3) quality-of-life interfering behaviors, and (4) skills acquisition (Linehan, 1993a, b). These goals are identified and targeted in the adolescent's individual sessions. In DBT-A, family goals are based on these individual targets and mirror this same hierarchy. They include (1) reducing family interactions that lead to suicidal and self-harm behavior, (2) decreasing family behaviors that interfere with treatment, (3) shifting family behaviors that interfere with quality of life, and (4) increasing family member's skills, with a focus on finding a "middle path" (see middle path section in this chapter as well as Miller et al., 2002).

Goals are behaviorally specific, measurable, and coincide with modules of DBT (Coyle et al., 2019). For example, "I want my child to be happier and have higher self-esteem" would need to be more behaviorally defined and concretized to track progress (e.g., "I want my child to initiate plans with friends"). Similarly, goals that highlight avoidance of emotions (e.g., "to not feel anxiety") also require psychoeducation around the importance of emotions as well as increasing behavioral specificity (e.g., "to attend school three days per week even if experiencing anxiety while at school"). Caregivers are asked to create goals that demonstrate awareness of family dynamics and are also goals for themselves, not for the adolescent (Fruzzetti & Hoffman, 2004). For example, setting a goal of, "I want my daughter to be less angry" is not a goal that a caregiver can work on specifically. Rather, setting a goal of "I want to learn how to regulate my emotions when I notice my daughter is dysregulated," focuses on the caregiver's skills and the dynamic interplay between the caregiver and adolescent. Many caregivers identify improving communication, increasing transparency (i.e., adolescents being more open and honest with caregivers about struggles), increasing validation, and setting clear boundaries and expectations.

There are times when caregivers and the adolescent are polarized on a goal or topic in session. In these moments, it is beneficial to encourage everyone to be open and honest about their rationale, provide space for validation, and collaboratively brainstorm a shared goal. In the example below, Mina and her mother discuss goals during the intake session.

> Mina's mother immediately responded with her goals for the DBT PHP. "I want Mina to be able to focus on school. She is in her junior year of high school and these grades matter for college! I want her to be able to have a future where she has choices." Mina rolled her eyes. "That's what YOU want. I want to get my GED and be able to spend more time on what I love-caring for animals. I don't see the purpose of high school; all it does is make me anxious." The clinician wrote down these goals and noted out loud that both Mina's mother's and Mina's goals' involved Mina taking steps towards a future that looks different than the past several months. Mina had been having difficulty leaving her room, hadn't been able to go to her volunteer job at the animal shelter, and was avoiding school. With some prompting, Mina was able to articulate a goal of "leaving my room every day even if I feel anxious" by the end of the PHP program. The clinician clarified with Mina's mother, that she should find goals that she, herself, could work on. Mina's mother looked confused for several moments. "I'm not sure...I guess I don't always know what to do when Mina seems angry, I just get so upset seeing her so distressed."

In this example, the clinician works with Mina and her mother to set goals for themselves, rather than setting goals for one another. The clinician looks for a middle path, or synthesis, for everyone to work toward shared, behaviorally specific goals. Of note, goals around self-harm and suicidality are often created in the first individual session as it is common for caregivers to not have much awareness of the extent of suicidality and self-harm occurring, and it may be challenging for the adolescent to share this information during intake.

11.2.1.2 Family System Conceptualization

Families are conceptualized through the transactional biosocial model (Fruzzetti et al., 2005; Linehan, 1993a), which is a compassionate and nonjudgmental theory to explain pervasive emotion dysregulation. The biosocial model is foundational to DBT and posits that biological predispositions to intense emotional experiences coupled with an invalidating environment and a lack of skills can lead to more chronic emotion dysregulation (Linehan, 1993a). The transactional model points to the ongoing transaction between emotion dysregulation exacerbating invalidating environments and invalidating environments, leading to more emotion dysregulation (Fruzzetti et al., 2005).

Within the "bio" part of the biosocial model, individuals may be born predisposed to feeling stronger emotions or have learned a more intense emotional reaction due to traumatic experiences, which led to increased reactivity (Linehan, 1993a). Due to this biological predisposition, similar presentations may be evident in one or both caregivers (e.g., Amad et al., 2014). Therefore, adolescents and caregivers may have similar skills deficits around regulating emotions and communicating effectively (Wilks et al., 2017). Due to the transactional nature of emotional experiences, heightened reactivity in both a caregiver and an adolescent may lead to further conflict between caregivers and the adolescent.

The other important part of the biosocial model is the social component. In DBT, validation means expressing that an emotion makes sense (Linehan, 1993a). An invalidating environment can range from more subtle invalidation to traumatic invalidation. Traumatic invalidation is the extreme or repetitive invalidation of a person's experiences, characteristics, and reactions (Linehan, 2014a). Traumatic invalidation attacks a person's sense of self by communicating that they are bad, inferior, and unacceptable. Alternatively, invalidation can also be more subtle and inadvertent. For example, if an adolescent's caregiver tells them to "just calm down," it may inadvertently signal that their emotion is incorrect for the situation and that fixing it should be easy. Invalidation tends to increase emotional intensity and leads individuals to have more difficulty identifying and understanding their emotions as well as how to cope (Yap et al., 2008). Furthermore, parental invalidation has also been shown to be predictive of adolescent self-harm and self-harm severity in high-risk youth (Adrian et al., 2018). Environments may also become invalidating over time due to familial stress when one family member is more emotionally reactive (Miller et al., 2002).

Families are conceptualized through this dynamic, transactional biosocial model. Each family member's biological predisposition for emotional reactivity, sensitivity, and return to baseline becomes part of the case conceptualization. Inadvertent, as well as more blatant, forms of invalidation are also identified. In this way, the conceptualization of the adolescent necessitates family interactions and dynamics.

In the example below, the clinician observes an unintentionally invalidating interaction between Mina and her mother.

> "Since a young age, Mina felt big emotions. I remember dropping her off at preschool when she was four, and she just cried and yelled. Her teachers said she didn't calm down the whole day until I picked her up. And this happened day after day!" Mina's mother described at the intake. "I just don't know what to do anymore. I try to be happy and cheery each day to her and tell her to wake up with a smile! But lately it feels like I am just walking on eggshells, ready to be yelled at." Mina slumped down in her chair and rolled her eyes. "My mom just doesn't get it. It makes me so angry when she tells me to 'be happy,' it's not that easy! There's just no point in even talking to her about it. I just keep my mouth shut and go to my room to be alone."

Here we see both a description of Mina's biological vulnerability to emotions (reactivity, sensitivity, slow return to baseline) as well as an example of inadvertent invalidation. Mina's mother instructing Mina to "just be happy" may tell Mina that her emotions do not make sense, that there is something wrong with her, and that she should be feeling something else. Furthermore, it also makes problem solving seem easier than it may be for Mina. Mina's mother expressed not being emotionally reactive and being able to re-regulate quickly, so she was confused that Mina couldn't "shift" her emotions and step away from feeling angry and sad. For Mina, she felt like "the problem in the family" and began feeling hopeless about feeling understood or finding ways to reduce the intensity of her anger, except through self-harm.

Based on initial sessions, a clinician's formulation of Mina and her caregivers might include each of their emotional sensitivity, reactivity, and return to baseline, coupled with specific examples of invalidation. For Mina, relying on self-harm and suicidality to cope with the big emotions that result from invalidation has only compounded her emotion dysregulation. The clinician must maintain a nonjudgmental stance toward all, blaming neither the adolescent nor the caregiver but rather understanding the transactional nature of behaviors and emotions within the family setting (Miller et al., 2002).

11.2.1.3 Family-Based Components of Treatment

Caregiver Skills Groups

Caregiver skills groups teach skills to regulate emotions, tolerate distress, and improve their relationship with their child. Family involvement in an outpatient DBT setting typically includes a multi-family skills group. In a PHP setting, the treatment length is brief, and adolescents attend upwards of 30 hours of skills groups each week. Instead of a weekly multi-family skills group as would be conducted in an outpatient adherent DBT setting, skills groups with only the caregivers offer a chance to focus on skills for caregivers in a bootcamp style. The McLean 3East PHP offers a virtual caregivers group that is held once a week for two hours. This is the one service that families get "for life." While all other services stop after the adolescent is discharges, caregivers can continue to join this group for a skills refresher and additional support. Caregivers receive a skills manual, which includes the psychoeducational topics foundational to DBT: mindfulness, emotion regulation, distress tolerance, and interpersonal effectiveness (Linehan, 1993a, b). The middle path skill, described later in this chapter, is also covered (Rathus & Miller, 2015). Additionally, skills groups teach caregivers to take a nonjudgmental and dialectical attitude toward situations that may have previously led to quick judgments, heightening emotional reactivity (Rathus & Miller, 2015). The structure of the group involves reviewing past homework, learning new DBT material, and then assigning homework to practice new material between sessions (Linehan, 1993a, b).

Research demonstrates the importance of caregivers learning these perspectives and skills alongside their children to allow the entire family system to shift in their interactions (Hoffman et al., 2007; Miller et al., 2007). The goal is for caregivers to learn and generalize the skills, convey the transactional nature of therapeutic work, and consequently ensure that the work in therapy is shared equally among the family (Fruzzetti et al., 2021).

Family Therapy

In traditional DBT-A outpatient settings, there are different clinicians who facilitate individual therapy and family therapy (Rathus & Miller, 2015); however, in the 3East PHP setting, the same clinician does the individual and family work, allowing for consistency and the ability to emphasize common themes between the individual and family sessions. For a review of the benefits and challenges of having the same family and individual therapist, see Fruzzetti et al. (2021). Due to the brevity of a PHP setting, family work is circumscribed, and goals must be specific. These sessions can serve as preparation for continued family work post-discharge to an outpatient setting (Fruzzetti et al., 2021).

One important element of preparation for continued work after the PHP is practicing the emotional exposure of talking about challenging topics such as self-harm, suicidality, and other risky behaviors. As previously stated, in DBT-A, there are four main family targets, with the initial target being to decrease familial interactions that lead to suicidal or self-harming behaviors (Miller et al., 2002). This is especially salient due to interpersonal challenges being one of the most common precipitants for suicide attempts (Miller & Glinski, 2000). For many families, this is their first experience having in-depth conversations about these topics with a clinician. Talking about these topics in a family meeting can be an exposure to experiencing and tolerating emotions. Caregivers may not know how to react when hearing about significant and stressful topics or may have an invalidating response (Fruzzetti, 2006). Adolescents may similarly have difficulty sharing these topics for a variety of reasons (e.g., fear of punishing or negative responses). Clinicians often emphasize to caregivers that the main goal is increasing transparency in the family. Family validation may include specific skills to allow for this greater transparency and nonjudgmental understanding while rebuilding relationships (Fruzzetti, 2006; Fruzzetti & Iverson, 2004). Thus, it is important that clinicians structure sessions to both allow space to discuss difficult topics and teach and coach effective skills use.

Family sessions are typically organized around several behaviorally structured skills including: (1) family chain analysis, (2) opportunities for skillful accurate emotion expression and disclosure of target behaviors (on the part of the adolescent), (3) validation and holding a nonjudgmental stance (on the part of the caregiver), and (4) chances to problem solve around skills deficits and cope ahead for difficult situations in the future (Rathus & Miller, 2015). We will briefly review these areas of family involvement in the DBT skills section of the chapter.

Caregiver Skills Coaching

In addition to the family sessions, caregivers at the 3East PHP have access to several ancillary clinical services for supplemental family support and guidance and in adherence to DBT-A structure (Rathus & Miller, 2015). Like the adolescent, caregivers are provided with an on-call clinician's contact information for skills coaching outside of program hours including nights/weekends. These brief calls (10–15 min) help caregivers identify their emotions, thoughts, and/or action urges that may interfere with their effectiveness and skillfulness in interacting with their adolescent.

Caregiver guidance sessions, without the adolescent, are also offered if caregivers are struggling to participate skillfully in treatment and act wise-mindedly within the home setting. These may include a deeper dive on validation, processing traumatic events, marital issues, co-parenting difficulties, and other related challenges.

11.2.1.4 DBT Family-Based Skills

In family sessions, there are several tools that are particularly helpful in aiding goals such as improving communication, decreasing conflict, and improving trust. Some of these tools include: chain analysis, accurate emotion expression, validation, walking the middle path, understanding dialectical dilemmas, and behaviorism.

Chain Analysis

The main structure of family therapy revolves around a family chain analysis or "double chain" (Fruzzetti & Payne, 2020; Fruzzetti et al., 2021). Chain analyses aim to improve emotional awareness, understand the transactional nature of conflictual moments, and review what skills to use and when to use them (for a complete review of chain analyses as well as the components of a chain analysis, see Rizvi, 2019). Family chain analysis is a nonjudgmental forum to understand the links that exist between different individuals and the functions behind problematic behavior.

Although a chain analysis in an individual session usually analyzes a problematic behavior (e.g., self-harm or a suicide attempt), a family chain analysis more often details a problematic interaction or conversation that took place that led to dysregulation and ineffectiveness (Fruzzetti & Payne, 2020). Each family member describes their observations and experiences throughout the interaction while the other family members refrain from interjecting. The clinician may point out moments where judgmental language or assumptions arise and help individuals to reframe thoughts in more descriptive and factual ways. Once everyone has had a chance to speak and process what each person has shared, the clinician will coach everyone on identifying moments that would have benefited from specific skills to lead to a more effective outcome. The clinician will provide psychoeducation around these skills, usually encouraging the adolescent to teach the skill to their caregiver in the session. The clinician will also facilitate role-plays of those moments to practice validation or provide feedback.

A vital part of the family (or double) chain analysis, as opposed to an individual chain analysis, is noticing the transaction between family members (Fruzzetti & Payne, 2020). Below, we see an example of this for Mina's family.

Mina's chain	Mom's chain
Mina returns home from school	Mina walks in the door from school
Thought (T): I want to tell my mom how bad the day was	T: I want to make things feel positive and have a good day after school
Emotion (E): Sadness, relief at coming home from school	B: "Did you have a wonderful day? Did you see that nice girl Samantha whose mom I met?"
T: My mom expects me to always be perfect and happy. She'll just be upset if she knows I was miserable all day and that Samantha and her friends hate me	E: Hopeful, anxious that I've said something wrong
Behavior (B): Told mom to shut up and swore at her. Went up to room	B: Made a shocked face, began to tear up
E: Misery, guilt, shame, sadness	E: Confusion, fear
B: Looking through bedside table for self-soothe kit, throwing items on floor	T: What if Mina cuts because she's so angry at me
T: Mom won't even give me space to cope with this. She's making me feel so guilty	B: Follow Mina to her room and try to block her from shutting the door
B: Start yelling that I hate my life and my mom makes everything worse	B: Start to cry
E: More intense guilt since my mom is crying	E: Sadness and fear

The inadvertent invalidation that Mina experienced led her to express anger rather than share sadness with her mother. This display of anger led Mina's mother to feel scared that Mina would self-harm. Mina's mother then tried to exert more control, in turn leading Mina to further push away her mother. Although both Mina and her mother wanted to connect and look to one another for support, they were left feeling more distant and confused by this interaction. Discussing this transaction, while avoiding blaming either individual, the double-chain allows for a better understanding and thus clearer problem-solving and skills coaching for potential future scenarios. For example, Mina's mother did not know about the guilt that Mina was experiencing or what triggered her anger. Similarly, Mina did not realize that her mother was not trying to invade her privacy but rather that she felt scared that Mina might hurt herself. Completing this chain allowed for compassion and vulnerability between Mina and her mother, as well as clear ways to improve communication going forward.

Accurate Emotion Expression

As seen in the chain analysis example, two key components that arise within family chain analysis are accurate emotional expression and validation (Fruzzetti & Payne, 2020). Accurate emotional expression is where an individual identifies what they are feeling, thinking, and experiencing and then communicates that information in a clear and direct way. This allows the person they are talking to an opportunity to understand and validate (Fruzzetti & Payne, 2020). Inaccurate expression of emotions tends to minimize the emotional experience ("I'm fine"), name a secondary emotion rather than a primary emotion ("I'm angry at you," when sadness and hurt are felt), or avoid the emotion ("I don't know" or "I don't care"). These are ineffective and indirect ways of communicating emotions. It leaves the person on the receiving side unsure of what the other individual is feeling and thus unable to accurately validate what they are experiencing (Fruzzetti & Payne, 2020). Many times, individuals are so accustomed to using inaccurate expressions of emotion that they have difficulty labeling and understanding their own emotions. Thus, one of the first steps to accurately express emotions is to use mindfulness to nonjudgmentally observe and identify the internal emotional experience.

Accurate emotional expression involves vulnerability and, depending on the environment, may not always be met with validation. In the example below, Mina is encouraged to use accurate expressions to directly communicate to her mother.

> Mina's brow furrowed, and tears filled her eyes. "I was so upset last night, and you didn't even care. You just left my dinner on my desk and walked away!" Mina's mother looked alarmed. "I asked you how you were doing, and you kept saying 'I'm fine!' I didn't know what else to do when you were telling me you were okay." The clinician prompted Mina to be more accurate and share her experience with her mother, "Mina, what were you feeling last night? Can we practice accurately expressing this now, so that your mom has a chance to try and validate you?" "I just don't even know. I was upset," Mina stated. "Let's try to dig a little deeper and try to figure this out. What was going on last night? Let's use mindfulness and nonjudgmentally describe what you were feeling in your body and the thoughts going through your mind." Upon further reflection, Mina was able to share that she was feeling deep sadness about not being invited to a close friend's house and then seeing pictures posted from the event on social media. Her mother then validated how painful it must have been to feel excluded in that way. Mina let out a big sigh, "I wish I had just told you that last night. I somehow thought you knew why I was so upset and thought you just didn't care."

An important part of family therapy is not only increasing the adolescent's accurate emotional expression, but also teaching caregivers how to validate in response to this expression. In this example, Mina's mother was able to skillfully validate after Mina disclosed her emotions.

Validation

Throughout the PHP duration, the clinician will assess caregivers' ability to validate. An abundance of research demonstrates how familial invalidation may contribute to increased emotion dysregulation (Fruzzetti, 2006; Fruzzetti & Worrall, 2010), and familial validation may lead to greater treatment gains and emotion regulation (Fruzzetti & King, 2019; Fruzzetti & Payne, 2020). Validation not only is a vital skill within DBT, but also is a critical part of conceptualizing how emotion dysregulation is maintained and increases over time (Linehan, 1993a; Miller & Glinski, 2000; Rajalin et al., 2009).

Caregivers are taught the six levels of validation within DBT (Linehan, 1993a), and this skill is practiced both within session and between sessions as homework. Psychoeducation and role-playing in sessions are important for helping caregivers practice validation while understanding that it does not condone any problematic behaviors. Rather, validation and curiosity will likely lead to deeper connection, greater understanding, more effective problem solving, and increased accurate expression from both caregivers and adolescents (Fruzzetti & Payne, 2020).

Validation is an acceptance-based strategy, and it is often a challenging exposure for caregivers to validate without jumping in with problem solving, which may be inadvertently invalidating or not allow the adolescent to learn how to solve the problem themselves. Allowing an individual to practice problem solving and cope with the natural consequences of their choices, rather than treating them as fragile is an important part of DBT (Linehan, 1993a). Below is an example with Mina and her mother where her mother uses validation to help reduce emotional intensity before discussing problem solving:

> Mina's face looked angry. "School makes me so stressed! I just don't know what to do. I am too anxious to do my homework, and I'm scared I'm going to fail!" Mina's mother noticed the urge to jump in with problem solving. She wanted to tell Mina, "Let's make a schedule and start step by step, first with the easiest work and then tackle the next piece of homework," but she knew how this typically ended. Mina would become increasingly angry at her and become even less likely to complete work. "Of course, you're anxious!" her mother exclaimed, "School is so important to you, and you've been trying harder than ever this past semester." Mina nodded. Her face softened and her eyes welled with tears. "Let me know if you want any help at planning this out," Mina's mother softly said. "I know I need to start with my English work. I know what I need to do," Mina shared.

In this example, Mina knew how to solve the problem, even without her mother's coaching. She needed validation to help her regulate her emotions to begin to solve the challenge on her own. Mina's mother's ability to refrain from problem solving allowed Mina a chance to solve this situation herself. Her mother's use of validation also strengthened the relationship between Mina and her mother and was noticeably regulating for Mina.

Parenting Dialectical Dilemmas and Middle Path

Dialectical dilemmas are patterns of behaviors that are common in individuals with BPD; they can coexist and may appear opposing to one another. Individuals sensitive to emotions often find themselves metaphorically swinging from one end to the other of each of the core dialectics (apparent competence-active passivity; emotional vulnerability-self-invalidation; inhibited grieving-unrelenting crisis). A complete description of these dialectical dilemmas can be found in Linehan (1993a, b, 2014a, b).

DBT-A has added additional dialectical dilemmas that arise within adolescent-caregiver relationships (Rathus & Miller, 2015). The three dialectical dilemmas unique to adolescents are: (1) excessive leniency versus authoritarian control, (2) pathologizing normative behaviors versus normalizing pathological behaviors, and

(3) fostering dependence versus forcing autonomy (Rathus & Miller, 2015). Within DBT-A, skills groups also include an additional module entitled "Walking the Middle Path," which helps families identify where they fall within these dialectical dilemmas, notice behavioral patterns, and teach a "middle path" approach that balances validation with behavioral modification.

The goal of this module is to increase dialectical perspectives or to be able to see one situation through multiple lenses and find solutions that "walk the middle path" between the extremes of the dialectics. Caregivers may fall at different points on the dialectical dilemmas; for example, one caregiver may be too strict while another is overly permissive. This further complicates the family work as one caregiver may be reinforcing problematic behaviors while the other caregiver takes on the role of the disciplinarian. The goal is to reach the middle path for both caregivers' interactions with one another in addition to the adolescent (Rathus et al., 2015).

In Mina's family, there were several dialectical dilemmas targeted. Mina's mother believed marijuana use was typical for teenagers. On the other hand, Mina's father, who had a family history of substance abuse, believed any substance use was unacceptable and often appeared angry and confused when discussing this:

> Mina's mother jumped into the conversation. "Smoking marijuana isn't that big of a deal, she's a teenager, they all do it! She's just too anxious right now." Her father stood up, appearing tense, "None of this is normal. It's just crazy. She's using drugs, and I just can't understand why!" Mina sat between her parents, eyes downcast and quiet. The clinician prompted Mina to share her thoughts on the function of her marijuana, something they had been discussing in individual therapy. "When I get really anxious, it definitely makes me feel calmer for a while; it brings me relief. Afterwards, I feel really ashamed and guilty though, and it's not something I want to do forever. I feel like I've been using it more and more, which I don't like." The clinician demonstrated holding the dialectic of validating the function of using this behavior while encouraging change. "Anxiety is really hard for you to tolerate and causing so much distress, and you also want to find some new skills to use for anxiety. Could we pay close attention to tracking anxiety and marijuana use on your diary card? Let's start a cope ahead plan now for what skills you could use instead of smoking."

In this example, Mina's father would be encouraged to find the middle path through using curiosity and validation to understand Mina's substance use, even if he does not agree with it, while her mother would be encouraged to also find a middle path in helping Mina change these behavioral patterns of using marijuana to decrease anxiety.

Behaviorism

DBT is rooted in behaviorism, and an important part of DBT-A involves balancing behavioral change with validation. Behaviorism pervades DBT from initial assessment (e.g., setting behaviorally specific goals), to increasing emotional awareness (e.g., noticing conditioned learned responses within the family environment via family chain analyses), and creating change (e.g., reinforcing skills use). Within the "middle path" module of DBT-A, tenets of behaviorism, including conditioning and learned responses, are taught to families (Rathus et al., 2015).

When describing behaviorism to caregivers, principles of conditioning including reinforcement and punishment are described. The benefits of positive reinforcement are also discussed from a caregiver lens as well as how behaviors like self-harm may be negatively reinforcing by providing short-term relief (Rathus et al., 2015. Family interactions are examined through a behavioral lens to better understand how certain behaviors may have increased or decreased over time (Fruzzetti & Payne, 2020). For example, if an adolescent only receives attention and validation from their caregivers when they are escalated, this may inadvertently reinforce dysregulated behaviors. Conditioning, reinforcement, and shaping all occur within the family systems and within the PHP setting; and therefore, one of the initial goals of family work is to increase awareness of the interactions that affect the problematic behavior. Although a full review of DBT behavioral strategies is outside the purview of this chapter, the following vignette describes how behaviorism may inform a discussion of target behaviors within a family session:

> "You never share your emotions with me," Mina's father angrily stated, "I just want to know what's going on, but you push me away and only talk to your friends. I wish you could share more with me, so I could understand." Mina inhaled sharply and a pained expression came over her face. "Do you want to know about my emotions? I'm suffering, Dad. I feel guilty all the time, and anxious, and sad. That's why I've been self-harming for so long," Mina's father's face hardened, "How can you say these things? You have a home, you have loving parents, I just don't understand you." The clinician gently paused this moment to explain reinforcement. "It sounds like when Mina shares about her emotions and mentions self-harm, it leads to a negative consequence, not being understood, and potentially being called ungrateful, which leads to her sharing less and less. We need to find a way to positively reinforce sharing accurate emotions, since it is a goal of yours to understand Mina's perspective more. This is a moment to practice validation."

Here in this example, subtle reinforcement, conditioning, and punishment is taking place. Mina and her father had to understand the behaviorism principles to change these interactions moving forward. In this example, Mina's accurate expression led to a withdrawal of warmth and an increase in sadness from Mina's father. Mina then felt guilt, which decreased the likelihood of her being forthcoming in the future. Even though Mina's father wanted to know more about Mina's experience, he was unaware of the subtle conditioning that was often occurring when Mina shared her emotions.

11.2.1.5 Common Challenges When Working with Families in a DBT PHP

Every family has unique characteristics and difficulties that arise in treatment. There are several challenges that can complicate sessions and become therapy destroying if not addressed in these sessions. Families begin treatment with differing structures, emotional reactivities, and vulnerabilities. It is a delicate balance to flexibly meet each member at their skill level to provide supportive change. For example, caregivers who are divorced or separated may have difficulty attending family meetings together and need separate sessions. Similarly, they may have inconsistent limits between households, for example, different rules around substance use. Some families may also display caregiver under-involvement in treatment for a variety of reasons (e.g., work demands, not being allowed to participate by the client). In these moments, clinicians hold the goal of being flexible, as well as of disseminating skills as widely as possible, while respecting the current family configuration.

11.2.1.6 Caregiver Over-Involvement and Over-Accommodation

Caregiver over-involvement creates numerous challenges and may take different forms. First, caregivers may jump into problem solving too quickly to protect the adolescent or prevent them from experiencing discomfort or consequences. Although well-intentioned, this can lead to adolescents feeling helpless as they do not develop the skills set to solve their own problems, cope with distress, or learn from natural consequences. Frequent surveillance is another type of overinvolvement. Caregivers may be overly involved with monitoring, even tracking the adolescent's phone usage (e.g., reading text messages and monitoring social media) due to concerns about risk. This can lead to anger and further secrecy from the adolescent as well as continued mistrust between the caregiver and adolescent.

Caregiver over-involvement can also lead to over-accommodation, which involves modifying routines or helping with the avoidance of emotion-provoking situations (see review in Lebowitz et al., 2013)). For example, if the adolescent has social anxiety, their caregiver may intervene in the environment in an ineffective way, such as calling school for a sick day when the adolescent is avoiding due to anxiety. Although well-intentioned and relieving anxiety in the short-term, these behaviors can increase anxiety in the long-term as the adolescent does not learn how to tolerate anxiety (Lebowitz et al., 2013). Additionally, caregivers may accommodate the adolescent's anger by "walking on eggshells" in their behaviors and what they say to prevent dysregulating the adolescent (Lebowitz et al., 2013; Mason & Kreger, 2020). Caregivers will often say they do not want the adolescent to get in trouble, or to feel distress and overwhelmed in handling difficult situations. This often leads to fragilizing the adolescent. They will also not experience and learn the natural consequences of their actions. Instead, the goal is for caregivers to support the adolescent in taking steps to face their emotions, little by little.

11.2.1.7 Caregiver Psychopathology and Trauma

During intake, caregivers provide family psychiatric history including their own psychiatric history. Many caregivers of adolescents with BPD also display or endorse symptoms of several psychiatric diagnoses and personality traits (e.g., Distel et al., 2008; Skoglund et al., 2021). These symptoms may contribute to difficulties with validation and executive functioning skills. Thus, family/caregiver history and clinician observations will inform treatment as to what skills to emphasize, what skills may be difficult to utilize, and what behavioral interventions to add.

For example, some caregivers may need more scaffolding (e.g., reminders to follow up with discharge referrals) or written/email summaries of to-do items. When appropriate, the clinician may recommend further therapeutic support for the caregiver. It is important to balance being direct and not fragilizing the caregiver while also talking about their mental health in a nonjudgmental and supportive way.

It is very common for adolescents and their family members to have experienced traumatic events (i.e., Criterion A traumas). For example, in this population, caregivers often have the traumatic experience of learning about or finding their adolescent after a suicide attempt or significant self-harming incident. In cases where trauma is present for the adolescent or caregivers, and it is currently impacting the family, ancillary consultations may be beneficial for psychoeducation around trauma, PTSD, and specific parenting recommendations around these topics.

11.2.2 Discharge Planning

Given that PHPs are time-limited and brief treatments, discharge planning is a crucial part of family work within a PHP setting. Standard recommendations typically include continuing outpatient, adherent DBT-A. Although some families opt to pursue family therapy after the PHP, others may be referred for a caregiver skills coach first, to generalize their DBT skills, work on contingency management, and improve interpersonal responses. Additional elements of discharge planning include setting expectations and coping ahead for life after the program. During this transition, old behavior patterns and target behaviors can re-emerge for both the adolescent and caregivers. Additionally, certain events, stressors, and situations (e.g., attending school, seeing certain friends, sports games) that were less common during their time at the PHP can bring up intense emotions, thoughts, urges, and impulsive behaviors. Cope ahead plans and discussions of these potential challenges are an integral part to discharge planning.

11.3 Research Evidence

There is little research examining DBT in PHP settings and even fewer studies in adolescent populations. In a pilot study of DBT-A in a six-week PHP for adolescents, results revealed decreased anxiety and depressive symptoms at discharge, as well as endorsement of fewer maladaptive ways to cope with stressors (Del Conte et al., 2016). In a secondary data analysis of this project, skills acquired from the emotion regulation and the interpersonal effectiveness modules predicted lower self-reported anxiety and depression at the time of discharge (Lenz et al., 2016). Additionally, this study found that adolescents reported more engagement in mindfulness practices, acceptance of emotional experiences, and effective strategies for problem solving and self-control after participating in the PHP. Another research investigation of DBT-A at this same PHP found decreased depressive symptoms and interpersonal sensitivity following treatment compared to treatment as usual, but no differences on anxiety and hostility (Lenz & Del Conte, 2018). A separate analysis of this PHP found that half of the participants reported clinically significant treatment gains, as well as equivalence of treatment response across age, gender, and ethnicity (Lenz et al., 2021). These studies support the use of DBT in a PHP as an effective treatment modality for adolescents struggling with significant mental health concerns. However, the described studies were conducted at the same treatment center (Del Conte et al., 2016; Lenz & Del Conte, 2018; Lenz et al., 2016, 2021). Thus, further research is needed to confirm the efficacy of DBT for adolescents in various PHPs.

11.4 Clinical Considerations For Diverse Identities

There may be cultural differences, such as language, race, ethnicity, religion, and generational differences, between the clinician and the family, as well as between the adolescent and their caregivers, that can impact treatment. These differences can lead to difficulties in communication and understanding, which can fuel disconnection. Additionally, differences in cultural emotional expression and cultural expectations need to be considered. For example, while accurate expression and validation are pillars in DBT family work, some clients and family members may struggle with these due to cultural norms such as conformity and filial piety (Cheng & Merrick, 2016). Within these cultural differences, it is crucial for clinicians to aim for cultural humility and recognize the adolescents and their caregivers as the experts on their family, while simultaneously challenging the norms that may not be effective. This dialectic is important to hold and name with families. There have been several examples of culturally adapted DBT programs implemented among different racial, ethnic, and cultural groups (Haft et al., 2022), and it is crucial for clinicians to continue to make efforts to optimize evidence-based therapies such as DBT for these groups (Haft et al., 2022).

Of note, a common area for more chronic or consistent invalidation from both families and culturally within the United States is around gender identity or sexual orientation (Sloan et al., 2017; Skerven et al., 2019). For example, adolescents who identify as non-binary or transgender may be consistently misgendered by caregivers, teachers, or peers who use incorrect pronouns. When caregivers engage in this misgendering, it can be especially emotionally painful. Whether due to caregivers' forgetting or refusing to use the adolescent's pronouns, this is one example of consistent invalidation. For misgendering, it is important for caregivers to "get curious" and ask questions to understand better (Sloan et al., 2017). In these situations, the interaction between accurate emotional expression and validation is again vital.

11.5 Case Vignette

In the case below, we more formally present Mina and her family's case conceptualization and treatment plan. Mina is a 15-year-old Latinx, nonbinary (pronouns: she/they) individual with diagnoses of social anxiety disorder and major depressive disorder. She has a history of several suicide attempts that have resulted in inpatient hospitalizations, as well as self-harm (i.e., cutting) and daily marijuana use. Mina presented to the PHP following an assessment at the emergency department (ED) where her parents found a suicide note along with pills that she had been hoarding. In the ED, Mina denied imminent and active suicidality and was therefore not admitted to an inpatient program. Mina's parents described feeling afraid and lost, and they believed that weekly outpatient therapy was not an adequate level of care. A social worker at the ED recommended participating in a DBT PHP.

During the interview, Mina described feeling overwhelmed with emotions like anxiety, guilt, and shame and not knowing how to cope with them. Her parents would tell her to "think about the positive side of life" and to "just push away these negative thoughts," when she became dysregulated. As a result, Mina would mask her emotions, self-invalidate, and minimize her problems to others. She felt shame that she struggled to see the positive side of things. "I feel like something is really wrong with me," Mina said in the interview, "Even when I start feeling happy, something can shift my mood so quickly, and it's like that happiness never even existed." Mina felt that the only way to cope with her emotions was via self-harm (cutting), considering suicide, and smoking marijuana. "If I wasn't invited to a social thing with my friends, I would hate myself and them. I would think about what they would say at my funeral and how badly they would feel. The only way I could get over the anger was by cutting." Mina had some insight about the function of her behaviors; however, overall, she appeared confused by the intensity of her emotions and the resulting behaviors.

Mina's clinician conceptualized her challenges through the biosocial model. Biologically, Mina was a highly emotionally sensitive and reactive individual and was slow to re-regulate to her emotional baseline. Mina also found it very hard to restrain from impulsive behaviors when feeling intense emotions. Socially, Mina's parents inadvertently invalidated her emotional experience by telling her that she "should" be happy and that it was easy to push the "bad" emotions away. This led Mina to feel intense shame and anger and rely on maladaptive coping skills such as self-harm, marijuana, and suicidal ideation. Given Mina's emotional sensitivity and impulsivity, she had difficulties maintaining friendships and worried about judgment from others. She feared that her current friends would leave her, which exacerbated her hopelessness about the future. Using the biosocial model to explain Mina's symptoms helped Mina understand her emotional experience and frame her problematic coping as a skills deficit. Additionally, her parents were made aware of the transactional role they unknowingly played in maintaining Mina's sense of shame about her emotional experiences while bringing attention to everyone's skills deficits in emotion-provoking situations.

Family treatment goals centered around increasing open and effective communication, which were broken down into the core DBT family goals and included:

1. Decreasing family interactions that lead to suicidal and self-harming behaviors.
   (a) Increasing Mina's accurate emotional expression and transparency (e.g., disclosing more of her problematic behaviors and emotional experiences) to give parents opportunities to validate.
   (b) Parents sitting with the urges to cheerlead, reassure, or problem-solve when Mina is dysregulated, and instead validate.
   (c) Using on-call skills coaching and practicing distress tolerance skills.
2. Decreasing family behaviors that interfere with treatment.
   (a) Reducing "walking on eggshells" behavior by parents (e.g., parents avoiding conversations about school, as it tended to often lead to conflict and risk of self-harm).
   (b) Coping ahead for conflicts and interruptions (e.g., work and school commitments) in treatment.
3. Decreasing family behaviors that interfere with quality of life.
   (a) Improving awareness around one's own dysregulation.
   (b) Each member discussing problematic interactions in the form of a chain analysis to learn how to be more effective.
4. Improve familial communication, effectiveness, and ability to find a "middle path".
   (a) Mina more effectively asking for what she wants.
   (b) Parents more effectively setting limits (e.g., screen time, time spent in room, expectations around chores and family time).
   (c) Mina and parents reinforcing effective communication and providing direct feedback around moments that were ineffective.

In the first half of family treatment, Mina and her parents reviewed problematic interactions over the past week. These interactions usually entailed Mina's parent assuming something about Mina's emotional experience or inadvertently invalidating what she was experiencing. Mina would then shut down or engage in a problematic behavior (e.g., self-harm or marijuana use) to deal with the emotions. Mina's parents were unaware of the resulting problematic behavior stemming from said conversation. Their clinician used chain analyses to aid each family member's understanding of what had transpired by having each person share their experience (e.g., emotions, thoughts, urges, behaviors). The clinician would share observations of these transactions to bring attention to the effect everyone had on each other. In these chains, parents and Mina's assumptions were challenged, judgments were reframed, and interpretations were checked. The clinician would also highlight moments where skills could have been used to prevent the escalation of the conflict. The clinician would validate how each member's emotions made sense given the context, history, and their vulnerabilities *and* would hold the dialectic that each member needed to be more skillful in regulating their emotions and communicating more effectively to improve their relationships.

In the latter part of the family work, sessions focused more on how the communication patterns had shifted, highlighting skillfulness, and reinforcing effective communication. Mina began expressing gratitude when she felt that her parents were validating her emotions. Similarly, parents were encouraged to provide feedback and appreciation when they felt that Mina was forthcoming about a problem. These latter sessions also included discussions about post-discharge topics around transitioning back to school, limit setting (e.g., curfew, expectations around substance use), and the new outpatient treatment team.

At discharge, Mina described feeling that she better understood the function of her emotions, how to practice self-validation to decrease her emotional intensity, how to accurately ask for help, and which skills helped her tolerate impulsive urges. She recognized the progress her parents had made in being more validating with fewer attempts at unsolicited problem-solving. Mina and her parents committed to ongoing outpatient DBT therapy post-discharge. Mina and her parents were also reminded that progress is not always linear and that there will be slips and relapses into old behavioral patterns. Progress can be reframed as noticing these slips earlier in the chain of events and employing skills sooner to avoid emotion dysregulation and problematic behaviors.

References

Adrian, M., Berk, M. S., Korslund, K., Whitlock, K., McCauley, E., & Linehan, M. (2018). Parental validation and invalidation predict adolescent self-harm. *Professional Psychology: Research and Practice, 49*(4), 274–281. https://doi.org/10.1037/pro0000200

Amad, A., Ramoz, N., Thomas, P., Jardri, R., & Gorwood, P. (2014). Genetics of borderline personality disorder: Systematic review and proposal of an integrative model. *Neuroscience & Biobehavioral Reviews, 40*, 6–19. https://doi.org/10.1016/j.neubiorev.2014.01.003

Batejan, K. L., Van der Feen, J., & Worden, P. (2022). Dialectical behavior therapy. In J. M. Leffler & E. Frazier (Eds.), *Handbook of evidence-based day treatment programs for children and adolescents* (pp. 157–173). Springer.

Cheng, P., & Merrick, E. (2016). Cultural adaptation of dialectical behavior therapy for a Chinese international student with eating disorder and depression. *Clinical Case Studies, 16*(1), 42–57. https://doi.org/10.1177/1534650116668269

Coyle, T. N., Brill, C. D., Aunon, F. M., Peterson, A. P., Gasser, M. L., Kuehn, K. S., & Harned, M. S. (2019). Beginning to envision a life worth living: An introduction to pretreatment sessions in dialectical behavior therapy. *Psychotherapy, 56*(1), 21–27. https://doi.org/10.1037/pst0000205

Curtin, S. C. (2020). State suicide rates among adolescents and young adults aged 10–24: United States, 2000–2018. *National Vital Statistics Reports, 69*(11).

Del Conte, G., Lenz, A. S., & Hollenbaugh, K. M. (2016). A pilot evaluation of dialectical behavior therapy for adolescents within a partial hospitalization treatment milieu. *Journal of Child and Adolescent Counseling, 2*, 16–32. https://doi.org/10.1080/23727810.2015.1134008

Distel, M. A., Trull, T. J., Derom, C. A., Thiery, E. W., Grimmer, M. A., Martin, N. G., Willemsen, G., & Boomsma, D. I. (2008). Heritability of borderline personality disorder features is similar across three countries. *Psychological Medicine, 38*(9), 1219–1229. https://doi.org/10.1017/S0033291707002024

Fruzzetti, A. E. (2006). *The high conflict couple: A dialectical behavior therapy guide to finding peace, intimacy, and validation*. New Harbinger Publications.

Fruzzetti, A. E., & Hoffman, P. D. (2004). *Family connections workbook and training manual*. National Education Alliance for Borderline Personality Disorder.

Fruzzetti, A. E., & Iverson, K. M. (2004). Mindfulness, acceptance, validation and "individual" psychopathology in couples. In S. C. Hayes, V. M. Follette, & M. M. Linehan (Eds.), *Mindfulness and acceptance: Expanding the cognitive behavioral tradition* (pp. 168–191). Guilford Press.

Fruzzetti, A. E., & King, A. (2019). Borderline personality disorder in couple and family therapy. In J. Lebow, A. Chambers, & D. C. Breunlin (Eds.), *Encyclopedia of couple and family therapy* (pp. 304–308). Springer. https://doi.org/10.1007/978-3-319-49425-8_442

Fruzzetti, A. E., & Payne, L. G. (2020). Assessment of parents, couples, and families in dialectical behavior therapy. *Cognitive and Behavioral Practice, 27*(1), 39–49. https://doi.org/10.1016/j.cbpra.2019.10.006

Fruzzetti, A. E., & Worrall, J. M. (2010). Accurate expression and validation: A transactional model for understanding individual and relationship distress. In K. Sullivan & J. Davila (Eds.), *Support processes in intimate relationships* (pp. 121–150). Oxford University Press.

Fruzzetti, A. E., Shenk, C., & Hoffman, P. D. (2005). Family interaction and the development of borderline personality disorder: A transactional model. *Development and Psychopathology, 17*(4), 1007–1030. https://doi.org/10.1017/S0954579405050479

Fruzzetti, A. E., Payne, L. G., & Hoffman, P. D. (2021). DBT with families. In L. A. Dimeff, S. L. Rivzi, & K. Koerner (Eds.), *Dialectical behavior therapy in clinical practice: Applications across disorders and settings* (2nd ed., pp. 366–387). The Guilford Press.

Haft, S. L., O'Grady, S. M., Shaller, E. A. L., & Liu, N. H. (2022). Cultural adaptation of dialectical behavior therapy: A systematic review. *Journal of Consulting and Clinical Psychology, 90*(10), 787–801. https://doi.org/10.1037/ccp0000730

Hiller, A. D., & Hughes, C. D. (2022). Dialectical behavior therapy for adolescents: Treatment outcomes in an outpatient community setting. *Evidence-Based Practice in Child and Adolescent Mental Health, 8*(4), 488–505. https://doi.org/10.1080/23794925.2022.2056929

Hoffman, P. D., Fruzzetti, A., & Swenson, C. (1999). Dialectical behavior therapy-family skills training. *Family Process, 38*(4), 399–414. https://doi.org/10.1111/j.1545-5300.1999.00399.x

Hoffman, P. D., Fruzzetti, A. E., & Buteau, E. (2007). Understanding and engaging families: An education, skills and support program for relatives impacted by borderline personality disorder. *Journal of Mental Health, 16*(1), 69–82. https://doi.org/10.1080/09638230601182052

Koerner, K. (2013). What must you know and do to get good outcomes with DBT? *Behavior Therapy, 44*(4), 568–579. https://doi.org/10.1016/j.beth.2013.03.005

Lazarus, S. A., Cheavens, J. S., Festa, F., & Rosenthal, M. Z. (2014). Interpersonal functioning in borderline personality disorder: A systematic review of behavioral and laboratory-based assessments. *Clinical Psychology Review, 34*(3), 193–205. https://doi.org/10.1016/j.cpr.2014.01.007

Lebowitz, E. R., Woolston, J., Bar-Haim, Y., Calvocoressi, L., Dauser, C., Warnick, E., Scahill, L., Chakir, A. R., Shechner, T., Hermes, H., Vitulano, L. A., King, R. A., & Leckman, J. F. (2013). Family accommodation in pediatric anxiety disorders. *Depression and Anxiety, 30*(1), 47–54. https://doi.org/10.1002/da.21998

Lenz, A. S., & Del Conte, G. (2018). Efficacy of dialectical behavior therapy for adolescents in a partial hospitalization program. *Journal of Counseling and Development, 96*(1), 15–26. https://doi.org/10.1002/jcad.12174

Lenz, A. S., Del Conte, G., Hollenbaugh, M., & Callendar, K. (2016). Emotional regulation and interpersonal effectiveness as predictors of treatment outcomes within a DBT treatment program for adolescents. *Counseling Outcome and Research Evaluation, 7*(2), 73–85. https://doi.org/10.1177/2150137816642439

Lenz, A. S., Del Conte, G., Douglas, C., Crenshaw, A., Dobbs, C., Stogner, E., & Williford, V. (2021). A pre-experimental evaluation of treatment gains associated with a DBT-A partial hospitalization program. *Journal of Counseling and Development, 100*, 146–156. https://doi.org/10.1002/jcad.12416

Linehan, M. M. (1993a). *Cognitive-behavioral treatment of borderline personality disorder*. Guilford Press.

Linehan, M. M. (1993b). *Skills training manual for treating borderline personality disorder*. Guilford Press.

Linehan, M. M. (2014a). *DBT skills training manual* (2nd ed.). Guilford Press.

Linehan, M. M. (2014b). *DBT skills training handouts and worksheets* (2nd ed.). Guilford Press.

Marshall, P., Sansom, K., Jagfeld, G., Jones, S., & Lobban, F. (2023). Caring for a friend or family member who has experienced suicidal behaviour: A systematic review and qualitative synthesis. *Psychology and Psychotherapy, 96*(2), 426–447. https://doi.org/10.1111/papt.12449

Mason, P. T., & Kreger, R. (2020). *Stop walking on eggshells: Taking your life back when someone you care about has borderline personality disorder* (3rd ed.). New Harbinger Publications.

Miller, A. L., & Glinski, J. (2000). Youth suicidal behavior: Assessment and intervention. *Journal of Clinical Psychology, 56*, 1131–1152. https://doi.org/10.1002/1097-4679(200009)56

Miller, A. L., Glinski, J., Woodberry, K. A., Mitchell, A. G., & Indik, J. (2002). Family therapy and dialectical behavior therapy with adolescents: Part I: Proposing a clinical synthesis. *American Journal of Psychotherapy, 56*(4), 568–584. https://doi.org/10.1176/appi.psychotherapy.2002.56.4.568

Miller, A. L., Rathus, J. H., & Linehan, M. M. (2007). *Dialectical behavior therapy with suicidal adolescents*. Guilford Press.

Mochrie, K. D., Lothes II, J., Guendner, E., & John, J. S. (2020). DBT-informed treatment in a partial hospital and intensive outpatient program: the role of step-down care. *Research in Psychotherapy: Psychopathology, Process and Outcome, 23*(2).

Moos, R. H. (2018). *Evaluating treatment environments: The quality of psychiatric and substance abuse programs*. Routledge. https://doi.org/10.4324/9781351291804

Neuhaus, E. C. (2006). Fixed values and a flexible partial hospital program model. *President and Fellows of Harvard College, 14*, 1–14. https://doi.org/10.1080/10673220500519706

Panos, P. T., Jackson, J. W., Hasan, O., & Panos, A. (2014). Meta-analysis and systematic review assessing the efficacy of dialectical behavior therapy (DBT). *Research on Social Work Practice, 24*(2), 213–223. https://doi.org/10.1177/1049731513503047

Perepletchikova, F., Axelrod, S. R., Kaufman, J., Rounsaville, B. J., Douglas-Palumberi, H., & Miller, A. L. (2011). Adapting dialectical behavior therapy for children: Towards a new research agenda for pediatric suicidal and non-suicidal self-injurious behaviors. *Child and Adolescent Mental Health, 16*, 116–121. https://doi.org/10.1111/j.14753588.2010.00583.x

Rajalin, M., Wickholm-Pethrus, L., Hursti, T., & Jokinen, J. (2009). Dialectical behavior therapy-based skills training for family members of suicide attempters. *Archives of Suicide Research, 13*(3), 257–263. https://doi.org/10.1080/13811110903044401

Rathus, J. H., & Miller, A. L. (2015). *DBT skills manual for adolescents*. Guilford Press.

Rathus, J., Campbell, B., Miller, A., & Smith, H. (2015). Treatment acceptability study of walking the middle path, a new DBT skills module for adolescents and their families. *American Journal of Psychotherapy, 69*(2), 163–178. https://doi.org/10.1176/appi.psychotherapy.2015.69.2.163

Rheinberger, D., Shand, F., McGillivray, L., McCallum, S., & Boydell, K. (2023). Parents of adolescents who experience suicidal phenomena: A scoping review of their experience. *International Journal of Environmental Research and Public Health, 20*(13), 6227. https://doi.org/10.3390/ijerph20136227

Rizvi, S. L. (2019). *Chain analysis in dialectical behavior therapy*. Guilford Press.

Skerven, K., Whicker, D. R., & LeMaire, K. L. (2019). Applying dialectical behaviour therapy to structural and internalized stigma with LGBTQ+ clients. *The Cognitive Behaviour Therapist, 12*, e9. https://doi.org/10.1017/S1754470X18000235

Skoglund, C., Tiger, A., Rück, C., Petrovic, P., Asherson, P., Hellner, C., Mataix-Cols, D., & Kuja-Halkola, R. (2021). Familial risk and heritability of diagnosed borderline personality disorder: A register study of the Swedish population. *Molecular Psychiatry, 26*(3), 999–1008. https://doi.org/10.1038/s41380-019-0442-0

Sloan, C. A., Berke, D. S., & Shipherd, J. C. (2017). Utilizing a dialectical framework to inform conceptualization and treatment of clinical distress in transgender individuals. *Professional Psychology: Research and Practice, 48*(5), 301–309. https://doi.org/10.1037/pro0000146

Tebbett-Mock, A. A., Saito, E., McGee, M., Woloszyn, P., & Venuti, M. (2020). Efficacy of dialectical behavior therapy versus treatment as usual for acute-care inpatient adolescents. *Journal of American Academy of Child and Adolescent Psychiatry, 59*(1), 149–156. https://doi.org/10.1016/j.jaac.2019.01.020

Waitz, C., Tebbett-Mock, A., D'Angelo, E., & Reynolds, E. K. (2021). Dialectical behavior therapy in inpatient and residential settings for adolescents: A systematic review. *Evidence-Based Practice in Child and Adolescent Mental Health, 6*(4), 497–515. https://doi.org/10.1080/23794925.2021.1970052

Wilks, C. R., Valenstein-Mah, H., Tran, H., King, A. M., Lungu, A., & Linehan, M. M. (2017). Dialectical behavior therapy skills for families of individuals with behavioral disorders: Initial feasibility and outcomes. *Cognitive and Behavioral Practice, 24*(3), 288–295. https://doi.org/10.1016/j.cbpra.2016.06.004

Yap, M. B., Allen, N. B., & Ladouceur, C. D. (2008). Maternal socialization of positive affect: The impact of invalidation on adolescent emotion regulation and depressive symptomatology. *Child Development, 79*(5), 1415–1431. https://doi.org/10.1111/j.1467-8624.2008.01196.x

Part IV
Interventions with Peers

Chapter 12
Peer-Supported Treatment for Adults

Madeline J. Bruce, Melba A. Hernandez-Tejada, and Ron E. Acierno

12.1 Introduction

Social support may take a variety of forms, from a sympathetic ear providing affirmation and comfort, to additional sets of working hands bringing community resources to bear on behalf of someone experiencing hardship. Peers, specifically those who share some aspect of unique experience with a given individual, may be a particularly relevant and powerful source of social support. In this chapter, we will describe current research on peer-based interventions for adults who are in individual treatment, how social support derived from peers may enhance a range of psychotherapeutic efforts, and highlight current research on peer-based interventions for adults who are in individual treatment. Peers refer to those with relevant lived experiences who may have the same diagnosis as an individual in treatment or have completed a similar kind of psychotherapeutic treatment. Patients connected with those who have "been there" tend to fare better after treatment for a variety of reasons.

In this chapter, we first review theories that underlie predictions related to effectiveness of integrating peer support into treatment, and then provide guidance for integrating this kind of support based on the current empirical evidence, especially

M. J. Bruce (✉)
Department of Psychology, Webster University, Webster Groves, MO, USA

Faillace Department of Psychiatry, McGovern Medical School at UTHealth Houston, Houston, TX, USA
e-mail: madelinebruce@webster.edu

M. A. Hernandez-Tejada · R. E. Acierno
Faillace Department of Psychiatry, McGovern Medical School at UTHealth Houston, Houston, TX, USA
e-mail: Melba.A.HernandezTejada@uth.tmc.edu; Ronald.acierno@uth.tmc.edu

L. Reuman, J. Thompson-Hollands (eds.), *Enhancing CBT Through Family and Peer Engagement*, CBT: Science Into Practice, https://doi.org/10.1007/978-3-031-74838-7_12

with a consideration for culture. We conclude with an illustrative example of peer-supported interventions derived from our own experiences: the Prolonged Exposure for PTSD (PE) + Peers program. Overall, this chapter will shed light on the significance of peer-based interventions and how incorporating peers into evidence-based treatments can be a valuable approach, particularly in engaging individuals at risk of dropout or who are hesitant to continue treatment.

12.2 How Peers Help People Navigating Psychotherapy

Numerous theories across social and behavioral psychology offer insights into how peer support can effectively enhance psychotherapy outcomes. These theories encompass various aspects, such as increasing motivation to engage in psychotherapeutic behaviors, enhancing learning during these behaviors, and fostering a sense of support, mutual belonging, and shared responsibility. In this review, peer support is defined as the provision of social-emotional support, in the form of encouragement, and instrumental support, such as giving advice about how to get better, provided by people who have experience with a similar diagnosis and/or treatment plan (Gartner & Riessman, 1982; Solomon, 2004). This support is typically asymmetrical, with a peer being further along in their recovery or treatment plan compared to the current patient (Barton & Henderson, 2016). Recognizing this disparity in knowledge and experience is crucial from the outset, as it represents a natural power differential, with the peer often assuming the role of a mentor rather than a pure equal.

12.2.1 Increasing Motivation

12.2.1.1 Self-Determination Theory

Ryan and Deci (2000) proposed a meta-theory of motivation called "self-determination theory." This theory asserts that increased autonomy, sense of competence, and sense of relatedness were key factors that foster the highest motivation to engage in a specific behavior. In the context of explaining the impact of peer support on psychotherapy, the relationships motivation theory suggests that we are motivated to engage in behavior that leads us toward belonging to a group and developing close personal relationships, which stems from the basic psychological need for social connection (Ryan & Deci, 2000). According to this theoretical framework, peer support programs would ideally promote both social connection and patient autonomy (Fortuna et al., 2019). For instance, a preliminary feasibility, acceptability, and effectiveness study showed promising results for a peer-delivered intervention designed to assist adults with serious mental illness with a primary goal of psychiatric and medical self-management (Fortuna et al., 2018).

12.2.1.2 Social Comparison Theory

This theory proposed by Festinger (1954) posits that we have an innate drive to compare ourselves against others to determine if our abilities are good enough, if our opinions are correct, and to set a benchmark of what we can achieve. Festinger identified two distinct types of comparisons: upward social comparison, which can inspire us to improve to a standard set by someone we understand as doing well, and downward social comparison, which can boost our self-esteem by feeling better off than someone we understand to be worse than us. In the context of peer support, the peer-to-patient interactions would encourage an upward comparison, inspiring the patient toward activities that help meet their goals (Salzer et al., 2013).

12.2.2 Enhancing Learning

12.2.2.1 Social Learning Theory

Bandura built upon behaviorist learning theories of classical and operant conditioning by incorporating the idea that behavior can be learned through the environment via the processes of observation, imitation, and reinforcement (1977). Within this framework, peer support is thus understood as offering a vicarious learning experience where patients can observe the peer engage in behaviors that can improve their shared condition. Patients then try to replicate the actions that led the peer towards recovery (Miller, 2010). Positive feedback and praise from peers can be especially reinforcing. For example, a study of a peer-support community program for substance abuse showed significant reduction of risk of relapse, and qualitative analysis pointed to the supportive behaviors of fellow community members as a major factor in preventing relapse (Boisvert et al., 2008).

12.2.2.2 Experiential Learning and Knowledge

Experiential learning (Kolb, 1984) is a style of learning that progresses through a four-stage cycle:

1. Concrete Experience: A learner faces a concrete experience, which may be a new event or reinterpretation of a previous experience that is being examined in light of new information.
2. Reflective Observation: A learner reflects upon the new experience, with a focus on inconsistencies between the experience, existing knowledge, and new information.
3. Abstract Conceptualization: The reflection catalyzes new ideas or changes in existing knowledge.

4. Active Experimentation: The new ideas or modified concepts are tested through experimentation by seeking further concrete experiences.

Experiential learning has become a cornerstone of instructional design in formal education (Kolb & Kolb, 2017). Yet, Borkman (1999) linked these same processes to mutual aid support groups. In these settings, peers narrate and openly reflect upon their life experiences in a socially validating group, which serves as a catalyst for both the sharer's further experimentation and represents a new concrete experience for other group members. Borkman (1999) referred to such experiential knowledge and learning as the main resource and product of support groups.

12.2.3 Mutual Belonging

12.2.3.1 Attachment Theory and Presence of Social Support

Bowlby (1980) asserted that children become self-reliant, have a decreased likelihood of psychopathology, and learn to function as social support to others in their community if they develop what he coined "secure attachments" to their parental figures. Secure attachments are developed when the child's basic physiological and psychological needs are met in a loving environment. This experience then would serve as a model for relationships as the child ages into adulthood (Hazan & Shaver, 1994). Generally speaking, the presence of social support, which is fostered through appropriate attachment to others, acts as a protective factor for various mental health concerns and diagnoses, ranging from PTSD (Wang et al., 2021) to depression (Rueger et al., 2016).

12.2.3.2 Helper Therapy Principle

The helper therapy principle states that those who provide assistance to others are likely to redeem benefits themselves (Riessman, 1965). Perhaps one of the most recognizable examples of this principle is through the mutual support group, Alcoholics Anonymous, which describes in its "Big Book" that "Helping others is the foundation stone of your recovery" (Alcoholics Anonymous World Services, Inc., 2001, p. 97). Although many mechanisms can explain behavior change in Alcoholics Anonymous participants, the group is well regarded for its sense of community and reciprocal responsibility "to the alcoholic who still suffers" (Alcoholics Anonymous World Services, Inc., 2001, p. 562). This type of relationship among individuals facing shared struggles differs from the patient-professional relationship due to ethical boundaries regarding self-disclosure. Twelve-step programs have been shown to be cost-effective and produce high rates of continuous abstinence, with the potential to outperform cognitive behavioral therapy in the long term (Kelly et al., 2020).

12.3 Research Evidence

Recent studies have examined treatment programs that incorporate peer support as an adjunct to established therapies, such as medication trials or psychotherapy. Overall, the inclusion of peer support consistently improves outcomes for patients across a variety of presenting concerns. The type of support that the patient receives from the peer can influence outcomes differently. Emotional support, characterized by affirmations and the presence of a warm and empathetic person, has been associated with improved psychosocial outcomes but may not directly impact clinical outcomes (White et al., 2020). Instrumental support, where peers provide guidance and instruction on engaging in psychotherapeutic behaviors, has shown potential for improving clinical outcomes and treatment adherence (Hernandez-Tejada et al., 2021). Of course, these types of support do not have to be mutually exclusive. Elucidating what type of support is most helpful toward which end and under what context represents an area for future research. What follows are recent studies categorized in terms of populations served and the type of peer support predominantly delivered in the intervention.

12.3.1 Peer Support in Inpatient Populations

12.3.1.1 Instrumental Support

Johnson and colleagues (2018) conducted a study of adult patients from the caseloads of psychiatric crisis resolution teams in England. Those assigned to the peer support intervention group ($n = 221$) had ten sessions with a peer support worker who helped them to complete a personal recovery workbook, which guided the user through identifying personal recovery goals and developing crisis plans. The control group ($n = 220$) completed the workbook themselves. The peer intervention group evinced a significantly lower remission to acute care and significantly longer time to readmission to the hospital compared to the control group. They also reported more satisfaction with mental health services after 4 months. There were no group differences in measures of self-reported self-management, symptom severity, loneliness, and social network size following the intervention.

12.3.1.2 Emotional Support

Simpson and colleagues (2014) examined how patients in England who were in the process of discharging from acute inpatient hospitalization could benefit from a peer support program, in addition to community mental health services ($n = 23$) compared to those who received these community mental health services without a peer adjunct ($n = 23$). In this study, peer support involved a trained peer support worker (who had lived experience and had achieved significant recovery); these peers provided emotionally supportive telephone calls for up to 4 weeks after the patients' discharge. Results showed no differences between these groups on the patients' sense of loneliness and quality of life. The peer support group, however, reported a significantly higher sense of hope. The authors demonstrated a high probability of a peer support adjunct being a more cost-effective intervention compared to care as usual given this increase in hope (Simpson et al., 2014).

Mahlke and colleagues (2017) conducted a randomized controlled trial comparing peer support in addition to mental health care as usual (n = 114) to a care as usual control (n = 112) for patients with severe mental illness. Inclusion criteria encompassed diagnoses such as schizophrenia and related disorders, severe affective disorders, or personality disorders with a duration of illness of at least 2 years. In this study, peers were provided with a specific role description, asking them to use "their own experiences as a resource, to make it visible for the user [patient]," (Mahlke et al., 2017, p. 105). Results demonstrated that the peer adjunct group reported higher scores of self-efficacy at follow-up, but there were no group differences on quality of life, social functioning, or hospitalizations.

12.3.2 Peer Support in Mood Disorders

12.3.2.1 Instrumental Support

Proudfoot and colleagues (2012) examined the comparative effectiveness of an online psychoeducation intervention aimed to increase perceived control over bipolar disorder symptoms in an Australian sample. Intervention groups included those who completed the program with peer support (n = 134), alone (n = 139), and an attentional control condition, whose participants received "simple facts about bipolar disorder" and provided daily mood monitoring (n = 134). Peer support in this study included emails with coaches who had effectively managed their own bipolar condition for at least 2 years, who provided examples of how to apply the material learned in the online program to the patient's own life. All groups evidenced increased perceptions of control, decreased perceptions of stigmatization, and significant improvement of depression and anxiety symptoms. Notably, the peer support group demonstrated higher adherence to the intervention.

Seeley and colleagues (2017) also studied instrumental support in their study of peer-supported cognitive-behavioral bibliotherapy in older adults in the United States. A total of 31 adults between the ages of 55 and 96 were assigned to a group that provided peer-mentoring sessions as the group completed cognitive-behavioral self-help workbooks. Another 31 adults were randomized to a wait-list control condition. Results demonstrated feasibility, acceptability, and potential efficacy of this intervention. Although the treatment group exhibited clinically meaningful reductions in depressive symptoms, the effect did not reach statistical significance, possibly due to the small sample size.

12.3.2.2 Emotional Support

Hunkeler and colleagues (2000) studied the additive benefits of nurse telehealth care and peer support in the pharmacological treatment of depression with a selective serotonin reuptake inhibitor (SSRI) in the United States. Participants were assigned to one of three groups: SSRI only (n = 123), SSRI with nurse telehealth care (n = 117), and SSRI with nurse telehealth care and peer support (n = 62). The nursing telehealth care involved phone calls where the nurse answered medication-related questions, emphasized the importance of the medication, and offered ideas for the patient to re-engage in value-driven behavior (instrumental support). Peer support was provided by volunteers who had a successfully treated episode of major depression or dysthymia. These volunteers contacted the patients to express their interest in the patients' well-being (emotional support). Patients with any nursing telehealth care saw improvement in their depression symptoms, improved mental functioning, and higher treatment satisfaction. Peer support did not provide any additive benefits. This important study raises questions about the relative impact of instrumental vs. emotional support.

In all, recent advancements in peer supported treatments show great promise in improving outcomes for a diversity of people and presenting concerns. Patients who receive peer support report more satisfaction with their mental health care, more hope and self-efficacy, more adherence to, and perceived acceptability of the treatment, and, at times, better symptom response. Future research would benefit from clarifying which form of peer support (e.g., instrumental; emotional support) is most helpful for which type of patient and which outcome.

12.4 Clinical Considerations for Diverse Identities

12.4.1 Collectivistic and Individualistic Cultures

The idea of giving back to others and sacrificing time for others' benefit is a salient value in collectivistic cultures (Kagitcibasi, 1997). Although adherence to collectivistic versus individualistic cultural norms has not been a tested moderator in the aforementioned studies, peer support has been a successful intervention and adjunct to psychotherapy in several countries with differing cultural narratives about responsibility to others. For example, Yamaguchi and colleagues (2017) created a peer support adjunct program for patients receiving services from case managers in Tokyo. In this study, a peer support specialist who had personal experience with mental illness helped the patient learn a shared decision-making tool, which provided a framework to help patients and mental health professionals make treatment decisions together. This support is an instrumental support that helps the patient communicate their goals to a mental health professional. A total of 26 patients received peer support before a medical consultation compared to 27 patients who received medical consultation alone. The intervention group reported more positive views of their relationship with their doctor as compared to the control group.

Conceptualizing helping someone with a mental health concern as an endeavor for one person and their therapist may be uniquely individualistic. Psychologist and writer Andrew Solomon studied cross-cultural approaches to treating depression, and he quoted a Rwandan mental health worker providing services after the 1994 genocide in his acclaimed TedTalk:

> We've had a lot of trouble with Western mental health workers… they would do this bizarre thing. They didn't take people out in the sunshine where you begin to feel better. They didn't include drumming or music to get people's blood going. They didn't involve the whole community…Instead, what they did was they took people one at a time into dingy little rooms and had them talk for an hour about bad things that had happened to them…We had to ask them to leave the country (Solomon, 2013).

Engaging the community is an effective and perhaps obvious approach to help someone.

12.4.2 Sex and Gender

The extant literature, perhaps serendipitously, features samples that tend to be separated based on sex, or the studies are conducted in a context that is primarily masculine or feminine. For example, peer support in the case of maternal depression will feature a predominately female sample with cultural narratives about motherhood (Letourneau et al., 2015). Another commonly featured sample in peer support studies includes veterans. Although there are many women who served the country and are in need of services, military culture remains predominantly masculine, and only 17.3% of active-duty military members are women (Department of Defense, 2021). Future research may consider gender-related match and other sensitivities' effects on treatment outcomes.

12.4.3 Stigmatized Situations

Peer support might be particularly helpful in situations where the patient's primary concern is related to stigmatization. For example, Meng and colleagues (2023) studied peer-led, community-based support services for people living with HIV in Wuxi, China. Those who received peer support ($n = 430$) were more likely to adhere to their viral treatments, achieve viral suppression, and saw a reduction in AIDS-related mortality and all-cause mortality compared to the control group ($n = 430$). Further, in the case of substance use, the combination of 12-step mutual support and professional outpatient services shows promise, and increasing the "dose" of 12-step group activities correlates to more abstinence (Costello et al., 2019). Proudfoot and colleagues (2012) also found decreased perception of stigma in their study of bipolar disorder treatment. Receiving social support when one expects rejection due to their condition can be a transformative experiential learning opportunity. Bolstering the benefits of social support in serving stigmatized groups remains an active area of research.

12.5 Treatment Overview: Integrating Peers in Prolonged Exposure Therapy (PE) for PTSD

12.5.1 Rationale

We have presented compelling evidence regarding the significant impact of social support on individual's lives, particularly when they are facing physical or mental health challenges. To understand the rationale behind introducing peers into one of the most effective treatments for PTSD, it is useful to review components of the therapy and identify challenges a patient may encounter. PE (Foa et al., 2007) is a highly researched and recommended evidence-based treatment for posttraumatic stress disorder (PTSD; Ostacher & Cifu, 2019). PE involves four main treatment components:

1. Psychoeducation: providing information about common reactions to traumatic events, which integrates the treatment rationale,
2. In Vivo Exposures: repeated, prolonged exposures to trauma reminders, or stimuli that trigger memories of the traumatic event that, while emotionally charged, are objectively safe. These exposures are conducted outside of therapy sessions.
3. Imaginal Exposures: repeated, prolonged exposure to traumatic memories by imaginal retelling to the therapist during therapy sessions.
4. Relapse prevention strategies: implementing strategies to prevent relapse and maintain treatment gains.

The underlying theory of PE, known as emotional processing theory, proposes that traumatic events are incompletely and inaccurately encoded as "fear networks" within long term memory (Foa et al., 2006). According to this cognitive-based theory, fear networks are "pre-programmed" cognitive structures with information that makes maintaining safety efficient. These fear networks can be helpful, but they at times integrate unhelpful information that could create anxiety-based psychopathology. In individuals with PTSD, fear networks contain pathological information, such as cognitive biases that distort reality, conditioned fear responses in objectively safe situations, and subsequent avoidance that are core features of the disorder. Changing the fear structure is done by introducing corrective information which competes with and disproves the pathological information in the fear network, thus stopping the pathological conditioned fear responses. In PE, gradual exposure to situations that activate the pathological fear structure allow for such corrective information to be learned during imaginal and in vivo exposures. PE is supported by several outcome studies demonstrating large effect sizes. In a meta-analytic review, the average PE patient showed greater reduction in PTSD symptoms compared to 86% of those in control groups (Powers et al., 2010). Despite these promising outcome results, PE has a high dropout rate, which often exceeds 30% and regularly reaches 50% in some clinical settings (Hernandez-Tejada et al., 2020). Asking patients to act against the core behavioral tendency of the disorder they are experiencing (i.e., avoidance of feared stimuli) presents a significant challenge.

Patients dropping out of PE is costly because untreated PTSD has significant consequences. PTSD symptoms take on average 11.2 years to remit by themselves (Pietrzak et al., 2011) all while symptoms of other disorders typically catalyze (Zlotnick et al., 2004) and costs of related healthcare increase (Priebe et al., 2009). Introducing a peer into PE can decrease dropout or re-engage those who have left into another trial of therapy, likely through increased motivation to create and maintain a relationship with the peer (Ryan & Deci, 2000). Encouragement from the peer to either continue with PE or try PE again may be particularly meaningful for patients (Boisvert et al., 2008).

Introducing peers to specific components of PE may be more productive than other components. In researching barriers to PE completion, Hernandez-Tejada et al. (2021) found that the veterans found telepsychology to be more convenient and felt less stigmatizing than in-person therapy, but the in vivo exposures were very anxiety provoking, and the resulting avoidance was too difficult to overcome. The in vivo exposures are notably the only aspect of PE that are traditionally done independently, as the therapist provides guidance and support during the imaginal exposure and conducts the psychoeducation and relapse prevention phases. Peers in the in vivo can provide both instrumental support, such as scheduling the exposure and providing ideas that can help them complete the trial, and emotional support in the form of supportive words and a kind presence. This combination was particularly helpful for patients being treated for depression (Hunkeler et al., 2000).

12.5.2 Who Are the Peers?

Many investigators have integrated some form of peer support, usually involving specific peer training within various programs addressing a range of challenges, spanning from general community integration issues, to specific health and mental health concerns (Fortuna et al., 2022; Hernandez-Tejada et al., 2021; Shalaby & Agyapong, 2020; Ziegler et al., 2022). A recent meta-analysis of one-to-one peer support in mental health services revealed a positive impact on psychosocial outcomes but not necessarily clinical outcomes (White et al., 2020). One attempt at improving outcomes involves patient to peer "match," often in terms of basic characteristics, such as race, gender identification, or age. One form of matching peers to patients that seems particularly meaningful is when peer has "been there," meaning there is some 'shared experience' between patient and peer in the form of a similar experienced stressful or traumatic event, cultural background or upbringing, complications of a diagnosis, or treatment plan (Hundt et al., 2015). Thus, peers may not need to always share the same specific characteristics with the patient, but a common key characteristic related to the therapeutic focus may enhance the connection. Most studies of peer supported intervention, whether in the area of physical or mental health, have used peer support professionals with specific training, while a minority have opted for peers who share a common characteristic with the individual receiving treatment. For example, in the case of peer supported Prolonged Exposure for PTSD, Hernandez-Tejada et al. (2020) selected peers based on shared characteristics: peers were veterans who had a diagnosis of PTSD, and successfully completed treatment (either Cognitive Processing Therapy or Prolonged Exposure Therapy). Peers were not matched by gender or age, except for those cases of military sexual trauma (Hernandez-Tejada et al., 2020).

12.5.3 Peer Orientation and Training

When peers are introduced into the psychotherapy context, the first rule for them to understand is that they are providing support to patients: they are not psychotherapists, and their training and orientation to peer support programs does not qualify them to replace psychotherapists or conduct psychotherapy. Rather, their training emphasizes that their role is to provide hope, empowerment, and increase treatment engagement to maximize therapy benefits (Jain et al., 2016). Along these lines, Sells and colleagues (2006) matched peer case managers with clients with severe mental illness to study the quality of peer-patient relationships and patient service use and motivation. Peers in this study attended lectures about patient engagement and professional boundaries before being matched with their patients and engaged in ongoing supervision during this study.

In the case of peer support being directly integrated into PE for PTSD: once peers were selected (on the basis of having completed PE for PTSD themselves) and consented, they underwent orientation and training regarding their role within the treatment protocol (Hernandez-Tejada et al., 2021). The peer's role and assigned activities were to provide instrumental support for in vivo exposure homework; specifically, they were to meet with fellow veteran patients to help provide encouragement and problem-solving advice as the veteran completed their in vivo exposure homework. As with prior efforts, peer training emphasized boundaries and limits of responsibility but also included specific role-playing supportive language and behaviors for use during the in vivo interaction. These peers brought to bear their successful approaches to in vivo tasks that could be valuable to share with the participant in order to help them achieve their own goals. All peers in our study attended a 2-h training session. Several metaphors were effective in helping the peers better understand and adhere to their role. The veterans displayed a strong affinity to the metaphor of a "PE workout buddy." Furthermore, drawing a comparison between their role to that of a group member in group counseling emphasized the supportive nature of the relationship, as well as set a tone of respect for the patient. Most importantly, the group therapy analogy provided a clear direction toward dealing with the issue of confidentiality with which many veterans are already familiar. Moreover, the decision to limit peer compensation solely to reimbursement for travel expenses (not time), served to reinforce the boundaries between roles of peer and therapist.

12.5.4 Logistics for the Peers Helping In Vivo

In the study conducted by Hernandez-Tejada et al. (2020), clinic professionals were asked to contact those who had successfully completed PE therapy for PTSD, and who they thought would be interested in serving as peers. This program specifically targeted military veterans who had dropped out of PE, or who had indicated that they intended to drop out, but who agreed to re-engage PE treatment, this time with peer support during a limited number of in-vivo exposure homework assignments. Peers and veterans were matched based on their geographical proximity to each other. During the height of the COVID-19 pandemic, peers and veterans met via televideo, This virtual adaptation proved extremely useful in resolving scheduling and distance barriers to peer assisted treatment and was the preferred modality by both groups. Thus, televideo peer support has the potential to significantly increase access to similar peer support programs, provided that further research supports its efficacy.

Once the peer and patient were successfully matched, the project coordinator facilitated the peer to join the veteran's upcoming psychotherapy session. During this session, the therapist introduced everyone and proceeded to review the veteran's in vivo exposure hierarchy. The selected exposure activity was thoroughly discussed, including the description, the time, the location, and the parameters of the assignment, such as how long the veteran needed to remain in the exposure for it to be a useful extinction trial. When the veteran, peer, and therapist were clear on these details, the veteran and peer made arrangements to meet (in person, or with the peer virtual) at a specific time and place to conduct the exposure trial.

The peer and patient agreed to only complete activities listed in the veteran's exposure hierarchy, as discussed by all parties (patient, peer, and therapist). The exposure homework exclusively comprised clearly safe activities conducted in safe places. Confronting these triggers and subsequent anxiety in a supportive environment is the very core of both PE and of peer-accompanied in vivo exposures (as opposed to creating "safe" situations with little to no anxiety). If the peer or therapist felt that there was more than minimal risk to physical safety, regardless of the potential anxiety the veteran might experience, then the activity was not conducted.

Peers and veterans scheduled activities about three to four times a week for about a month during the joint session described above. This schedule allowed for the veteran to progress on their own independent exposure trials on days they were not with their peers, and to continue independently for the second half of PE therapy without the peer. Overtly limiting peer accompaniment from the beginning thus allowed for “phasing out” of the program, which also encouraged the veteran to become increasingly independent in their homework.

12.6 Case Vignette

What follows is a case vignette to illustrate how peer support can be integrated into the in vivo exposure component of PE. The idea of including peers in evidence-based treatment for PTSD was suggested by veterans seeking services in a test of an entirely remote PE telehealth therapy program (Hernandez-Tejada et al., 2021). These veterans indicated that, while telehealth delivery removed logistical obstacles to care, specific aspects of treatment, namely in vivo exposure homework, seemed harder to complete without any human contact related to treatment. In response, the PE + Peers program, pairing veterans who had dropped out of PE with peers who had completed this same treatment, was developed. This program has had much success in helping reduce PTSD symptoms in veterans who otherwise would not have completed treatment.

12.6.1 Background and Case Description

JL, a 34-year-old mixed-race Army Veteran, sought help at the VA PTSD clinic approximately 5 years after returning from deployment to Operation Iraqi Freedom. During his time in service, he fought in the second Battle of Falluja, facing over 40 firefights and witnessing the deaths and severe injuries of fellow soldiers. Additionally, JL was injured by an IED in a crowded market, where he lost consciousness for about 7–10 min. JL completed high school and community college. He was employed by his uncle, who was also a veteran, and who accommodated JL’s PTSD symptoms (e.g., requiring workers to call out “nail gun” before starting to use the tool so as not to startle JL). JL was married with two children, ages 7 and 11. He reports his relationship with his wife was severely strained due to his ongoing “problems” with PTSD. He felt incapable of being the father he wanted to be, citing frequent irritability and inability to attend his children’s sporting events due to the crowds.

Structured clinical assessment indicated that JL suffered from severe PTSD and depression, with concomitant functional impairment across all major life roles including spousal, parental, and vocational. He also experienced significant guilt due to having killed or injured very young fighters during his deployment. He reported that he avoided all reminders of military events, celebrations, or honors; yet at the same time, he missed the comradery he had in service. He specifically described an inability to relate to civilians who had not seen or been through conflict, but at the time of beginning the PE + Peers program, he had not reached out for any support from friends who served with him for fear of stirring up unwanted memories.

12.6.2 Symptom Presentation

JL's primary PTSD symptoms included extreme hypervigilance and heightened startle response to loud or unexpected noises, pervasive avoidance of reminders of traumatic events (e.g., avoiding markets, crowded stores, movie theatres, public sporting events, and public transportation from which escape might be delayed or difficult), and significant affective problems (e.g., sadness, guilt, feelings of worthlessness, and high levels of irritability). Reexperiencing symptoms were also pervasive, including nightmares several times each night and frequent intrusive ideation. He indicated that he was entirely unable to sleep through the night, leading to higher levels of irritability and feelings of malaise. He did not report suicidal ideation or intent, but on self-report measures of depression and suicidal ideation, he did endorse sometimes feeling that he would be better off dead. JL's symptoms started about 2 months following deployment and had consistently worsened since that time.

12.6.3 Treatment History

JL had attempted to engage in therapy for PTSD on three prior occasions. The first attempt was in group format at a Vet Center; he specifically selected the Vet Center rather than seeking services at the VA due to negative feedback he had heard from others about the VA. Regrettably, after attending just one session his symptoms worsened significantly, prompting him to discontinue further participation. One year later, at his wife's insistence, JL sought an evaluation at the VA, where he was diagnosed with PTSD and depression. He was offered evidence-based therapy which was scheduled to begin a month later. His anxiety and fear of discussing his traumatic experiences became so intense the night before the appointment that he experienced severe physical stress, including vomiting and lying on the floor, ultimately causing him to miss the session. In a subsequent attempt, about a year prior to beginning the PE + Peers program, JL tried to initiate therapy through a non-profit program that provided evidence-based treatment. Once again, he encountered severe physical stress and anxiety reactions the night before his first scheduled session of treatment, leading him to cancel this appointment. He finally presented to the VA PTSD clinic for assessment due to an ultimatum given by his wife. His wife has stated that unless he actively engages in care, she will file for divorce. His motivation is also enhanced by his desire to attend his children's school functions and reduce his overall irritability.

12.6.4 PE for PTSD with Peer Support During In Vivo Exposure

Given JL's repeated dropout from treatment, he was identified as a suitable candidate for a new program wherein another veteran peer would accompany him at in vivo exposure homework sites and engage in the exposure trials with him 2–3 times per week for 2–3 weeks, starting the third session of treatment after the in vivo hierarchy was created with his therapist. He enthusiastically endorsed this option for treatment, stating that "this is how we would do something in the Army." He was made clearly aware that the program was extremely time and frequency limited, and to ensure a successful transition and completion of treatment, he was encouraged to seek out other sources of social support available to him in his environment once he became accustomed to the exposure homework assisted by the peer. Importantly, JL's job required extensive travel time, it was agreed that some peer-accompanied in vivo homework assignments were to be facilitated virtually using televideo platforms. In these instances, the peer would observe and interact with JL during the exposure trial, providing support and assistance remotely.

At the end of the third session, the peer joined the therapist and JL via televideo. They reviewed and discussed the in vivo exposure hierarchy, along with specific selection of homework assignments for the week, three of which would be joined by the peer. As a large and routinely crowded store was located centrally between JL and the peer, they decided to meet there for in vivo exposure to crowds. This exposure focus was graded insofar as initial trials involved going to the parking lot, parking, and walking up to the front door on a weekday before 10 am (i.e., on a day and at a time before it became too crowded), followed by going into the store near the door, then further inside away from the door, for extended periods until anxiety levels diminished. Grading also involved going to the store in the afternoon when it was more crowded, and on a weekend, and repeating the steps above (parking lot, front door outside, front door inside, further into the store). JL was instructed to move through the hierarchy, and that the peer would offer advice and support while he was doing so.

For the first two assignments, JL and the peer met at a large store in person, and the third assignment featured the peer joining via televideo on JL's smartphone. On the day of the first exposure, JL called the peer to cancel, saying he just was not feeling up to it. The peer suggested they just drive there and see how he felt when he was there, so at least he would feel like he tried. The peer let him know that he had already canceled his morning plans to do this, and framed it as "the only worthwhile thing I really had planned." JL agreed to this, and after talking to the peer, actually suggested that they try to go in the door. "I haven't been inside this store since the first week I was back, and that time, I ended up leaving a bunch of stuff in my cart and jogging the hell out with my kid crying that we were leaving his toys. I felt so bad but I just couldn't deal with the crowds and the noise.... But here I am. It's not crowded but it's not empty, and for some reason I'm feeling ok.... I'm stressed and I want to leave, but I'm ok with it." The peer suggested they stay for a while and just see how things progressed, which they did for about 90 min in total.

The next assignment was at the same store, 2 days later. Once again, JL called the peer a half hour before they were to meet to call it off, to which the peer responded that he was already on his way. JL stated that he didn't want the peer to go through all that trouble for no reason and said he would meet him there. This time when he arrived, JL suggested they do a little shopping, as his wife told him that if he were already going to the store that he could pick up some things for her. JL was surprised that the store was much more crowded this time, but the peer suggested they push through to see if shopping gave him something to focus on and also so that he would not disappoint his wife. JL agreed and successfully found the things his wife wanted, albeit avoiding aisles or locations that were crowded. When the peer noticed JL was shifting around the shopping list to get items in sections that had no people, he jokingly stated that he knew what was up, and that for the next two items, they were going to go "looking for trouble" in the crowded aisles and challenged JL to push it. JL agreed and reported that he was surprised that it was not as overwhelming as he thought: "It was horrible, yes, I was stressed out of my mind for a few minutes, but it was possible. I did it, and we stayed in those areas until I got a little used to it, and then I started to actually get bored."

For the third assignment, JL and the peer had agreed to meet virtually, with the peer calling him on his phone's televideo app when JL was at the exposure site. The peer suggested that JL try another store closer to him as the one they were going to seemed to be "getting too easy for him." This closer store was larger and likely more crowded, but JL's confidence was tremendously increased. JL initiated the televideo session from the parking lot of the store. His wife had given him another shopping list, but JL felt overwhelmed at the thought of going deep into a new store. The peer suggested he put the list in his back pocket, and instead start over at the beginning of the hierarchy and move through it as he got used to each one, rather than starting so intensely. JL did this along with the peer on televideo, and was surprised that after about 5 min of standing inside the store near the door, he was no longer anxious and started to get bored again. At this point, the peer suggested that he keep going, noticed on the video feed that there were people near a sample give-away stand, and said, "JL, maybe you should go over there and get some free food as you are already doing the exposure homework. It'd be a twofer: therapy and breakfast." JL laughed and said, "Well, it is breakfast sausage they're giving away, so yes, I think I will." JL then decided that he was going to get his wife's shopping list done, and with the peer on televideo, completed both his therapy homework and his errands.

After the first week of 3 peer assisted exposure homework trials, JL attended his next PE therapy session. The therapist asked JL how the exposure homework with the peer went and if he wanted to continue with the peer (the therapist also asked the peer this question, separately). JL was extremely happy to report that the exposure homework, "sucked hard, but that having a guy who had also been through it over there doing these damn homework assignments with me made it doable, and actually I sort of enjoyed the last part of the homework on the second day, just hanging out in the store shooting the shit with him." The therapist pointed out that anxiety and enjoyment did not need to be mutually exclusive and educated JL on the point that if he stayed in these anxiety provoking situations, he would become less anxious, and he might actually be able to enjoy himself, despite the residual anxiety. When the therapist asked JL if things were any different or less useful when the peer was with him on televideo, instead of in person, JL responded, "To tell you the truth doc, no, not at all. He was basically there with me. He could see and hear what I could see and hear, and this is what made him tell me to go get some free breakfast sausage. I really think that it's a lot more convenient for the peers this way, but of course, it was nice to start in person." Following this quick debrief, imaginal exposure was conducted per protocol, followed by determining the next week's in vivo exposure homework assignment. JL and his peer met twice that next week, once in person and once virtually. For the third and final week with a peer, they decided to change to the second hierarchy involving crowded school events, as JL's nephew had a football game that weekend, and a homecoming parade the day before. These were both attended virtually by the peer, and JL reported that after about 15 min, he let the peer go each time because he was actually focusing on the events around him and felt guilty for not interacting with the peer. The peer insisted that this was great, and that JL was in the moment and in the situation with his family, and that this was a clear indication he was ready to handle these exposures on his own.

The next week the therapist prepared JL for engaging in the in vivo exposure homework on his own, suggesting he move to one easier, previously practiced item on each of the exposure hierarchies he was working on. JL reported that he did this for the first one, quickly got bored, and that he had the peer's voice in his head telling him to go ahead and push a little harder, so that's what he did. JL stated, "I was actually a little worried I wouldn't be able to do it without my guy there with me, but I think the fact that we had a few homeworks with the peer on Facetime got me used to doing it a little bit more on my own. I had to push through my initial anxiety, and then it was just like normal. I felt like shit when it started, got bored after 5 min, and pushed myself harder until I got used to it. Pretty basic now." JL completed 12 sessions of PE therapy and did not meet criteria for PTSD at either the conclusion of treatment or at the 3-month follow-up assessment. He expressed interest in serving as a peer himself, stating that he needed to do this for the next brother down the line. Indeed, JL transitioned into the peer role, helping several other veterans.

12.7 Conclusion

Incorporating peer support into mental health care, either in a generally supportive manner, or specifically to achieve treatment homework goals as demonstrated in the case presented in this chapter, represents an innovative approach to augmenting treatment. The latter case approach leverages the veteran patients' military background and foster a supportive environment that enhances engagement in therapy and promotes successful clinical outcomes. By incorporating peers, the program sought to create a sense of understanding and empathy while tackling the patients' PTSD symptoms through therapy. The use of virtual platforms also provided flexibility in accommodating patients' work-related travel and/or Covid-19 related changes in their environment, ensuring that they could maintain consistent progress throughout treatment. The outcomes of this peer supported treatment for PTSD may hold promise for addressing other mental health conditions, and could serve as an effective option to bolster treatment engagement for patients facing difficulties or lacking motivation to complete the tasks between sessions. Certainly, this area presents significant opportunities for further research and practical application.

References

Alcoholics Anonymous World Services, Inc. (Ed.). (2001). *Alcoholics anonymous* (4th ed.). Alcoholics Anonymous World Services, Inc.

Bandura, A. (1977). *Social learning theory*. Prentice Hall.

Barton, J., & Henderson, J. (2016). Peer support and youth recovery: A brief review of the theoretical underpinnings and evidence. *Canadian Journal of Family and Youth, 8*, 1–17. https://doi.org/10.29173/cjfy27140

Boisvert, R. A., Martin, L. M., Grosek, M., & Claire, A. J. (2008). Effectiveness of a peer-support community in addiction recovery: Participation as intervention. *Occupational Therapy International, 15*(4), 205–220. https://doi.org/10.1002/oti.257

Borkman, T. J. (1999). *Understanding self-help/mutual aid: Experiential learning in the commons*. Rutgers University Press.

Bowlby, J. (1980). *Attachment and loss* (Vol. 3. Loss). Basic Books.

Costello, M. J., Li, Y., Remers, S., MacKillop, J., Sousa, S., Ropp, C., Roth, D., Weiss, M., & Rush, B. (2019). Effects of 12-step mutual support and professional outpatient services on short-term substance use outcomes among adults who received inpatient treatment. *Addictive Behaviors, 98*, 106055. https://doi.org/10.1016/j.addbeh.2019.106055

Department of Defense. (2021). *2021 Demographics: Profile of the military community*. https://download.militaryonesource.mil/12038/MOS/Reports/2021-demographics-report.pdf

Festinger, L. (1954). A theory of social comparison process. *Human Relations, 7*, 117–140. https://doi.org/10.1177/001872675400700202

Foa, E. B., Huppert, J. D., & Cahill, S. P. (2006). Emotional processing theory: An update. In B. O. Rothbaum (Ed.), *Pathological anxiety: Emotional processing in etiology and treatment* (pp. 3–24). The Guilford Press.

Foa, E. B., Hembree, E. A., & Rothbaum, B. O. (2007). *Prolonged exposure therapy for PTSD: Emotional processing of traumatic experiences, therapist guide*. Oxford University Press.

Fortuna, K. L., DiMilia, P. R., Lohman, M. C., Bruce, M. L., Zubritsky, C. D., Halaby, M. R., Walker, R. M., Brooks, J. M., & Bartels, S. J. (2018). Feasibility, acceptability, and preliminary effectiveness of a peer-delivered and technology supported self-management intervention for older adults with serious mental illness. *The Psychiatric Quarterly, 89*(2), 293–305. https://doi.org/10.1007/s11126-017-9534-7

Fortuna, K. L., Brooks, J. M., Umucu, E., Walker, R., & Chow, P. I. (2019). Peer support: A human factor to enhance engagement in digital health behavior change interventions. *Journal of Technology in Behavioral Science, 4*(2), 152–161. https://doi.org/10.1007/s41347-019-00105-x

Fortuna, K. L., Solomon, P., & Rivera, J. (2022). An update of peer support/peer provided services underlying processes, benefits, and critical ingredients. *The Psychiatric Quarterly, 93*(2), 571–586. https://doi.org/10.1007/s11126-022-09971-w

Gartner, A. J., & Riessman, F. (1982). Self-help and mental health. *Psychiatric Services, 33*(8), 631–635. https://doi.org/10.1176/ps.33.8.631

Hazan, C., & Shaver, P. R. (1994). Attachment as an organizational framework for research on close relationships. *Psychological Inquiry, 5*(1), 1–22. https://doi.org/10.1207/s15327965pli0501_1

Hernandez-Tejada, M. A., Muzzy, W., Price, M., Hamski, S., Hart, S., Foa, E., & Acierno, R. (2020). Peer support during in vivo exposure homework to reverse attrition from prolonged exposure therapy for posttraumatic stress disorder (PTSD): Description of a randomized controlled trial. *Trials, 21*(1), 366. https://doi.org/10.1186/s13063-020-04302-5

Hernandez-Tejada, M. A., Acierno, R., & Sánchez-Carracedo, D. (2021). Re-engaging dropouts of prolonged exposure for PTSD delivered via home-based telemedicine or in person: Satisfaction with veteran-to-veteran support. *The Journal of Behavioral Health Services and Research, 48*, 171–182. https://doi.org/10.1007/s11414-020-09734-0

Hundt, N. E., Robinson, A., Arney, J., Stanley, M. A., & Cully, J. A. (2015). Veterans' perspectives on benefits and drawbacks of peer support for posttraumatic stress disorder. *Military Medicine, 180*(8), 851–856. https://doi.org/10.7205/MILMED-D-14-00536

Hunkeler, E. M., Meresman, J. F., Hargreaves, W. A., Fireman, B., Berman, W. H., Kirsch, A. J., Groebe, J., Hurt, S. W., Braden, P., Getzell, M., Feigenbaum, P. A., Peng, T., & Salzer, M. (2000). Efficacy of nurse telehealth care and peer support in augmenting treatment of depression in primary care. *Archives of Family Medicine, 9*, 700–708. https://doi.org/10.1001/archfami.9.8.700

Jain, S., McLean, C., Adler, E. P., & Rosen, C. S. (2016). Peer support and outcome for veterans with posttraumatic stress disorder (PTSD) in a residential rehabilitation program. *Community Mental Health Journal, 52*(8), 1089–1092. https://doi.org/10.1007/s10597-015-9982-1

Johnson, S., Lamb, D., Marston, L., Osborn, D., Mason, O., Henderson, C., Ambler, G., Milton, A., Davidson, M., Christoforou, M., Sullivan, S., Hunter, R., Hindle, D., Paterson, B., Leverton, M., Piotrowski, J., Forsyth, R., Mosse, L., Goater, N., et al. (2018). Peer-supported self-management for people discharged from a mental health crisis team: A randomized controlled trial. *The Lancet, 392*(10145), 409–418. https://doi.org/10.1016/S0140-6736(18)31470-3

Kagitcibasi, C. (1997). Individualism and collectivism. In M. H. S. J. W. Berry & C. Kagitcibasi (Eds.), *Handbook of cross-cultural psychology* (Vol. 3. Social behavior and applications). Allyn & Bacon.

Kelly, J. F., Humphreys, K., & Ferri, M. (2020). Alcoholics anonymous and other 12-step programs for alcohol use disorder. *Cochrane Database of Systematic Reviews, 3*, CD012880. https://doi.org/10.1002/14651858.CD012880.pub2

Kolb, D. A. (1984). *Experiential learning: Experience as the source of learning and development* (Vol. 1). Prentice-Hall.

Kolb, A. Y., & Kolb, D. A. (2017). Experiential learning theory as a guide for experiential educators in higher education. *Experiential Learning & Teaching in Higher Education, 1*, 7–44. https://nsuworks.nova.edu/elthe/vol1/iss1/7

Letourneau, N., Secco, L., Colpitts, J., Aldous, S., Stewart, M., & Dennis, C.-L. (2015). Quasi-experimental evaluation of a telephone-based peer support intervention for maternal depression. *Journal of Advanced Nursing, 71*(7), 1587–1599. https://doi.org/10.1111/jan.12622

Mahlke, C. I., Priebe, S., Heumann, K., Daubmann, A., Wegscheider, K., & Bock, T. (2017). Effectiveness of one-to-one peer support for patients with severe mental illness – A randomized controlled trial. *European Psychiatry, 42*, 103–110. https://doi.org/10.1016/j.eurpsy.2016.12.007

Meng, X., Yin, H., Ma, W., Gu, J., Lu, Z., Fitzpatrick, T., & Zou, H. (2023). Peer-led community-based support services and HIV treatment outcomes among people living with HIV in Wuxi, China: Propensity score-matched analysis of surveillance data from 2006 to 2021. *JMIR Public Health and Surveillance, 9*, e43635. https://doi.org/10.2196/43635

Miller, P. H. (2010). *Theories of developmental psychology*. Macmillan.

Ostacher, M. J., & Cifu, A. S. (2019). Management of posttraumatic stress disorder. *JAMA, 321*(2), 200–201. https://doi.org/10.1001/jama.2018.19290

Pietrzak, R. H., Goldstein, R. B., Southwick, S. M., & Grant, B. F. (2011). Prevalence and Axis I comorbidity of full and partial posttraumatic stress disorder in the United States: Results from Wave 2 of the National Epidemiologic Survey on alcohol and related conditions. *Journal of Anxiety Disorders, 25*, 456–465. https://doi.org/10.1016/j.janxdis.2010.11.010

Powers, M. B., Halpern, J. M., Ferenschak, M. P., Gillihan, S. J., & Foa, E. B. (2010). A meta-analytic review of prolonged exposure for posttraumatic stress disorder. *Clinical Psychology Review, 30*(6), 635–641. https://doi.org/10.1016/j.cpr.2010.04.007

Priebe, S., Matanov, A., Janković Gavrilović, J., McCrone, P., Ljubotina, D., Knezević, G., Kucukalić, A., Franciskovič, T., & Schützwohl, M. (2009). Consequences of untreated post-traumatic stress disorder following war in former Yugoslavia: Morbidity, subjective quality of life, and care costs. *Croatian Medical Journal, 50*(5), 465–475. https://doi.org/10.3325/cmj.2009.50.465

Proudfoot, J., Parker, G., Manicavasagar, V., Hadzi-Pavlovic, D., Whitton, A., Nicholas, J., Smith, M., & Burckhardt, R. (2012). Effects of adjunctive peer support on perceptions of illness control and understanding in an online psychoeducation program for bipolar disorder: A randomized controlled trial. *Journal of Affective Disorders, 142*, 98–105. https://doi.org/10.1016/j.jad.2012.04.007

Riessman, F. (1965). The "helper" therapy principle. *Social Work, 10*(2), 27–32.

Rueger, S. Y., Malecki, C. K., Pyun, Y., Aycock, C., & Coyle, S. (2016). A meta-analytic review of the association between perceived social support and depression in childhood and adolescence. *Psychological Bulletin, 142*(10), 1017–1067. https://doi.org/10.1037/bul0000058

Ryan, R. M., & Deci, E. L. (2000). Self-determination theory and the facilitation of intrinsic motivation, social development, and well-being. *American Psychologist, 55*, 68–78. https://doi.org/10.1037/0003-066X.55.1.68

Salzer, M. S., Darr, N., Calhoun, G., Boyer, W., Loss, R. E., Goessel, J., Schwenk, E., & Brusilovskiy, E. (2013). Benefits of working as a certified peer specialist: Results from a statewide survey. *Psychiatric Rehabilitation Journal, 36*(3), 219–221. https://doi.org/10.1037/prj0000016

Seeley, J. R., Manitsas, T., & Gau, J. M. (2017). Feasibility study of a peer-facilitated low intensity cognitive-behavioral intervention for mild to moderate depression and anxiety in older adults. *Aging Mental Health, 21*(9), 968–974. https://doi.org/10.1080/13607863.2016.1186152

Sells, D., Davidson, L., Jewell, C., Falzer, P., & Rowe, M. (2006). The treatment relationship in peer-based and regular case management for clients with severe mental illness. *Psychiatric Services, 57*(8), 1179–1184.

Shalaby, R. A. H., & Agyapong, V. I. O. (2020). Peer support in mental health: Literature review. *JMIR Mental Health, 7*(6), e15572. https://doi.org/10.2196/15572

Simpson, A., Flood, C., Rowe, J., Quigley, J., Henry, S., Hall, C., Evans, R., Sherman, P., & Bowers, L. (2014). Results of a pilot randomized controlled trial to measure the clinical and cost effectiveness of peer support in increasing hope and quality of life in mental health patients discharged from hospital in the UK. *BMC Psychiatry, 14*, 30. https://doi.org/10.1186/1471-244X-14-30

Solomon, P. (2004). Peer support/peer provided services underlying processes, benefits, and critical ingredients. *Psychiatric Rehabilitation Journal, 27*(4), 392–401. https://doi.org/10.2975/27.2004.392.401

Solomon, A. (2013, December). *Depression, the secret we share* [Video]. Ted Conferences. https://www.ted.com/talks/andrew_solomon_depression_the_secret_we_share?language=en

Wang, Y., Chung, M. C., Wang, N., Yu, X., & Kenardy, J. (2021). Social support and posttraumatic stress disorder: A meta-analysis of longitudinal studies. *Clinical Psychology Review, 85*, 101998. https://doi.org/10.1016/j.cpr.2021.101998

White, S., Foster, R., Marks, J., Morshead, R., Goldsmith, L., Barlow, S., Sin, J., & Gillard, S. (2020). The effectiveness of one-to-one peer support in mental health services: A systematic review and meta-analysis. *BMC Psychiatry, 20*, 534. https://doi.org/10.1186/s12888-020-02923-3

Yamaguchi, S., Taneda, A., Matsunaga, A., Sasaki, N., Mizuno, M., Sawada, Y., Sakata, M., Fukui, S., Hisanaga, F., Bernick, P., & Ito, J. (2017). Efficacy of a peer-led, recovery-oriented shared decision-making system: A pilot randomized controlled trial. *Psychiatric Services, 68*(12), 1307–1311. https://doi.org/10.1176/appi.ps.201600544

Ziegler, E., Hill, J., Lieske, B., Klein, J., & dem, O. V., & Kofahl, C. (2022). Empowerment in cancer patients: Does peer support make a difference? A systematic review. *Psycho-Oncology, 31*(5), 683–704.

Zlotnick, C., Rodriguez, B. F., Weisberg, R. B., Bruce, S. E., Spencer, M. A., Culpepper, L., & Keller, M. B. (2004). Chronicity in posttraumatic stress disorder and predictors of the course of posttraumatic stress disorder among primary care patients. *Journal of Nervous and Mental Disease, 192*(2), 153–159. https://doi.org/10.1097/01.nmd.0000110287.16635.8e

Chapter 13
Peer-Supported School-Based Treatment for Adolescents

Samantha Coyle-Eastwick, Jeremy K. Fox, Talita Ahmed, Liora Steinberg, Avi Kalver, and Carrie Masia Warner

13.1 Introduction

Adolescence marks a critical transition during which social development occurs. During this period, adolescents spend the majority of their time with peers, play a more active role in the selection of their friend groups, and look to their peers as key sources of social support (Brown & Larson, 2009; Coyle & Malecki, 2018; La Greca & Lopez, 1998). Not surprisingly, positive relationships with peers are associated with several indicators of adjustment, such as self-esteem, academic performance, and social functioning (Parker et al., 2006; Wentzel, 2009). Thus, understanding ways to facilitate the development of healthy peer relationships is essential.

In addition, likely due to increased academic and social pressures, adolescence is the peak time for the onset of anxiety disorders. In fact, research indicates that approximately 32% of youth will meet diagnostic criteria for an anxiety disorder by the age of 18, making anxiety among the most prevalent mental health conditions in youth (Merikangas et al., 2010). This is concerning, as anxiety disorders are associated with significant negative interpersonal and academic outcomes and increased risk for other mental health difficulties, such as depression, suicidality, and substance use (Balázs et al., 2013; Buckner et al., 2021; Cummings et al., 2014; de Lijster et al., 2018).

Despite the high prevalence and significant impairment associated with anxiety disorders, the majority of children with significant anxiety go unidentified and untreated (Masia Warner & Fox, 2012). Understanding ways to address the unmet

S. Coyle-Eastwick · J. K. Fox · T. Ahmed · L. Steinberg · A. Kalver · C. M. Warner (✉)
Psychology Department, Montclair State University, Montclair, NJ, USA
e-mail: coyles@montclair.edu; foxjer@montclair.edu; ahmedt11@montclair.edu; kalvera1@montclair.edu; masiac@montclair.edu

L. Reuman, J. Thompson-Hollands (eds.), *Enhancing CBT Through Family and Peer Engagement*, CBT: Science Into Practice, https://doi.org/10.1007/978-3-031-74838-7_13

mental health needs of anxious youth is critical. Delivering evidence-based interventions, such as cognitive-behavioral therapy (CBT), in the school setting may be an effective strategy to meet this need. Indeed, research suggests that school-based CBT is effective in treating anxiety disorders in youth (Ginsburg & Drake, 2002; Masia Warner et al., 2016; Sanchez et al., 2018). In addition to providing unparalleled access to youth that can support early identification and intervention efforts, the school environment allows for the implementation of interventions that can incorporate peers into treatment. Youth with anxiety often experience significant peer difficulties, and their fears commonly occur in school and are connected to peer interactions (Blöte et al., 2015). Thus, school-based interventions that facilitate positive peer relationships in an authentic group setting may be especially supportive (Masia Warner et al., 2005, 2007).

This chapter addresses the role of peers in treating anxiety disorders in youth, with a focus on the benefits of including peers in CBT interventions at school. One specific school-based intervention that emphasizes peer involvement is described, along with evidence to support its effectiveness. Considerations for implementation of interventions with diverse youth are discussed, as well as a case example highlighting the benefits of including peers in CBT.

13.2 Treatment Overview: Rationale for Peer-Based Treatments

13.2.1 Anxiety and Peer Relationships/Social Functioning

Significant work highlights that youth with anxiety disorders experience impaired peer relationships (de Lijster et al., 2018). Much of this research has focused on social anxiety, given that its related impairment centers around social interactions. Youth with greater social anxiety symptoms report that they spend less time with their peers, have less intimate and lower-quality peer relationships, and fewer positive interactions than their less anxious peers (Biggs et al., 2012; Chiu et al., 2021; La Greca & Lopez, 1998; Motoca et al., 2012). Positive and supportive peer relationships are consistently associated with fewer social anxiety symptoms (Coyle & Malecki, 2018; Coyle et al., 2021), and longitudinal research has suggested that peer difficulties can increase social anxiety symptoms over time (Tillfors et al., 2012).

Anxiety disorders are also associated with increased risk for negative interpersonal experiences, such as bullying-victimization (Coyle et al., 2021; Spence et al., 2022; Stapinski et al., 2014; Storch & Masia-Warner, 2004). For example, one meta-analysis by Chiu et al. (2021) found bidirectional associations between social anxiety symptoms and peer rejection/victimization. Victimization experiences can increase risk for social avoidance behaviors, which may also limit the frequency of positive peer interactions and serve as a contributor to greater anxiety over time (Biggs et al., 2012; Storch & Masia-Warner, 2004). Further, victimization may also impact how youth perceive more positive aspects of peer relationships. For instance, Coyle et al. (2021) found that peer victimization increased risk for anxiety by eroding perceived support from peers. In sum, it is clear that both positive and negative peer experiences are implicated in the development and maintenance of social anxiety.

Difficulties in peer relationships are also evident for youth with other anxiety disorders (e.g., generalized anxiety, specific phobias; Early et al., 2017). For example, one study of adolescents between the ages of 12 and 14 explored differences in social functioning between youth with social anxiety disorder (SAD) ($n = 59$), other anxiety disorders (e.g., generalized anxiety disorder [GAD; $n = 95$]), and a community-based sample of youth without any anxiety disorder ($n = 116$). Results of this study indicated that although youth with SAD had the greatest deficits, perceived peer acceptance was also lower among youth with other anxiety disorders when compared to non-anxious peers (Early et al., 2017). Moreover, research has demonstrated that youth with generalized anxiety have fewer friends (Scharfstein et al., 2011) and greater emotional reactivity to peer interactions than non-anxious youth (Herres et al., 2018). Further, one large meta-analysis including 165 empirical studies found evidence that the negative impact of victimization is not unique to social anxiety, but extends to other anxiety and related disorders (Moore et al., 2017). Together, these findings highlight the important role of peers in relation to anxiety disorders.

13.2.2 Anxiety and Social Skills in Adolescence

Social struggles for youth with anxiety may be partially related to deficits in social skills (Beidel et al., 2007; Inderbitzen-Nolan et al., 2007; Miers et al., 2009; Scharfstein et al., 2011). Observational studies indicate that youth with social anxiety exhibit lower levels of friendliness, assertiveness, and overall social performance compared to non-anxious peers (Beidel et al., 2007; Inderbitzen-Nolan et al., 2007), and other research has extended these deficits to youth with GAD (e.g., Scharfstein & Beidel, 2015).

Deficits in social skills may be intertwined with behavioral and cognitive experiences associated with anxiety. Youth who experience social anxiety and avoid social situations restrict their opportunities to practice social skills with peers and build social confidence, which can further exacerbate peer relationship difficulties (Biggs et al., 2012; Miers & Warner, 2023). For example, in a sample of over 300 youth ages 8–12, social anxiety symptoms were associated with lower teacher-reported social skills, and social skills mediated the association between social anxiety and peer acceptance (Greco & Morris, 2005). Additionally, deficits in social skills may be related to negative perceptual biases held by anxious youth. For instance, socially anxious individuals tend to report their social skills as lower compared to ratings by independent observers (Cartwright-Hatton et al., 2003, 2005). These findings are in line with cognitive-behavioral models of social anxiety, which suggest that anxious youth underestimate their social capabilities; in turn, these negative biases are thought to impair social performance and contribute to anxiety symptoms (e.g., Leigh & Clark, 2018; Rapee & Heimberg, 1997). One of the goals of anxiety treatment is to lessen negative expectations of social competence and skills (i.e. improve social self-efficacy) by exposing youth to feared situations and allowing them to experience successful social interactions. Therefore, interventions that involve peers in naturalistic settings may be a promising avenue for addressing social anxiety and building social confidence, as well as generalizing these gains to the real world (Beidel et al., 2005; Miers & Warner, 2023).

13.2.3 School Based Cognitive Behavioral Therapy for Anxiety in Youth

CBT has been widely supported in treating anxiety disorders in children and adolescents (Beidel et al., 2000; Scaini et al., 2016). Although CBT can be delivered effectively in an individual or group format (Silverman et al., 2008), evidence suggests that recovery rates following CBT are lower for youth with a primary diagnosis of social anxiety compared to those with other anxiety disorders (Evans et al., 2021). It is possible that group-based treatment that incorporates peers and explicitly targets feared situations and repeated exposure to peer interactions may be more effective for socially anxious youth (Ryan & Masia Warner, 2012; Scaini et al., 2016). Youth with anxiety often feel embarrassed by their fears, worry about being rejected by others, and believe that others do not share their social difficulties; thus, group-based CBT where youth have opportunities to share their feelings and experiences with peers facing similar challenges may help adolescents feel less isolated and help normalize experiences of anxiety (Masia Warner et al., 2018). Further, implementing CBT in a group format allows socially anxious students to practice important social skills and engage in exposure exercises in a safe environment (Masia Warner et al., 2005; Ryan & Masia Warner et al., 2012; Silverman et al., 2019). Groups conducted in the school setting can be especially effective, as many common situational triggers of fears and worries for anxious youth occur at school (e.g., asking questions during class, eating lunch with peers, making friends, and giving presentations; Blöte et al., 2015). School-based CBT provides opportunities for youth with social anxiety to engage in scaffolded exposures to these fears in the environment where they occur (Masia Warner et al., 2007, 2016). Groups at school may be more helpful in generalizing and maintaining treatment outcomes to other settings and may help build positive relationships with peers at school that can be maintained after treatment (Masia Warner et al., 2005; Ryan & Masia Warner, 2012; Silverman et al., 2019).

In addition, clinical and community settings must address challenges to organizing and implementing groups, such as variability in student needs, availability and scheduling of groups, and the developmental level of children seeking treatment

(Masia Warner et al., 2005, 2016). The school setting can uniquely address these challenges. For example, the intervention can be built into the school day, which helps address scheduling and time constraints. Further, schools have unparalleled access to a large number of children, which facilitates greater identification of youth who need support but may not be identified in other settings. The school setting increases the ease in which students are matched or grouped together according to their needs (Masia Warner et al., 2005, 2016). Group treatment is also a cost-effective approach to addressing the mental health needs of a large number of youth (Ryan & Masia Warner, 2012).

Furthermore, school-based interventions are ideally suited to address the barriers to treatment commonly reported within the field. For instance, issues that often impede utilization of community-based services, such as financial costs, insurance coverage, transportation, and childcare needs, are not concerns for school-based services; Families are not charged for services received in the school setting, and since students are already in school, there is no need to travel to therapy sessions at inconvenient times (Bannon Jr. & McKay, 2005). School-based group treatment may also help address stigma, a common barrier to engagement in community-based mental health services, by promoting groups as a routine part of activities and services offered by schools (Masia Warner et al., 2018). Thus, the school setting seems to be an ideal environment to enhance prevention and intervention efforts targeting anxiety while also capitalizing on peer involvement in treatment.

13.2.4 Skills for Academic and Social Success (SASS; Masia Warner et al., 2005)

Because of the benefits of delivering support in the school setting, researchers have been interested in developing CBT-based interventions for schools. One such intervention targeting SAD that has been supported in the literature is *Skills for Academic and Social Success* (SASS; Masia Warner et al., 2005). Adapted from Social Effectiveness Therapy for Children (SET-C; Beidel et al., 2000), a group intervention for use in clinical settings, SASS was modified for delivery in the school environment by school counselors (Masia Warner et al., 2016). SASS includes 12 group sessions lasting approximately 40 min. Each session coincides with the typical length of one class period and helps enable delivery in the school setting. The group sessions consist of one psychoeducation session, one realistic thinking session, four social skills training sessions, five exposure sessions, and one session on relapse prevention. Importantly, SASS utilizes peers within the groups, as well as prosocial peer assistants, to help facilitate social activities and address social challenges reported by youth throughout the intervention. A series of four social events are held outside of the group to facilitate generalization of skills in authentic social settings. Finally, the intervention includes individual sessions, booster sessions, two parent meetings, as well as meetings with teachers as needed.

13.2.4.1 Psychoeducation and Realistic Thinking

The first two group sessions focus on psychoeducation and realistic thinking. The psychoeducation session begins with an explanation of anxiety and highlights that anxiety is a universal process, which is meant to help normalize the experiences of students in the group. The group setting also helps students understand that others have similar worries and helps facilitate discussion and group participation among group members who may be more reserved initially. During this session, the connection between the physical, behavioral, and cognitive symptoms of SAD are discussed, including how these three factors maintain symptoms of anxiety. Group leaders ask group members to provide specific examples from their own experiences and encourage more hesitant students to engage by asking them whether they have had similar experiences to those who are willing to share, which can help build comfort and establish connections within the group.

The second session focuses on realistic thinking, where group leaders discuss common thinking traps associated with social anxiety, such as how socially anxious individuals overestimate the negative outcomes of a social situation (e.g., being perceived as "dumb" for making a mistake during a class presentation) or adopt rigid social rules (e.g., thinking they can't go to a friend's party with their sports team friends because they are not on the team). Group leaders challenge these negative assumptions and help students evaluate their social experiences more realistically. By challenging these thought patterns and replacing them with more reasonable ones, it can increase the likelihood that youth will approach anxiety-provoking situations rather than avoid them. Capitalizing on the group setting where peers can interact and learn from each other, group participants are able to discuss their feelings in a safe environment and begin to think about ways to address their challenges in this setting. Since youth often have a hard time identifying their negative thought patterns on their own, the group format can help facilitate conversations that may help youth better identify their own thinking traps and relate to their peers in the group who report similar difficulties (Masia Warner et al., 2018).

13.2.4.2 Social Skills Training

SASS targets four specific social skills as part of this treatment: (1) initiating conversations, (2) maintaining conversations and establishing friendships, (3) listening and remembering, and (4) assertiveness. Each skill addresses a deficit that is common among socially anxious teens and tends to impede their social interactions (Masia Warner et al., 2018). Each session begins with an overview of the skill, as well as a discussion about why it is important and how it can help promote effective social interactions. Next, group leaders model the skill for students and break down the steps for students to learn, followed by role-play activities in which students practice using each skill with their peers in the group. Throughout the social skills sessions, students participate in at least two role-plays.

Peer involvement in the social skills group sessions is especially valuable. Rather than role playing with an adult counselor or therapist, social skills training with peers allows for repeated practice using skills with individuals similar to their peers in social situations (Masia Warner et al., 2018). Adults have less knowledge about peer culture and therefore may find it more difficult to understand the most relevant topics or interests for youth during role-play exercises. Role-playing with adults can also feel inauthentic, and youth who are successful with adults may discount their success in those interactions because of their adult or therapist status, making it less likely that those skills will generalize to real life situations (Masia Warner et al., 2018). Thus, peer support from other students participating in the group and peer assistants can address this limitation and facilitate repeated practice using skills with varied peers. Role plays are selected based on encounters that students in the group are likely to experience, which may build social confidence when presented with similar situations in their day to day life. In addition to practicing the skills, group leaders also provide feedback to help address some of the non-verbal behaviors (e.g., avoiding eye contact, low tone of voice) that often impede social interactions and make anxious youth appear unfriendly or disengaged (Masia Warner et al., 2018). After reviewing and practicing the four skills, students are provided with homework assignments in which they are expected to practice using the skills outside of the group.

13.2.4.3 Facing Your Fears: Exposure Sessions

Exposure is a critical component of anxiety treatment. Five exposure sessions are included in SASS to allow youth to gradually engage in interactions that they have typically avoided. Explaining the rationale of exposure (i.e. that practice facing one's fears can help to reduce anxiety over time) is important to ensure that students understand why they are being asked to do things that may be distressing to them (Masia Warner et al., 2018). To facilitate exposure activities, each student creates a fear ladder of the social situations that make them most anxious. Fear ladders should have clearly defined steps that increase in difficulty. To capitalize on the school-based delivery and the support of peers in this setting, exposures should include activities that can be practiced within the school environment, such as asking questions in class, eating lunch in the cafeteria with a group, or joining a club or sports team. Finally, given that extending invitations can be very uncomfortable for socially anxious teenagers, it is recommended that this is included as an exposure exercise.

Peers can be a helpful resource during exposure sessions, as students are able to share and discuss their goals and identify fears that they may have in common, providing opportunities to talk about how to handle the situation and offer feedback to support each other. Further, peers can help each other during exposure activities at school. For example, they may be able to attend school events together and return to the group to discuss their experiences (Masia Warner et al., 2018). Finally, observing others with similar challenges experience social success during these activities can build confidence in the other participating students and help them to learn that they too can be successful.

13.2.4.4 Peer Assistants and Social Events in SASS

One of the unique aspects of this intervention is the use of peer assistants to facilitate group activities and promote positive interactions/social engagement throughout treatment. Peer assistants can include students who have participated in the group previously or other prosocial peers outside of the group. Including peers who have struggled with social anxiety in the past can be a powerful tool to show how facing fears can help overcome anxiety, and can reinforce students' motivation to build their skills and participate in the intervention (Masia Warner et al., 2018). Thus, oftentimes, peer assistants have participated in the groups and are already familiar with the curriculum. Peer assistants serve as role models for students in the group to help practice social skills and build social confidence throughout the intervention. Prior to their involvement in the group, they meet with group leaders twice to discuss their role in the intervention and responsibilities. Further, confidentiality is discussed and peer assistants are asked to sign a confidentiality statement prior to being involved (Fisher et al., 2004). Once they have met with group leaders, peer assistants support group participants with exposure activities and other skills as necessary throughout sessions. However, the exact number of sessions they attend during treatment may vary according to the needs of the group. Furthermore, peer assistants may aid outside of groups sessions by having conversations with group members in the hallways at school or accompanying them to school clubs or activities. Peer assistants also participate in the social events (described below) to provide opportunities for real-life exposure and skills generalization.

In addition, because socially anxious youth report that unstructured social activities are among their most distressing social experiences, SASS includes four 90-min social events that further support socially anxious youth in facing feared situations and generalize the skills learned in the intervention to other settings (Masia Warner et al., 2018). These events highlight the program's emphasis on cultivating positive relationships with peers throughout the intervention. Social events often occur outside of school hours and include activities such as going bowling, having a picnic, or playing games with a group. Peer assistants are key to supporting students during social events and promote positive interactions/engagement during these events that increase the chance that they will be successful. These events also provide a venue for students to connect in a more casual atmosphere while also gaining real life exposure to feared situations.

13.2.4.5 Relapse Prevention and Booster Sessions

In the last group session, group leaders inform students of the potential occurrence of relapse and how to target these emerging social anxiety symptoms by using learned techniques. Relatedly, group leaders may administer booster sessions 1–2 months following the end of the program. Booster sessions are indicated based on feedback obtained from the participating students and information related to how the student is doing/their anxiety symptoms (i.e., using social anxiety rating scales) after completing the program (Masia Warner et al., 2018). The purpose is to reinforce learned skills, monitor student progress, and help to overcome barriers to symptom improvement (Masia Warner et al., 2005, 2007). This can also serve as an opportunity for peers to connect and hear about the success or challenges of others and an opportunity to provide support to one another.

13.2.4.6 Individual, Teacher and Parent Meetings

In addition to the group meetings described above, this intervention includes two 15-min individual meetings with students to discuss issues that may impact treatment progress and tailor the intervention to individual student needs. The individual meetings occur within the first half of the intervention and focus on concerns that students may not feel comfortable disclosing in the group (e.g., overprotective parenting) or to tailor treatment strategies to the needs of the student (i.e., refining fear hierarchy, conducting additional individual exposures; Fox et al., 2018). In addition, two parent meetings teach parents about social anxiety and how to support their children in using the skills learned in the group. The first meeting occurs in the first few weeks and provides parents with psychoeducation about social anxiety and a rationale and overview of the intervention. At the second meeting, which occurs about a month after the intervention, parents are taught specific strategies to help manage their child's anxiety, such as encouraging cognitive reappraisal and facing fears, decreasing reassurance and avoidance, and reinforcing non-anxious behaviors (Fox et al., 2018). Finally, because students conduct exposures at school, meetings with teachers may also be beneficial to support students as they complete exposures and practice skills in classes.

13.3 Research Evidence

Research supports SASS as an effective treatment in reducing social anxiety in adolescents (Masia et al., 2001, 2005). Following a small open pilot study (Masia et al., 2001), a randomized controlled trial was conducted with 35 adolescents randomly assigned to receive the SASS intervention or to a wait list control group (Masia Warner et al., 2005). Results of the RCT revealed that 12 of the 18 students in the intervention group no longer met criteria for SAD, compared with 1 of the 17 students in the waitlist group. These promising findings were replicated in another study including 36 adolescents randomized to receive the SASS intervention or an attention control (Masia Warner et al., 2007). Results of the study found that symptom severity ratings were significantly lower in the SASS group compared to the attention control group. Importantly, findings indicated that treatment outcomes were maintained at 6 months post treatment (Masia Warner et al., 2007). In addition to promising improvements in outcomes, attrition rates in this study were low (11%). Given that studies have found high and variable rates of treatment dropout in services delivered in outpatient clinic settings (ranging from 35% to 75%), this suggests that school-based treatment may be more effective in promoting treatment engagement in youth (Gonzalez et al., 2011).

Although these studies provided evidence to support the use of SASS when delivered by clinical researchers, it is important to understand whether the benefits of SASS would be maintained when the intervention is delivered by school counselors who are typically conducting groups in the school setting. To answer this question, Masia Warner et al. (2016) investigated the effectiveness of SASS delivered by school counselors. In this study, 138 adolescents with SAD were randomly assigned to one of three groups: the SASS intervention delivered by a psychologist, the SASS intervention delivered by a school counselor, or the Skills for Life intervention, a general school counseling program. Results indicated that participants who received SASS experienced significantly greater improvement in anxiety symptoms following treatment and 5 months post-treatment. In addition, there was no significant difference between the participants in the SASS intervention delivered by school counselors or psychologists in terms of symptom severity, indicating that the intervention can be effectively delivered in schools by school counselors (Masia Warner et al., 2016). Similar to the findings of Masia Warner et al. (2007), attrition rates were low (11.5%), again suggesting benefits of treatments delivered in the school setting. Finally, one meta-analysis by Mychailyszyn (2017) reported that, across five studies, evidence supported the effectiveness of SASS in reducing anxiety symptoms in youth.

13.3.1 Other School-Based Interventions with Peers

As is clear, there is evidence that the SASS program, which focuses on facilitating positive social relationships, can improve social functioning. There is also evidence to support the use of peer-supported school CBT for other psychological challenges, including general anxiety, trauma, and depression. For example, the FRIENDS program (Barrett et al., 1999) is a school-based preventive intervention that addresses anxiety and depression in youth, with three main goals: to increase resilience skills, to build confidence, and to establish positive relationships with both family and peers. Similar to SASS, this intervention discusses strategies to help improve peer interactions (e.g., by maintaining eye contact, using a confident voice, showing empathy towards each other, approaching new groups of peers to make friends, and problem solving) and uses role play and exposure activities to facilitate practice (Barrett et al., 2014). The extensive research on the FRIENDS program has shown it to be effective in reducing self-reported anxiety and depression, increasing resilience, and improving peer relationships (Barrett et al., 2014). Recently, evidence supporting this program been supported in studies including students from various cultural and socioeconomic backgrounds (see Barrett et al., 2014 for a review).

Another peer-supported intervention is the Cool Kids Anxiety program (Rapee et al., 2000), which targets children ages 7–17 who are experiencing symptoms of anxiety. The program utilizes a group format to deliver a CBT-based intervention that can be administered in school and other settings. Like SASS, Cool Kids includes role play exercises and group activities that facilitate peer interactions where students can practice their social skills and build positive peer relationships (Rapee et al., 2000). Research has supported the use of this program as a targeted intervention for at risk youth (Haugland et al., 2020) as well as a universal intervention to prevent anxiety in school settings (Scaini et al., 2022).

Finally, school-based CBT interventions that facilitate the development of supportive peer relationships have also shown promise for psychological conditions such as posttraumatic stress disorder (PTSD). The Cognitive Behavioral Intervention for Trauma in Schools (CBITS; Jaycox et al., 2009) is a secondary or tertiary school-based group intervention designed for students ages 11–15 who have experienced trauma and are experiencing symptoms of PTSD or any related emotional or behavioral problems. CBITS utilizes a cognitive-behavioral approach to accomplish three goals: decreasing symptoms related to trauma, building skills to cope with stress and anxiety, and increasing peer and family support. Specifically, the group serves as a place to obtain social support from peers and normalize students' experiences following exposure to traumatic events. There has been a great deal of empirical support for CBITS as an effective school-based intervention (Jaycox et al., 2009). Together, these findings support that school-based CBT treatments that facilitate peer interactions in a structured and supported environment are effective in addressing a range of anxiety and related disorders.

13.4 Clinical Considerations for Youth with Diverse Identities

Although there has been research supporting the use of peer-supported CBT in schools, this work has included predominantly White, middle class, cisgender, general education samples. However, less work has focused on understanding treatment for youth with marginalized identities. Minoritized youth face additional stressors that likely impact symptoms of anxiety, such as racial discrimination, which is linked to increased risk for mental health difficulties (Benner et al., 2018). A recent study found that Black teenagers report that racism is a main contributor to social fears and avoidance (Masia Warner et al., 2024). Further, experiences with racism can increase risk for the internalization of these negative racial messages (Kline et al., 2021). Research has also suggested that factors such as immigration history, family documentation status, and acculturation can impact symptoms of anxiety in youth, warranting a need for cultural factors to be included in anxiety treatment (Huang et al., 2012; Potochnick & Perreira, 2010). In addition to considerations related to race/ethnicity, other identity considerations are critical to consider when working with youth with diverse backgrounds/identities. For instance, LGTBQ+ youth also face unique stressors, such as concealment of identity, internalized homonegativity, and internalized transphobic beliefs (Chodzen et al., 2019; Mahon et al., 2021). In addition, children with disabilities are at risk for negative social experiences such as bullying-victimization (Rose et al., 2012), which may increase anxiety symptoms in youth. Thus, understanding how to ensure that identity specific factors are incorporated into anxiety treatment is important in addressing the needs of a diverse student body.

Despite increased social risk, limited work has investigated the effectiveness of CBT treatment for youth with marginalized identities who may benefit from school-based programs. Relatedly, few programs have investigated culturally or identity modified (e.g., LGBTQ affirming) interventions that can address some of the unique risk factors faced by marginalized youth. Recommendations have been provided to adapt such interventions and ensure that treatment is aligned with the lived experiences and needs of those receiving support (Chapman et al., 2013; Graham-LoPresti et al., 2017). For example, it is recommended that clinicians address identity-based issues (e.g., discrimination, identity-based bullying) early in treatment and that such experiences are not discounted during cognitive restructuring activities. Instead, validating these experiences and attributing them to external oppressive systems can help reduce the likelihood that youth will internalize these negative messages related to one's identity. It may also help to include identity-based fears in exposure activities to challenge expectations related to negative interactions and increase opportunities for social success (Chapman et al., 2013; Graham-LoPresti et al., 2017).

Although these recommendations may be valuable in working with individuals with diverse identities, little is known about whether such modifications can effectively address anxiety in minoritized youth receiving school-based treatments. There are active efforts to address this gap in the field. For example, there have been some efforts to create LGBTQ-affirming CBT interventions (e.g., Craig et al., 2021). In addition, one ongoing study aims to assess a culturally responsive adaptation of evidence-based interventions for Black adolescents (Masia Warner et al., 2024). Using the cultural adaptation model outlined by Barrera Jr. and Castro (2006), interviews with key experts, parents, students and educational professionals within the Black community were conducted and modifications were made to incorporate discrimination and fear of evaluation based on race, as well as cultural strengths, such as strengthening racial identity. Should this effort yield promising results, the hope is that it will encourage additional intervention research focused on youth with marginalized identities that is currently lacking in the field.

13.5 Case Vignette

Below we provide an example of a student engaged in the SASS intervention to showcase the potential benefits of this treatment in facilitating social confidence and reducing social anxiety.

Jane is a 15-year-old high school sophomore who has always been more reserved than her peers. Jane feels uncomfortable with approaching unfamiliar teens, inviting others to hang out, and making small talk. She often worries that she will sound boring when talking with her classmates and that they will think she is "weird." Jane is more sociable in structured settings and when comfortable with the activity, such as when she participates in the lighting crew for her school's theater performances. However, before a party to celebrate the latest production, Jane had a "panic attack" because she was not sure how the party would be and whether anyone would talk to her. She also hates having her picture taken since she thinks she looks "weird" in pictures and will hide photos of herself so that others cannot see them.

Lately, Jane has been feeling lonely. Jane had two close friends growing up who moved away in recent years. She currently has one close friend, Lacey, who she met in seventh grade. Jane said they like to go to movies about twice per month and text each other occasionally. Otherwise, Jane mostly spends her free time at home. During lunch, Jane sits with other students but she has never asked them to hang out outside of school. Overall, Jane described her main difficulty as not "reaching out enough" to other people. She would like to attend more parties and have more friends.

13.5.1 Diagnostic and Functional Assessments

To confirm that Jane may be a good fit for the SASS intervention and establish a diagnosis of Social Anxiety Disorder (SAD), a multimethod assessment was conducted with Jane and her parents. Assessment included a clinical interview to gather background information, along with the Anxiety and Related Disorders Interview Schedule for DSM-5, Child and Parent Version (ADIS-5-C/P; Brown & Barlow, 2014), a semi-structured diagnostic interview that provides guided questions about social anxiety, including severity, associated distress and impairment, specific social fears, and situational triggers. The ADIS-C/P was administered before and after treatment to evaluate change in diagnostic status. A standardized questionnaire, the Social Phobia and Anxiety Inventory for Children (SPAI-C; Beidel et al., 1995), was also completed by Jane and her mother to evaluate somatic, cognitive, and behavioral markers of social anxiety. The SPAI-C was administered before treatment, at the midpoint of treatment, and at the end of treatment to evaluate change in social anxiety severity.

13.5.2 Case Formulation

Based on the completed assessment, Jane was diagnosed with SAD, with a clinician severity rating (CSR) of six out of a possible range of 0–8 (indicating moderate severity), and received scores on the self-rated and parent-rated SPAI-C that exceeded the clinical threshold. Her background and history pointed to a biopsychosocial explanation of her social anxiety informed by cognitive-behavioral theory. Jane was described by her mother as having shown reticence to play with unfamiliar children and enter new situations from an early age. Although Jane gradually became more comfortable socializing with peers and making friends in elementary school, she experienced a setback in middle school when she was bullied by some of her classmates.

As Jane developed fears of criticism and rejection, she often experienced negative expectations of social situations, such as predicting that other teens would laugh at her if she tried to speak with them. This led her to either leave feared situations early or avoid them completely, which ultimately led her to miss social opportunities that could have resulted in new friendships and challenged her expectations. Taken together, this suggests that Jane is a good candidate for a school-based intervention to address her anxiety.

13.5.3 Session-by-Session Overview

Jane participated in the entire 12-week SASS program (at her high school), which features peer involvement in skills training and exposure exercises. In the first group session, Jane was provided with an overview of the program and psychoeducation about the symptoms of SAD. She also learned to recognize the interaction between the emotional, cognitive, and behavioral manifestations of her social anxiety, including the important role of avoidance. Listening to her peers in the group discuss their own social anxiety caused Jane to think that her experiences were more normal than she realized.

The second session focused on cognitive reappraisal. Jane learned about two types of thoughts associated with SAD: exaggerated negative expectations and exaggerated feared consequences. When asked to identify one of her feared social situations and associated negative thoughts, she described being uncomfortable with starting conversations with her classmates in the cafeteria, noting that she often thinks, "If I try to talk to them, I will stumble over my words." She also acknowledged that she imagines the consequences if her prediction came true, such as "If I stumble over my words, my classmates will laugh at me and tell everyone that I'm weird." Next, Jane was taught to ask herself questions to assess the reality of her predictions and think more flexibly by proposing alternative explanations. For example, she asked herself, "Am I exaggerating?" and "How many times has this happened in the past?" Based on this, she could only recall one time in the past year when she stumbled over her words, which led her to realize that she may have been overestimating the likelihood of this happening again. Jane was encouraged to practice these cognitive strategies at home and in future sessions as needed. Jane felt validated when she heard that other kids in the group shared her fears, and it helped make her feel more comfortable talking about her own social discomfort with others.

Social skills training was the focus of four group sessions, with each session covering a different skill: initiating conversations (session three), maintaining conversations and establishing friendships (session five), listening and remembering (session seven), and assertiveness (session nine). The goal of these sessions is to increase the confidence of adolescents with SAD in facing social situations they might otherwise avoid. In each session, group leaders explained the concept and rationale of each skill, modeled them for group members, and facilitated role-play exercises so they could practice each skill with their peers. For example, in the session dedicated to initiating conversations, group leaders reviewed good opportunities for starting conversations and body language that conveys friendliness. Jane also learned that conversation starters can include commenting on something around you or that you have in common with the other person. In the session dedicated to maintaining conversations, Jane was taught to use open-ended questions. When it came time for the role-play in that session, the group leaders paired Jane with a group member named Michael and gave them a scenario:

Group Leader: Jane, I want you to pretend that you're at a school play. Another student, played by Michael, is sitting next to you by himself. You've had some classes with Michael, and he seems nice, but you've only spoken with him once or twice in class. It's now the show's intermission, and you'd like to have a conversation with him. Go for it.

Jane: I've really liked the show so far. Comedic plays like this are usually my favorite.

Michael: Yeah, me too, this show has been very funny.

Jane: Definitely. What were your favorite parts?

The group leaders praised Jane for using the strategies they taught and encouraged her to practice them between sessions. Jane left this session feeling good, as she thought that the interaction with Michael went well and that she could have similar conversations with other peers.

Exposure was the focus of five group sessions. Group leaders provided the rationale for exposure, explaining that avoidance of social situations reinforces fear, whereas facing these situations decreases anxiety over the long term. Next, group leaders noted that effective exposure is gradual and requires staying in the situation and repeated practice. Jane then created a fear hierarchy by ranking her feared social situations, in order from least anxiety-provoking (e.g., talking with her friend, Lacey) to most anxiety-provoking (e.g., starting a conversation with an unfamiliar peer). Jane progressed up her fear hierarchy by completing exposure exercises during and between sessions. Before each exercise, group leaders asked Jane for her predictions (e.g., "What are you expecting will happen?") and fear rating (from 0 to

8). Conducting exposures in school allowed Jane's group leaders to create realistic situations targeting social fears involving peers. For example, one exposure session featured a "speed chatting" exercise, in which students paired up with fellow group members to practice conversations and confront their discomfort. Other exposure exercises for Jane included starting a conversation with a peer in the cafeteria, as well as walking around the school hallways while wearing brightly colored clothing with large patterns to target her fears of looking weird. Jane reported feeling moderately anxious before each task (fear ratings of 5 or 6) but afterwards reported that she felt less anxious (fear ratings of 3) and that the exercises were not as scary as she expected. She felt that the other group members were very supportive and also had similarly positive experiences, which made her feel more confident with each passing activity.

To facilitate skill practice and generalization between sessions, Jane participated in four weekend social events as part of the SASS program. Events involved different activities (e.g., bowling, laser tag) and were attended by group leaders and members, along with several peer assistants, who were friendly and prosocial students invited by group leaders to promote a positive experience and help group members engage in the activities and practice skills. Jane became increasingly comfortable interacting with her peers at these events and began a friendship with a fellow group member, Olivia. At one event, Jane expressed to a peer assistant that she was nervous to ask Olivia to hang out. The peer assistant encouraged Jane to use this as an opportunity to face her fear of extending invitations. Despite being nervous, Jane asked Olivia if she wanted to go to the mall the following weekend, and Olivia happily agreed. Jane was grateful for the peer assistant's encouragement and sensitivity toward her anxiety.

The final group session focused on maintenance of gains and relapse prevention. Additional components of SASS included two brief individual sessions, which allowed group leaders to check in with Jane, and two parent sessions, which provided Jane's parents with psychoeducation about the program and strategies for responding to her anxiety.

13.5.4 Review of Outcomes

Based on Jane's ADIS-5-C/P after the end of the program, Jane no longer met criteria for a diagnosis of SAD (CSR of 3, indicating mild social anxiety). Jane's self-rated and parent-rated SPAI-C scores also fell to below the threshold for clinical significance. Overall, Jane reported feeling more comfortable talking with unfamiliar peers and less self-conscious about being perceived as weird. Because of her increased confidence, she had begun developing multiple new friendships and overall felt less lonely than she had before treatment.

13.6 Conclusion

There is a great deal of support for the use of CBT in addressing youth anxiety. Peer-supported CBT within the school setting can be especially valuable in reducing anxiety and building social confidence. One school-based intervention, *Skills for Academic and Social Success (SASS)*, facilitates social interactions through the use of a group format and peers at school who assist with social skills practice, exposures, and outside of school social events. Including peers in this way promotes the generalization of learned strategies in treatment to real-world contexts. A great deal of research has supported school-based interventions that focus on facilitating positive peer relationships. This work holds significant potential for reaching or increasing access to services for youth, including those with marginalized identities who may be at increased risk for anxiety.

Acknowledgement This chapter was supported by a grant from the Institute of Education Sciences (R305A200013) awarded to Dr. Carrie Masia Warner.

References

Balázs, J., Miklósi, M., Keresztény, Á., Hoven, C. W., Carli, V., Wasserman, C., et al. (2013). Adolescent subthreshold-depression and anxiety: Psychopathology, functional impairment and increased suicide risk. *Journal of Child Psychology and Psychiatry, 54*(6), 670–677. https://doi.org/10.1111/jcpp.12016

Bannon, W. M., Jr., & McKay, M. M. (2005). Are barriers to service and parental preference match for service related to urban child mental health service use? *Families in Society, 86*(1), 30–34. https://doi.org/10.1606/1044-3894.1874

Barrera, M., Jr., & Castro, F. G. (2006). A heuristic framework for the cultural adaptation of interventions. *Clinical Psychology: Science and Practice, 13*(4), 311–316. https://doi.org/10.1111/j.1468-2850.2006.00043.x

Barrett, P. M., Webster, H. M., & Wallis, J. R. (1999). Adolescent self-esteem and cognitive skills training: A school-based intervention. *Journal of Child and Family Studies, 8*, 217–227. https://doi.org/10.1023/A:1022044119273

Barrett, P. M., Cooper, M., & Guajardo, J. G. (2014). Using the FRIENDS programs to promote resilience in cross-cultural populations. In S. Prince-Embury & D. Saklofske (Eds.), *Resilience interventions for youth in diverse populations* (pp. 85–108). Springer. https://doi.org/10.1007/978-1-4939-0542-3_5

Beidel, D. C., Turner, S. M., & Morris, T. L. (1995). A new inventory to assess childhood social anxiety and phobia: The social phobia and anxiety inventory for children. *Psychological Assessment, 7*(1), 73–79. https://doi.org/10.1037//1040-3590.7.1.73

Beidel, D. C., Turner, S. M., & Morris, T. L. (2000). Behavioral treatment of childhood social phobia. *Journal of Consulting and Clinical Psychology, 68*(6), 1072–1080. https://doi.org/10.1037/0022-006X.68.6.1072

Beidel, D. C., Turner, S. M., Young, B. J., Ammerman, R. T., Sallee, F. R., & Crosby, L. (2007). Psychopathology of adolescent social phobia. *Journal of Psychopathology and Behavioral Assessment, 29*, 46–53. https://doi.org/10.1007/s10862-006-9021-1

Beidel, D. C., Turner, S. M., Young, B., & Paulson, A. (2005). Social effectiveness therapy for children: Three-year follow-up. *Journal of Consulting and Clinical Psychology, 73*(4), 721. https://doi.org/10.1037/0022-006X.73.4.721

Benner, A. D., Wang, Y., Shen, Y., Boyle, A. E., Polk, R., & Cheng, Y. P. (2018). Racial/ethnic discrimination and well-being during adolescence: A meta-analytic review. *American Psychologist, 73*(7), 855–883. https://doi.org/10.1037/amp0000204

Biggs, B. K., Vernberg, E. M., & Wu, Y. P. (2012). Social anxiety and adolescents' friendships: The role of social withdrawal. *The Journal of Early Adolescence, 32*(6), 802–823. https://doi.org/10.1177/0272431611426l4

Blöte, A. W., Miers, A. C., & Westenberg, P. M. (2015). The role of social performance and physical attractiveness in peer rejection of socially anxious adolescents. *Journal of Research on Adolescence, 25*(1), 189–200. https://doi.org/10.1111/jora.12107

Brown, T. A., & Barlow, D. H. (2014). *Anxiety and related disorders interview schedule for DSM-5 (ADIS-5)-adult and lifetime version: Clinician manual*. Oxford University Press.

Brown, B. B., & Larson, J. (2009). Peer relationships in adolescence. In R. M. Lerner & L. Steinberg (Eds.), *Handbook of adolescent psychology* (pp. 74–100). John Wiley & Sons, Inc.

Buckner, J. D., Morris, P. E., Abarno, C. N., Glover, N. I., & Lewis, E. M. (2021). Biopsychosocial model social anxiety and substance use revised. *Current Psychiatry Reports, 23*, 1–9. https://doi.org/10.1007/s11920-021-01249-5

Cartwright-Hatton, S., Hodges, L., & Porter, J. (2003). Social anxiety in childhood: The relationship with self and observer rated social skills. *Journal of Child Psychology and Psychiatry, 44*(5), 737–742. https://doi.org/10.1111/1469-7610.00159

Cartwright-Hatton, S., Tschernitz, N., & Gomersall, H. (2005). Social anxiety in children: Social skills deficit, or cognitive distortion. *Behaviour Research and Therapy, 43*, 131–141. https://doi.org/10.1016/j.brat.2003.12.003

Chapman, L. K., DeLapp, R. C., & Williams, M. T. (2013). Cognitive-behavioral treatment of social anxiety among ethnic minority patients, Part 2: Bridging the gap in treatment. *Directions in Psychiatry, 33*(3), 163–176.

Chiu, K., Clark, D. M., & Leigh, E. (2021). Prospective associations between peer functioning and social anxiety in adolescents: A systematic review and meta-analysis. *Journal of Affective Disorders, 279*, 650–661. https://doi.org/10.1016/j.jad.2020.10.055

Chodzen, G., Hidalgo, M. A., Chen, D., & Garofalo, R. (2019). Minority stress factors associated with depression and anxiety among transgender and gender-nonconforming youth. *Journal of Adolescent Health, 64*(4), 467–471. https://doi.org/10.1016/j.jadohealth.2018.07.006

Coyle, S., & Malecki, C. K. (2018). The association between social anxiety and perceived frequency and value of classmate and close friend social support. *School Psychology Review, 47*(3), 209–225. https://doi.org/10.17105/SPR-2017-0067.V47-3

Coyle, S., Malecki, C. K., & Emmons, J. (2021). Keep your friends close: Exploring the associations of bullying, peer social support, and social anxiety. *Contemporary School Psychology, 25*, 230–242. https://doi.org/10.1007/s40688-019-00250-3

Craig, S. L., Eaton, A. D., Leung, V. W. Y., Iacono, G., Pang, N., Dillon, F., Austin, A., Pascoe, R., & Dobinson, C. (2021). Efficacy of affirmative cognitive behavioural group therapy for sexual and gender minority adolescents and young adults in community settings in Ontario, Canada. *BMC Psychology, 9*(1), 1–15. https://doi.org/10.1186/s40359-021-00595-6

Cummings, C. M., Caporino, N. E., & Kendall, P. C. (2014). Comorbidity of anxiety and depression in children and adolescents: 20 years after. *Psychological Bulletin, 140*(3), 816. https://doi.org/10.1037/a0034733

de Lijster, J. M., Dieleman, G. C., Utens, E. M., Dierckx, B., Wierenga, M., Verhulst, F. C., & Legerstee, J. S. (2018). Social and academic functioning in adolescents with anxiety disorders: A systematic review. *Journal of Affective Disorders, 230*, 108–117. https://doi.org/10.1016/j.jad.2018.01.008

Early, M. C., Biggs, B. K., Makanui, K. P., Legerski, J. P., Van Allen, J., Elledge, A. R., & Whiteside, S. P. (2017). Specificity of peer difficulties to social anxiety in early adolescence:

Categorical and dimensional analyses with clinical and community samples. *Anxiety, Stress, & Coping, 30*(6), 647–660. https://doi.org/10.1080/10615806.2017.1348296

Evans, R., Chiu, K., Clark, D. M., Waite, P., & Leigh, E. (2021). Safety behaviours in social anxiety: An examination across adolescence. *Behaviour Research and Therapy, 144*, 103931. https://doi.org/10.1016/j.brat.2021.103931

Fisher, P.H., Masia-Warner, C. & Klein, R.G. (2004). Skills for social and academic success: A school-based intervention for social anxiety disorder in adolescents. *Clinical Child and Family Psychological Review, 7*, 241–249. https://doi.org/10.1007/s10567-004-6088-7

Fox, J., Masia-Warner, C., & Drew, M. (2018). School-based intervention for adolescents with impairing social anxiety. In A. W. Leschied, D. H. Saklofske, & G. L. Flett (Eds.), *Handbook of school based mental health promotion: An evidenced informed framework for implementation* (pp. 411–428). Springer. https://doi.org/10.1007/978-3-319-89842-1

Ginsburg, G. S., & Drake, K. L. (2002). School-based treatment for anxious African-American adolescents: A controlled pilot study. *Journal of the American Academy of Child & Adolescent Psychiatry, 41*(7), 768–775. https://doi.org/10.1097/00004583-200207000-00007

Gonzalez, A., Weersing, V. R., Warnick, E. M., Scahill, L. D., & Woolston, J. L. (2011). Predictors of treatment attrition among an outpatient clinic sample of youths with clinically significant anxiety. *Administration and Policy in Mental Health and Mental Health Services Research, 38*, 356–367. https://doi.org/10.1007/s10488-010-0323-y

Graham-LoPresti, J. R., Gautier, S. W., Sorenson, S., & Hayes-Skelton, S. A. (2017). Culturally sensitive adaptations to evidence-based cognitive behavioral treatment for social anxiety disorder: A case paper. *Cognitive and Behavioral Practice, 24*(4), 459–471. https://doi.org/10.1016/j.cbpra.2016.12.003

Greco, L. A., & Morris, T. L. (2005). Factors influencing the link between social anxiety and peer acceptance: Contributions of social skills and close friendships during middle childhood. *Behavior Therapy, 36*, 197–205. https://doi.org/10.1016/S0005-7894(05)80068-1

Haugland, B. S. M., Haaland, A. T., Baste, V., Bjaastad, J. F., Hoffart, A., Rapee, R. M., Raknes, F., Himle, J. A., Husabo, E., & Wergeland, G. J. (2020). Effectiveness of brief and standard school-based cognitive-behavioral interventions for adolescents with anxiety: A randomized noninferiority study. *Journal of the American Academy of Child & Adolescent Psychiatry, 59*(4), 552–564. https://doi.org/10.1016/j.jaac.2019.12.003

Herres, J., Caporino, N. E., Cummings, C. M., & Kendall, P. C. (2018). Emotional reactivity to daily events in youth with anxiety disorders. *Anxiety, Stress, & Coping, 31*(4), 387–401. https://doi.org/10.1080/10615806.2018.1472492

Huang, K. Y., Cheng, S., Calzada, E., & Brotman, L. M. (2012). Symptoms of anxiety and associated risk and protective factors in young Asian American children. *Child Psychiatry and Human Development, 43*(5), 761–774. https://doi.org/10.1007/s10578-012-0295-0

Inderbitzen-Nolan, H. M., Anderson, E. R., & Johnson, H. S. (2007). Subjective versus objective behavioral ratings following two analogue tasks: A comparison of socially phobic and non-anxious adolescents. *Journal of Anxiety Disorders, 21*(1), 76–90. https://doi.org/10.1016/j.janxdis.2006.03.013

Jaycox, L. H., Langley, A. K., Stein, B. D., Wong, M., Sharma, P., Scott, M., & Schonlau, M. (2009). Support for students exposed to trauma: A pilot study. *School Mental Health, 1*, 49–60. https://doi.org/10.1007/s12310-009-9007-8

Kline, E. A., Warner, C. M., Grapin, S. L., Reyes-Portillo, J. A., Bixter, M. T., Cunningham, D. J., Farah, M., Tanya, S., & Weeks, C. (2021). The relationship between social anxiety and internalized racism in Black young adults. *Journal of Cognitive Psychotherapy, 35*(1), 53–63. https://doi.org/10.1891/jcpsy-d-20-00030

La Greca, A. M., & Lopez, N. (1998). Social anxiety among adolescents: Linkages with peer relations and friendships. *Journal of Abnormal Child Psychology, 26*(2), 83–94. https://doi.org/10.1023/A:1022684520514

Leigh, E., & Clark, D. M. (2018). Understanding social anxiety disorder in adolescents and improving treatment outcomes: Applying the cognitive model of Clark and Wells (1995).

Clinical Child and Family Psychology Review, 21(3), 388–414. https://doi.org/10.1007/s10567-018-0258-5

Mahon, C. P., Pachankis, J. E., Kiernan, G., & Gallagher, P. (2021). Risk and protective factors for social anxiety among sexual minority individuals. *Archives of Sexual Behavior, 50*(3), 1015–1032. https://doi.org/10.1007/s10508-020-01845-1

Masia Warner, C., & Fox, J. K. (2012). Advances and challenges in school-based intervention for anxious and depressed youth: Identifying and addressing issues of sustainability. *School Mental Health, 4*, 193–196. https://doi.org/10.1007/s12310-012-9087-8

Masia Warner, C., Colognori, D., & Lynch, C. (2018). *Helping students overcome social anxiety: Skills for academic and social success (SASS)*. Guilford Publications.

Masia Warner, C., Colognori, D., Brice, C., Herzig, K., Mufson, L., Lynch, C., Reiss, P. T., Petkova, E., Fox, J., Moceri, D. C., & Klein, R. G. (2016). Can school counselors deliver cognitive-behavioral treatment for social anxiety effectively? A randomized controlled trial. *Journal of Child Psychology and Psychiatry, 57*(11), 1229–1238. https://doi.org/10.1111/jcpp.12550

Masia Warner, C., Fisher, P. H., Shrout, P. E., Rathor, S., & Klein, R. G. (2007). Treating adolescents with social anxiety disorder in school: An attention control trial. *Journal of Child Psychology and Psychiatry, 48*(7), 676–686. https://doi.org/10.1111/j.1469-7610.2007.01737.x

Masia, C. L., Klein, R. G., Storch, E. A., & Corda, B. (2001). School-based behavioral treatment for social anxiety disorder in adolescents: Results of a pilot study. *Journal of the American Academy of Child & Adolescent Psychiatry, 40*(7), 780–786. https://doi.org/10.1097/00004583-200107000-00012

Masia Warner, C., Klein, R. G., Dent, H. C., Fisher, P. H., Alvir, J., Marie Albano, A., & Guardino, M. (2005). School-based intervention for adolescents with social anxiety disorder: Results of a controlled study. *Journal of Abnormal Child Psychology, 33*, 707–722. https://doi.org/10.1007/s10802-005-7649-z

Masia Warner, C., Escobar, M., Thomas, H., Ahmed, T., Ndubuisi, I., Perrone, L., & Coyle-Eastwick, S. (2024). A universitycommunity partnership to develop a culturally responsive school intervention for Black adolescents with social anxiety. *School Mental Health*. https://doi.org/10.1007/s12310-024-09658-6

Merikangas, K. R., He, J. P., Burstein, M., Swanson, S. A., Avenevoli, S., Cui, L., Benjet, C., Georgiades, K., & Swendsen, J. (2010). Lifetime prevalence of mental disorders in US adolescents: Results from the National Comorbidity Survey Replication–Adolescent Supplement (NCS-A). *Journal of the American Academy of Child & Adolescent Psychiatry, 49*(10), 980–989. https://doi.org/10.1016/j.jaac.2010.05.017

Miers, A. C., Blöte, A. W., Bokhorst, C. L., & Westenberg, P. M. (2009). Negative self-evaluations and the relation to performance level in socially anxious children and adolescents. *Behaviour Research and Therapy, 47*(12), 1043–1049. https://doi.org/10.1016/j.brat.2009.07.017

Miers, A. C., & Warner, C. M. (2023). Adolescent social anxiety: Bridging cognitive and social behavioral perspectives through a developmental lens. In *Handbook of lifespan cognitive behavioral therapy* (pp. 89–100). Academic Press. https://doi.org/10.1016/B978-0-323-85757-4.00042-0

Moore, S. E., Norman, R. E., Suetani, S., Thomas, H. J., Sly, P. D., & Scott, J. G. (2017). Consequences of bullying victimization in childhood and adolescence: A systematic review and meta-analysis. *World Journal of Psychiatry, 7*(1), 60. https://doi.org/10.5498/wjp.v7.i1.60

Motoca, L. M., Williams, S., & Silverman, W. K. (2012). Social skills as a mediator between anxiety symptoms and peer interactions among children and adolescents. *Journal of Clinical Child & Adolescent Psychology, 41*(3), 329–336. https://doi.org/10.1080/15374416.2012.668843

Mychailyszyn, M. P. (2017). Systematic review and meta-analysis of the Skills for Social and Academic Success (SASS) program. *Advances in School Mental Health Promotion, 10*(2), 147–160. https://doi.org/10.1080/1754730X.2017.1285709

Parker, J. G., Rubin, K. H., Erath, S., Wojslawowicz, J. C., & Buskirk, A. (2006). Peer relationships, child development, and adjustment: A developmental psychopathology perspective. In D. Cicchetti (Ed.), *Developmental psychopathology: Vol. 2: Risk, disorder, and adaptation* (pp. 419–493). Wiley.

Potochnick, S. R., & Perreira, K. M. (2010). Depression and anxiety among first-generation immigrant Latino youth: Key correlates and implications for future research. *Journal of Nervous & Mental Disease, 198*(7), 470–477. https://doi.org/10.1097/NMD.0b013e3181e4ce24

Rapee, R. M., & Heimberg, R. G. (1997). A cognitive-behavioral model of anxiety in social phobia. *Behaviour Research and Therapy, 35*(8), 741–756. https://doi.org/10.1016/S0005-7967(97)00022-3

Rapee, R. M., Wignall, A., Hudson, J. L., & Schniering, C. A. (2000). *Treating anxious children: An evidence based approach*. New Harbinger.

Rose, C. A., Swearer, S. M., & Espelage, D. L. (2012). Bullying and students with disabilities: The untold narrative. *Focus on Exceptional Children, 45*(2), 1–10. https://doi.org/10.17161/foec.v45i2.6682

Ryan, J. L., & Warner, C. M. (2012). Treating Adolescents with Social Anxiety Disorder in Schools. *Child and Adolescent Psychiatric Clinics of North America, 21*(1), 105–118. https://doi.org/10.1016/j.chc.2011.08.011

Sanchez, A. L., Cornacchio, D., Poznanski, B., Golik, A. M., Chou, T., & Comer, J. S. (2018). The effectiveness of school-based mental health services for elementary-aged children: A meta-analysis. *Journal of the American Academy of Child & Adolescent Psychiatry, 57*(3), 153–165. https://doi.org/10.1016/j.jaac.2017.11.022

Scaini, S., Belotti, R., Ogliari, A., & Battaglia, M. (2016). A comprehensive meta-analysis of cognitive-behavioral interventions for social anxiety disorder in children and adolescents. *Journal of Anxiety Disorders, 42*, 105–112. https://doi.org/10.1016/j.janxdis.2016.05.008

Scaini, S., Rossi, F., Rapee, R. M., Bonomi, F., Ruggiero, G. M., & Incerti, A. (2022). The cool kids as a school-based universal prevention and early intervention program for anxiety: Results of a pilot study. *International Journal of Environmental Research and Public Health, 19*(2), 941. https://doi.org/10.3390/ijerph19020941

Scharfstein, L. A., & Beidel, D. C. (2015). Social skills and social acceptance in children with anxiety disorders. *Journal of Clinical Child & Adolescent Psychology, 44*(5), 826–838. https://doi.org/10.1080/15374416.2014.895938

Scharfstein, L., Alfano, C., Beidel, D., & Wong, N. (2011). Children with generalized anxiety disorder do not have peer problems, just fewer friends. *Child Psychiatry & Human Development, 42*, 712–723. https://doi.org/10.1007/s10578-011-0245-2

Silverman, W. K., Marin, C. E., Rey, Y., Kurtines, W. M., Jaccard, J., & Pettit, J. W. (2019). Group-versus parent-involvement CBT for childhood anxiety disorders: Treatment specificity and long-term recovery mediation. *Clinical Psychological Science, 7*(4), 840–855. https://doi.org/10.1177/2167702619830404

Silverman, W. K., Pina, A. A., & Viswesvaran, C. (2008). Evidence-based psychosocial treatments for phobic and anxiety disorders in children and adolescents. *Journal of Clinical Child & Adolescent Psychology, 37*(1), 105–130. https://doi.org/10.1080/15374410701817907

Spence, S. H., Lawrence, D., & Zubrick, S. R. (2022). Anxiety trajectories in adolescents and the impact of social support and peer victimization. *Research on Child and Adolescent Psychopathology, 50*(6), 795–807. https://doi.org/10.1007/s10802-021-00887-w

Stapinski, L. A., Bowes, L., Wolke, D., Pearson, R. M., Mahedy, L., Button, K. S., Lewis, G., & Araya, R. (2014). Peer victimization during adolescence and risk for anxiety disorders in adulthood: A prospective cohort study. *Depression and Anxiety, 31*(7), 574–582. https://doi.org/10.1002/da.22270

Storch, E. A., & Masia-Warner, C. (2004). The relationship of peer victimization to social anxiety and loneliness in adolescent females. *Journal of Adolescence, 27*(3), 351–362. https://doi.org/10.1016/j.adolescence.2004.03.003

Tillfors, M., Persson, S., Willén, M., & Burk, W. J. (2012). Prospective links between social anxiety and adolescent peer relations. *Journal of Adolescence, 35*(5), 1255–1263. https://doi.org/10.1016/j.adolescence.2012.04.008

Wentzel, K. R. (2009). Peers and academic functioning at school. In K. H. Rubin, W. M. Bukowski, & B. Laursen (Eds.), *Handbook of peer interactions, relationships, and groups* (pp. 531–547). The Guilford Press.

Index

L. Reuman, J. Thompson-Hollands (eds.), *Enhancing CBT Through Family and Peer Engagement*, CBT: Science Into Practice, https://doi.org/10.1007/978-3-031-74838-7

SPRINGER NATURE

GPSR Compliance

The European Union's (EU) General Product Safety Regulation (GPSR) is a set of rules that requires consumer products to be safe and our obligations to ensure this.

If you have any concerns about our products, you can contact us on ProductSafety@springernature.com

In case Publisher is established outside the EU, the EU authorized representative is:

Springer Nature Customer Service Center GmbH
Europaplatz 3
69115 Heidelberg, Germany

The manufacturer's authorised representative in the EU is Springer Nature Customer Service Centre GmbH, Europaplatz 3, 69115 Heidelberg, Germany. If you have any concerns regarding our products, please contact ProductSafety@springernature.com

Printed and bound by CPI Group (UK) Ltd, Croydon, CR0 4YY
23/09/2026
02221528-0014